DREAM WORK IN THERAPY

Dream Work in Therapy

FACILITATING EXPLORATION, INSIGHT, and ACTION

EDITED BY
Clara E. Hill

American Psychological Association • Washington, DC

Copyright © 2004 by the American Psychological Association. All rights reserved. Except as permitted under the United States Copyright Act of 1976, no part of this publication may be reproduced or distributed in any form or by any means, or stored in a database or retrieval system, without the prior written permission of the publisher.

First Printing July 2003
Second Printing September 2007

Published by
American Psychological Association
750 First Street, NE
Washington, DC 20002
www.apa.org

To order
APA Order Department
P.O. Box 92984
Washington, DC 20090-2984
Tel: (800) 374-2721; Direct: (202) 336-5510
Fax: (202) 336-5502; TDD/TTY: (202) 336-6123
Online: www.apa.org/books/
E-mail: order@apa.org

In the U.K., Europe, Africa, and the Middle East, copies may be ordered from
American Psychological Association
3 Henrietta Street
Covent Garden, London
WC2E 8LU England

Typeset in Goudy by Page Grafx, Inc., St. Simons Island, GA

Printer: Data Reproductions, Auburn Hills, MI
Cover Designer: Berg Design, Albany, NY
Technical/Production Editor: Dan Brachtesende

The opinions and statements published are the responsibility of the authors, and such opinions and statements do not necessarily represent the policies of the American Psychological Association.

Library of Congress Cataloging-in-Publication Data
Dream work in therapy: facilitating exploration, insight, and action / edited by Clara E. Hill.
    p. cm.
  Includes bibliographical references.
  ISBN 1-59147-028-5
  1. Dreams—Therapeutic use. 2. Dream interpretation. 3. Cognitive–experiential psychotherapy. 4. Hill, Clara E., 1948– I. Hill, Clara E., 1948–

RC489.D74D723 2003
616.89'14—dc21

2003044403

British Library Cataloguing-in-Publication Data
A CIP record is available from the British Library.

Printed in the United States of America

CONTENTS

Contributors vii

Foreword ix
Alan B. Siegel

Preface xiii

Acknowledgments xv

Introduction 3
Clara E. Hill

I. **Overview of the Hill Cognitive–Experiential Dream Model** ... 17

    Chapter 1. The Exploration Stage 19
                  Clara E. Hill

    Chapter 2. The Insight Stage 41
                  Clara E. Hill

    Chapter 3. The Action Stage 71
                  Clara E. Hill

II. **Extensions of the Hill Cognitive–Experiential Dream Model** 95

    Chapter 4. Working With Dreams in
                  Ongoing Psychotherapy 97
                  Mary C. Cogar

Chapter 5. Working With Dreams in Groups 115
Teresa L. Wonnell

Chapter 6. Self-Guided Methods for Working With Dreams ... 133
Jason S. Zack

Chapter 7. Incorporating Spirituality Into Dream Work 149
Timothy L. Davis

Chapter 8. Dreams of the Bereaved 169
Shirley A. Hess

Chapter 9. Using Dreams To Work With Male Clients 187
Aaron B. Rochlen

Chapter 10. Working With Nightmares 203
Kristin J. Heaton

III. Training and Research on the Hill Cognitive–Experiential Dream Model 223

Chapter 11. Training Therapists To Work With Dreams in Therapy 225
Rachel E. Crook

Chapter 12. Research on the Hill Cognitive–Experiential Dream Model 245
Clara E. Hill and Melissa K. Goates

Appendix A: Steps of the Dream Interpretation Model 289

Appendix B: Attitudes Toward Dreams Scale 291

Appendix C: Gains From Dream Interpretation Measure 293

Appendix D: Therapist-Rated Adherence Measure 295

Index 297

About the Editor 305

CONTRIBUTORS

Mary C. Cogar, independent practice, Baltimore
Rachel E. Crook, College of Education, Brigham Young University, Provo, UT
Timothy L. Davis, Counseling Center, University of Dayton, OH
Melissa K. Goates, Department of Psychology, University of Maryland, College Park
Kristin J. Heaton, School of Public Health, Department of Environmental Health, Boston
Shirley A. Hess, College of Education and Human Services, Shippensburg University, Shippensburg, PA
Clara E. Hill, Department of Psychology, University of Maryland, College Park
Aaron B. Rochlen, College of Education, University of Texas at Austin
Alan B. Siegel, Department of Clinical Science, University of California, Berkeley
Teresa L. Wonnell, Harford Community College, Harford, MD
Jason S. Zack, JSZ Behavioral Science, Coral Gables, FL

FOREWORD

ALAN B. SIEGEL

At the beginning of the 20th century, the groundbreaking work of Freud (1900/1965) and Jung (1974) created a wave of interest in the therapeutic value of dreams. Interpreting dreams was the essence of the treatment, and generations of psychoanalysts learned the gospel of the technique while free-associating on their analysts' couches and through training analyses and dream seminars. They faithfully applied what they learned to illuminate the meaning of their patients' dreams, to effect change, and to build and revise theories about the meaning and function of dreams and dreaming.

The impact of these early psychological theories of dreaming was not limited to the psychoanalyst's consulting room. From the Surrealist poets and artists of the 1920s and 1930s to contemporary artists, musicians, filmmakers, and scientists, the creative aspects of dreams were appreciated; used for artistic inspiration and license; and even, in the case of the Surrealists, revered. In the wake of the dream revolution of the early part of the century, popular media portrayed dream analysis as being nearly synonymous with psychotherapy.

A mid-century watershed in our understanding of dreams was the 1953 discovery of the cycles of rapid eye movement, or REM, sleep by Aserinsky and Kleitman (Shafton, 1995). Awareness of the discrete neurophysiological stages of sleep and the high correlation of dreaming with REM periods reshaped our understanding of the biology of sleep and dreams (Moffitt, Kramer, & Hoffman, 1993). This breakthrough led to extensive public and private funding for the study of the biology of sleep and dreaming. Among the results of this research was the development of treatment strategies for sleep and dream disorders, such as apnea and narcolepsy, that have plagued humanity over the centuries (Moorcroft, 2003). It is regrettable that the dramatically increased funding of sleep research did not translate into equal funding for research on dream interpretation. Pharmaceutical companies saw no immediate source of revenue from medicines to treat dream disorders, and research into the meaning and therapeutic value of dreams proceeded slowly, with meager funding.

Nevertheless, in the second half of the 20th century, the scientific study of the meaning and functions of dreams was greatly advanced by the adoption of content analysis methods developed by Hall and Van de Castle (1966) and refined by Domhoff (2003) and others. Hundreds of studies with content analysis established a scientific basis for studying patterns in the overt or manifest content of dreams. Content analysis research has illuminated crucial aspects of personality and cognitive development; the unconscious impact of trauma, illness, and other crises; and the inner reverberations of normal turning points in the life cycle, such as pregnancy, marriage, midlife, and grieving (Siegel, 2003).

In the final decades of the 20th century, a number of promising events and trends set the stage for greater scientific investigation of dreaming and renewed psychotherapeutic use of dreams. The founding in 1984 of the Association for the Study of Dreams, an international multidisciplinary organization, has led to increased dialogue, research, and communication regarding the meaning and use of dreams in the scientific, mental health, and academic communities (Shafton, 1995). The Association for the Study of Dreams has advanced professional and public awareness and education through its academic journal, *Dreaming*; its international and regional conferences; its educational Web site (http://www.asdreams.org); and its magazine, *Dream Time*.

Today, the tide may be turning back toward both clinical and scientific interest in dreams. Psychotherapists who have been trained to work with dreams continue to be impressed with their therapeutic value (Cartwright, 1993; Delaney, 1993). Beneficial uses pioneered by practitioners have included using dreams to identify feelings and conflicts that are not easily accessible, enhance the therapeutic alliance and reinvigorate treatment, diagnose and resolve issues linked to transference (Fosshage & Loew, 1987), work through blocks related to unresolved grief and trauma (Barrett, 1996), bridge cultural identity, and affirm transcendent experiences emerging from dreams (Shafton, 1995).

Despite a renaissance of scientific interest in dreams and dreaming, until very recently there were no systematic attempts to demonstrate the effectiveness of working with dreams as a therapeutic intervention. The work of Clara Hill establishes a framework for proving what we have "known" all these years: that dream work is one of the most valuable tools in the psychotherapist's repertoire. Hill has spent her career developing empirical models for demonstrating the effectiveness of psychotherapy, developing innovative training methods, and mentoring a generation of young researchers who have helped her develop and extend her work.

The Hill method for dream work is both synthetic and integrative. It synthesizes key features from a variety of theoretical approaches without asking for an oath of allegiance to a particular school of psychotherapy. I believe Hill's technique for dream work is a valuable integration of the best elements from a variety of theories. After examining a wide range of clinical and personal growth approaches to dreams, she has developed a technique that happily marries divergent approaches. Hill calls her method *cognitive–experiential*, and its influences include contemporary Freudian and Jungian psychoanalytic models; cognitive–behavioral techniques; and experiential techniques that have been developed by humanistic, existential, client-centered, and gestalt psychologists and tested in traditional psychotherapy, personal growth and expressive-arts workshops, and self-help techniques.

Hill distills these divergent influences into a flexible three-stage process that includes exploration, insight, and action. The dreamer is guided through the stages and encouraged to participate actively. Hill dispels the myth of the psychotherapist as the "expert" who dispenses dream interpretations to the receptive client. She reframes the process as *dream work*, an active collaboration between dreamer and therapist. The metaphor for the therapist is a facilitator, or a kind of oneiric midwife who guides the dreamer to give birth to transformative ideas, affects, and insights that flow from the conjoint dream work.

Embedded in her collaborative philosophy of dream work is a deep respect for the dreamer's ideas and associations. Perhaps this is best explained by exercising poetic license on a classic saying: "If you give a person a dream interpretation, she will feel enlightened for a day, but if you teach her to explore her own dreams, she will have a source of inner wisdom for a lifetime."

Although the Hill method was designed as a research technique and a vehicle for exploring and scientifically proving the value of using dreams in psychotherapy, it is accessible and will appeal to both psychotherapists and the public. For psychotherapists working with clients in short- or intermediate-term psychotherapy or under the time limits of managed care, Hill and her colleagues have evidence to show that working with dreams can be beneficial even in shorter forms of psychotherapy.

In addition, many psychotherapists have dismissed dream work because it is usually packaged tightly with some variation of psychoanalytic or Jungian theory. By offering an eclectic and relatively flexible approach that is theoretically inclusive, many more psychotherapists may feel they can try the Hill method without dismissing or contradicting their orientation and without having to pledge allegiance to a theory that may contrast with their prior orientation and training. In fact, in the introduction to this volume,

Hill invites readers to learn and practice her model and then tailor it to the needs of their clients, to particular kinds of dreams, and to their own therapeutic styles.

Another advantage of Hill's work on dreams builds on her extensive research on effective methods for teaching psychotherapists how to work with dreams. By applying her methodological expertise to developing and refining training techniques, she is filling another gap in the field. That aspect of her work may help to revive teaching the art and science of dream work in graduate schools and postgraduate continuing education courses.

Hill's work on dreams pioneers a crucial new direction for the psychotherapy of the 21st century. Psychotherapists no longer have to rely on dazzling case vignettes of experts interpreting patients' dreams that always seem to neatly confirm their own methods and theories. With Hill's work, psychologists are on the threshold of establishing exactly how dreams work in psychotherapy, for whom they work best, and at what stage in the treatment process they work best.

REFERENCES

Barrett, D. (Ed.). (1996). *Trauma and dreams*. Cambridge, MA: Harvard University Press.

Cartwright, R. (1993). Who needs their dreams? The usefulness of dreams in psychotherapy. *Journal of the American Academy of Psychoanalysis, 21*, 539–547.

Delaney, G. (1993). *New directions in dream interpretation*. Albany: State University of New York Press.

Domhoff, G. W. (2003). *The scientific study of dreams*. Washington, DC: American Psychological Association.

Fosshage, J. L., & Loew, C. (1987). *Dream interpretation: A comparative study*. New York: PMA.

Freud, S. (1965). *The interpretation of dreams*. New York: Avon. (Original work published 1900)

Hall, C., & Van de Castle, R. (1966). *The content analysis of dreams*. New York: Appleton-Century-Crofts.

Jung, C. G. (1974). *Dreams* (R. F. C. Hull, Trans.). Princeton, NJ: Princeton University Press.

Moffitt, A., Kramer, M., & Hoffman, R. (1993). *The functions of dreaming*. Albany: State University of New York Press.

Moorcroft, W. (2003). *Understanding sleep and dreaming*. New York: Plenum.

Shafton, A. (1995). *Dream reader: Contemporary approaches to the understanding of dreams*. Albany: State University of New York Press.

Siegel, A. B. (2003). *Dream wisdom: Uncovering life's answers in your dreams*. Berkeley, CA: Celestial Arts.

PREFACE

When I first became interested in working with dreams, I searched for a good model to use for studying the effects of dream work. Many theories existed on working with dreams, but there were problems selecting one to use. First, several models seemed valid and useful, and it was difficult to choose one over the others. Second, the existing models were vague, which made it difficult to teach them to therapists and to determine whether therapists were adhering to them for research purposes. Hence, my students and I set out to develop a model that included the most useful aspects of the available models. We placed the existing models into an integrative theoretical structure to guide the client progressively through exploration, insight, and action stages. A major emphasis was on developing a model that would be clear and easy to teach and use for research and clinical purposes.

It took us a long time to make the model workable. My students and I started working on developing the model after training therapists for Mary Cogar's dissertation and revised it many times, trying to get it right.[1] Finally, after much feedback from colleagues and students who were involved in the training and participated in studies as therapists, the model came together in book form.[2]

Since publication of the 1996 book, we have conducted a lot more training and research, and these experiences have helped us refine our thinking about the model. The time seemed ripe for an updated version of the model. The basic structure of the model (i.e., the stages of exploration, insight, and action) is the same as in the 1996 version, but the present model

---

[1]Cogar, M. C., & Hill, C. E. (1992). Examining the effects of brief individual dream interpretation. *Dreaming, 2,* 239–248.
[2]Hill, C. E. (1996). *Working with dreams in psychotherapy.* New York: Guilford Press.

is clearer and easier to follow. The steps of the model have been modified somewhat (e.g., we added an acronym to help therapists explore the images in the exploration stage, deleted the level of past experiences and added the level of inner conflicts to the insight stage, and clarified the steps of the action stage).

The timing for another book on dream work is also good. When I first became interested in working with dreams, many of my colleagues were taken aback because dream work was not well accepted within academic circles. Since then, attitudes toward dream work have shifted in a positive direction, as is evidenced by the growing number of people joining the Association for the Study of Dreams. I believe this attitude change has come about for several reasons. First, the cognitive revolution of the last 30 years or so has filtered down to dreams, leading to a recognition that working with dreams in therapy can be valuable. Furthermore, the discovery of the connection between nightmares and posttraumatic stress disorder has led therapists to a realization of the need to work with some dreams in therapy.[3] Third, a number of brief approaches to working with dreams[4,5] have begun to appear, countering the widespread belief that dream work is appropriate only in long-term therapy. I hope that a final reason for the positive attitude shift is the growing evidence from our research that working with dreams is beneficial.

I hope that this book will provide the impetus for more people to work on their own dreams, for more therapists to incorporate dreams into their therapy work, and for more researchers to tackle some of the fascinating questions about the hows and whys of dream work.

---

[3]Barrett, D. (Ed.). (1996). *Trauma and dreams*. Cambridge, MA: Harvard University Press.
[4]Delaney, G. (Ed.). (1993). *New directions in dream interpretation*. Albany: State University of New York Press.
[5]Krippner, S., & Waldman, M. R. (Eds.). (1999). *Dreamscaping*. Chicago: Lowell House.

ACKNOWLEDGMENTS

I thank all my students who have gone through the training and have challenged many components of the cognitive–experiential model. They have helped me expand my thinking through their questions and experiences.

In particular, I want to recognize and thank several students and colleagues who have worked closely with me on the model: Mary Cogar, Jamila Codrington, Rachel Crook, Tim Davis, Roberta Diemer, Keith Eiche, Dana Falk, Charlie Gelso, Melissa Goates, Julie Goldberg, Jim Gormally, Kristin Heaton, Shirley Hess, Ann Hillyer, Mary Ann Hoffman, Frances Kelley, Sarah Knox, Misty Kolchakian, Daniela Ligiero, Leslie Lobell, Tim McCready, Leslie Muldanado, Emilie Nakayama, David Petersen, Peggy Rios, Aaron Rochlen, Robyn Seeman, Meredith Tomlinson, Maria Turkson, Sutha Veerasamy, Barbara Vivino, Teresa Wonnell, and Jason Zack.

I also thank the hundreds of clients who have taken part in our research sessions—they are the real tests of how well the model works. I extend thanks to Peggy Barott for typing many of the transcripts from the dream sessions for this book.

DREAM WORK IN THERAPY

INTRODUCTION

CLARA E. HILL

Dreams often leave people feeling puzzled and fascinated when they wake up. Consider the following dream, told by a participant in a recent study:

> I am getting ready to swim in a swim meet, and I'm scared that I am going to do badly. My friend is swimming with me, and so to swim fast I cheat and put on fins. This helps me go a 2:06, which isn't my best time, but still is fast. I beat my friend but feel terribly guilty for cheating. Then, I come back to my home and see my grandmother hammering nails into wood. She is building something. I leave the room to take a shower, and when I come back I notice that my grandma has hammered the wood and nail into her hand. I try to pry it off her hand, and I notice that she is not responding. I look up at her eyes and they are shut, so I shake her profusely to try to wake her up, but she won't budge.

After dreams like this one, people wonder why they had the dream, what it means, and what they should do about it.

If you listen on the subway or at work in the morning, you will often hear people say that they just had a bizarre dream that they cannot figure out. If you tell someone at a party that you are a psychologist, they often begin telling you a dream (e.g., flunking a test, appearing naked, falling) that they vividly remember but do not understand. Students often major in psychology thinking that they will learn about themselves and their dreams (and they are often quite disappointed to learn that psychologists do not study dreams much). These examples show that many people are fascinated by and curious about their dreams, and so it is important to figure out ways to help people understand their dreams.

Over the years, my students and I have developed a cognitive–experiential approach to working with dreams so that we can help people figure out what their dreams mean. The model is a straightforward approach that can be easily learned by therapists to help clients understand their dreams.

ASSUMPTIONS OF THE MODEL

Before I describe the theoretical overview of the model, several critical underlying assumptions should be noted. First, I assume that *dreams are a continuation of waking thinking without input from the external world* (see also Breger, 1967, 1969; Cartwright, 1990; Garma, 1987; R. Greenberg, 1987; Koulack, 1991; Kramer, 1982; Kramer, Hlasny, Jacobs, & Roth, 1976). When people go to sleep, and during non-rapid eye movement (REM) sleep, they continue to think about issues that have been on their minds during the day. As they begin to dream, they think about these issues in a more metaphorical manner, weaving in related memories and associations. In essence, they create a story out of what is currently most pressing on their minds. People typically star in their dreams and use the dreams to think about and work on their personal issues.

The second assumption flows from the first. Given that I believe that dreams are a reflection of a person's waking thoughts and memories, feelings, and behaviors, it follows that I believe that *the meaning of the dream is personal for the client*. Hence, standard dream dictionaries and standard symbolic interpretations (such as Freudian sexual symbolism or Jungian archetypes) are not typically helpful when applied without knowledge of the individual's associations. Although standard interpretations may be generally applicable to a population, they are not necessarily helpful when trying to understand an individual, because each individual has had unique experiences. For example, an elephant might represent a lucky charm for most people in a particular culture but might be a very negative symbol for an individual within that culture who narrowly escaped being trampled by an elephant. I assert that these individual experiences shape the dreams and dream interpretations. Therefore, because dreams reflect individual experiences, I stress that therapists cannot rely on standard interpretations; rather, they need to help clients access their personal thoughts and memories about dream images.

The assumption that only the dreamer has the "key" to the meaning of the dream leads to the third assumption, that *working with dreams in therapy should be a collaborative process between the therapist and client*. The therapist is *not* the expert who knows the meaning of the dream but rather is an expert at helping the client explore the dream, come to a new understanding of the meaning of the dream, and make decisions about action based on the dream. The meaning of the dream, as well as what the client chooses to do differently in waking life, should come as a surprise to both the client and the therapist (Reik, 1935). The meaning should emerge through the exploration process of the two people working together, with the therapist serving as the coach who facilitates the process.

Even if a therapist can see themes within or across dreams (cf. Kramer, 1993), I assert that it is not as useful for the therapist to explicate these themes as it is for the client to discover these themes alone or through the facilitation of the therapist. There is a sense of empowerment that comes when one puts together all the information and finds a new meaning for oneself.

The fourth assumption is that *dreams are a useful tool for helping people understand more about themselves*. Although dreams may also serve other functions (e.g., to maintain sleep, to discharge energy in the brain; see Hunt, 1989), they provide a window into the dreamer's psyche. Because dreams come from the individual, they help therapists learn more about the individual, often revealing things of which the individual is not consciously aware. Therapists cannot know whether they ever actually get to the "true" meaning of the dream, or even whether there is a single meaning to a dream, but they do assume that dreams provide information about the person that therapists might not obtain otherwise.

Another assumption is that *dreams involve cognitive, emotional, and behavioral components*. We know that cognition is involved, because people are thinking during their dreams. We also know that emotions are involved, because people wake with their hearts pounding and feeling afraid, being sexually excited, or being happy. We also know that behaviors are involved, because dreams involve actions and doing things. Hence, because dreams involve cognitive, emotional, and behavioral components, it makes sense to target all three of these variables in working with dreams.

Finally, effective implementation of the model by therapists is based on the assumption that *therapists need to have expertise in using the basic helping skills and therapeutic techniques* (see Hill & O'Brien, 1999) *before they do dream work*. In particular, therapists need to be empathic and skilled at helping clients explore thoughts and feelings (through reflection of feelings, open question, and restatement), construct insights (through interpretation, confrontation, self-disclosure, and immediacy), and develop action ideas (through information and direct guidance) before they work on dreams with clients. Furthermore, they need to know how to manage sessions (e.g., how to begin and end a session; how to establish a therapeutic relationship; how to develop a focus; how to determine when clients have explored enough, gained enough insight, and developed a good-enough action plan; how to determine when to pursue the dream vs. when to go into other therapeutic issues; how to deal with cultural issues). They also need to know how to conceptualize client pathology and how to manage difficult client situations (e.g., clients who are angry, depressed, borderline, schizophrenic). Finally, therapists need to have a good understanding of the theory underlying the dream interpretation model so that they are not just applying techniques but also have a solid understanding of why they are doing whatever they are doing. Because lots of other therapeutic issues arise when dealing with dreams, therapists must have a solid foundation in theory, clinical skills, and conceptualization abilities in addition to knowing how to work with dreams.

THEORETICAL FOUNDATION

The cognitive–experiential model of dream work evolved from a number of different theoretical orientations (e.g., humanistic–experiential, Gestalt, psychoanalytic, cognitive, and behavioral). In particular, I have been strongly influenced (see review in Hill, 1996) by the dream interpretation models of Adler (1936, 1938, 1958), Cartwright (1977; Cartwright & Lamberg, 1992), Craig and Walsh (1993), Delaney (1991, 1993), Faraday (1972, 1974), Freud (1900/1966), Gendlin (1986), Johnson (1986), Jung (1964, 1974), Mahrer (1990), Ullman (1979, 1987, 1993; Ullman & Zimmerman, 1979), and Weiss (1986). Furthermore, my approach to dream work has been heavily influenced by my graduate school training in client-centered therapy (Rogers, 1951, 1957) and behavioral therapy (Goldfried & Davison, 1994; Kazdin, 2001; Rimm & Masters, 1974) and by my subsequent reading of psychodynamic (Basch, 1980; Book, 1998; Greenson, 1967; Malan, 1976; Mann, 1973; Mitchell, 1993) and interpersonal theorists (Cashdan, 1988; Strupp & Binder, 1984; Teyber, 2000).

Because all these approaches make sense and the literature finds no outcome differences across types of therapy (see Wampold, 2001), the key is to sequence approaches together into a theoretically consistent structure. The structure that makes most sense to me is a sequence in which the person goes from exploring the dream thoroughly to trying to make sense of the meaning of the dream to then figuring out what to do differently in waking life based on what he or she has learned about the dream. This three-stage model is similar to those proposed by Carkhuff (1969), Egan (1986), and myself (Hill & O'Brien, 1999) for therapy.

This model involves three stages: (a) exploration, (b) insight, and (c) action. In the exploration stage, the therapist guides the client through an examination of the individual images of the dream, encouraging the client to re-experience the thoughts and emotions in the dream. In the insight stage, the therapist and client collaborate to construct an understanding of the dream. In the action stage, the therapist works with the client to use what he or she has learned to think about making changes in waking life.

The model can be considered to be cognitive–experiential, because both cognitions and emotions are worked on throughout all three stages. The cognitive part of the model comprises the thorough exploration of thoughts, associations, and memories in the exploration stage; the fostering of insights in the insight stage, and the exploration of thoughts about making changes in the action stage. The experiential component involves an arousal of emotions throughout all three stages, because emotional arousal is posited to be a prerequisite for gaining emotional insight and making good decisions about changes in waking life. In the next section, I provide a brief overview of each of the three stages.

The Exploration Stage

The goal of the exploration stage is to activate the client's cognitive schema (or memory structures) so that the feelings, thoughts, memories, and experiences that fueled his or her dream are activated. We want the schemas activated so that we can help the client change his or her way of thinking (i.e., to gain insight) in the next stage. We also want to heighten the client's emotional arousal so that he or she is energized and motivated to understand the dream and make changes. Furthermore, we want to build an alliance so that the client trusts us, and we want to learn more about the client's world so that we have a foundation for understanding the client and offering input in the coming stages. Finally, we want to learn as much as we can about the client to provide a foundation for giving feedback in the insight and action stages.

The theoretical foundation for the exploration stage is client-centered therapy (Bohart & Tallman, 1999; Bozarth, 1998; Gendlin, 1986; L. Greenberg, 2002; L. Greenberg, Rice, & Elliott, 1993; Rogers, 1942, 1951, 1957). The therapist tries to help the client explore the dream but does not act as the expert who has the answers. We assume that the client has the answer to the dream and needs support (empathy, warmth, genuineness) to get unblocked and work through to self-healing. The therapist, however, follows a more structured approach than is typical in client-centered therapy. Along with Bohart and Tallman (1999), we believe that therapists can accomplish the task of providing a supportive environment through a variety of interventions. The provision of empathy and collaboration and the belief that the client is self-healing make this stage (and the whole model) client centered. Furthermore, it is important that the therapist structures the process in this stage but does not add any input (e.g., does not offer associations). Hence, the structure allows the therapist a framework through which to help the client explore and the therapist get to know the client. The client is the one, however, who does the work of exploring the dream.

To encourage exploration, we work with the client to carefully examine each image. In effect, we take a magnifying glass and try to magnify each image so we can discover what it means to the person. We assume that we cannot ever know another person completely, and so we try to get the client to explore as much as possible about the image. We do this through encouraging clients to proceed sequentially through the images by describing the scene; re-experiencing the feelings; associating to the thoughts, feelings, and memories; and searching for waking life triggers. We use the acronym DRAW (description, re-experiencing, associations, waking life triggers) to help therapists remember the four steps.

The Insight Stage

The desire for insight often energizes clients to want to work on their dreams. They have a puzzling dream that begs for illumination. They want to figure out why they had the dream and what it means for their lives. They want to know the "message" from their inner selves (recall the quote from the Talmud that a dream is like an unopened letter). In the insight stage, we take the material generated in the exploration stage and help clients expand on initial understandings and search for new ways to understand the dream. In particular, we aim for emotional insight—understanding things at a deep, emotional level rather than at just a dry, sterile, intellectual level.

The insight stage is based on psychodynamic dream theory (e.g., Adler, 1936, 1938, 1958; Beebe, 1993; Bonime, 1987; Bosnak, 1988; Fosshage, 1983, 1987; Freud, 1900/1966; Garma, 1987; Glucksman, 1988; Glucksman & Warner, 1987; Johnson, 1986; Jung, 1964, 1974; Natterson, 1980, 1993; Schwartz, 1990). The main goal of psychodynamic dream work is to understand the meaning of the dream. Insight is considered the "pure gold" of psychodynamic treatment and is thought to be crucial for helping clients make sense of their world.

Insight can occur at a number of levels. At the most surface, or transparent level, the therapist can help the client understand the experience (or theme, or story) of the dream and think about what the story reflects about him or her. At the middle level, the therapist can work with the client to help her or him understand how the dream relates to events in waking life. At the deepest level, the therapist can help the client understand how the dream relates to inner personality dynamics (e.g., parts of self, conflicts originating in childhood, existential or spiritual concerns).

Although the goal shifts from pure exploration to insight in this stage, the process remains collaborative, and the therapist continues to be empathic. Often the therapist poses questions to stimulate the client's thinking about meanings. In addition, the therapist sometimes judiciously and collaboratively offers his or her thoughts about meanings to provide input and jumpstart further client thinking. The process is similar to brainstorming, by which two people can come up with better ideas through the interaction than one person can on his or her own.

The Action Stage

Action is important to help clients consolidate the insights from the preceding stage. When clients have to figure out what to do about the insights, it makes the insights gained during the preceding stage more immediate and real. Furthermore, action is especially important when the dream reveals problems that need to be addressed.

The theoretical foundation for the action stage is behavioral theory. Although behavioral theorists have not developed specific approaches to working with dreams (with the very recent exception of Eschenröder, 2003), several nonbehavioral dream theorists (Gendlin, 1986; Mahrer, 1990) have proposed that a thorough understanding of a dream leads to a new growth direction. Also, Jungian theorists (e.g., Johnson, 1986) have discussed the importance of using rituals to intensify the meaning of the dream and help the person change habits and attitudes. It makes sense to bring behavior therapy into dream work to help people make changes in their lives when these changes are suggested by the dream work.

Insight often directly leads to action, but at other times therapists need to help clients explore their thoughts about action. Many clients are ambivalent about action and need to talk through the benefits and drawbacks about making changes. Other clients are eager to change but need to be taught specific skills (e.g., assertiveness training, how to increase positive behaviors or decrease negative behaviors, methods to continue to work with the dream). Others just need encouragement to maintain their current change programs.

As in the previous two stages, the process in the action stage remains collaborative, and the therapist continues to empathize with the client. The therapist most often asks questions to facilitate the client's thinking about action. The therapist also occasionally offers his or her thoughts about possible client actions when the client is stuck or has a hard time thinking of possible actions. Even when the therapist makes suggestions, though, the process remains collaborative, with the therapist being tentative about the suggestions, attentive to client reactions, and eager to turn the process back to the client.

FORMAT OF THE BOOK

Part I of this book is a manual of how to do cognitive–experiential dream work. In separate chapters I explicate the steps of the exploration, insight, and action stages. In Part II, several former students who are very familiar with this model have contributed chapters about applications of the model. Cogar writes in chapter 4 about using the model in ongoing therapy. In chapter 5, Wonnell discusses use of the model in groups. In chapter 6, Zack writes about self-help applications of the model. Davis describes in chapter 7 a modification of the model for inspiring spiritual insights. Hess discusses in chapter 8 using the model to help people cope with loss. Rochlen presents ideas about how to use the model when working with men in chapter 9. In chapter 10 Heaton applies the model to work with nightmares. Part III involves discussions of training and research. Crook writes in chapter 11 about training therapists to use the model and, finally, in chapter 12, Goates and I review the research on this model. In the Appendixes readers can find an outline of the steps of the model and reprints of several measures that my students and I have used for assessing the effects of dream work.

It is also important to mention that the history of dreams, research on sleep and dreaming, and the formation of dreams are not covered in this book. Readers are referred to Hill (1996) and Van de Castle (1994) for good summaries of that literature.

Furthermore, readers should know that most of the examples in this book involve actual dreams and dream work with clients and students, although some are composites of several dreams. We have obtained permission from clients to use their material, and we have changed names to protect identities. In addition, the content of the real dreams and dream work has also been altered sometimes to increase readability and illustrate points more clearly.

I need to say a few words about the terms used in this book. The term *client* is used, rather than *patient*, to emphasize that the client is an active agent in the dream work rather than a person with a disease, as in the medical model. The term *dream work* is used to represent the range of activities in which therapists and clients engage in the model. I used to use *dream interpretation* because of the long history of this term in regard to working with dreams, but the term has too often been misunderstood by people who assumed that it meant that therapists were the experts providing the interpretations for clients (reflecting a traditional psychoanalytic manner of using interpretations; Mitchell, 1993). I acknowledge that the term *dream work* might be confusing to some psychoanalytic people, because Freud used it to represent the movement of latent dream content into manifest content, but it is the best term I have come up with to reflect the range of activities in the model.

WHO SHOULD READ THIS BOOK?

Therapists who want to help clients work with dreams should read this book. Therapists should also read this book to learn more about working on their own dreams. Furthermore, therapists should give this book to clients to educate them about why and how they are working with dreams. Finally, people who want to understand more about themselves and their dreams should read this book.

My students and I have found that most people prefer to work with therapists and that they get more out of working with therapists to understand their dreams, but this approach also works well as a self-help approach to working with dreams (Heaton, Hill, Petersen, Rochlen, & Zack, 1998; Hill, Rochlen, Zack, McCready, & Dematatis, in press). The ideal is for clients to first work with therapists on a dream and then use the model to work by themselves on their dreams. However, this model is also appropriate for people who have no access to therapists or who do not wish to seek therapy. I recommend, however, that people working alone on their dreams seek professional help when the emotions or insights from dream work become too intense or overwhelming.

I present this model as a self-contained therapeutic intervention, or therapeutic module or mini-therapy. In other words, a person comes to therapy with a dream that he or she wants to understand, and a therapist works with him or her to understand the dream. This intervention can take place in one or two sessions for a relatively healthy person whose goal is primarily self-discovery or growth. The model can also be used in single sessions or within the course of brief or long-term therapy.

HOW TO USE THIS BOOK

The steps of the dream interpretation process are outlined in Appendix A. When initially practicing the model, therapists can take this page into sessions with them as a "cheat sheet" to provide an outline of the steps. Therapists should plan on 60 to 90 minutes for conducting the full dream model, although in chapter 4 Cogar offers some suggestions for modifying the model for ongoing therapy.

It is important to note that this book is meant to serve as a guideline rather than as a rigid structure. I suggest that therapists become familiar with the theory behind the model and then try to use the model as presented here with a range of clients. After practicing the model several times, therapists will find ways to personalize the approach to their own individual styles, to the needs of different clients, and to different types of dreams. Obviously, there are many ways to work with dreams, none of which have been proven to be superior to others, so therapists need not adhere slavishly to this or any other model.

I also encourage therapists to work with their own dreams, either by working with another trainee or by using the computer program Jason Zack and I have developed (see chap. 6). Working on one's own dreams can provide convincing evidence of the value of working with dreams. It also helps one learn the steps of the model more effectively.

The question often comes up about whether there are certain clients with whom it is not advisable to do dream work. Research (see chap. 12) and clinical experience suggest that dream work is not appropriate for everyone. First, the choice about whether to use dream work depends on attitudes of the therapist and client toward working with dreams. Therapists and clients with positive attitudes toward dreams are most likely to want to work with dreams. If clients are not eager to work with their dreams, or if they seem resistant, then it is not a good idea to force dream work on them. Furthermore, if clients do not have a pressing dream that they want to understand, it does not make sense to force them to work with their dreams. Finally, therapists will probably want to be more cautious about doing dream work with clients who have a tenuous grasp on reality (i.e., who cannot distinguish dreams from waking life), who are psychotic, or who cannot concentrate on the dream interpretation process.

REFERENCES

Adler, A. (1936). On the interpretation of dreams. *International Journal of Individual Psychology, 2,* 3–16.

Adler, A. (1938). *Social interest: Challenge to mankind.* London: Faber & Faber.

Adler, A. (1958). *What life should mean to you.* New York: Capricorn.

Basch, M. F. (1980). *Doing psychotherapy.* New York: Basic Books.

Beebe, J. (1993). A Jungian approach to working with dreams. In G. Delaney (Ed.), *New directions in dream interpretation* (pp. 77–102). Albany: State University of New York Press.

Bohart, A. C., & Tallman, K. (1999). *How clients make therapy work: The process of active self-healing.* Washington, DC: American Psychological Association.

Bonime, W. (1987). Collaborative dream interpretation. In M. L. Glucksman & S. L. Warner (Eds.), *Dreams in a new perspective: The royal road revisited* (pp. 79–96). New York: Human Sciences Press.

Book, H. E. (1998). *How to practice brief psychodynamic psychotherapy: The core conflictual relationship theme method.* Washington, DC: American Psychological Association.

Bosnak, R. (1988). *A little course in dreams: A basic handbook of Jungian dreamwork.* Boston: Shambhala.

Bozarth, J. (1998). *Person-centered therapy: A revolutionary paradigm.* Ross-on-Wye, England: PCCS Books.

Breger, L. (1967). Function of dreams. *Journal of Abnormal Psychology Monographs, 72*(5, Pt. 2, Whole No. 641).

Breger, L. (1969). Dream function: An information processing model. In L. Breger (Ed.), *Clinical–cognitive psychology* (pp. 192–227). Englewood Cliffs, NJ: Prentice-Hall.

Carkhuff, R. R. (1969). *Human and helping relations* (Vols. 1 & 2). New York: Holt, Rinehart & Winston.

Cartwright, R. D. (1977). *Nightlife.* Englewood Cliffs, NJ: Prentice Hall.

Cartwright, R. D. (1990). A network model of dreams. In R. Bootzin, J. Kihlstrom,

& D. Schachter (Eds.), *Sleep and cognition* (pp. 179–189). Washington, DC: American Psychological Association.

Cartwright, R. D., & Lamberg, L. (1992). *Crisis dreaming: Using your dreams to solve your problems*. New York: HarperCollins.

Cashdan, S. (1988). *Object relations therapy*. New York: Norton.

Craig, E., & Walsh, S. J. (1993). The clinical use of dreams. In G. Delaney (Ed.), *New directions in dream interpretation* (pp. 103–154). Albany: State University of New York Press.

Delaney, G. (1991). *Breakthrough dreaming*. New York: Bantam Books.

Delaney, G. (1993). The dream interview. In G. Delaney (Ed.), *New directions in dream interpretation* (pp. 195–240). Albany: State University of New York Press.

Egan, G. (1986). *The skilled helper* (3rd ed.). Monterey, CA: Brooks/Cole.

Eschenröder, C. T. (2003). Ueber den umgang mit traeumen in der verhaltenstherapie. *Verhaltenstherapie und Psycholsoziale Praxis, 35,* 73–85.

Faraday, A. (1972). *Dream power*. New York: Coward, McCann & Geoghegan.

Faraday, A. (1974). *The dream game*. New York: Harper & Row.

Fosshage, J. L. (1983). The psychoanalytic function of dreams: A revised psychoanalytic perspective. *Psychoanalysis and Contemporary Thought, 6,* 641–669.

Fosshage, J. L. (1987). New vistas in dream interpretation. In M. L. Glucksman & S. L. Warner (Eds.), *Dreams in a new perspective: The royal road revisited* (pp. 23–44). New York: Human Sciences Press.

Freud, S. (1966). *The interpretation of dreams*. New York: Avon. (Original work published 1900)

Garma, A. (1987). Freudian approach. In J. L. Fosshage & C. A. Loew (Eds.), *Dream interpretation: A comparative study* (pp. 16–51). New York: PMA.

Gendlin, E. (1986). *Let your body interpret your dream*. Wilmette, IL: Chiron.

Glucksman, M. L. (1988). The use of successive dreams to facilitate and document change during treatment. *Journal of the American Academy of Psychoanalysis, 16,* 47–69.

Glucksman, M. L., & Warner, S. L. (Eds.). (1987). *Dreams in a new perspective: The royal road revisited*. New York: Human Sciences Press.

Goldfried, M. R., & Davison, G. C. (1994). *Clinical behavior therapy* (expanded ed.). New York: Wiley.

Greenberg, L. S. (2002). *Emotion-focused therapy: Coaching clients to work through their feelings*. Washington, DC: American Psychological Association.

Greenberg, L. S., Rice, L. N., & Elliott, R. (1993). *Facilitating emotional change*. New York: Guilford Press.

Greenberg, R. (1987). The dream problem and problems in dreams. In M. L. Glucksman & S. L. Warner (Eds.), *Dreams in a new perspective: The royal road revisited* (pp. 45–57). New York: Human Sciences Press.

Greenson, R. R. (1967). *The technique and practice of psychoanalysis* (Vol. 1). Madison, CT: International Universities Press.

Heaton, K. J., Hill, C. E., Petersen, D. A., Rochlen, A. B., & Zack, J. S. (1998). A comparison of therapist-facilitated and self-guided dream interpretation sessions. *Journal of Counseling Psychology, 45,* 115–122.

Hill, C. E. (1996). *Working with dreams in psychotherapy.* New York: Guilford Press.

Hill, C. E., & O'Brien, K. (1999). *Helping skills: Facilitating exploration, insight, and action.* Washington, DC: American Psychological Association.

Hill, C. E., Rochlen, A. B., Zack, J. S., McCready, T., & Dematatis, A. (in press). Working with dreams using the Hill cognitive–experiential model: A comparison of computer-assisted, therapist empathy, and therapist empathy + input conditions. *Journal of Counseling Psychology.*

Hunt, H. (1989). *The multiplicity of dreams: Memory, imagination, and consciousness.* New Haven, CT: Yale University Press.

Johnson, R. (1986). *Inner work.* San Francisco: Harper & Row.

Jung, C. G. (Ed.). (1964). *Man and his symbols.* New York: Dell.

Jung, C. G. (1974). *Dreams* (R. F. C. Hull, Trans.). Princeton, NJ: Princeton University Press.

Kazdin, A. E. (2001). *Behavior modification in applied settings* (6th ed.). Belmont, CA: Wadsworth/Thomson Learning.

Koulack, D. (1991). *To catch a dream: Explorations of dreaming.* Albany: State University New York Press.

Kramer, M. (1982). Psychology of the dream: Art or science? *Psychiatric Journal of the University of Ottawa, 7,* 87–100.

Kramer, M. (1993). Dream translation: An approach to understanding dreams. In G. Delaney (Ed.), *New directions in dream interpretation* (pp. 155–194). Albany: State University of New York Press.

Kramer, M., Hlasny, R., Jacobs, G., & Roth, T. (1976). Do dreams have meaning? An empirical inquiry. *American Journal of Psychiatry, 133,* 778–781.

Mahrer, A. R. (1990). *Dream work in psychotherapy and self-change.* New York: Norton.

Malan, S. H. (1976). *The frontier of brief therapy.* New York: Plenum.

Mann, J. (1973). *Time-limited psychotherapy.* Cambridge, MA: Harvard University Press.

Mitchell, S. (1993). *Hope and dread in psychoanalysis.* New York: Basic Books.

Natterson, J. M. (1980). The dream in group psychotherapy. In J. M. Natterson (Ed.), *The dream in clinical practice* (pp. 434–443). New York: Jason Aronson.

Natterson, J. M. (1993). Dreams: The gateway to consciousness. In G. Delaney (Ed.), *New directions in dream interpretation* (pp. 41–76). Albany: State University of New York Press.

Reik, T. (1935). *Surprise and the psychoanalyst.* London: Routledge.

Rimm, D. C., & Masters, J. C. (1974). *Behavior therapy: Techniques and empirical findings.* New York: Academic Press.

Rogers, C. R. (1942). *Counseling and psychotherapy.* Boston: Houghton Mifflin.

Rogers, C. R. (1951). *Client-centered therapy: Its current practice, implications, and theory*. Boston: Houghton Mifflin.

Rogers, C. R. (1957). The necessary and sufficient conditions of therapeutic personal change. *Journal of Consulting Psychology, 21*, 95–103.

Schwartz, W. (1990). A psychoanalytic approach to dreamwork. In S. Krippner (Ed.), *Dreamtime and dreamwork: Decoding the language of the night* (pp. 49–58). Los Angeles: Tarcher.

Strupp, H. H., & Binder, J. L. (1984). *Psychotherapy in a new key: A guide to time-limited dynamic psychotherapy*. New York: Basic Books.

Teyber, E. (2000). *Interpersonal process in psychotherapy* (4th ed.). Pacific Grove, CA: Brooks/Cole.

Ullman, M. (1979). The experiential dream group. In B. B. Wolman (Ed.), *Handbook of dreams* (pp. 407–423). New York: Van Nostrand Reinhold.

Ullman, M. (1987). The dream revisited: Some changed ideas based on a group approach. In M. L. Glucksman & S. L. Warner (Eds.), *Dreams in a new perspective: The royal road revisited* (pp. 119–130). New York: Human Sciences Press.

Ullman, M. (1993). Dreams, the dreamer, and society. In G. Delaney (Ed.), *New directions in dream interpretation* (pp. 11–40). Albany: State University of New York Press.

Ullman, M., & Zimmerman, N. (1979). *Working with dreams*. Los Angeles: Tarcher.

Van de Castle, R. L. (1994). *The dreaming mind*. New York: Ballantine Books.

Wampold, B. E. (2001). *The great psychotherapy debate: Models, methods, and findings*. Mahwah, NJ: Erlbaum.

Weiss, L. (1986). *Dream analysis in psychotherapy*. New York: Pergamon.

I

OVERVIEW OF THE HILL COGNITIVE–EXPERIENTIAL DREAM MODEL

1

THE EXPLORATION STAGE

CLARA E. HILL

In the exploration stage, the therapist serves as a coach, helping the client explore the dream images. The therapist avoids having expectations about what content will emerge but focuses instead on guiding the exploration process. Clients learn a lot about themselves by responding to the questions, and therapists learn a lot about clients through the exploration of the images. After all, therapists do not often ask clients about things such as dragons, butterflies, and spaceships, yet such images occur in dreams and often have significance, both literally and metaphorically. A complete exploration of the major images in a dream is crucial for setting the foundation for understanding the dream and using it to make changes in waking life.

The primary skills that therapists use in this stage are open questions, restatements, and reflections of feelings (see Hill & O'Brien, 1999). They use open questions to introduce each new step, direct the process, seek clarification, and ask about thoughts and feelings. They use restatements and reflections of feelings to mirror what the client has said, demonstrate that they are listening and understanding, and encourage further exploration.

In this chapter I describe the five steps of the exploration stage: (a) explaining the model, (b) retelling the dream, (c) exploring overall feelings and the timing of the dream, (d) exploring images using DRAW (description, re-experiencing, associations, waking life triggers), and (e) summarizing exploration. I provide extensive examples of the process so that therapists can understand how to proceed through this stage.

EXPLAIN THE MODEL

Clients need to know what will occur in dream sessions so that they have realistic expectations about the process. They need to know that the therapist expects them to take an active role in working with the dream rather than expecting that the therapist will be the expert who takes in all the information and then spits out "the" interpretation. Hence, clients can be told very briefly about the three-stage model for working with dreams:

> *Therapist:* Today we're going to explore the individual images of your dream. Then we'll work together to figure out the meaning of the dream. And finally, we'll work together to explore what you would like to do differently in your waking life based on what you think the dream is telling you.

ASK THE CLIENT TO RETELL THE DREAM

The therapist needs to hear the content of the dream so that he or she can begin working on it, and the therapist also wants to get the client re-immersed in the immediate experience of the dream to become involved in the whole process. When clients are involved in the process, they are likely to work to understand their dreams and make changes in their waking lives. For this reason, we ask clients to tell the dream in the first-person present tense as if they are experiencing the dream currently.

Therapist (T): Tell me the dream in the first-person present tense.

Client (C): What do you mean?

T: Pretend you are actually in the dream, and tell it to me as if it is happening right now. For example, "I am walking down the hall and I see this monster jump out."

C: Oh, okay. The dream begins when I was in the desert last spring.

T: "I am in the desert..."

C: I am in the desert, and I see this armadillo...

If, after adequate explanation and examples, the client cannot or will not tell the dream in the first-person present tense, the therapist should not insist but should let the client tell it in his or her own way. If this occurs, however, the therapist might want to take a moment to conceptualize what is going on. It may be that the therapist is being too coercive and should back off, or perhaps the client resists too much direction. If this is the case, the therapist might want to proceed cautiously and modify the structure if other signals of resistance appear.

Generally, we suggest that the therapist take notes to record the major images as the client tells the dream; otherwise it is difficult for the therapist to remember all the images and the twists and turns that dreams often take. It is not possible (or even desirable) to get all the text verbatim, but it is possible to get the major images. I scribble the images on a pad of paper while maintaining eye contact with the client. For example, in response to a woman's dream about being in the garden behind her house and pushing her sisters on swings when a yellowjacket stung one of the sisters and her mother got mad at her for not protecting her sister, I might write the following images from the dream:

> garden
> sisters on swing
> yellowjacket stings
> mother gets mad.

After writing down the images, I put down the pen and take no more notes during the remainder of the session because I want to focus completely on the client. The notes about the images are just meant to be my cue sheet for where to go next as the client and I review the images. It is tempting to write notes to capture all the details of what the client says throughout the session, but it usually distracts one from the immediacy of the process.

When clients first tell their dreams, most therapists have no idea about what the dreams mean. For therapists who feel a need to control the therapy process, not knowing the meaning can be anxiety provoking; however, the client-centered stance of focusing on the clients and helping the clients explore their dreams takes the pressure off therapists to know what the dream means. Therapists can go into the process with a sense of confidence that they know how to guide the process even if they do not know the outcome of the process.

Even if therapists think they know what the dream means, we encourage them to hold off saying anything during the exploration stage so that clients have the opportunity to explore thoroughly and come to the meaning on their own. Thorough exploration of the dream images allows clients to get involved in the process and enables therapists to learn something new about their clients.

Several issues can come up in this step. Some clients ask whether they can read a written copy of the dream. We discourage reading written copies of dreams because it can have a distancing effect and makes it more difficult for clients to reenter the dream experience. What seems to work better is asking the client to take a minute to scan the written copy and recollect the dream and then to tell the dream as if she or he is experiencing it currently.

Another issue is that it can be difficult to work with lengthy dreams, especially ones that have many different scenes or segments. As an example, a client might have a dream that starts with a complicated fight in the desert, then moves to a lot of details about a big family dinner, then moves to a long flight in a hot air balloon over the ocean, and then switches yet again to a detailed exchange between the dreamer and a neighbor. Although these segments are probably connected, it would be hard to deal competently with such a long dream in a single session. As another example, one client brought a dream that was three typed pages long into a workshop. It took her 20 minutes just to tell the dream. There was no way that we could get through the whole dream in one session without shortchanging the experience.

Therapists can handle the problem of overly long dreams in several different ways. If it is clear at the beginning of the session that the dream is too long, the therapist can ask the client to pick a scene or segment of the dream and tell only that part. Alternatively, if the client feels that the whole dream is important, the therapist can ask the client to tell the whole dream, and then they can decide together which segment to work on, preferably the segment that is the most salient. If therapists do not know initially that the dream is too long, but the retelling goes over 5 minutes, the therapist might stop the client and ask him or her to choose just a segment of the dream to work with in the session. Another option is to go through all three stages on one part of the dream in one session and then do another part in one or more separate sessions.

At the other extreme, short dreams are usually not a problem, even if the client can remember only a fragment of a dream, as long as he or she is motivated to understand the dream. The therapist can focus in depth on each individual image. For example, one client had a dream about falling. At first she was apologetic because the dream was short and she could not remember many details. She felt silly talking about the dream because she thought that falling dreams were very common and did not mean anything in particular. However, the therapist took the dream seriously and asked the client to describe the dream in as much detail as possible. Additional details emerged through the exploration process. They were able to get a lot of meaning for her personally from even that brief dream.

Another issue that often comes up regards the recency of the dream. Freud (1900/1966) suggested that it is preferable for clients to discuss dreams that are less than 24 hours old so that the waking life triggers are readily available to the client. In our experience, clients get annoyed with the restriction to tell only recent dreams, because they often do not remember recent dreams and want to discuss dreams that are more salient to them, sometimes ones that have haunted them for years. For example, a college student from India talked about a dream from when she was 10 years old. In the dream, she went out into her backyard in India and found thousands of snakes hanging down all over the yard about 10 ft above the ground. The dream terrified her, and she wanted to understand it. Of interest is that the details from her life at the time of the dream were relatively clear, because it immediately preceded her move to the United States. However, even if the waking life triggers are not available to memory, therapists can still work with the dream, as I describe in the *Waking Life Triggers* section. Thus, it seems to be okay for clients to present any dreams, as long as the dreams are vivid and clients are motivated to work on them.

Therapists often ask about the importance of clients accurately remembering dreams as they actually occurred. People typically forget all but the most salient and vivid dreams on awakening (Koulack, 1991), and details of dreams are lost unless they are rehearsed or written down immediately. As time progresses and people think about their dreams, they make them more palatable and logical and smooth over the rough parts, often unaware that they are changing it. There is also some evidence for selectivity in terms of which dreams are presented. Whitman, Kramer, and Baldridge (1963) obtained dream reports from two people in a sleep laboratory and then studied which dreams were reported later to a psychiatrist. Not surprisingly, dreams that might have elicited a negative response from the psychiatrist (e.g., sexuality dreams) were not reported. For our purposes in working with dreams therapeutically, however, these issues about the accuracy of dream recall are not of major importance. The client brings in dreams with which he or she is comfortable or on which he or she is ready to work, and we work with whatever the client brings into the session.

Another question that comes up is whether the dream has to be real. Could it be a daytime fantasy? Yes. Could it be totally made up? Yes. Even if a client makes up the dream, it still comes from his or her mind. Could it be someone else's dream? Yes, if the client can project onto the dream as if it were his or her own dream. In group dream work, all group members are asked to project onto one person's dream, and typically all the group members benefit from the projections (see chap. 5).

ELICIT OVERALL FEELINGS AND DETERMINE WHEN THE DREAM OCCURRED

After the dream has been told, the therapist asks how the client felt during the dream, to facilitate re-entry into the emotions in the dream and build arousal and motivation for change. The idea here is not to examine the feelings for each of the individual images in the dream (that comes later) but to obtain an overall sense of the emotional climate of the dream. It is important for therapists to encourage clients not only to say feeling words but also to immerse themselves in the emotions involved in the dream experience. Therapists can also ask clients about feelings when they woke up and as they are telling the dream, again to encourage clients to become aware of and talk about their feelings.

T: What were you feeling during the dream?

C: I felt scared. I have never had such anxiety. It was just awful.

T: You sound scared just talking about it.

C: Yeah, it has really stayed with me.

T: And how did you feel when you woke up from the dream?

C: Strangely enough, when I woke up, I wasn't that scared. I could see that the monster was that old suitcase sitting in the corner, and I felt a little silly. But I was still shaking a little and had to calm myself down.

T: And how do you feel now, as we're talking about it?

C: I feel a little silly, like I'm wondering what you're thinking of me. But when I get back into the dream itself, I feel scared all over again. I don't like being in that situation.

Sometimes the client spontaneously tells the therapist when the dream occurred as he or she is retelling the dream, but sometimes the timing is not clear, and the therapist needs to ask. Knowing when the dream occurred can help the therapist plan how to approach the exploration process. If the dream is old, the therapist may not be able to gain much information about waking life triggers but will want to be curious about whether there were any significant events going on at that point in the client's life. It can also be useful to know whether the dream is a recurrent one, particularly if it is a nightmare or unpleasant dream. This information can help the therapist assess the situation and determine how troubling the dream is for the client.

T: When did you have this dream?

C: I had the dream last week, but I have had similar dreams before.

T: How often have you had this dream?

C: Every couple months. It started when I went to college, and I've had it every couple months for the last 10 years.

T: Sounds like that must be hard for you.

C: It is. It upsets me for a whole day after I have the dream. I really want to understand what's going on so I'm not so upset afterwards.

EXPLORE IMAGES

Therapists then move to exploring 5 to 10 major images as they appear sequentially in the dream. We define an *image* as any object, person, action, thought, or feeling in the dream. An image should be fairly concrete, though, or else it is difficult for the client to explore (e.g., the brown house on the corner rather than houses in general). For example, in the following dream, the major images that the therapist might choose to explore in depth are highlighted:

> I am with this **man with blond hair**. He invites me to tour his **house**. He takes me through this majestic, overwhelmingly beautiful house. It has an **outside aviary** with big **birds**. There is dark marble all over, big windows, and the latest in technology—all that anyone could want. He has very expensive taste. As we're on the tour, I have the thought that **my mother** would not be pleased that I am here. Then my mother is here, and several other friends and relatives are here looking at the house too.

Although it would be wonderful to cover every image of this dream in great detail, that would take a long time. I have seen some beginning therapists take 3 hours for a dream session. Because therapists usually do not have that long, and it can be very exhausting to spend that much time, they need to choose a few images. It is better to do a thorough exploration of a few images rather than a meager exploration of many images. One does not want to shortchange this exploration because it allows the client to get a lot of issues out in the open and allows the therapist to learn about the client.

We suggest that the images be explored sequentially, because this seems to allow the client to become more immersed in the dream. They relive the dream as they go through and think about each of the images sequentially. In contrast, if they jump around, getting into the narrative process is more confusing and difficult.

The question arises as to how to choose the 5 to 10 images. Some therapists choose the images that they perceive to be most salient; other therapists ask clients to choose the images. It seems to be a matter of personal style and also a matter of clinical judgment about which way seems best for individual clients. With the above dream about the blond-haired man, the therapist might begin with the first image (man with blond hair), or the therapist might say:

> T: In this dream, you had a number of images: the man, house, outside aviary, big birds, marble, big windows, technology, your mother, other friends. We need to pick about five images to work with today. Which ones would you choose?
>
> C: Definitely the man—he seems very significant. And the house because it was so magnificent—definitely I was attracted to that house. And the aviary we should do because birds are very important to me. And my mother, of course—it's no big surprise that she showed up there.
>
> T: How about the other friends and relatives at the end of the dream? Did they seem as important as the other images?

C: Not really. If we have time we could do them, but I think the others are the most important images.

T: Okay, then, let's start sequentially and go through those images.

DRAW Acronym

The acronym DRAW can be used to describe the steps we use to help clients explore each major image. The therapist should go through each of the DRAW steps for one image and then move to the next image, with a thorough exploration of each image taking about 5 minutes. The therapist should be curious and try to learn as much as possible about the client's thoughts and feelings in relation to each image. The therapist should not interpret or make any suggestions but rather should absorb what the client says. The therapist guides the client through each of the steps for each image sequentially and tries to empathically enter into each image with the client.

Description

This step is based on phenomenological methods of working with dreams (e.g., Craig & Walsh, 1993. We ask the client to provide a thorough description of the dream image, verbally re-create the scene for us, live inside the image, and give us a tour of the scenery. Reliving the dream can help the client capture the immediacy of the dream and communicate to the therapist what it is like. This step also helps the client remember additional details that can be useful in understanding the dream.

The client is asked for all the details that she or he can remember about the image as it appeared in the dream. The therapist can say something such as, "Paint the picture for me of this moment in the dream so that I can see the image as clearly as you do." Follow-up questions might focus on the different senses (smell, touch, hearing, visual, tasting).

The description should focus on the image in the dream rather than the reality of the object in waking life. So, if the person dreams about his or her mother, we want to know about the mother in the dream, not about the real mother in waking life (that is covered in the upcoming association and waking life trigger steps).

T: Tell me about the man with the blond hair.

C: He is cute. I like him in the dream.

T: Tell me more about how he looks in the dream. Paint the picture for me so that I can see him through your eyes.

C: He has the 70s-style feathered hair look. He has bad skin and pronounced features. He isn't much taller than me. He has on an

T: expensive black custom-made suit with a gray cashmere turtleneck sweater. He looks very chic.

T: What do you mean by pronounced features?

C: He has kind of a hooked nose. Maybe he looks Arabic. He's got very intense eyes that make me feel like he can see through me. His hair is just beginning to gray on the top, so he looks very distinguished.

T: Any smells?

C: He wears some type of cologne, but it's very faint and tasteful.

T: Anything else that you can think of to describe how he looked in the dream?

C: Now that I think about it, at the beginning of the dream he and I are in this new fancy Plymouth touring car, and then he invites me to tour his house. The car made him seem even more elegant—kind of like an Italian count.

Re-Experiencing

Therapists should always be alert for opportunities to help the client talk about and experience feelings because of the importance of getting the client maximally involved in the dream affect. For each image, therapists want clients to focus on what they are feeling at that moment in the dream so that the feelings become more immediate, real, and significant for the client. Therapists typically use open questions to probe for the feelings (e.g., "What are you feeling at this moment in the dream?") and then follow up with reflections of feelings (e.g., "You sound a bit pensive as you talk") to help clarify the feelings as well as expand on and deepen the feelings. Therapists can vary the way they ask for feelings (e.g., "What's it like for you as you talk about this image?", "What are you experiencing right now talking about this image?") and reflect feelings ("I wonder if you feel detached from this man?", "I might feel annoyed if I were you at this point in the dream", "You feel attracted to him") so that they do not sound like robots.

T: What are you feeling at this moment in the dream when you see this man?

C: I'm attracted to him.

T: How are you feeling, though?

C: I think I'm happy. I'm certainly curious.

T: You sound a bit apprehensive as you talk about it.

C: I guess I am, because I'm not sure what this guy wants from me. I also feel a little uncomfortable in this house. It's a lot bigger and grander than anything I'm used to.

T: So, a little unsure of yourself.

C: Yeah.

An alternative method for getting clients into re-experiencing emotions is to ask them to go back into the image and relive it, stating their feelings as they go through the image. For example:

T: Let's play back the scene again where you first see this man, and tell me what you feel as you go through it.

C: Okay, for some reason I am at the front door of this beautiful house. I feel a bit apprehensive as I look at the house because it's so grand. I feel a little out of place. I knock anyway, and this gorgeous guy answers the door. I immediately feel attracted to him—he is so good-looking. He invites me to tour the house. I feel so happy that he has invited me in.

T: So you feel pretty good right now.

C: Yeah, I'm kind of all tingly and excited.

Ways to Increase the Emotional Temperature

Some clients have a hard time getting into their feelings, and the therapists need to help free them up to experience their emotions. To facilitate emotional processing, therapists can use Gestalt exercises such as the empty-chair technique (see also Greenberg, 2002; Greenberg, Rice, & Elliott, 1993). Therapists can ask clients to stay with the feeling and try to experience the sensation somewhere in their bodies, again to facilitate the immediacy of the experiencing.

T: Stay with that feeling of discomfort for a moment. Where do you feel the sensation in your body?

C: My head feels a little dizzy.

T: What is that dizziness like for you?

C: I have a pounding in my head. I feel light-headed.

The therapist can also ask the client to "be the image" and talk from the perspective of the image about the experience.

T: Be your head. Tell me how you feel.

C: I feel angry. I want to yell at the guy.

T: Go ahead. Yell at him.

C: Who do you think you are, making me so uncomfortable? You make me so mad. You look just like my father standing there with that scowl on your face. Go away.

T: How do you feel right now?

C: I feel a bit lighter. Yeah, I liked telling him to go away.

Ways to Decrease the Emotional Temperature

Some clients, especially those who are presenting nightmares, become hyperaroused and panicked when talking about the dream, and so therapists need to help them reduce and manage their anxiety. In such cases, the therapist might ask the client to relax by focusing on his or her breathing, taking deep breaths, or "grounding" (i.e., focusing on where the person's body connects with the chair and floor). These exercises can help the client settle down until he or she can handle going back into the dream (for more detail, see chap. 10). Of course, therapists should make sure that it is not their own anxiety about strong feelings (i.e., countertransference) that makes them want to avoid going with the client into these feelings.

C: (hyperventilating). I can't handle this.

T: (speaking softly and slowly) Take a moment and focus on your breathing. Take a deep breath. Breathe in. Breathe out. Breathe in. Breathe out. As you breathe in, focus on taking in fresh air. As you breath out, think about all the bad air going out. Close your eyes and just relax your whole body. Breathe in. Breathe out. Feel your feet connecting to the floor. Feel your body sitting on the chair. How do you feel now?

C: Much better.

T: Ready to go back to the dream? We'll take it slowly.

C: I'm ready, thanks. I'm eager to learn more about what makes me so anxious.

T: Okay. Let me know at any time if you want to slow down.

Associations

Gathering associations to the image is a very important part of the exploration stage, because it provides clues for what the image is related to. Therapists cannot assume that they know the meaning of images for clients; neither can they use standard interpretations or dream dictionaries to determine what the images mean. Rather, they want to help clients search their memory banks for what the images mean. To any given image, a person has a myriad associations built up based on his or her past experiences. Therapists need to help each individual client search his or her memories for past experiences related to the image.

The core of both Freudian and Jungian dream interpretation lies in associations. In Freudian associations, the client is asked to say whatever comes to mind about the images. The idea is that with the chain associations, something significant eventually emerges. For example:

house → White House → President → terrorist attacks → safety → fearing travel

Jung (see Johnson, 1986) had concerns about this type of chain association, because he felt that the significant association that eventually emerges might not be related to the original dream image. He recommended instead that therapists continually go back to the specific dream image. For example, in asking the client to associate to *house*, he would constantly come back to the image of "What else do you think of when you think of a house?" The yield here is like spokes on a wheel, with lots of different associations leading out from the dream image, with the focus always returning to the original image (see Figure 1.1).

Extended Associations

My position on the process of doing associations is closer to Jung's. I want the client to associate to the specific image rather than associate until she or he gets to some crucial issue that may or may not be related to the dream. However, more than just a one-word or one-phrase association is needed. The therapist needs to learn what this image means to the person and hear about the associated memories. Therapists need to be curious and learn as much as possible about what the client thinks about each image. It is more important to get lots of information about a few associations than to just get lots of associations.

Associations are the therapist's major avenue to learning about the client's schema, so they ask a lot of questions to help clients expand on the associations. Therapists also, of course, still attend carefully to reflecting feelings so that clients feel supported and understood. Therapists are aiming for what might be called *extended associations*, which are the thoughts, feel-

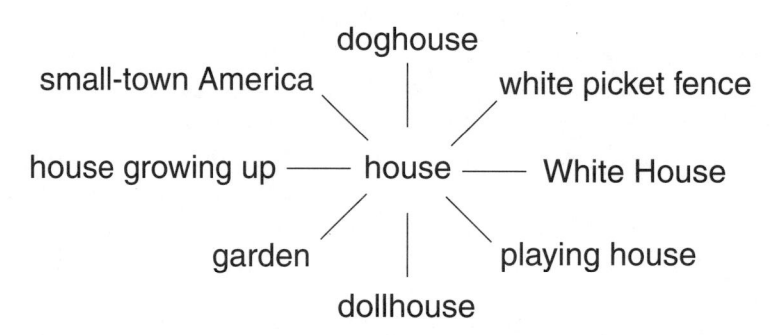

Figure 1.1. Different associations focus on the original image.

ings, and memories that come to mind in relation to the image along with what those thoughts, feelings, and memories mean to the individual. The difference between regular and extended associations, then, is the amount of exploration, such that the client explores a lot of material related to each association. Rather than just saying the word, therapists learn about what that word means to the client. Using the same words as described above, a client might say the following:

> *Doghouse:* I had this wonderful dog when I was young. My mother wouldn't let me have him in the house, so we built him this doghouse. It was cool—it looked just like our house. I used to go out there and hang out with the dog.
>
> *Small-town America:* We lived in a small town for awhile before we moved East. I liked it so much more than the big, crowded city. Our family was happier then.
>
> *White picket fence:* Our house had a white picket fence. It was so quaint; it reminded me of the stories I read about Tom Sawyer and Huckleberry Finn when I was a kid. Somehow a white picket fence seems related to stability and family life.
>
> *House growing up:* It was big farmhouse type of house in the small town. Lots of neighbor kids running in and out, lots of good memories. I'm really fond of that house and want to live in one just like it when I buy my own house.
>
> *White House:* Where the President lives when he's there. I didn't vote for him, but he's doing an okay job. I'm not much into politics.
>
> *Garden:* I want to have a garden when I grow up. I like growing things. My dad is a gardener. I've had some thoughts about going into plant sciences in graduate school.
>
> *Playing house:* I hated that game. My sister always tried to make me play with her. I was always more of a tomboy and hated playing girl games.
>
> *Dollhouse:* I made a dollhouse for my sister when I took shop class. I was really proud of that dollhouse because it was so well done. I learned how to be a carpenter doing that.

It is not possible to know which associations are going to be the crucial ones for helping the client construct an understanding about the dream, so therapists need to go for as much depth as possible for the 5 to 10 chosen images, hoping to stimulate recollections of critical issues for the client.

It is fascinating to hear the different associations people have to similar images, which makes sense given that all people have had different experiences. In training workshops, I ask people to go around and say the first thing that comes to mind when they think of some familiar image, such as a pumpkin. A variety of associations come out, such as Halloween, pumpkin pie, trick-or-treating, Thanksgiving, pumpkin soup, jack o' lanterns, and gardens. When I then ask people to expand on their associations, it is quickly obvious that even when people have similar associations, they have very different experiences related to these associations. For one person, pumpkins reminded her of Halloween and wonderful hours spent with her mother carving pumpkins. But pumpkins reminded another person of a Halloween incident in which someone threw a pumpkin at his car and broke his windshield, which made him very angry. So even though both individuals associated pumpkins with Halloween, they had very different extended associations. Again, it is crucial to get as much personal detail about the experiences as possible to understand what the images mean to the client.

Varied Methods for Eliciting Associations

Many clients, especially those who are not psychologically sophisticated, do not understand what is meant by *associations*, so therapists should provide a simple definition (e.g., "the first thing that comes to your mind"). In addition, clients get bored or annoyed when therapists use the same phrases repeatedly, so it is good for the therapist to vary how he or she asks for associations. The most straightforward way to ask is to say something like:

- "What is the first thing that comes to mind when your think about a house?" or
- "What do you associate with a house?" or
- "What do you think of when you think of houses?"

To learn more about (i.e., extend) an association, we can ask the client to expand on it, using probes such as:

- "Tell me more about that" or
- "What does that mean for you personally?" or
- "What's it like for you to talk about your memories of houses?"

To get the associations going, the therapist can also ask, "What is a house?" or "What is the purpose of a house?" This question forces the client to back up, explore, and articulate his or her implicit definitions and meanings. Therapists often assume that they know what a house (or any other object) is, but in fact it might mean something different to the client. A "door" to one person is just an entryway, whereas to another person it is a means of keeping others out. By asking the client to define the image, the therapist enables him or her to bring the idiosyncratic meaning to the surface.

Delaney (1991) offered another approach that can be useful and fun and help the client who feels silly exploring things that seem obvious: Say to the client, "Pretend I'm from Mars, and I don't know what a house is. Tell me what a house is." Through this probe, we let clients know that we want to hear from them about their thoughts, and we acknowledge that we do not know what they mean by their words.

Another particularly useful way of extending associations is to ask for memories related to the image (e.g., "What memories do you have of aviaries?", "What's your first memory of aviaries?", "What's your strongest memory of aviaries?"). Asking about memories brings up significant events from the past that may have influenced the dream. One of the major theories about the function of dreams is that people are trying to compare current life concerns with past memories (Palombo, 1978, 1980, 1987). Asking about memories brings past experiences out into the open so that clients can begin to assimilate these into their memory banks.

There are no right or wrong associations—therapists simply help the client explore the images. Therefore, the therapist needs to take a stance of curiosity rather than judging or blaming the client. People are fascinating, and we want to draw each person out to learn about him or her through associations to the images.

T: What is the first thing that comes to mind when you think about a house?"

C: I grew up in a house with lots of marble. There was a lot of marble where I grew up, but it always seems cold to me. Not surprisingly, my mother likes a lot of marble.

T: What associations do you have to houses?

C: Houses are places you live in. It's where families are together, unless they are divorced. But a house is not necessarily a home. It takes a loving family to make it a home, to make it a place you want to be.

T: What memories do you have of houses?

C: The one I remember most is the house we grew up in over in Italy.

T: Tell me more about that house.

C: It was big and spacious. I remember my room there—I loved it. I felt safe there. I had birds there. I've always liked birds.

T: You sound almost wistful when you talk about your childhood house.

C: I miss it. Those were simpler times. I kind of wish I could go back. But there were also parts that weren't so good. It seems like my mother was always angry when I was younger. I had to try to stay out of her way.

T: So there were both good and bad parts to the house where you grew up. Any other associations to houses, particularly to big, majestic, elegant houses?

C: I think of those women's magazines and the pressure to have this elegant house. It's a sign of wealth, of having attained some special status. I would like to have a house like that, but I clearly won't be able to get one on my salary unless I meet some man who makes a lot of money. So I feel like a failure that I don't have a big house like those.

Waking Life Triggers

We assume that each image is connected to some issue in waking life (past, present, or future), so we ask the client to explore possible waking life triggers to each image. The therapist should ask for waking life triggers to the *particular* image rather than for what might have triggered the whole dream, because he or she is still focused on the individual image and is gathering the building blocks to use in constructing meaning for the whole dream in the insight stage. Waking life triggers sometimes emerge spontaneously during earlier steps, and therapists can skip this step, but at other times therapists have to probe specifically for triggers. Even if waking life triggers have emerged spontaneously earlier in the process, it can sometimes be useful to probe further for more triggers.

T: What might have triggered the image of your mother at this particular time?

C: My mother is a constant presence in my life. We are changing roles right now from her being the mother to my taking care of her more. She wants me to take care of all the business matters. And she gets much too intrusive in my love life.

T: Tell me more about that.

C: She just recently asked me if I had met anyone yet. She really wants me to get married so that she can have grandchildren. She seems to live her life through mine.

One issue that arises in working with dreams that are not very recent is that the client may not know about waking events at the time of the dream. Therapists can handle this issue in one of two ways. First, they can ask about whatever memories of events the client remembers from the time of the dream. Clients often do remember details of waking events from that time because the dream reflects a significant event (recall the earlier example of the client who vividly recalled a dream from when she was 10 years old because it was right before a major move).

Alternatively, therapists can ask about current events, with the assumption that the client still remembers the dream because of current concerns. For example, a male client might dream about his parents' divorce because he is troubled by it or because he is having problems in relationships, and his template for relationships is his parents' relationship. Both methods (focus on time of dream or current waking life) seem to work relatively well because they allow the therapist to learn more about the client and the client's life.

Example of the DRAW Steps

Especially when first learning the model, it is helpful to go through all four DRAW steps for each image. Of course, therapists need not cover them in a rigid manner, because this gets very annoying for clients. Hence, therapists might want to vary the way that they ask about each of the steps. Here is an example of all the steps for one image (highlighted) in a dream:

Dream: I am in the dorm where I worked over the summer. I see some green and blue **beanbag chairs** and decide to take one for my room. I am trying to drag it out when this girl I know walks in and starts a conversation with me. I attempt to talk to her while pretending that I am not trying to steal the chair.

T: Describe this beanbag chair for me.

C: It is very big and heavy, like it's full of sand.

T: Can you describe that more?

C: It was cute in this lime green shade, and it looked really comfortable. I expected it to be heavy. I was just frustrated that I had to drag it, and it was a pain.

T: How do you feel when you think about this beanbag chair?

C: I mostly feel greedy, like I really want it. I'm angry that someone is in my way and might prevent me from getting it.

T: When you think of beanbag chairs, what do you think of?

C: I don't have one now in my apartment, but I want one in real life. My parents have some beanbag chairs at home, but I don't have any here.

T: So you associate it with home.

C: Maybe. More with my parents—more of a hippy attitude, more free. Their mentality is from the 70s culture; they are free spirits.

T: Any other things you think of?

C: I don't have enough money to buy one (laughs).

T: So it's something you want.

C: Something I want, but I don't have the space or money for it.

T: What about the sand or the heavy part?

C: I don't know. It's something else that keeps me from getting the beanbag.

T: What might have triggered this image at this particular time in your life?

C: I don't have much furniture in my apartment. I just moved into my apartment. My parents didn't really want me to move in there, because I don't have enough furniture. I really would like to have a beanbag chair.

Subsequent Images

Once the therapist and client have explored the first image in depth, they use the DRAW steps on subsequent images (i.e., do the four DRAW steps on the first image, then do the four DRAW steps on the second image, etc.). Each image takes about 5 minutes to explore in depth, so it is crucial for therapists to plan to have enough time to focus on all 5 to 0 images (usually 30–45 minutes). Sometimes therapists focus too extensively on initial images, and then they do not have enough time or emotional energy for exploring later images.

SUMMARIZE THE EXPLORATION STAGE

Some therapists like to summarize the exploration process by restating the dream and inserting what has been learned about the images through exploration. In this summary, the therapist briefly retells the highlights of the dream, inserting the central descriptions, feelings, associations, and waking life triggers revealed by the client for the major images in the dream. It is important for therapists to keep the summary relatively short and then turn the focus back to the client; otherwise, the summary can detract from the flow of the session and take the attention away from the client. Hearing the dream retold in this manner can be very revealing for some clients, because it allows them to hear what they have been saying. In essence, it provides clients with a mirror. Sometimes just hearing the dream and the associations repeated back succinctly can be enough to help the client put it all together and figure out the meaning (at which point client and therapist can move right into the insight stage).

How should the therapist decide whether to do a summary? If the client seems almost ready to move into insight, with just a little nudging, then a brief summary can be helpful. If, however, the summary would take the flow away from the client, or if the exploration process has already been long, it is sometimes better to move right into the insight stage. Furthermore, if the therapist does not feel confident of having a good, brief summary, it is probably better to skip it. This is an example of a summary provided by a therapist after about 30 minutes of exploration of the short dream mentioned earlier about falling:

So, you were walking along slowly during this pleasant, peaceful day when you had this sensation of sinking and falling. You associate falling with being clumsy and not in control. To break the fall, you clutch your comforter, which you associate with saving yourself and being comforted. You have a memory of snuggling with your brother under your comforter after you heard about the September 11 terrorist attacks. How does this fit for you?

Here is another example from a longer dream:

Dream: I'm somewhere on campus, maybe the mall, with my Mom, stepfather, and boyfriend. We're walking around looking at the landscape. It's a nice day; the sun is shining. Then, all of a sudden we see a huge tornado and the sky turns black. I say, "We have to go to a building and run to the basement." So we run into a building that has glass windows. I say, "We've got to go downstairs!" My stepfather and boyfriend run down towards the stairs, but my mother says she wants to look out the window at the tornado. I'm halfway down the stairs, and I have to run back to get her. I'm looking out the window the whole time I'm trying to get her, and the tornado splits. Now there's two of them coming right toward our building. So, I grab my mom and run down toward the stairs where there's this room with a whole bunch of cots and bunk beds. There are a lot of other families with kids, fathers, and mothers. Some of them are hiding under the beds, some are hiding on the beds, and some are hiding in corners. I'm sitting on a bed. For the most part the wind is not blowing, and it's not raining. But then the wind starts blowing really hard and my hair is blowing all over the place, and I hear glass shattering.

Therapist summary (after about 45 minutes of exploration): So you're on the campus mall on this bright, sunny, beautiful day. When you think of campus, you think of a peaceful place where you can relax and see people. Sometimes you have lunch on the mall, so it's one of your favorite places on campus. You're with your mom, stepfather, and boyfriend, and it's really important to you to have them together, because you love them very much. You talked about your mom as being a very wonderful, caring person. It seems like you feel really taken care of by all these people. And then this huge tornado hits quickly. A tornado is something that destroys, so something that destroys things is coming. You're scared that you may die and feel that you have to take charge. Taking charge is something you do a lot in your life, and especially in the dream you are trying to take care of your mom. You feel like you want to protect her, because she has always protected you. You're in the basement and glass windows are shattering. You think of windows as something like visibility through barriers, as sort of a door to the outside world, sort of an association to danger. Again, you can hear the sirens and the windows. (This led naturally to the therapist saying as the beginning of the insight stage, "I wonder what you make of the dream after hearing back your associations to the images?")

THOUGHTS ABOUT DOING THE EXPLORATION STAGE

As a guideline, we suggest that about half of the time in a session be spent in the exploration stage, one quarter in the insight stage, and one quarter in the action stage. Because thorough exploration takes a lot of time, therapists need to plan accordingly.

It is important for the therapist not to feel a sense of urgency to have an interpretation of the dream during the exploration stage; rather, he or she should assume an attitude of curiosity and try to learn as much as possible about the client. This stage is truly client centered, in that the therapist has no idea what will emerge but wants to facilitate the client's exploration. The exploration stage is an opportunity for clients to think deeply about the dream images and for therapists to learn about the client's world. Although the therapist might have some ideas about what images mean in a given culture, or might have some projections based on what the images mean for him or her personally, he or she cannot completely know what the images mean for the individual client. Even if the therapist did know exactly what the images related to, as might be the case if the therapist had been seeing the client for some time, it would not likely be helpful for the therapist to tell the client what the dream means. It seems to be more helpful for clients to discover the meaning for themselves.

The exploration stage is often not gratifying for therapists who want to have a brilliant interpretation of the dream as soon as they hear it or who want to go directly to the insight stage. But yet it can be crucial for clients to have an opportunity to explore the images, and exploration sets the stage for the client to discover the meaning of the dream.

Another issue is that focusing on the images sometimes leads the client to talk about other things outside the dream. For example, if the dream is about one's child, the client might shift the topic from the dream to talking in detail about the latest crisis with the child and then proceed to talking about the marital relationship. Although the marital relationship might be an important topic for the client, it might be a tangent that takes away from the task of understanding this particular dream. I suggest that therapists take some latitude in exploring these connections for their relevance to the dream but then bring the client back to the dream so that the client can reach some closure about the meaning of the dream. Having a focus is important so that the client can leave with something tangible that he or she has learned about the dream (see Budman & Gurman, 1988, for issues about developing a focus in brief therapy).

If the client is not able to tolerate the gentle structure of the model, then the therapist should abandon dream work and move into regular therapy. This is a rare occurrence, however. Of the many people who have participated in our research, therapists have been able to use the model with all but a very few. One woman could not focus on a single dream and kept going off on irrelevant tangents, so the therapist finally abandoned the model and just let her talk. In addition, when working with nightmares (see chap. 10), we sometimes modify procedures by slowing down so that the client can tolerate the feelings. Most clients, though, are willing to follow the structure, because it provides a gentle, clear way to work with the dream.

REFERENCES

Budman, S. H., & Gurman, A. S. (1988). *Theory and practice of brief therapy*. New York: Guilford Press.

Craig, E., & Walsh, S. J. (1993). The clinical use of dreams. In G. Delaney (Ed.), *New directions in dream interpretation* (pp. 103–154). Albany, NY: SUNY Press.

Delaney, G. (1991). *Breakthrough dreaming*. New York: Bantam Books.

Freud, S. (1966). *The interpretation of dreams*. New York: Avon. (Original work published 1900)

Greenberg, L. S. (2002). *Emotion-focused therapy*. Washington, DC: American Psychological Association.

Greenberg, L. S., Rice, L. N., & Elliott, R. (1993). *Facilitating emotional change*. New York: Guilford Press.

Hill, C. E., & O'Brien, K. M. (1999). *Helping Skills: Facilitating exploration, insight, and action*. Washington, DC: American Psychological Association.

Johnson, R. (1986). *Inner work*. San Francisco: Harper & Row.

Koulack, D. (1991). *To catch a dream: Explorations of dreaming*. Albany: State University of New York Press.

Palombo, S. R. (1978). *Dreaming and memory*. New York: Basic Books.

Palombo, S. R. (1980). The cognitive act of dream construction. *Journal of the American Academy of Psychoanalysis, 8*, 186–201.

Palombo, S. R. (1987). Can a computer dream? In M. L. Glucksman & S. Warner (Eds.), *Dreams in a new perspective: The royal road revisited* (pp. 59–78). New York: Human Science Press.

Whitman, R., Kramer, M., & Baldridge, B. (1963). Which dream does the patient tell? *Archives of General Psychiatry, 8*, 277–282.

2

THE INSIGHT STAGE

CLARA E. HILL

The main goal of the insight stage is to help clients construct meanings for their dreams. I use the term *construct* purposely to acknowledge that it is not possible to ever know for sure the true meaning of the dream. I believe that the therapist and client work together to develop or create the meaning that makes the most sense at the moment, given the information that they have at hand.

Some clients spontaneously come to understand their dreams through the exploration process. Just thinking about the memories and experiencing the feelings associated with the images leads them directly to what the dream means. Other clients need encouragement and then are able to explore their ideas about the meaning of the dream. Yet other clients need more input from someone else to help them figure out the meaning of the dream either because the dream is not clear or because they are blocked. They may need guidance through the process of gaining insight or may even need interpretations from the therapist to stimulate their insight processes.

Hence, depending on the needs of the client, the therapist may switch from the client-centered stance that was used in the exploration stage to offering somewhat more input in this stage, although the input is still offered in a very collaborative manner. At this point, the therapist has gathered a lot of data and is in a more informed position from which to help the client figure out the meaning of the dream and to offer input about the dream. Of course, any input is tentative because the therapist can never understand the dream or client completely, but the therapist joins with the client to brainstorm ideas about what the dream might mean.

Because it is often easier to think of ideas with another person who has a different perspective, this stage allows the therapist to use her or his creativity to help the client think of meanings of the dream. This stage is often exciting and fun, with the therapist and client working together to figure out the meaning of the dream. Of course, the therapist always needs to be respectful and work with the client rather than act as the expert who has the answers; the client always has the final say about what the dream means.

In addition to the skills used in the exploration stage (open questions, restatements, reflections of feelings), the therapist sprinkles in a few challenges, interpretations, self-disclosures of insight, and immediacy skills to help the client construct an interpretation of the dream (see Hill & O'Brien, 1999). Because these skills require more risk than do the exploration skills, therapists have to be carefully trained in these skills, be aware of how clients are reacting, and be prepared to deal with misunderstandings that may arise.

In this chapter I describe the three steps of the insight stage: (a) asking for an initial understanding of the dream, (b) constructing the meaning of the dream (including several possible levels of insight), and (c) summarizing insights. I also provide extensive examples of the process so that therapists can get an idea of how to foster insight.

ASK THE CLIENT FOR AN INITIAL INTERPRETATION

The insight stage begins with the therapist asking the client to say what she or he thinks the dream means. As the client responds, the therapist listens carefully to indicate a valuing of the client's introspection, to assess the client's current level of functioning, to make an assessment of the client's current level of understanding of the dream, and to determine the level of interpretation to which the client is naturally drawn.

Indicate a Valuing of the Client's Perspective

It is important for the therapist to respect what the client thinks about the dream. Clients have often spent a lot of time thinking about the dream and have an idea about what the dream means. If the therapist does not acknowledge the client's interpretation, the client can feel annoyed and devalued and refuse to cooperate in the work of this stage. Given that this method emphasizes collaboration, it is important for the therapist to value the client's input and work together with the client to understand the dream.

Assess the Client's Level of Functioning

The therapist has observed the client during the exploration stage and in the initial part of the insight stage, where the client states an initial interpretation, and hence, can make some conceptualizations about the client's functioning. This information provides the therapist with some guidelines about how to approach the client in the insight stage. If the client seems anxious and fragile, for example, the therapist might be cautious about being too interpretive.

In addition, an examination of dream content can tell the therapist a lot about the individual's level of functioning (see also Kramer, 1993). Looking at a client's actions in a dream can reveal whether she or he takes an active or a passive approach, is the aggressor or the victim, is happy versus sad, and is associated with others or a loner. There is a sizable body of research about dreams of people with different diagnoses. For example, dreams of people with depression are filled with masochism, dependency needs, and self-defeating thoughts and behaviors (Beck & Hurvich, 1959; Beck & Ward, 1961; Cartwright, 1986; Kramer, Whitman, Baldridge, & Lansky, 1966; Langs, 1966). Dreams of people with schizophrenia involve feelings of loneliness, a lack of human contact, sterility, limited and/or bizarre imagery, danger, morbidity, a sense of emergency or stress, and feelings of hopelessness and helplessness (Biddle, 1963; Carrington, 1972; Dement, 1955; Kant, 1942; Noble, 1951). People with hysteria have dreams that are characterized by poor impulse control, exhibitionism, and aggressive sexual acting out, whereas people with paranoid schizophrenia have dreams characterized by paranoia and filled with delusional thinking (Langs, 1966). Dreams of sex offenders contain strong sexual elements (Goldhirsh, 1961). I caution therapists, however, to use this diagnostic literature with care, because it would be easy to lose sight of focusing on the individual client and allowing him or her to come to an understanding of the dream. The dream content can be a source of clues, however, that can be explored later.

Assess the Client's Current Level of Understanding of the Dream

Listening to the client's initial interpretation allows the therapist to assess how much the client understands about the dream. The client might not understand the dream at all, might understand it partially, or might have a very complete understanding of the dream. If the client has no understanding of the dream and is eager to go further, the therapist can proceed to the next step. For example, one client had a dream about riding in a bus with a group of Mexican immigrants who did not speak any English. He was totally stumped and could not think of anything the dream could mean, even after extensive exploration. He was eager to have the therapist help him understand the dream.

If the client understands the dream partially, it is important for the therapist to listen for what parts of the dream were left out in the client's interpretation. The example I like best here is of a graduate student who had a dream that he was in a prison walking down the aisle between the cells. The prisoners were spitting at him and making fun of him. He was feeling very uncomfortable and trying to keep as far away from the prisoners as possible. As he was walking, he saw his brother sitting on the top bunk in one of the cells, with a monkey on his shoulder. When asked his initial thoughts about the meaning of the dream, he said he thought that it was related to his working in the prison for a summer placement and that he felt very uncomfortable there. Although it was obvious that he felt uncomfortable about working in the prison, he left out the part about the brother and the monkey. Our initial task was to help him incorporate the piece about his brother into his interpretation to seek additional understanding of the dream.

If the client has an understanding of the dream, the therapist can assess whether the client is satisfied with that interpretation. If the client is satisfied with his or her interpretation of the dream (regardless of whether the interpretation is the most elegant or best possible), the therapist can help the client explore the interpretation completely and then move on to the action stage. If the client is satisfied with the current interpretation, he or she is not likely to be open to additional work at this time for whatever reason, and so working further with the insight stage will probably not be fruitful. It is better for the therapist to recognize that the client is satisfied with his or her interpretation (and often quite proud of it) than to try to force the client to come up with additional insights. An example might be a client who believes his or her dream can be interpreted according to a dream dictionary (e.g., in India, riding an elephant is lucky, whereas riding a donkey is unlucky). To dissuade the client of his or her interpretation in favor of one's own values would dishonor the client and would probably be ineffective.

If however, the client has an interpretation but is not completely happy with it or is eager to keep working for additional understanding, the therapist can suggest that they work together to understand the dream using another level of interpretation given that most dreams can be interpreted in several ways. This practice does not negate the client's initial interpretation but suggests that there are many possible ways of approaching dreams.

Sometimes the client jumps directly to action and is not immediately concerned with insight. For example, a client who was asked about the meaning of a flying dream responded that she thought it meant that she needed to make a change in her career so that she could soar instead of plodding along as she had been doing. Because action was most salient to her at that moment, we pursued the idea of a career change and later came back to tying it into insight.

Similarly, if after being asked, the client says something like "I don't think it means anything," the therapist might stop the process and talk with the client about his or her attitude toward dreams. Research has indicated (see chap. 12, this volume) that there is a subgroup of people who do not value their dreams or dream work. Rather than try to convince such a person of the value of dream work, it is usually better to go with the resistance and ask them about their reactions. It could be helpful to educate them about the research, or it might be more respectful to ask them whether they want to continue with the process or whether they would rather try something other than dream work.

Assess the Level of Interpretation to Which the Client Is Drawn

Listening to the client's initial interpretation can also provide clues as to the appropriate level of interpretation for the client. If the initial interpretation is about an intense fantasy-type experience (e.g., flying), the therapist might aim for the experiential level. If the initial interpretation closely reflects waking life (e.g., concern about an upcoming presentation), the therapist has a clue that it would be important to start with the waking life level. If the initial interpretation seems more related to deep-seated personality conflicts or existential concerns, the therapist might orient the subsequent work toward looking at inner conflicts.

In our experience, most initial interpretations reflect waking concerns, because most people are aware of the theory that dreams reflect waking life. It is helpful to go with the client's chosen level first and proceed to other levels only if there is time or inclination on the client's part.

Example of Working With an Initial Client Interpretation

The following is an example of how a therapist asked a college-aged woman for her initial interpretation of a dream. Note that the therapist asked for an interpretation and then tried to help the client explore and expand on this initial interpretation. In this example, the therapist did not need to offer any interpretations of her own but needed only to facilitate the client's process of understanding the dream in more depth. Had the client been less psychologically minded and motivated to understand the dream, the therapist might have had to offer more interpretations.

> ***Dream:*** There is a man chasing my sister and me and trying to get into the house. We try to lock the door, but it won't lock. And every time we looked, he was standing there trying to get in. We would tell him to get away from the door, but he didn't. Finally, he just barged toward the door and took it off its hinges. Then we're running through different buildings, first an apartment, then a house I used to live in, then we're in this really, really white hospital. In the last part he takes me by the neck. I tell him to put me down, and he does. Then, he catches my sister, and I never see her after that.

[*After exploration stage*]

T: After all the exploration you've done on the dream, what do you think it all means?

C: Sometimes you actually can say something, get your voice heard. You definitely want your voice to be heard. If somebody does something and you know it's wrong, you have to say something, do something, protest.

T: If someone has you up against the wall, you have to do something.

C: You can't just sit and flop, "All right, I'm done. I can't do anything." You have to actually say something. Fight for your right to be alive.

T: Literally, in that part of your dream it was a fight for your life. You were dead if you didn't stand up for yourself.

C: Right.

T: Go with that, you're dead if you don't stand up. What could that be related to?

C: The thing I think of is my sister—letting her fight her own battles sometimes.

T: Say more about that.

C: There's going to be a point when I'm not going to be there, or my mom's not going to be there, for my sister. She's going to have to do something for herself. She's going to have to be able to take care of herself. I can always help her or be there to assist her, but she's going to have to do her own thing. She's going to have to be able to stand up for herself and say, "I'm going to do this. I don't want to do that. What you're saying is wrong. What I'm saying is wrong." Basically be able to say what she does and doesn't want to do. But, let her have a chance to say it. Let her have a chance to be wrong. Let her have the chance to experience that she can take care of herself.

T: So, you can't protect her all the time. How does that feel?

C: I can learn. I don't want anything bad to happen to her knowing that I could have helped her, but I didn't.

T: Anything else this dream could mean? You've got this guy who's trying to get into your house. The lock doesn't work. What else could that be about?

C: It's not like I have any secrets or anything. It seems as if I'm trying to keep everyone out. And hold something in. But, I can't think of anything I'm trying to hold in. I can't think of anything I'm trying to keep away from everybody else.

T: He's trying to get in, to batter you down.

C: The only thing I can think of is in high school when people were talking about me to my friends. The fact that they were always talking, I thought, "Stop, this is ridiculous." And with my sister. The fact that I didn't say anything in high school, I guess is another thing. I had the chance. I didn't want to hurt anybody. You get along in school, you go home, you do your homework, go back to school the next day. You don't want to have to bother with anybody.

T: You get along and go along.

C: You get along. Even though my friends gave me a hard time by saying, "Don't let those people get away with it," I still felt, "Forget about it. Don't worry about what they're saying because sooner or later it will jump back over. They'll find out sooner or later how ridiculous they sounded." I had the chance to say something, but I didn't.

T: And that bothers you?

C: Yes, it does. That's just the way I am that I don't fight too many battles. That's the way my mom was in the beginning. She always tells me I was her version when she was younger. And my sister is the version of the way she is now. When my mom was younger, with my dad, she couldn't do or say anything or he'd get angry at her. Now she doesn't think anything about saying, "You're wrong. I can tell you why you're wrong." That's not the way it is with me. I don't want to say anything because I don't want anybody telling me that I'm wrong. My sister will say anything. She'll say, "I can tell you you're wrong and I can give you so many good reasons why you're wrong, and you can't prove me wrong." We are the split version of my mother. I think that's the way I was brought up. I don't know why we are so different, but there is some reason why we are so opposite when it comes to fighting. The fact that I don't need to fight my own battles is maybe why I think I have to fight my sister's. I don't usually talk back to anybody. I probably take it home with me in my head and think that I could have said or done something, even though my sister would love to say something, making sure she doesn't get in those situations. It makes me feel bad about the fact that if she didn't get in those situations, then she wouldn't have to say anything. And it feels bad that I didn't fight that battle and I could have.

T: Anything else that this dream could mean?

C: Before I went to sleep, something happened that's related to the part about the man being at the door. Somebody came and knocked on the door about 3 in the morning. His face was wrapped up, because it was cold outside. He was knocking on the door, saying, "Is <man's name> there?" We peeked out the window to see him. Every time we peeked out the window, he was looking up at the window. He was probably thinking to himself, "I know he's in that apartment!" That's how I think the whole thing started with the man at the door. But I don't know why the lock was that way, or why my sister was so much smaller, or why everything was so white in the hospital.

T: We're not going to get a chance to do all of those, but can you take any one of those and explore it some more?

C: I think I know why my sister seemed smaller. Because I always have to protect her because she's smaller than me.

T: That makes sense. What about the white hospital?

C: I'm aware of a contrast.

T: What comes to your mind? Free associate.

C: That we're different. We're from <another country>, so when we first came up here, no one wanted to be around us because we were different, we were foreign. "My daddy told me you can't play with me because you're different." It's not possible that we were the only different ones there, but we were new and….I guess people are always afraid of what they don't know. My mom would tell me that it was because we are foreign, and I thought, "But that's not possible because we are all human! How is that going to work? Who was I going to play with? I can't play with my sister all the time. She's going to have her own friends." It was in my grade and above. Not people in her grade. I don't know what it is about kids that they…. My grade and above, everybody was very conscious of me being different. I know I felt different because when I was born I had clubfeet, feet that turned in. So I had to go through a lot of operations, and I have scars on my legs. The thing is, my legs never got the chance to develop. The left leg was weaker than the right and never developed to the capacity of the right leg, so it is smaller. I wore these brace boots, and everybody always asked me what they were. When I told them that I had to wear them because I had a condition, they just couldn't understand. They would ask if I was going to get some real shoes soon. I tried to explain, but they didn't understand.

T: So you were kind of discriminated against.

C: Yeah, because I'm foreign, because I'm different.

T: It doesn't feel good.

C: No, it doesn't.

EXPANDING ON THE CLIENT'S INITIAL UNDERSTANDING OF THE DREAM

As indicated earlier, the therapist and client can work together to expand on the client's initial understanding of the dream. There are a number of levels at which dreams can be understood, ranging from the most concrete and noninterpretive level, where dreams represent only themselves, to the most abstract, symbolic level, where dreams are metaphoric representations of deep inner personality dynamics. Hence, the therapist can talk about understanding the dream in terms of the experience itself, in terms of waking life, and in terms of inner personality dynamics. All can lead to valid interpretations, even though they might be quite different. To illustrate the different interpretations that can emerge using these different levels of interpretations, I offer an example of the following dream of a middle-aged married woman:

> **Dream:** My husband is having an affair. I am surprised that I am not as angry as I would expect myself to be. I tell him that he better stop the affair.

The Experience Itself

Rather than thinking of the dream as reflecting something else, it can be understood in terms of the experience itself (see also Craig & Walsh, 1993). The dream is an experience that the client lived through, albeit during sleep rather than waking life, and thus is important in and of itself. In this case, the dream does not need to be "interpreted"; rather, it needs to be experienced and understood for what it is. By examining this level, clients can learn more about the depths of their wishes, desires, fears, doubts, and feelings.

In dreams, people do things that they ordinarily might not do. In waking life, they might not have an affair, go off on a wild adventure, murder someone, invent something, or solve the world's problems, but they often do these very things in dreams. These dreams reflect aspects of the person and what he or she is capable of doing, given the assumption that most people are capable of doing many things given the right circumstances. Reflecting on these actions offers clients opportunities to see what their feelings and reactions would be if they were to find themselves in these situations. They might not act on these things in waking life, but dreams allow people the freedom to try on new roles and behaviors without the consequences that would occur in waking life.

Using the above example of the woman's dream of her husband having an affair, the therapist might ask the woman what she has learned about herself:

> T: If we just take this dream as an experience that you have lived through, what did you learn about yourself?
>
> C: I am surprised that I was not as upset as I thought I would have been. If you had asked me before this session, I would have said I would be devastated if my husband had an affair, but I really wasn't in the dream.

T: How did you feel about yourself in the dream?

C: I was pretty pleased that I talked back to him. Again, I often think of myself as passive, but I really wasn't in the dream. I seemed to know what I wanted and that I wasn't going to put up with him having an affair. Maybe I'm stronger than I think of myself as being.

T: You sound pleased when you say that.

C: I am pleased. I like feeling strong. That's neat.

Waking Life

During their dreams, people often continue thinking about waking concerns but do so without the influence of external cues. For example, if a student has a test the next day, she might dream about what she has or has not studied for the test, try to imagine what the questions will be, and rehearse how to answer the questions. She might also incorporate into her dream thoughts about how she has done on past tests, what tests mean to her realistically and symbolically, and what might happen in the future if she does or does not do well on the test. Similarly, if a man has a fight with his wife, he might continue to ruminate over the fight as he goes to sleep and incorporate his feelings about his wife and the fight into his dream. He might also associate during sleep to other fights and other women and weave those into his dream.

People often pick up on subtle cues during the day that they ignore because the cues are too uncomfortable or unpleasant, or because they are too busy, but these emerge during dreams. Paying attention to one's dreams provides clues about feelings of which one may not have been aware. Faraday (1974) gave the example that she might dream that the brakes were failing on her car. She might have subliminally or subconsciously picked up on clues during the day about her failing brakes but had time to process this information only in her dreams.

It is also important to recognize that dreams may use metaphors to portray feelings, given that people often think in metaphorical terms. From the previous example of the student worried about a test, she might dream of a soccer competition, because she has been on soccer teams most of her life. The man might dream of his wife as a tiger, because he associates tigers as being ferocious creatures. A client who experienced anxiety about her husband abandoning her started dreaming about coming home only to find that her house had been uprooted and carted away, because that was a recurrent fear she had as a child. Hence, it is sometimes important not to take all the images literally but to think about what they might represent in waking life.

Given that some dreams reflect waking life, it makes sense that these dreams can be used to help people understand how they feel about aspects of waking life. Therapists can look to the dream to find out how the person feels about waking events. The key here is to pay attention to what the dream might mean about waking life. A rat attacking a person's throat might reflect anxiety about speaking; an affair with a friend might indicate an underlying attraction to the friend. It is important to emphasize at this point, however, that becoming aware of feelings (such as attraction to a friend) during dreams does not mean that the person must act on these feelings. Although feelings are involuntary, people have choices over how they come to understand the feelings and what they do about them (see also Greenberg, 2002).

Another point to make is that the waking life level of insight can include thoughts and feelings about the past and future as well as about the present. In the Hill (1996) model, past experiences were considered to be a separate level of insight, but we discovered that past experiences can not easily be distinguished from current waking life. Memories of past experiences are often actively present in one's thoughts in waking life. Similarly, future events can be just as salient as present events if the person is actively thinking about them. Therefore, anything that is actively present in one's thinking can be considered appropriate material for waking life insights.

On a related note, I am often asked by therapists about how to work with old dreams in terms of waking life insights considering that the dreams were about issues with which the person was dealing at another time. I contend that old dreams can often have relevance to current waking life as well as to understanding the past experiences. An old dream can mean something about the past experience as well as about one's current life situation in that the past experience might serve as a metaphor or reminder for a current personal conflict. In fact, one could argue that the person remembers the specific dream at the present time because of unresolved conflicts. For example, one therapist brought a dream about a spaceship to a workshop. He had worked on the dream a number of times before and each time had come to a different understanding—and indeed, during the workshop he came to a new understanding. Certainly the new insight could have been due to different methods of working with the dream, but I also postulate that the new understanding was due to the fact that he was at a different emotional place in his current life.

Using the example about the woman's dream of her husband having an affair, the woman might come to recognize that there are underlying tensions in her relationship with her husband about which she has not consciously allowed herself to think:

T: Could you think about how this dream reflects what's going on in your waking life?

C: Well, I am concerned that my husband is not as interested in me as he was before. The bloom definitely seems to be off our relationship. He hardly ever says anything to me anymore. He just watches TV. I worry that he doesn't love me anymore.

T: How do you feel about him?

C: I'm not sure anymore. It's not very rewarding. I find myself more interested in work and being with friends. I'm not getting much out of the relationship.

An interesting twist when the dream is about a relationship is to have all the people in the dream come to the session to work on the dream. Doing this assumes that the dream reflects some degree of reality about all the people in the dream, and therefore all should be involved in the interpretation. In the preceding example, the therapist could ask the client to bring the husband into the session so that they could work on the dream together (see Kolchakian & Hill, 2000).

Understanding Dreams in Terms of Inner Personality Dynamics

There are undoubtedly many ways in which one can understand dreams as reflecting inner personality dynamics, but I focus here on just three of them: (a) parts of self, (b) conflicts originating in childhood, and (c) spiritual–existential concerns. These three foci clearly overlap, but I present them separately to indicate the range of possibilities when working on inner personality dynamics.

Parts of Self

One could view the images in dreams as representing parts of the dreamer, given that the dreamer has identified with and introjected parts of significant others into him- or herself. Psychoanalytic therapists (e.g., Greenson, 1967) have discussed the construct of *projective identification*, in which unresolved historical conflicts are projected onto current significant others, who then play out the part. So, dreams can reflect a projecting of one's issues onto other people or objects. Gestalt therapists (e.g., Perls, 1969) have suggested that all the different parts of the dream are a projection of the self. Jungians (see Johnson, 1986) believe that all the parts of dreams are parts of self, in that each person has many parts (e.g., persona, anima, animus, shadow, trickster, etc.). By imagining that specific dream images represent parts of ourselves, we can explore the many facets of our personalities.

My students and I thought previously that only psychologically minded people (i.e., people who value insight and introspection) could profit from the parts-of-self level of insight, because it seemed to require an ability to think deeply about oneself. However, we recently tested this hypothesis (Hill et al., 2001) by comparing waking life and parts-of-self levels of interpretation and found that clients profited equally from them, regardless of their level of psychological-mindedness. We speculated that clients profited equally from both foci because a coherent rationale was provided for both. Because the idea of dreams representing parts of the self is an unfamiliar concept to many people, some rationale and education are often needed for why the therapist thinks that a parts-of-self focus is appropriate.

In the example of the woman's dream of her husband having an affair, the husband might reflect a part of the woman that is aggressive and thinking about having an affair (her animus, from a Jungian perspective). The part played by herself may represent her victim side, the part of her that feels that others are taking advantage of her (her anima, from a Jungian perspective). Hence, the dream might represent a conflict between her active and passive sides.

T: Would you like to try a parts-of-self level to try to understand this dream?

C: What do you mean?

T: The idea here is that each of the images in the dream represents a part of you. Theory suggests that we incorporate important persons, ideas, events, or feelings into ourselves, and these get enacted in the dream as different characters or objects. By understanding and accepting the different parts of ourselves, we can begin to integrate all the parts and develop a more cohesive sense of self. So, what do you think the dream means if you think of the images as representing different parts of yourself?

C: Well, I guess maybe it means that a part of me is like my husband—inattentive, maybe wanting to have an affair. And part of me is the victim.

T: Sounds like there's some battle between the two parts.

C: Yeah. I guess I don't really know what I want right now. I thought I wanted to get married so badly, but now I'm just not sure. We wanted kids, but couldn't have any, and the marriage just doesn't feel really good right now.

If the insight involves a conflict, such as in the above example, the therapist can conduct a two-chair exercise (see also Greenberg, Rice, & Elliott, 1993) to help the client explore and understand this conflict more experientially. Several studies have demonstrated the efficacy of two-chair work (Greenberg, 1979; Greenberg & Clarke, 1979; Greenberg & Dompierre, 1981; Greenberg & Webster, 1982), especially when therapists can get the two sides to soften and listen to each other, thus allowing for negotiation. For example:

T: If you're willing, I'd like to try something. I'd like you to take the part of yourself in the dream and talk to your husband.

C: I am so angry at you for having an affair. How could you shame me so much?

T: Now be your husband. Sit in that chair and talk back to you.

C: Maybe I wouldn't have had an affair if you had paid more attention to me.

T: Now be you again. Move over to the other chair.

C: What? I pay plenty of attention to you. I don't know what you expect. I suppose you want me to be like your mother and dote on you completely. Well, let me tell you, that isn't going to happen. I have my own life.

T: Be your husband.

C: Well, that's what I want. If you don't want to do that, maybe we shouldn't be together. Maybe we should get divorced.

T: Be you.

C: Well, that's certainly a possibility. We do seem to be incompatible in some ways. But you know, I just want to tell you that you're not the only one who's not completely happy in this relationship. You don't pay much attention to me, either. I would really like to spend more time with you.

T: Be your husband.

C: Really? I didn't know that. You always seem so busy.

C (to therapist): Hmm, that's interesting. I begin to see what you're talking about. Sometimes I feel like me, angry that my husband is having an affair. And sometimes I feel like my husband—wanting to break free and do whatever I want. Sometimes I want to stay in the relationship; sometimes I want out. I've never really put myself in his place before and tried to understand how I might be like him. It gives me a lot to think about.

Conflicts Originating in Childhood

Dreams might also reflect conflicts that developed early in life in relation to interactions with primary caregivers, such as parents. Psychoanalytic theorists have been particularly eloquent in articulating how early childhood experiences develop into unconscious motivations and then influence current behavior (e.g., Greenson, 1967; Malan, 1976). Freud (1900/1966) in particular described how these influences emerge in dreams. In this case, dreams might reflect the Oedipal or Electra conflict (i.e., the dream might reflect the person's struggle to work through entangled relationships with attraction to the opposite-sex parent and competition with the same-sex parent), or dreams might represent the person's attempt to establish an identity separate from his or her parents (Mahler, 1968), to replay interpersonal maladaptive cycles (Book, 1998; Strupp & Binder, 1984; Teyber, 2000), or to challenge and master interpersonal patterns (Weiss, Sampson, & The Mount Zion Psychotherapy Research Group, 1986). I cannot do justice to the wealth of psychoanalytic and interpersonal applications to dream work, but it is important to note that psychoanalytic dream work involves more than just providing standard symbolic interpretations (e.g., all umbrellas are penises). The most important aspect is using the dream to help the client become aware of deep-seated personality conflicts, most of which originated in relation to early attachment figures and then were perpetuated through current interpersonal interactions.

A good example is a terrifying recurrent dream that a young woman had of being chased through the woods by a hooded man who kept getting closer. Her house (all lit up) is in the distance, but she cannot quite get there. In the most recent rendition of the dream, she climbed a tree to get away, and when she looked down, she saw that the face on the hooded figure was her own. The client, who was quite psychologically sophisticated, immediately associated the house with her feminine side, the tree as a phallic symbol, and the hooded figure as her shadow. She interpreted the dream as a struggle between her masculine and feminine sides and between her persona and shadow. She felt she was running away from herself, clinging to her masculinity but wanting to reach the safety of her femininity. She reflected on early relationships with her parents and how, to please her father, she had been a tomboy while growing up. Now that she was living away from her parents and had started college, she began to acknowledge her feminine side but was uncertain how to integrate the different parts into a coherent whole.

In the example of the woman whose husband had an affair, a Freudian interpretation might be that the woman chose a husband as a substitute for her father, of whom she had never completely let go. The husband may be an inadequate substitute, and she may need to resolve her relationship with her father and get a solid identity separate from men before she can have a satisfactory adjustment. A therapy session might proceed as follows:

> T: I wonder if your dream might reflect your feelings toward your father rather than toward your husband.
>
> C: Hmm, that's interesting. I did feel very angry at my father for having affairs. I never really trusted men because of how my father messed around with these floozies. And my mother just passively put up with it. She seemed to pretend that it never happened. I don't know how she really felt, though, because she never talked about it.

T: So some of your feelings about your husband may be transferred from your feelings about your father?

C: I suppose that could be true. I always wanted to feel special with my father, but he was never really there for me.

Spiritual–Existential Concerns

The dream can also be understood in terms of what the dream reflects about the person's relationship with a higher power, or existential issues, such as the meaning of life (see also chapter 7). Yalom (1980, 1992) has suggested that people are driven not so much by past childhood events as by existential fears (e.g., the meaning of life, isolation, freedom, death anxiety). Therapists often ignore existential issues because of their own fears about the purpose of life and anxiety about death, but these are very real issues that everyone must face.

A pertinent example is of a graduate student who had a dream that he and his wife were hiking in the mountains. They came to a juncture where they could follow his wife's family over the desert trail, or he could go kayaking by himself down a mountain stream. Given that he loved kayaking and had frequent arguments with his wife about how often he should take time away from the family to enjoy this sport, the waking life interpretation was obvious. However, when asked for a possible spiritual interpretation, he immediately related to the idea that the mountains were in Utah and that following his wife's family meant following a traditional Mormon path, whereas going kayaking meant developing his own beliefs and desires. He strongly felt that the dream reflected his conflict over his religious–spiritual beliefs.

In the example of the woman whose husband is having an affair, the dream might reflect how the woman is worried about everyday concerns and not thinking about weightier spiritual or existential issues. Discussing the dream might help her realize that she needs to pause and think about who she is and what she really wants out of life:

T: I wonder if you could step back and think about how this dream could reflect on spiritual or existential concerns for you.

C: That's interesting, because I have been thinking a lot lately about how I need to work on my spirituality. Religion was important to me as a kid, but I've grown away from it, and I've been feeling kind of empty. Let's see, my main thought is that I am avoiding thinking about myself and what I want out of life by focusing on my husband and his life.

T: That's interesting. Can you say more about that?

C: Before I met my husband, I was seriously considering becoming a nun. I had been looking into it. I really wanted to dedicate myself to social justice issues and thought that being a nun would be a good way to do that. But then I met the man who became my husband, and I just quit thinking about other things. I devoted my life to making him happy. But I'm not too happy now. I feel like I'm just going through the motions. I need something else in my life.

Choosing Among Insight Levels

From the example of the woman's dream about the husband having an affair, it is readily apparent that working at the various insight levels yielded several different meanings, all of which are plausible. How does the therapist determine which level to use and whether the insight gained is accurate?

The following suggestions are extremely tentative, because no studies have been done to study this issue. As discussed earlier, the type of dream being explored might help the therapist decide which level to use (see Table 2.1). Dreams that are highly arousing and represent experiences in which the client is not likely to be engaged, or in which he or she has not ever been engaged, but has a desire to do or fears doing, seem ideal for experiential interpretations, because these interpretations help the client see what it would be like to be in these situations. For example, a young woman had a dream about an intruder entering her apartment. She heard the intruder, reached under her bed for an ax, and went out to confront the intruder, scaring him off. This event was not something that had ever happened to her, but by working on the dream she came to understand more about herself. She had thought of herself as someone who needed others to take care of her, but this dream helped her realize that she was more capable of self-defense than she had been aware.

Dreams that are very concrete and seem to be reflective of daily life seem suited for waking life interpretations, because it seems that the person is problem solving. For example, a male college student dreamed that he was

TABLE 2.1
The Relationship Between the Level of Insight and
the Appropriate Type of Dream

Level of insight	Most appropriate type of dream
Experiential	Dreams that reflect extraordinary experiences
Waking life	Dreams that reflect normal waking life experiences
Inner dynamics	Dreams that are distant from regular waking life
a. Parts of self	a. When an image is not owned or when there is a major conflict between two images
b. Conflicts from childhood	b. When the dreamer is struggling with past issues with parents, attachment, identity
c. Spiritual–existential	c. When the dreamer is struggling with spiritual or existential concerns, such as figuring out meaning of life, death

at a wedding banquet and saw an old girlfriend across the room. In the dream, he sat down and talked with his old girlfriend. His associations were all about how much he missed his old girlfriend and how much he wanted to reconcile with her. The dream did not seem to involve any metaphor or symbolism but rather seemed directly related to his waking wishes and fantasies.

Dreams that seem most appropriate for understanding in terms of inner dynamics are those that are bizarre, out of the ordinary, metaphoric, abstract, or symbolic. For example, one person had a dream in which an alien was whispering in his ear while he was dancing in a circus. Another had a dream about finding exotic oils in a small shop in Mexico. Yet another had a dream about being imprisoned in a mental hospital only to escape and float above the world on a green carpet. None of these dreams related to everyday experiences for these clients, and thus they were more likely representative of inner experiences. Even a dream about a specific person can be reflective of inner personality dynamics. For example, a man had a dream about his sister dying. On waking, he checked and found that his sister, who lived in another country, was well and happy. In this dream, he decided that the sister was a metaphor for an inner dynamic.

Furthermore, within the inner dynamics, a parts-of-self approach might be used when there are images that seem to be disowned or when there is a lot of conflict between two images. Inner conflicts might be the focus when the client is concerned about unresolved past issues, such as relationships with parents, attachment, or identity. The focus might be spiritual–existential if the dream and associations reflect spiritual or existential concerns or if the client expresses a lot of spiritual beliefs or interest in existential issues.

Furthermore, to make a decision about which level to use, therapists can assess the level to which clients seem drawn initially in terms of their understanding of dreams. Most clients automatically think about waking life interpretations, because it is common knowledge in U.S. culture that dreams reflect waking life. It is also less threatening to talk about one's waking life than about inner personality dynamics or spiritual issues. Thus, it seems appropriate to try waking life interpretations as a first tactic.

Some clients, however, will be willing to go further with the insight stage. Hill et al. (2001) learned that it is important for therapists to provide a credible rationale for these other levels of interpretations. Because most clients think of dreams as reflecting waking life, clients need to be educated that dreams could mean something else. Therapists can suggest another level of interpretation and see whether the client is interested in pursuing it.

Therapists can also use their clinical judgment based on their hunches about the meaning of the dream to suggest particular levels of interpretation. For example, if a dream has a symbol that seems blatantly suggestive of a Freudian (e.g., a hot dog) or Jungian (e.g., a mandala) interpretation, the therapist might want to pursue that level of interpretation (always being alert for a lack of agreement on the part of the client). Alternatively, if the therapist notices that the dream and the exploration of the dream are full of conflicts, an interpretation in terms of parts of self might be appropriate. Similarly, if the client has been talking about spiritual issues during the exploration stage, it seems reasonable to go with the spiritual level. If a client believes that the dream reflects cultural interpretations (i.e., dream dictionaries), it is wise to go with that. Hence, therapists match the level of interpretation to the client's immediate needs and dynamics.

THOUGHTS ABOUT DOING THE INSIGHT STAGE

In the insight stage, therapists focus on helping clients put things together and gain insight. However, they also might offer more of their own thoughts and reactions than they did during the exploration stage, if this is needed to help the client come up with new understandings. The therapist has more to offer in this stage and, in fact, clients have indicated that they value the different perspectives that therapists offer (Hill, Diemer, & Heaton, 1997). Some clients need to hear a different perspective because they get stuck trying to figure out their dreams on their own.

However, in offering their own ideas and insights, therapists need to remain attuned to the client's feelings and level of comfort. Therapists must remember that they are not the experts who have the answers to what the dream means but rather that their main role is to facilitate the client's involvement and understanding of the dream. Therapists must always be aware that they can never know clients completely, and hence their insights are always tentative and subject to revision based on feedback from clients. Therapists need to be creative and flexible and use their intuition and individual therapeutic style to provide the clients with possible interpretations, but they also need to be empathic and attentive to what the client can handle.

Therapists also need to be aware of their own personal issues and how these can negatively influence the therapeutic process. They need to think about their motivations for giving interpretations rather than helping clients arrive at their own insights. When therapists want to be viewed as brilliant and have clients hang onto their interpretations, the client's insight process is often stifled. I suggest that therapists change their criterion of success from being brilliant to being happy when they can coach clients in attaining their own understanding.

The task here is for the therapist and client to engage together in an insight-generating process to try to come up with new understandings of the dream. Reik (1935) wrote that the meaning of the dream should come as a surprise to both the client and therapist, and I heartily agree. The key is to recognize that the client is the expert on him- or herself. The therapist, rather than saying what the dream means, can say something like, "I wonder if it might mean…" and encourage the client to modify and correct the meaning. By working together, therapists and clients can often construct a better interpretation than either could alone. The client is ultimately the arbiter of the meaning of the dream, so the therapist needs to listen very attentively for client disagreement or feelings of being misunderstood. Given that clients often hide negative reactions and disagreement from therapists (Hill, Thompson, Cogar, & Denman, 1993; Regan & Hill, 1992; Rennie, 1994; Thompson & Hill, 1991), it is incumbent upon therapists to ask clients for their reactions.

Another method that works well comes from Ullman (1979, 1987, 1993; Ullman & Zimmerman, 1979). The therapist says something like, "If it were my dream, it might mean...." In this way, the therapist owns that the interpretation may be a projection and hence may not be accurate or work for the client. Clients often feel more permission to refute an interpretation phrased tentatively (e.g., "No, it's not quite that; it's more....") than if the therapist states "the" meaning.

Another caveat about working in this stage is that it is important to match the depth of interpretation to what the client can handle. As Speisman (1959) suggested, moderate levels of depth are better than interpretations that are too shallow or too deep. If the interpretation is too shallow, the client might dismiss it (and the therapist) because it adds nothing new. If the interpretation is too deep, the client may not be able to handle the insight (or it could be wrong). It is important to be attuned to what clients can handle and to offer interpretations that are similar to what clients are thinking and trying to articulate or that are just half a step beyond what clients are thinking. In this way, the therapist helps the client by stretching him or her to think about other possibilities that are just a bit beyond thoughts the client has already had.

Another issue to note is that it is wonderful and exhilarating for therapists and clients when clients have breakthrough "aha" insight experiences (i.e., "Oh, so that's what the dream is about. Wow!! That's amazing!!"). However, not all clients, not even those who are psychologically minded, have breakthrough insights during every dream session. For some clients, the issues are too deep, and defenses might be too strong. For other clients, the particular dream is just not compelling. In other situations, the process of working with the dream may not have been conducive to insight, either because of the therapeutic relationship or the therapist's techniques. Whatever comes out, comes out. Therapists should not keep pushing for more insight after a certain amount of concerted effort (i.e., 15–20 min) but should go on to the action stage.

Finally, beginning therapists often ask about how to determine the accuracy of an interpretation. Determining accuracy is not possible because therapist can neither trace back to the exact events in the client's life, nor examine how experiences are stored in the client's cognitive schemas. Furthermore, people's understanding of things changes with added information and in different contexts. Hence, it makes more sense to think about the therapist and the client *constructing* a meaning of the dream based on the information available at the time. Instead of talking about accuracy, it is more appropriate to think about the value of the interpretation for the therapeutic process. The interpretation is good if it fits most of the components of the dream, makes sense to the client, sparks an "aha" reaction in the client, and provides a sense of newness and satisfaction for the client. Furthermore, the real proof of the quality of the insight is in whether the insight leads directly to actions in the next stage and helps the client think differently or do something differently in waking life.

EXAMPLE OF THE INSIGHT STAGE

Dream: I am in the top room of this three-story house. It isn't my home or any house I've ever been in. There is a storm approaching, and it is going to flood the house room by room. I am not really that anxious about it, I guess, because I am just taking my time and hanging out doing my own thing. I am really waiting until the last moment. I finally see water coming into the room, so I start taking my personal things from the room. I take my cat and this other cat I used to have and put them in a separate room that is further away from where the flood is coming. Then I go downstairs and just wait for the house to fill up with water.

[After exploration stage]

T: What do you think the dream means?

C: It seems to be mirroring what I'm going through because there's a lot of facets in my life that are very unstable. At the same time, a side of me thinks that that's just the way things are and there's not much I can do about it right now. A lot of things are happening to me that I don't have a lot of control over, unfortunately. But I think in the dream, I realize that there's some major changes coming, and I'm not letting it affect me, or maybe I should be letting it affect me. Maybe I should take some more precautions or move a little bit quicker, but I'm just kind of accepting it because I'm used to these things happening and being out of control. Maybe I'm just feeling a little bit unsettled because there's no furniture and there's not a real lived-in feeling to this house. I feel like I'm moving again, but at this point it's kind of normal, because it's happened before. I definitely think there's something to the cleanliness of the place too.

T: You mentioned that there's so much going on—the cleanliness, the lack of organization, the pristine white house versus all that's going on that you can't control, the outside forces, this life, this cat that you can't control, the cat who wants to go back home…

C: Yeah, that's true.

T: ...And in the midst of all this, you're feeling kind of calm, not quite reacting, not quite sure what to make of not reacting. It's all so mysterious and wonderful and interesting, but you think you ought to be more organized. There's a lot going on.

C: It's true. I guess what I just realized, too, is that when the flood is finally coming in is when I rush to get all my personal things out, which to me, is ridiculous. I wait until the last minute before disaster strikes before I act. The other thing is that it's always hard for me to figure out what's important. What will I move from the flood?

T: What would be the most important things?

C: I think it would be first my journals and letters, and then my cat, and maybe my jewelry. That's probably it. I would leave everything else behind because the other stuff is too big and heavy.

T: So things that are really personal to you, things you've gotten very attached to.

C: Yeah. I think those are the things I just wouldn't be able to replace at all.

T: It sounds like the flood is going to wipe out stuff, but it could also cleanse.

C: I think it's a lot of things. I'm in a relationship right now, too, that's been stormy. I don't really know what's going on right now, maybe the calm after the storm. But at the time that this dream was occurring, I was caught up in lots of things. I was looking for a new job and wasn't getting many responses. My housemate had this big family emergency. I found out that I'd have to move. There was a lot going on, and I wasn't taking a lot of action, because I was thinking about graduate school and I was feeling a lot of pressure. My boyfriend was like, "Well, where do I fit into the picture? Because anything you decide from this point on is going to affect me is some way."

T: Where does he fit in?

C: He's a very significant part of my life, but we're trying to decide if we're right for each other. I don't think it really fit into the dream, maybe the storm side.

T: I'm struck that you were so alone and had to take care of it all by yourself.

C: Yeah, that's true. I think that's one of the major issues, that he's really busy with his own life, so I don't have a lot of support from him. That's probably why I was alone in my dream. But it's strange. I do have a lot of people who are very supportive in my life. Maybe

I put myself in those positions, too, like I just kind of want to be less dependent on others. I just keep that to myself.

T: That dichotomy between independence and dependence is interesting. You described yourself as being like your cat, who on the one hand attacks, and on the other hand follows you around all the time. What do you make of that?

C: Well, I am like that a little bit. It's interesting. But, I find that when I'm in a relationship, a lot of times, I'm kind of like my cat. I mean, I have to really make sure that I'm not becoming dependent on that other person. When I am, I'm very sensitive about things. That's when I become very angry, or explosive, or sensitive to criticism. So there's two dynamics going on.

T: So, back to these polarities. You want to be independent and able to travel wherever you feel like going, and yet there's part of you that's really dependent.

C: I'm not very good at balancing those two. I'm either–or, but not very often in the middle. Part of it, too, is that even in friendly kinds of relationships, I get to a certain point where I'm very close to a person and then it's like too much, so I go to the opposite extreme and try to break free of the whole situation. Then I realize it's kind of more finding a balance. I think I'm a very intense person when it comes to relationships. I'm not satisfied with knowing a little bit. I want to know more about the other person, or I want there to be more of a connection. But then I realize that that's too much to ask.

T: Why do you think it's difficult to find a middle ground?

C: I wonder if has to do with watching my parents' relationship when I was growing up, because I feel like they were very…I just don't understand their relationship; it seems very efficient.

T: That's an interesting word.

C: I know there's romance there, but I just can't even imagine them having a deep conversation about anything. It seems to be more about how can we get from Point A to Point B and still manage to have lunch together. I don't know, maybe it's sort of battling with that. I just don't want to be like that.

T: That's important to you.

C: It seems superficial to a certain extent and very disconnected in a way. They are connected by situational things. Sometimes I'm amazed that they're still together, because they're so different and I don't know how they could have connected. Maybe it's just not really my place to understand that, but…

T: But that's not what you want.

C: No, that's not what I want at all, but I know what I want is probably not good. It's probably not a very safe thing to want. I've had a couple of very close friends in the past. Some people have a lot of friends, and I always have like two or three really close friends. Usually there's one person who's very significant in my life, and you just don't ever see us apart. We're always together, the best of friends. And I think I search for that in my intimate relationships, and I'm just not getting that. Maybe it's a male–female thing. I don't know what it is.

T: It's not a safe thing to want?

C: I think that when you're too dependent on somebody that's not very good. It can be dangerous, because you're not thinking clearly about the situation. You're acting more on an emotional level. You're not able to see clearly.

T: So part of you wants that dependency, but part of you doesn't. You don't want to lose yourself in a relationship. It doesn't feel like it's possible to be close friends with a man like you are with your women friends. Somehow you lose yourself; you can't maintain your limits.

C: Yeah. When I do try to maintain my limits, it seems very awkward. The person might as well be a stranger. It just doesn't seem like there's a real connection going.

T: I keep coming back to the image of that white carpet. If the house is so pristine clean and the carpet is so white, how can you have a relationship? And either you really believe in something, or you lose it and don't care. Where's the in-between? This white carpet doesn't work too well.

C: Yeah, I know, I know. I don't know what the white carpet is all about.

T: And there's something in your parents' relationship that's efficient. Your mother's very organized, very clean, keeps everything very clean…

C: My dad is like an absent-minded professor. He loses things all the time, kind of like me. He leaves his keys behind. He'll be halfway to the office and realize he left his office key and turn around and go back. We'll be halfway on a trip someplace, and he forgot his passport. We have to turn around and go get his passport, little things like that. He's very distracted with his work.

T: Does that drive your mother crazy?

C: It does. But she's very good about it. She's very efficient, and goes down the list of the three of us. I guess it works out. I think to a certain extent, I'm kind of looking for, if I was looking from a Freudian perspective, I'm probably looking for somebody in my life who's a little bit like my dad in his characteristics, somebody who's different from my mom. I don't know how that works out.

T: It seems like there might be a step before that, though, of coming to accept yourself as you are. I'm not sure you're quite at that point.

C: Maybe that's true.

T: You want to embrace who you are, value who you are. That might be part of what's so confusing for you. When you're not sure who you are and what you want, it's hard to be with someone else because they might overwhelm you. It sounds like you're trying to figure out who you are.

C: Maybe so. I don't know that many people who have accepted themselves as they are.

T: Well, it's certainly an ongoing struggle.

C: I have a close friend who hasn't dated anybody for like 7 years! It amazes me because she's about my age and she is very anti-going out with anybody. She says that it's because she has to learn to accept herself first. To me, that seems like the other extreme. But I'll probably be trying to figure this out for the rest of my life. But I don't want to [end up] 30 years from now regretting that I was never in a relationship, either. I guess it is true that you have to decide whether you're spending too much energy in an area that is conflicting with what you're trying to do.

T: Oh, I agree with you. I don't think it happens separately. You have to work on both parts at once. And these are things that you keep working on all your life. Let's just come back to the subject of these cats. The attack versus dependency versus running away. It's like these cats represent you in some way.

C: Could be. Like the dependency and running away. Attack. I never thought about that before. That's really interesting.

ASK THE CLIENT TO SUMMARIZE HIS OR HER UNDERSTANDING OF THE DREAM

In ending the insight stage, the therapist can ask the client to summarize the major themes or meanings of the dream. It is better for the therapist to allow the client to summarize rather than doing the summarizing him- or herself, because summarizing allows the client to consolidate what she or he has learned about the dream. In addition, hearing the client summarize the interpretation of the dream provides an opportunity for the therapist to hear what the client has taken away from the interpretation process and to assess the client's readiness to move on to the action stage. I vividly recall a session in which the client and I had spent a long time working on insights, but when the client summarized what she had learned, she repeated her initial interpretation. I realized that she had not absorbed much of our exploration about new insights. I was alerted to slow down and proceed more at her pace.

Here is an example of summarizing based on the dream presented at the beginning of the chapter about the man chasing the young woman and her sister:

T: Can you summarize what you think this dream means? There's a lot of different phases and a lot of different threads. We could spend hours on this dream, but what do you think you've learned today?

C: I think the dream was about standing up for yourself. Being able to say "no." Being able to say, "Let go!" Being able to not keep everything in you uptight. To make sure you're able to let it go. And the fact that I couldn't lock the door in the door in the dream, that I'm not going to be able to protect my sister all the time. Because the fact is that she did get caught. Maybe she got away, maybe she didn't, but she has to fight that battle on her own.

T: Seems like a good metaphor. I keep coming back to the phrase you used about personal character. It sounds like you have personal character—you know when to stand up for yourself and how much you can take care of your sister.

CONCLUSION

The insight stage can be very exciting for both therapists and clients when they work together to discover the "pure gold" of the meaning of dreams. Clients present dreams because they want to understand them, so gaining insight is congruent with their expectations; also, insight is often a prerequisite for making changes in waking life.

The insight stage can be fun and creative. It can provide an opportunity to figure out a puzzling dream, to create new meaning, to get past defenses. I encourage therapists to use their intuition and enjoy the process of working collaboratively with clients to understand their dreams.

REFERENCES

Beck, A. T., & Hurvich, M. (1959). Psychological correlates of depression: I. Frequency of "masochistic" dream content in a private practice sample. *Psychosomatic Medicine, 21,* 50–55.

Beck, A. T., & Ward, C. (1961). Dreams of depressed patients: Characteristic themes in manifest content. *Archives of General Psychiatry, 5,* 462–467.

Biddle, W. E. (1963). Images. *Archives of General Psychiatry, 9,* 464–470.

Book, H. E. (1998). *How to practice brief psychodynamic psychotherapy: The core conflictual relationship theme method.* Washington, DC: American Psychological Association.

Carrington, P. (1972). Dreams and schizophrenia. *Archives of General Psychiatry, 26,* 343–350.

Cartwright, R. D. (1986). Affect and dream work from an information-processing POV. *Journal of Mind and Behavior, 7,* 411–427.

Craig, E., & Walsh, S. J. (1993). The clinical use of dreams. In G. Delaney (Ed.), *New directions in dream interpretation* (pp. 103–154). Albany: State University of New York Press.

Dement, W. C. (1955). Dream recall and eye movements during sleep in schizophrenics and normals. *Journal of Nervous and Mental Disease, 122,* 263–269.

Faraday, A. (1974). *The dream game.* New York: Harper & Row.

Freud, S. (1966). *The interpretation of dreams.* New York: Avon. (Original work published 1900)

Goldhirsh, M. L. (1961). Manifest content of dreams of convicted sex offenders. *Journal of Abnormal Social Psychology, 63,* 643–645.

Greenberg, L. S. (1979). Resolving splits: The two-chair technique. *Psychotherapy: Theory, Research, and Practice, 16,* 310–318.

Greenberg, L. S. (2002). *Emotion-focused therapy: Coaching clients to work through their feelings.* Washington, DC: American Psychological Association.

Greenberg, L. S., & Clarke, K. (1979). The differential effects of the two-chair experiment and empathic reflections at a conflict marker. *Journal of Counseling Psychology, 26,* 1–8.

Greenberg, L. S., & Dompierre, L. (1981). Specific effects of gestalt two-chair dialogue on intrapsychic conflict in counseling. *Journal of Counseling Psychology, 28,* 288–294.

Greenberg, L. S., Rice, L. N., & Elliott, R. (1993). *Facilitating emotional change.* New York: Guilford Press.

Greenberg, L. S., & Webster, M. C. (1982). Resolving decisional conflict by gestalt two-chair dialogue: Relating process to outcome. *Journal of Counseling Psychology, 29,* 468–477.

Greenson, R. R. (1967). *The technique and practice of psychoanalysis* (Vol. 1). Madison, CT: International Universities Press.

Hill, C. E. (1996). *Working with dreams in psychotherapy.* New York: Guilford Press.

Hill, C. E., Diemer, R., & Heaton, K. J. (1997). Dream interpretation sessions: Who volunteers, who benefits, and what volunteer clients view as most and least helpful. *Journal of Counseling Psychology, 44,* 53–62.

Hill, C. E., Kelley, F. A., Davis, T. L., Crook, R. E., Maldonado, L. E., Turkson, M. A., et al. (2001). Predictors of outcome of dream interpretation sessions: Volunteer client characteristics, dream characteristics, and type of interpretation. *Dreaming, 11,* 53–72.

Hill, C. E., & O'Brien, K. (1999). *Helping skills: Facilitating exploration, insight, and action.* Washington, DC: American Psychological Association.

Hill, C. E., Thompson, B. J., Cogar, M. M., & Denman, D. W., III. (1993). Beneath the surface of long-term therapy: Client and therapist report of their own and each other's covert processes. *Journal of Counseling Psychology, 40,* 278–288.

Johnson, R. (1986). *Inner work.* San Francisco: Harper & Row.

Kant, O. (1942). Dreams of schizophrenic patients. *Journal of Nervous and Mental Disease, 95,* 335–347.

Kolchakian, M., & Hill, C. E. (2000). A cognitive–experiential dream interpretation model for couples. In L. VandeCreek & T. L. Jackson (Eds.), *Innovations in clinical practice: A source book* (Vol. 18, pp. 85–101). Sarasota, FL: Professional Resource Press.

Kramer, M. (1993). Dream translation: An approach to understanding dreams. In G. Delaney (Ed.), *New directions in dream interpretation* (pp. 155–194). Albany: State University of New York Press.

Kramer, M., Whitman, R., Baldridge, B., & Lansky, L. (1966). Dreaming in the depressed. *Canadian Psychiatric Association Journal, 11,* 178–192.

Langs, R. J. (1966). Manifest dreams from three clinical groups. *Archives of General Psychiatry, 14,* 634–643.

Mahler, M. S. (1968). *On human symbiosis of the vicissitudes on individuation.* New York: International Universities Press.

Malan, S. H. (1976). *The frontier of brief therapy.* New York: Plenum.

Noble, D. (1951). A study of dreams in schizophrenia and allied states. *American Journal of Psychiatry, 107,* 612–616.

Perls, F. (1969). *Gestalt therapy verbatim.* New York: Bantam.

Regan, A. M., & Hill, C. E. (1992). An investigation of what clients and counselors do not say in brief therapy. *Journal of Counseling Psychology, 39,* 168–174.

Reik, T. (1935). *Surprise and the psychoanalyst.* London: Routledge.

Rennie, D. L. (1994). Clients' deference in therapy. *Journal of Counseling Psychology, 41,* 427–437.

Speisman, J. C. (1959). Depth of interpretation and verbal resistance in psychotherapy. *Journal of Consulting Psychology, 23,* 93–99.

Strupp, H. H., & Binder, J. L. (1984). *Psychotherapy in a new key: A guide to time-limited dynamic psychotherapy.* New York: Basic Books.

Teyber, E. (2000). *Interpersonal process in psychotherapy* (4th ed.). Pacific Grove: CA: Brooks/Cole.

Thompson, B., & Hill, C. E. (1991). Therapist perceptions of client reactions. *Journal of Counseling and Development, 69,* 261–265.

Ullman, M. (1979). The experiential dream group. In B. B. Wolman (Ed.), *Handbook of dreams* (pp. 407–423). New York: Van Nostrand Reinhold.

Ullman, M. (1987). The dream revisited: Some changed ideas based on a group approach. In M. L. Glucksman & S. L. Warner (Eds.), *Dreams in a new perspective: The royal road revisited* (pp. 119–130). New York: Human Sciences Press.

Ullman, M. (1993). Dreams, the dreamer, and society. In G. Delaney (Ed.), *New directions in dream interpretation* (pp. 41–76). Albany: State University of New York Press.

Ullman, M., & Zimmerman, N. (1979). *Working with dreams.* Los Angeles: Tarcher.

Weiss, J., Sampson, H., & The Mount Zion Psychotherapy Research Group. (1986). *The psychoanalytic process: Theory, clinical observation, and empirical research.* New York: Guilford Press.

Yalom, I. D. (1980). *Existential psychotherapy.* New York: Basic Books.

Yalom, I. D. (1992). *The Yalom reader.* New York: Basic Books.

3

THE ACTION STAGE

CLARA E. HILL

The purpose of the action stage is for therapists to help clients extend what they have learned during the previous stages to thinking about changes that they might want to make in waking life. Some clients spontaneously move to action after the insight stage. For example, one client had a dream in which she was wearing a see-through dress while walking down a dark alley in a bad section of town. By going through the insight stage, she recognized that she was engaging in some risky behaviors because of some self-destructive tendencies. She thought she had worked through these self-defeating attitudes but realized that they had come up again as she was becoming involved in a new relationship. She saw the dream as a message that she needed to be more careful in how she dressed, where she went, and with whom she got involved. She did not need the therapist's guidance to move her along to the action stage because her insight led her directly to want to change her behavior. In this case, the task in the action stage was for the therapist to help this client figure out how she wanted to go about making the changes.

Other clients, however, need more help moving on to the action stage. For various reasons, they make changes on their own—either they need someone to provide an opportunity for them to think about action, or they need someone to suggest ideas for action, or they need someone to teach them specific skills (e.g., study skills, job hunting skills).

I like to think of the idea of "exploring action" rather than "action," because our task as therapists is to help clients think about the possibility of changing, rather than being task masters who force changes on clients. In keeping with my client-centered emphasis on clients as self-healers, I believe that therapists should encourage clients to think about the benefits and drawbacks of change and help them make good decisions about what, if anything, they want to do. Therapists help clients establish or clarify intentions to carry out action ideas (see Wonnell & Hill, 2000, 2003). Whether clients carry out their intentions depends on how motivated they are as well as on external factors, such as opportunity. For example, a client might intend to talk to his parents, but he may not go home for some time, or something else may come up in the meantime on which it is more important to focus. The therapist's goal is to help clients formulate intentions about actions, but it is up to the clients to make the changes. In essence, therapists serve as consultants or coaches to facilitate the clients' change process.

Because the major task in the action stage is to help clients explore change, the primary skills that therapists use are the same ones they used in the exploration stage, most notably, open question, restatement, and reflection of feelings (see Hill & O'Brien, 1999). Therapists also use a smattering of action skills (information and direct guidance) to provide specific instructions or advice to clients, and they also use a sprinkling of insight skills (challenge, interpretation, self-disclosure of insight, and immediacy) to facilitate the client's understanding of blocks to action. Both insight and action skills are more difficult than exploration skills to use therapeutically, so therapists need to be very aware of how clients are reacting and be prepared to deal with misunderstandings as they arise.

In this chapter I describe the three steps of the action stage: (a) changing the dream, (b) translating changes to waking life, and (c) summarizing action ideas. I also provide extensive examples so that therapists can get an idea of how to facilitate the steps of the action stage.

CHANGING THE DREAM

The action stage can begin with the therapist asking the client to change the dream or create a sequel to the dream (i.e., continue the dream and give it a different ending). Because the client created the dream initially, she or he can change it or extend it. Encouraging clients to change dreams is important for three reasons. First, the task emphasizes that clients are the creators and directors of their dreams and can change their dreams, which can facilitate a sense of empowerment for the client. By realizing that they are not passive recipients of their dreams but rather are active players, clients can learn to take more responsibility for themselves. Second, making changes in the dream is often a fun and creative way to get the client started in thinking about making changes and can lead to specific behavioral changes.

Third, hearing what clients say about changing their dreams allows therapists an opportunity to assess readiness for change. Some clients immediately gravitate toward the idea of changing the dream, whereas others resist changing the dream because it seems silly or irrelevant. If clients act helpless and cannot change their dreams, chances are that they are not going to be willing to make changes in their lives. However, if clients readily think about changes that they could make in their dreams, they are more likely to be willing to make changes in their lives. For example, one woman dreamed that she was observing her dead body being carried down a flight of stairs by several strange men. When asked what she would like to change in the dream, she said she wanted to know who the men carrying her body were. It was very revealing that she did not want to change being dead and observing herself rather than being in her body. The work in this step then evolved to asking her about this omission and helping her think about what that was about. Thus, we do not just ask clients about the changes, but we explore these changes with them to help them understand themselves more (hence cycling back to insight).

I now describe two ways of working on changing dreams: in fantasy and in reality.

Changing Dreams in Fantasy

Therapists can ask clients to change their dreams in fantasy. If clients could change the dream any way they wanted, how would they change it? If they could imagine the dream continuing, what would they like to happen next? Therapists want clients to play with the dreams and warm up to the idea of change. They remind clients that clients created the dreams, so the dreams are theirs to change as they wish. Change is sometimes less threatening in fantasy than in reality, and therapists want to empower clients to begin thinking about the possibility of change.

Sometimes therapists suggest that clients invoke *dream helpers* when they feel helpless to cope on their own in the dream. For example, a young man had a dream in which several bad guys were following him and throwing plastic knives at him, clearly meaning to hurt him. I suggested that he invoke several policemen to help him battle the bad guys. Having the policemen at his side gave him confidence to fight.

The following is an example of asking a client to change a recurrent dream. I first present the dream and the insight gained in the insight stage.

> **Dream:** I wake up and am surprised to see a snake in a glass aquarium on my roommate's dresser. My roommate is sleeping, so I sit fearfully watching the snake and waiting for her to wake up. I notice while staring at the cage that the top is open and the snake can get out. I get up, and as

I'm moving towards my roommate's bed, the snake starts to raise his head out of the cage. The closer I get to her, the farther his head gets out of the cage. I get to her bed and wake her up, and he goes back down like he was sleeping the whole time. Then she closes the cage and we both go back to sleep. When I wake up again and look around, I notice that my roommate has gone to class and the snake is out of the cage. I look around and can't see him, so I sit in my bed silent and scared. I get up to run for the door, and when I get there, I notice that the snake has the perimeter of the room surrounded. I freeze, but I'm still able to scream. Two girls hear my scream and run into the room. They are able to get the snake and put him away. Later, he sneaks out again but this time, he's under my covers, and when I wake up his head pops out from under the covers and then he gets back in the cage before I have a chance to tell my roommate he is out.

[*Insight stage*]

C: It has to do with me feeling trapped socially. I feel like I can't socialize as much as I want to. I feel trapped in my living situation with my roommate. My schoolwork is constricting my social life. I miss my family in Louisiana. All of these aspects played a part in my dream.

[*Action stage*]

T: If you could change the dream in any way, how would you change it?

C: There wouldn't be a snake in it.

T: Why not?

C: It feels like the snake is restricting me, and I don't like that.

T: Who would be in it instead?

C: People I feel comfortable with.

T: Can you think of specific people you would like to have around?

C: I would rather have a roommate I can feel close to, someone more like me.

T: So no one specific. Any other changes?

C: I wouldn't have that feeling of being scared.

T: Say more about that.

C: I don't like being so paralyzed by this stupid snake. It's my room. I want to feel more comfortable there.

T: What would you like to do?

C: I'd like to tell my roommate that she can't have a snake in the room.

T: Go ahead and tell her.

C: Get that snake out of this room. What are you thinking of?

T: How did that feel?

C: It felt good. I need to talk to her about things going on in the room. I've just been too chicken to stir things up.

The client specifically mentioned changes that she could make in her own behavior. She said that would like to not feel scared and would like to feel more comfortable, which led her and the therapist to the next step of bridging to changes in waking life. If, however, clients talk only about external changes (e.g., the snake not being there), it is more difficult to bridge to changes in waking life, because people seldom have control over others' actions. In such a situation, therapists can ask clients to also think about changes that they would like to make to themselves in the dream.

T: Any changes that you would like to make in the way that *you* handled the situation with the snake?

C: I don't think there are any changes I could make. I just feel so helpless in this dream. And I keep having it. I'm getting really frustrated. I really don't want to feel as scared, though.

T: How would you like to be?

C: I would like to be more assertive in the way I handle the situation.

Sometimes clients have a hard time thinking of ways to change their dreams. Some feel overwhelmed by the emotions in the dream, some feel helpless to change the dream, and some feel anxious or silly changing the dream. In these cases, the therapist might suggest how he or she would change the dream if it were his or hers. Using such projections preserves the integrity of the client's feelings and yet provides some ideas for clients to get them unstuck.

T: If this were my dream, I would want to speak up for myself. I would want to tell her that snakes aren't allowed and she has to get it out of there. How would that feel for you?

C: I would like to do that, but I would be scared.

T: Try it right now and see how it feels.

C: You've got to get that snake out of here now. I'm not sleeping in here another night with that snake in the room.

T: How was that for you?

C: I felt really tense, but I liked telling her that.

Other people feel that dreams are gifts or messages from external sources and that it is wrong to change them. In such a case, I might suggest that the client think of a sequel to how she or he would like the dream to continue if that were possible. In this way, the dream as it occurred is preserved, but the client is freed to think about new possibilities.

T: If you could continue this dream, what would you like to happen next?

C: I would go to the resident assistant and ask to get a new roommate. I want to room with someone I really like so I would finally have a friend. There would no more snakes in the bed.

T: Sounds like a much better ending.

Of course, if clients do not want to change the dream or create a sequel, it is not wise to force the issue. As elsewhere in the model, the therapist follows the client's lead and does not pressure the client to do any step that he or she does not want to do. Rather, the therapist can move to behavioral changes or to a discussion of why the client does not want to do this step.

Teaching Clients to Change Troubling Nightmares

Some clients need active interventions to help them deal with troubling nightmares. A Vietnam veteran had vivid and horrible nightmares that awoke him; he did not want to go back to sleep for several nights for fear of having the nightmares again. He clearly needed some intervention to help him cope with this nightmare and get some sleep. (I provide some information on working with nightmares here but also refer interested readers to Cartwright & Lamberg, 1992, and chap. 10, this volume.)

Therapists can focus on three steps for helping clients manage their nightmares.

1. Teach the client to visualize the nightmare and stop it before it becomes too frightening.
2. Teach clients to relax so that they can reduce the anxiety. Benson's (1975, 1988) approach to relaxation is quite simple and useful. It involves two main components: (a) the repetition of any word, sound, prayer, thought, phrase, or muscular activity and (b) the passive return to repeating when other thoughts intrude.

The therapist uses a calm, slow voice and suggests that the client close his or her eyes, relax all over, and then pick a word or phrase and say it over and over slowly for a few minutes, passively letting all other thoughts go if they intrude.

3. Teach the client to change the nightmare into something more positive. Therapists can assess what might be a pleasant image for the client (i.e., skiing, sitting on a beach, talking to a friend) and ask the client to imagine this pleasant image right then. They can rehearse these changes several times with the client until the client becomes confident that she or he can implement the changes at the critical time during the nightmare.

The therapist then can coach the client about dealing with the actual situation of the nightmare. Following up with the client to assess difficulties in implementing the procedures is crucial, of course, and therapists need to modify procedures to fit with problems as they arise when clients are trying to implement the changes. Using the snake dream, a therapist might do this step in the following way:

T: Let's go through the dream again and try to help you plan how to deal with it the next time you have it. Where would you like to start?

C: Let's do the part where the snake is actually in my bed. That's the scariest part.

T: So start there and tell me what's happening. Remember to keep it in the present tense.

C: I wake up and feel this thing slithering around my ankles. I freeze and look and this snake's head pops out right next to my face. I start to scream, but I feel so panicked I can't even move. I feel panicked just talking about it—I'd like to run out of the room.

T: Okay; stop right there. Let's try something to help you relax. Focus on your breathing for a minute. [pause] Take a deep breath and let it out slowly. [pause] Close your eyes and let your whole body relax. [pause] Now pick a word or short phrase, like "one" or anything that has meaning to you and repeat that over and over for a few minutes. When other thoughts intrude, just passively let them go. Just take a couple minutes now and do that. [pause] How are you feeling now?

C: I feel much better now. Thanks.

T: Okay, let's go back to working on the nightmare. What would you like to do at this point of the nightmare?

C: I want to tell the snake to disappear.

T: Okay, try it.

C: Get out of here. This is my dream; you can't be here.

T: How was that for you?

C: I don't think I could do it. I'm still too frightened.

T: How about if you invoked someone else to come into your dream and help you get rid of the snake?

C: Hmm. I have a better idea. Maybe I could pretend I'm Harry Potter and wave my wand and make it disappear.

T: Okay, let's try that. Visualize that.

C: I see the snake's head pop out, and I call on my mystical powers to zap it. I wave my wand, and the snake disappears. Hey, that's great.

T: Let's practice it through again from the top. Close your eyes and try to visualize yourself sleeping in your bed and actually having this nightmare. And then add something different and positive instead.

C: Okay. I feel the snake slithering at my feet and I'm feeling scared. It pops its head up. I look it in the eye and wave my wand and poof, it disappears. I go back to sleep and dream about being a magician with unlimited powers.

T: What I'd like you to do is practice that a few more times before you go to sleep. Then the next time you have the nightmare, wake yourself up and make the snake disappear. Do you think you could do that?

C: I think I could. I want to try it.

Instead of battling the image in the dream, therapists can suggest to clients that they make friends with the terrifying image. Although the natural instinct is to attack the terrifying image, we typically do not want to encourage clients to resort to violence as a coping method. Furthermore, if one considers that parts of the dream might be parts of the self, then one does not want to encourage the person to self-destruct. Instead, the therapist might want to encourage clients to make friends with the terrifying object and get to know it. I used both methods (battling the monster and making friends with the monster) with my own children when they were young to help them cope with nightmares that woke them up. Both methods empowered them so that they did not feel as helpless and had skills to cope with the nightmares (note that nightmares are very common in young children). In regard to the snake dream:

T: Let's try another tactic with this nightmare. What I'd like you to do is try to talk to the snake and see if he has anything to tell you.

C: I don't even want that snake near me. But I'm willing to try it. What do I do?

T:	Say hello to the snake and try to make friends with it.
C [as self]:	Hello, snake. Who are you and what do you want from me?
C [as snake]:	Why are you always trying to get rid of me? It's warm and safe in here.
C [as self]:	You slither around and make me scared. You act like you own the room. Why do you have to be so sneaky?
C [as snake]:	That's just the way I am. I don't know how else to be. I'm a snake.
C [as self]:	Well, you can stay, but you can't be in my bed. You have to stay in your cage on the other side of the room.
T:	How did that feel?
C:	It wasn't so scary once I started talking to it.
T:	Do you think you could try that when you have the nightmare the next time?
C:	I don't think so yet. I think I need to stop the nightmare first, and then maybe later I'll be able to figure out what the snake is all about. I'm just not there yet.

Not all therapists do the changing-the-dream step (see Wonnell & Hill, 2003); some go directly to the next step of making changes in waking life. Some therapists do not like the step (although it is one of my favorite parts of dream work). At other times, the dream is not amenable to alteration, or the client is ready to work immediately on waking life changes.

The most common mistake that I have noted in beginning therapists is that they ask the client about how he or she would like to change the dream and then jump immediately to the next step. I suggest that therapists not only ask but also help the client expand on his or her ideas. Therapists need to spend enough time in this step to have it make an impact on the client.

COACHING THE CLIENT ABOUT MAKING CHANGES IN HIS OR HER WAKING LIFE

The next step involves working with the client to think about making changes in waking life. This may involve bridging from the changes to the dream that the client suggests to thinking about changes that the client can make in waking life. Alternatively, it may involve moving directly to this step without having changed the dream.

Sometimes changes in waking life are obvious after the extensive work that has been done prior to this point. For example, if a person has a recurrent dream about failing a class and the insight gained is that the person is anxious on the job, and the changes to the dream are talking to the boss, then a clear action is helping the client plan how to talk to his or her boss.

Not all dreams lead readily to behavioral changes, however. For example, if a person has a dream about wandering through a medieval forest with a parrot on his shoulder and wants to change the dream to wandering around a medieval town as a court jester, it is not readily apparent what a waking life action might be. It may take more time and therapeutic work to link the dream to current waking life.

As I have emphasized throughout this chapter, the therapist is not usually the one who prescribes actions. In fact, there is some evidence that clients come up with more action ideas when therapists use a client-centered approach of encouraging clients to think of their own ideas rather than offering any suggestions for action (Hill, Rochlen, Zack, McCready, & Dematatis, in press).

Instead of prescribing actions, the therapist works with the client to help him or her think about change. If the client wants to change, the therapist helps the client figure out how to go about changing. If the client, however, seems reluctant, the therapist might work with the client to assess the benefits and drawbacks of changing. Often people's dreams tell them where they are stuck, but it is difficult to get unstuck. For some clients, remaining in the stuck spot is familiar, and change is frightening. Therapists need to respect the client's right to choose to stay the same or change.

As in the insight stage, when the therapist sometimes offers interpretations, in the action stage therapists can offer some of their own suggestions for change, especially when clients have a hard time coming up with ideas. The key is to offer ideas tentatively without pushing them on the client; the therapist might say something such as, "I wonder if you might...", or "Have you considered...?", or "What would it be like if you...?"

Alternatively, the therapist might use the "If it were my dream..." intervention. If the therapist takes responsibility for the suggestion, the client is more likely to feel free to accept or reject it. Therapists might say something like, "If I were in your situation, I think I would either want to make friends with my roommate or try to move out and get a new roommate. It sounds like it's pretty miserable living with someone you don't like."

I next discuss three kinds of actions: (a) behavioral changes, (b) rituals, and (c) continued work on the dream. Therapists typically choose one kind of action to implement in any given session.

Specific Behavioral Changes

The therapist can choose to help the client explore how changes in the dream parallel actual changes the client wants to make in his or her life. For example, if a client wants to change his or her behavior in the dream to be more assertive with male authorities, the therapist might conduct some assertiveness training with the client and practice specific situations in which the client could be more assertive. Clients often lack specific skills for making changes, so therapists can use behavioral techniques (e.g., behavioral rehearsal, feedback, reinforcement) to help clients learn how to behave differently. Therapists need to be competent users of behavioral techniques so that they can help clients make these behavioral changes (see Goldfried & Davison, 1994; Hill & O'Brien, 1999; Kazdin, 2001; Watson & Tharpe, 2002):

T: Let's translate the changes that you made to the dream into how you would change things in your waking life. The first thing you said was there wouldn't be a snake. The snake represents restricting you, trapping you. So how would you translate that? So there's something restricting or trapping you.

C: Saying what's on my mind to my roommate about what a slob she is.

T: How would you do that?

C: Being more aggressive.

T: What would that be like for you?

C: It would be very different.

T: Is it something that would be easy or difficult?

C: Very difficult. I save everything up, and then I'm just furious and blow up.

T: It sounds like you're so worked up at that point, there's no choice.

C: Yeah. When I finally do, it's not good, I'm angry and frustrated. It shouldn't be like that. I should be able to speak my mind.

T: So what's the outcome when you do speak up?

C: Usually people listen to me because they see that I'm so upset.

T: You sound very angry and frustrated—can you say more about what that sounds like?

C: I talk very quickly, and sometimes I cry.

T: How would you like to be?

C: Not as confrontational, not as angry. Just talk it out. Say it sooner.

T: There wouldn't be as much build-up if you said something sooner.

C: Uh huh.

T: Let's say you are in the situation where you are frustrated with her hygiene; she smells really bad. What would you like to say to her?

C: It would probably be refreshing to get it off my chest. I make little comments, but I guess she doesn't get it.

T: I wonder if it would be helpful to have an intermediate step before saying something to her directly.

C: It wouldn't be scary to do it. I just wouldn't do it.

T: I wonder if it would be helpful to write down some of the things about her to get clear about what it is about her—like her lack of showering, her style, the different things that bug you. I wonder if that would make it easier to talk to her if you felt a little more confident about exactly what is was that was bothering you about her.

C: Mm-hmm.

T: So let's pick the one thing that bugs you most about her that's an infringement on your space and work on that.

C: She leaves her dirty clothes all over the room.

T: Okay. Can you say something to her about that?

C [to roommate]: Um, I kind of don't like it when you leave your stuff around.

T: Good, you said something. But you sounded very soft when you said it, and you didn't have any eye contact. Could you try it again? Take a deep breath first.

C [to roommate]: I really wish you wouldn't always leave your dirty clothes on my side of the room. They really smell. You're such a slob.

T: That was much clearer. I liked your eye contact and your tone of voice. You were clearer about what you want. I wonder if you could do it again, but this time maybe don't put her down so much by saying she's a slob. Maybe try to use a little empathy to see if you can put yourself in her place.

C [to roommate]: I know we're different people and have different styles, but I was hoping to talk with you so that we could come to some agreement about how we keep the room. How about if we make a line down the middle and I'll keep my stuff on my side and you keep your stuff on your side.

T: That sounded great. Do you think you could do it?

C: Yeah, I think so. I think it sounded pretty reasonable.

With dreams that are not recent, therapists can still work on changes in current life, under the assumption that the client remembers the dream or has a recurrent dream because there is some current unresolved issue. For example, a middle-aged woman brought in a recurrent dream that she had not had recently about flunking an exam. I asked what was going on her life at the moment that made her think about this dream. As it turned out, the woman was chronically anxious about success, and the dream served as a useful metaphor to remind her to take care of herself. We discussed that the next time she had the dream, she could use it as a sign to herself to slow down and see what she needed to be doing differently in her life.

To help the client implement the desired change, it is sometimes helpful for therapists to assign homework. Therapists, however, need to be careful about how they suggest homework. Research shows that clients most often do homework when it is relatively easy to accomplish, directly related to the problem, and based on the client's strengths (Conoley, Padula, Payton, Daniels, 1994; Scheel, Seaman, Roach, Mullin, & Mahoney, 1999; Wonnell & Hill, 2003). For example, if the client has talked about having trouble expressing her feelings and mentions that she used to write in a journal, it makes sense to suggest that she begin a dialogue expressing her feelings in her journal.

Rituals to Honor the Dream

If the dream is not amenable to specific behavioral changes, if the client is resistant to making changes in waking life, or if this additional step seems like it would be helpful, the therapist can discuss with the client how the dream could be "honored" in some way through a ritual (a symbolic act). I have found that often the dream and its interpretation have a very striking impact on the client that can be strengthened and expanded if the therapist suggests using a ritual to honor the dream (see also Johnson, 1986). Examples of rituals that our clients have used include the following: a client wore a ring that her grandmother had given her to remind herself to stand up to her mother, a client put up a sign with a big "NO" on it up on his bulletin board to remind himself not to take on too many tasks, a client placed a paper boat in a stream to symbolize letting go of a relationship, a client put a picture of a nose above his desk to remind himself that his nose (identity) would be chopped off if he were not careful, a client built a quiet spot in her garden that was similar to a spot she had seen in her dream, and a client placed flowers on her father's grave after she dreamed about talking with him.

T: Can you think of a symbol that you could use to remind you of this dream?

C: Well, obviously snakes are a pretty big part of the dream. Maybe I could do something with snakes. But I sure don't want to get a snake.

T: I wonder if you could get a picture of a snake and hang it over your bed.

C: Yuck, that would be terrible to have to see it all the time. But maybe I could get a picture of a snake and put it in my journal so that just I could see it.

T: Would that work for you?

C: Well, I would probably ignore it most of the time, so I'm not sure it would work. Maybe I could get a stuffed animal that's a snake and put it on my bed—I like that idea.

Continued Work With Dreams

Therapists can help clients think about how to continue to work on the specific dream worked on in the session or how to continue to work for future dreams. Clients who like to write might be asked to start a dream journal or to use the self-help manual in Hill (1996) or the interactive computer software program that Jason Zack and I developed (see chap. 6, this volume) to continue to work on understanding their dream. The client could be encouraged to work on different images in the exploration stage, different levels in the insight stage, and different actions in the action stage to obtain a different, perhaps richer understanding of the dream.

Clients who prefer other modalities might be asked to draw a picture of the dream or create a dance. After drawing or dancing, they might be asked to write down their reactions to the experience so that these reactions can be discussed in the next session. Heaton et al. (1998) provided an example of incorporating artwork into dream work. During the first session of brief therapy, the client described a graphic recurrent nightmare of standing in a white dress on top of a cliff against a gray background and then being swept out to sea by a huge wave. In the last of her 20 sessions of therapy that focused on this recurrent nightmare and other troubling dreams, she spontaneously brought in a painting that she had done of her nightmare. It is interesting that the picture was of her next to a river with lots of green trees and a small cliff in the distance. Her painting illustrated the changes she had made in her understanding and helped her express those changes in a way that made sense to her. These changes make sense in that memories often change as therapists and clients work on them and come to understand situations in new ways. Going back to the snake dream, the therapist might make the following suggestion:

T: I wonder if you would be interested in doing more with this dream. It's such a rich dream, and it seems like there are a number of things you could do with it. Just to throw out an example, from a Freudian perspective, the snake might represent a penis, and the snake is in your bed. It seems like there might be a lot of sexual innuendoes that we won't have time to even begin to get to today. But I wonder if you would want to keep playing with the dream.

C: How would I do that?

T: You could use a computer program and specifically go in and try to understand the snake more from a perspective of what else it could mean to you. Or you could write in a journal and perhaps have a dialogue with the snake to see more about what it has to tell you. You could make up a song or dance about the snake. Do any of those options sound appealing to you?

C: I love to write in my journal. And I'm intrigued that the snake might mean other things. And I think it might be easier to explore the sexual part on my own.

T: Maybe you could write in your journal and think about the dream more and then we could talk some more about it next week.

As with the previous step, we urge therapists to spend an adequate amount of time on this step so that clients gain a clear idea of how they could actually make changes in their lives. A frequent mistake that beginning therapists make is to speed through this step without giving it adequate attention. Change is complicated, however, so therapists need to work extra hard to help clients with this step.

SUMMARIZING ACTION

As a final step, therapists can ask clients to summarize their thoughts about action. Clients can talk about whether they want to make changes and talk specifically about what they want to do. As with the summary in the insight stage, it is better for clients to do the summarizing rather than therapists' doing it for them. Having clients summarize helps them clarify and consolidate what they learned and helps them make a commitment to change. In addition, it helps therapists assess what clients have taken away with them and determine what additional treatment might be needed.

As a part of the summary process, therapists might ask clients to make up a title that helps them remember the significance of the dream. The title can serve as a shortcut reminder later in therapy for therapist and client about what was learned during the dream work. Some titles from recent dreams include "The Chase to Save My Nose," "Swimming With the Elephants," and "Escaping the Mental Hospital." The therapist might say the following:

T: Can you think of a title that you could use to remind yourself of what you learned today about this dream?

C: I'm not sure. I don't know, maybe...."The Snake."

T: Can you could think of a title that captures more what you want to do about the snake?

C: Okay, how about "Making Friends With the Snake."

T: Sounds good to me.

THOUGHTS ABOUT DOING THE ACTION STAGE

Therapists need to keep in mind during the action stage that they are helping clients explore action rather than dictating action. In other words, therapists need to remain neutral ("caringly disconnected") about whether clients make plans to change or actually do anything different in their lives. Their task is to help clients think seriously about whether they actually want to change rather than pushing them to change. Clients are often not ready to change or have ideas about what change would involve that are very different from their therapists' ideas. The task for therapists is to help clients explore their options and make decisions about whether they want to change and then to help them with specific change strategies if they want to change.

From listening to many dream sessions, it seems to me that one of the biggest problems therapists have is running out of time and energy and then neglecting or shortcutting the action stage. Therapists need to plan ahead to leave themselves enough time (usually about 15–20 minutes) to do the action stage. My students and I have become more convinced over the years about the importance of the action stage (see Wonnell & Hill, 2000, 2003), so we urge therapists to give it full attention.

A related problem is leaving the action idea vague and not fleshing it out and making it concrete (e.g., "I'll think about it more" rather than "I am going to call my sister tonight and see how she's doing"). Therapists need to remember that it is more likely that clients will carry out an action if they have a specific, concrete idea about how to carry it out.

Another issue is that therapists might not be satisfied that the action idea is concrete enough or elegant enough. In one session, especially a first, it is not always possible to come up with an elegant, complete action idea.

We aim for one that is "good enough" to get the client thinking about action. With a little encouragement, most clients can continue the work of the dream session on their own and can begin to apply the model to work on other dreams.

Furthermore, it is important to note that therapists often cycle back to insight during the action stage. Some clients need to jump to action before doing insight. For other clients, action spurs them into thinking more about insight. The act of figuring out what they want to do or what they do not want to do sometimes stimulates clients into reflection about the reasons for their choices. Insight and action are often intertwined, with therapists going back and forth.

EXAMPLE OF THE ACTION STAGE

The following is an example of how a therapist facilitated a client through the action stage. I first present the dream and the insight gained in the insight stage.

Dream: I am Dorothy from the Wizard of Oz movie. I have already found my Scarecrow, Tin Man, and Lion. And even though I don't recognize them as friends, I know a lot about them. But we aren't trying to find the Emerald City. We're just searching. We wonder what happens if you don't take the yellow brick road, so we just wander around and talk. No one needs anything like a heart or brain. I want to get "home" but I can't really verbalize that to my friends, and I don't really know where we are.

Insight: Before coming here, I had no idea if the dream meant anything at all. I worked through images and feelings until I thought the dream could parallel what's going on in my life right now. I think I've been so involved in other things that I haven't had time to do enough outdoor sports and activities.

[*Action stage*]

T: If you could change anything in the dream, what would you change?

C: The thing that bothered me in the dream was that there was nothing there. We weren't on the yellow brick road, which I liked, and we didn't really have this ultimate goal, which I really want. We didn't really see anything. We were just on this straight path with trees. I wanted to see something, to be doing something. We just kept walking, and I think we were talking about it. I think it would be nice to have a house we could walk up to and go in and meet the people, see what's there and how the people live. Or just a change of scenery where it just wasn't all forest. Fields, mountains, or something new to look at.

T: So visually, you'd like something new, maybe a little more stimulating.

C: Yeah, I want something to happen instead of just walking around the same landscape.

T: So exactly how would you like the dream to be? Remember, it's your dream, and you can have it be any way you want it to be.

C: Oh, okay. I would like it to be where my friends and I have planned this trip and we are going hiking in the mountains. We go up this beautiful mountain and have a wonderful hiking trip.

T: You mentioned that a lot of things in the dream seem to match things in your life. How would you make changes in your life?

C: I just want to see what there is outside of where I've been living all my life. I keep talking to friends about going on trips, but we never seem to do anything.

T: Is there something that you could do in your life to make that happen?

C: I've been so busy with other things, because I have really focused on school this semester. I always focus on school, but last semester my grades weren't as high as I wanted them to be, so I've just been going to class and studying really hard, which is a good thing. I don't really want to cut that out of my schedule. And I belong to a sorority, and I've been trying to go there more, which I have been doing, and I work. So, by the time I work and do school and do the sorority and hang out with my friends who aren't in the sorority and hang out with my boyfriend, the weeks just keep going by, and I feel like I haven't had the opportunity to take any trips with the recreation club. I want to go hiking in the mountains. I need to come up with dates.

T: Sounds like you want that.

C: I've definitely been trying, and it just hasn't worked. I always sign up for something, and then it falls through.

T: You said you were planning this trip to Colorado, but is there something that you could do in your life on a smaller scale to create some change?

C: Well, I could do some day hikes. It would be easier to get through my homework if I knew I was going to get some outdoor exercise. I need to try to get that into my schedule. During the week there is always something else, or the people that I want to go with have something going on. So, there just isn't time.

T: What could you do to make this more a reality in your life?

C: I really want to do it. I should be able to, because I have classes on Tuesday through Thursday, so I should be able to get a day off work on one of the other days and get some people together. I feel like it's going to happen, I just don't know when. There's a bunch of kids from last year that we usually go camping with one weekend during the semester, and we haven't done that yet. So we're still trying to do that, too.

T: So, what kind of steps could you take to ensure something like that happens?

C: This semester I've kind of waited for other people to plan it and get the whole group together. And if I actually got on the phone and talked to people and said, "Let's do it this weekend," I think it might happen. I just have to take charge and do it.

T: Is that something you think you can do?

C: Definitely. I've done it before and things happened, so I can just do it again. I will.

T: So, it sounds like that would be something you could do. You could call your friends and get the trips together. Is there anything else that comes to mind?

C: Where I work there are so many opportunities. I work at the climbing wall in a store. There are people at the store who lead trips, and that's something that I'm actually interested in doing. There are people who hang out at the store, who are just there all the time. It seems like they have a really good time together. There are a lot of times when I could just go down and hang out with them if I wanted to.

T: So it sounds like there are a lot of opportunities in your life for doing different things. And it sounds like you feel confident that you'll be able to make some of these changes.

C: Yes, I do feel confident. I'm going to start calling some people tonight about the camping trip.

ANOTHER EXAMPLE OF THE ACTION STAGE

Dream: I am standing watching a train. My father and other family members are aboard the train. I hear a gunshot and look up to see that my father has shot my mother. Then the scene moves to another car on the train where my grandmother is sick. As I watch her moaning about, suddenly the train crashes, and I see her die right in front of me. Again, the scene changes and I am in the car with my father. Horrified at what he did, I begin to run. The train becomes a street in my town. I hear my father behind me chasing me as I run for the house. When I get to the corner around from my house, I wake up.

Insight: I think that the dream is showing how I feel about current life situations. I think it means that I feel isolated from my family and that

I don't have much control over what's happening in my life currently.

[*Action stage*]

T: If you could change anything in the dream, how would you change it?

C: My father not shooting my mother. I would also be able to help my grandma or get her help. I wouldn't want my grandmother to die, so I would change that. I would want it so that people would talk to me, that they would be able to see me.

T: So how would your dream go?

C: I'm not quite sure. I more know what I don't want to happen.

T: If it were my dream, I might want to be on the train with my parents and grandmother going to a nice resort someplace. How would that be for you?

C: I think I'd actually rather be with my friends going someplace.

T: That sounds good. Let's try to see if we can help you translate these changes to your waking life. In terms of the first one, you wish that your dad didn't shoot your mom—how could you translate that to your waking life?

C: My mom and dad don't get along. They're always fighting when they do talk to each other. When they fight, he'll leave because he doesn't want to hurt her. And I always seem to get put in the middle of their fights. I guess that's where that part of the dream came from.

T: What can you do to make changes about this in your real life?

C: I guess I could talk to them both about it and tell them how I feel about them putting me in the middle of everything. Ask them if they could be more conscious and not put me in the middle and try to work out their problems on their own.

T: Have you ever tried this before?

C: No.

T: When you see your dad and mom, how could you address this issue with them?

C: I would just bring it up by saying, "When you guys have a problem or an argument, could you try not to bring me into the middle of it? Could you work it out yourselves?"

T: So would you would do it when both of them are there?

C: Yeah.

T: Since you haven't tried this before, I'm wondering if you're ready to bring it up?

C: Yeah, I think I'm ready because I wanted to before, I just never did it.

T: Are there any potential barriers you can foresee?

C: No.

T: It sounds like you prefer to talk to your mom and your dad face to face.

C: Yeah.

T: When might you do that?

C: Well, I won't be going home until Thanksgiving.

T: Wow. One more month. So what would it take to bring it up with them? Would you do it first thing, or do you need a special setting?

C: It probably won't be the first thing, but it will probably happen the first day we're all together. I just want it to be the three of us with nobody else around.

T: How do you feel about that?

C: It might be kind of hard to get just the three of us together, but I'm pretty sure I could get one of my brothers to make sure nobody else is around.

T: What would you like to say?

C: That I hope they understand where I'm coming from and to try to not put me in between the two of them and that they shouldn't try to get me to choose sides about who I like more.

T: Will that be difficult for you?

C: Yeah, because I don't like being put in the middle.

T: Sounds tough, but I think you can do it. You sound clear on what you want to say.

C: It shouldn't be too hard to bring it up since I've been thinking about it for a while.

T: The second change you wanted to make in the dream is to help your grandma. Again, how would you translate that into your waking life?

C: I'm all the way down here now at school, and she's up in New York. So, it's not very easy to get to her because I can't have a car down here. Again, I want to help her, but there's nothing I can do because we're so far apart.

T: Is there any way you can contact your grandma?

C: I can't help her physically, but she likes to get stuff. I could try to send her cards and pictures as often as I can, because she says it makes her feel better.

T: Are you going to do that in the near future?

C: Yeah.

T: Just mail her a card?

C: Yeah.

T: What would you put in the card?

C: That I miss her and I love her and I hope she gets better and that I'm going to come see her as soon as I get a chance.

T: So when are you going to do that?

C: Probably this week I will mail her a card.

T: It sounds like it's not too difficult of a task. You have done that before?

C: Yeah.

T: The third one is that you hope someone notices you so you won't feel so isolated. How would you change that in your current life?

C: Because I'm down here, and it's long distance, I don't talk to my family as much as I did when I was home. My brothers don't call either, so I haven't talked to them since around the first couple weeks of school.

T: So you haven't contacted your family for awhile?

C: I talk to my mom once a week, but I haven't talked to any of my brothers.

T: What can you do to improve this situation?

C: I guess I could call my brothers or write to them, or I could e-mail them.

T: What is stopping you from doing that?

C: Nothing, really.

T: If you call your brothers, what are you going to say to them?

C: Why they don't call me? I'll ask them what's going on at home and what's going on with the family.

T: When do you want to do that?

C: I'll probably call them maybe tonight or tomorrow.

T: Can you summarize what you are going to do to make those changes happen?

C: I guess the biggest thing would be to talk to my mom and dad about not putting me in the middle. So that would be the biggest, but I wouldn't be able to do that one until I go home. So, the easiest one would be to get the card for my grandma and send it and I have pictures to send her. I can do that first. Then, I can call my brothers. If I call one of them, I can always tell them to tell the other one to call me.

T: Who would you like to call first?

C: I'll probably call my oldest brother first and see how he is doing, and then I'll call my nieces and nephews.

T: Sounds good. If you were to title this dream, what title would you give it?

C: I can't really think of a title for it. I guess "Reality."

T: I was thinking of something like "The Train Ride From Hell."

C: How about "Turn That Train Around?"

CONCLUSION

A complete dream interpretation process involves thorough exploration, gaining at least some insight into the meaning of the dream, and then figuring out what to do differently in one's life based on what one learned from the dream. We hope to help people make changes in their lives by listening to messages from their inner world.

We encourage therapists to have fun with the action stage. It can be challenging to figure out how to encourage clients who are stuck, but it can also be rewarding to see clients make connections and spontaneously figure out what to do with their lives. Being able to participate in this self-discovery and growth process is exciting. It can also be gratifying to see the change process get started relatively quickly given the powerful stimulus of dreams.

REFERENCES

Benson, H. (1975). *The relaxation response*. New York: Morrow.

Benson, H. (1988). Relaxation response, physiology, history, and clinical applications. In J. A. Hobson (Ed.), *States of brain and mind*. Cambridge, MA: Birkhauser.

Cartwright, R. D., & Lamberg, L. (1992). *Crisis dreaming: Using your dreams to solve your problems*. New York: HarperCollins.

Conoley, C. W., Padula, M. A., Payton, D. S., & Daniels, J. A. (1994). Predictors of client implementation of counselor recommendations: Match with problem, difficulty level, and building on client strengths. *Journal of Counseling Psychology, 41,* 3–7.

Goldfried, M. R., & Davison, G. C. (1994). *Clinical behavior therapy* (expanded ed.). New York: Wiley.

Heaton, K. J., Hill, C. E., Hess, S., Hoffman, M. A., & Leotta, C. (1998). Assimilation in therapy involving interpretation of recurrent and nonrecurrent dreams. *Psychotherapy, 35,* 147–162.

Hill, C. E. (1996). *Working with dreams in psychotherapy.* New York: Guilford Press.

Hill, C. E., & O'Brien, K. (1999). *Helping skills: Facilitating exploration, insight, and action.* Washington, DC: American Psychological Association.

Hill, C. E., Rochlen, A. B., Zack, J. S., McCready, T., & Dematatis, A. (in press). Working with dreams using the Hill cognitive–experiential model: A comparison of computer-assisted, therapist empathy, and therapist empathy + input conditions. *Journal of Counseling Psychology.*

Johnson, R. (1986). *Inner work.* San Francisco: Harper & Row.

Kazdin, A. E. (2001). *Behavior modification in applied settings* (6th ed.). Belmont, CA: Wadsworth/Thomson Learning.

Scheel, M. J., Seaman, S., Roach, K., Mullin, T., & Mahoney, K. B. (1999). Client implementation of therapist recommendations predicted by client perception of fit, difficulty of implementation, and therapist influence. *Journal of Counseling Psychology, 46,* 308–316.

Watson, D. L., & Tharp, R. G. (2002). *Self-directed behavior: Self-modification for personal adjustment* (8th ed.). Belmont, CA: Thomson Learing.

Wonnell, T., & Hill, C. E. (2000). The effects of including the action stage in dream interpretation. *Journal of Counseling Psychology, 47,* 372–379.

Wonnell, T., & Hill, C. E. (2003). *Predictors of action in dream interpretation.* Manuscript in preparation.

II

EXTENSIONS OF THE HILL COGNITIVE–EXPERIENTIAL DREAM MODEL

4

WORKING WITH DREAMS IN ONGOING PSYCHOTHERAPY

MARY C. COGAR

Working with dreams in psychotherapy can enliven the therapeutic process in many ways. Dreams evoke curiosity about the connection between waking life experience, past experience, and unconscious processes. Dreams allow clients to bring up thoughts and feelings that they think are unacceptable and must be hidden. Dreams mark progress, allowing clients to recognize subtle changes they have made before new behavior patterns are firmly established.

The Hill cognitive–experiential model of dream work, a three-stage model, is a thorough guide to the use of dream work in psychotherapy. Dream work contributes significantly to the therapeutic process of exploration of problems, gaining insight, and facilitating behavioral change. Because the model is intended to be used to interpret one dream in a 90- to 120-minute session, adaptation of the model to ongoing psychotherapy is necessary. The purpose of this chapter is to explore various ways of adapting the model to integrate dream work into the clinical process.

I also review practical aspects of introducing dream work to clients, such as timing, client selection, and education about dream work. Examples of dreams are based on those of actual therapy clients whose identifying data have been altered for purposes of confidentiality.

IDENTIFYING CLIENTS FOR WHOM DREAM WORK IS APPROPRIATE

On her first visit, a client reported the following dream: She was witnessing the birth of multiple human babies that actually appeared to be puppies. The first, second, and fourth puppies were healthy. The third puppy was still and not breathing. She wrapped up the third puppy and breathed into its face and noticed that it had a most beautiful human face. The client's interpretation of this dream was that the puppies (babies) represented stages in her life. She felt that the first two stages, childhood and parenthood, were "healthy." The still puppy represented the current stage of her life in which she felt that she needed "something to breathe life into her." She was struggling with numerous somatic symptoms and a difficult marriage that she felt would not sustain her in the fourth stage of her life, retirement. This dream had prompted her to seek therapy to work on issues in her marriage that had been troubling her for a long time. She felt hopeful that her life could change, as reflected in the dream image of the fourth puppy's being healthy, and she was motivated to use dream work to understand what would make her life better. This client had a lively interest in her dreams and had read books about interpreting dreams. She characterized her dreams as "the real me talking to the pretend me."

Although few clients are as sophisticated about understanding dreams as this client was, many clients are interested in their dreams and would like to understand more about the meaning of their dreams. Research on client characteristics that predict ability to work with dreams is limited. Diemer, Lobell, Vivino, and Hill (1996) found that clients who are cognitively complex, or able to think deeply and elaboratively, benefit most from dream work. Other clinicians have cited client interest in dreams as the primary indicator for using dreams in psychotherapy (Flowers, 1993). Introducing dream work early in therapy allows the therapist to assess the client's interest in dreams and the client's openness to the idea that dream imagery is connected to waking life issues. For example, a client who was a poet had great interest in imagery and responded enthusiastically to working with dreams. She reported a dream that had an image of a huge mouth in it. She had found the image of the disembodied mouth puzzling but easily accepted the idea that the image might be a metaphor for issues in her life. By associating to the image, she came to the interpretation that the mouth represented her failure to "speak up" in a relationship of hers that had just ended and in relationships in general. She was able to use this image to become more consciously aware of times when she was not expressing herself. This brief discussion of a dream early in therapy established that the client was interested in using dreams to understand herself and laid the groundwork for further dream work as the therapy progressed.

Clients who think concretely or are uncomfortable with symbolism and metaphor may have little interest in working with dreams. For example, one of my clients had a dream about dogs driving cars. I found the dream interesting, because the client had very strong relationships with her dogs, and I thought that exploration of the dream might be useful in understanding more about the client's current difficulties in relationships. However, the client thought that the image was silly and resisted analyzing it. She had the intellectual capacity to understand the metaphor, but she responded to the image literally and could not associate to it.

Other clients may be interested and able to work with metaphors but are too anxious or depressed by the material associated with the dream to actually engage in the dream work. One client who had been severely sexually and physically abused as a child reported that she had a disturbing dream about sexual abuse without being able to remember or identify the actual content of the dream. Identifying and associating to the images would have put the client at risk for being overwhelmed by her anxiety and depressive symptoms. The dream was used as a signal that something in the client's life was triggering the anxiety about sexual abuse, and the treatment was focused on helping the client to manage the anxiety.

Finally, dream work may be contraindicated in clients who are psychotic or have difficulty distinguishing reality from fantasy. If a client is likely to experience the dream images as real, or to confuse the images with events in real life, then dream work could intensify confusion and distress.

INTRODUCING DREAM WORK TO CLIENTS

The ideal time to introduce dream work to clients is during the initial assessment. In a typical initial assessment, problems and goals of the therapy are discussed and agreed on, and then the therapist describes the process of the therapy and the methods used to address the identified problems. Dream work can be discussed as one of several methods used to increase self-understanding and achieve the therapeutic goals. If a client is interested in dream work, further education about how dreams are used can be given. Some clients may be interested in dreams but fail to remember most of their dreams. Methods of increasing dream recall can then be introduced.

EDUCATING CLIENTS ABOUT DREAM WORK

Early in the therapy, it is helpful to provide specific education to clients about how dream work can be used in psychotherapy. Clients can be taught that dreams are connected to waking life and that dreams provide useful information about thoughts, feelings, memories, and experiences that affect current life issues and problems. Hill's (Introduction, this volume) idea of dreams weaving together a story about issues that are currently relevant for the client draws on the idea of storytelling, a concept that is familiar to most people. Teaching that dreams provide information about thoughts and feelings of which the client may not be consciously aware, or may be uncomfortable confronting, introduces the connection of dreams with the unconscious. As the client to whom I referred at the beginning of this chapter said, dreams are "the real me talking to the pretend me." Understanding dreams enables clients to know more about their "real" selves, which include both conscious thoughts and ideas and hidden or conflicted material, represented in dreams.

Another aspect of education about dreams consists of discussing ways of working with the imagery in dreams. Teaching clients to work with dream images as symbols and metaphors helps to decrease anxiety about the strange images in dreams and increases clients' curiosity about and interest in dream images. One client was scared by the frightful and bizarre images in her dreams and thought that the images meant that something was wrong with her, possibly that she was crazy. Understanding that the images served as symbols of previous traumatic experiences rather than psychosis helped her to feel better about herself and less fearful about the dreams.

It is also useful to teach clients that dream images that seem to represent familiar activity in waking life may actually be more meaningful as symbols or metaphors. For example, a client had a dream of throwing up while having dinner with a friend. The vomiting did not make sense to her as she rarely vomited and never thought of making herself vomit. When the client associated to the "throwing up" image in the dream, she thought of having "something thrown up in my face." She could relate the image to a recent experience with the same friend who had confronted her about something she did not want to think about. Similarly, familiar people in dreams may represent themselves or may be symbolic of many other issues, such as a particular trait of the person, a particular feeling the dreamer is having about the person, or an aspect of the relationship the dreamer has with the person.

TEACHING CLIENTS TO INCREASE DREAM RECALL

Once the therapist has determined that a client is interested in working with dreams, teaching practical aspects of remembering dreams is important.

Keeping a notepad by one's bed in which to write dreams immediately on awakening often increases dream recall. Waking up without an alarm clock, even a few mornings during the week, may also facilitate dream recall. Encouraging clients to record all dream images or fragments even when they do not make sense also contributes to the client's involvement in recording dreams. Stimulating interest in images that are not readily understandable may evoke curiosity and further exploration in therapy. Once the preliminary work of establishing the client's interest in dreams, ability to remember dreams, and understanding the basic principles of using dreams is accomplished, dream work can begin to be integrated into the ongoing process of therapy.

ADAPTING THE MODEL TO ONGOING PSYCHOTHERAPY

Because the goal of Hill's cognitive–experiential model of dream work is to provide a self-contained intervention to work with one dream in a 90- to 120-minute session, adaptation of the model is necessary to integrate the dream work into the 50-minute hour of ongoing therapy. Adaptation of the model can be done in several ways. First, the therapist and client can select relevant parts of a dream on which to focus, rather than analyzing an entire dream. Spending an entire session on a dream may occasionally be done, but more often parts of the dream that are salient to the current therapy themes are selected for investigation. Sometimes the fit between a dream image and an immediate theme in psychotherapy is obvious. At other times, work on the dream image is needed to clarify the relevance of the dream to the therapeutic process. For example, in working with the dream of the person vomiting while having dinner with a friend, the relationship of the dream image of vomiting to the therapy process was initially puzzling. When the client associated to the image, she came to understand vomiting as a symbol of being forced to think about something that she wanted to avoid. This insight opened a discussion of the client's feelings of discomfort about discussing angry feelings and stimulated exploration of her pattern of denial and avoidance when "negative" feelings came up.

Second, rather than working with the dream by systematically using all three stages of the model, the therapist may find it most effective to use the stages of the model that are relevant to the immediate therapeutic process. Decisions about what aspects of the dream interpretation model should be used are determined by assessments as to how the dream contributes to what is happening in the therapy at the time. For example, some dreams indicate that the client is ready to open up a new issue or work on an issue that has been too anxiety provoking to explore. Work on a dream that opens a new issue would typically start with the exploration stage of dream work to elicit as much of the client's thoughts, feelings, and experiences about the issue as possible. The new material that is elicited could then be further explored in the therapy process, and the therapist and client could return to the dream using the insight stage of the model when the client is ready. In another session, using the insight stage of dream work would help the client understand more about how the issue is affecting his or her current life and connect current life patterns to past experiences.

The insight stage of the model is also typically used with dreams that synthesize various aspects of a therapeutic focus. Using the insight stage of the model to work with this type of dream can help a client connect waking life experiences; insight into various aspects of the self and inner conflicts; and problems surfacing in therapy, such as transference issues.

The action stage of the model can be used with dreams that facilitate therapeutic process and behavior change. For example, a problem may have been fully explored in therapy, and the client may have salient insights about it but still be struggling with behavior change. A dream presented at this time may offer the insight and prescription for action that have been missing. Use of the action stage of the dream interpretation model would help the client translate insight into behavior change.

The third component of selecting stages of the model to use with the dream work depends on when the dream is presented in the therapeutic process. The way dream work is done is influenced by whether the client is exploring a problem, developing insight about the problem, or working on an action plan. Using the exploration stage of the model with a dream early in therapy may facilitate the explication of thoughts, associations, and memories about the focal problem. Later in therapy, approaching the same dream in the insight stage contributes to new understanding about current life experiences, personality dynamics, and unconscious conflicts. Consequently, the same dream may be worked with differently at various times in the therapy, yielding information that is relevant to the client's progress at each stage of therapeutic work.

In the next several sections I further explore how to use the model to work with dreams and to integrate dream work in the psychotherapeutic process. The sections are organized according to how dream work functions in therapy to open new areas of work, synthesize various elements of an issue, facilitate therapeutic process and action, and summarize progress.

DREAMS THAT OPEN NEW AREAS OF THERAPY

The reporting of certain dreams may open issues that have not been raised as goals in the therapeutic contract. Clients may be anxious about directly opening up certain issues or be unconsciously repressing aspects of unresolved conflicts. A 23-year-old woman who worked in an office and lived at home with her parents presented problems of self-esteem. She had difficulty feeling good about herself, although she was functioning well in several areas of her life. The main focus of the therapeutic work was her relationship with her mother, who had extremely rigid expectations of the client and was often critical toward her. The client also alluded to problems with a former boyfriend but had not discussed it further.

After 6 weeks of work on understanding how her views of herself were influenced by her mother's behavior toward her, the client presented her first dream in therapy. The dream was extremely disturbing to her and stirred up considerable anxiety when she retold it. In the dream, the client was pursued by a very scary monster that reached inside her and pulled out her "guts." Given the intensity of the client's anxiety, the description and re-experiencing stages of exploration were modified so that the client was not asked to retell the dream in the first person, and breathing exercises were done to help the client reduce her anxiety after telling the dream. The client was able to relax and discuss the dream after doing the breathing exercises. Having the client associate to each image seemed too likely to raise the anxiety level again, so the first step of the insight stage was done by asking the client what her thoughts about the meaning of the dream were. The client connected the dream to traumatic experiences with a former boyfriend, whom she had dated 4 years previously. The client was able to tell the therapist that she wanted to talk about the relationship but that she was afraid to do so. This insight suggested a plan of action for the continuing therapy. Together the therapist and client discussed a structure that would help the client talk about the experience but feel safe doing so.

In this example, the reporting of a dream allowed the client to open an issue on which she wanted to work but about which she was fearful. Discussion of the dream alerted the therapist to how scared and anxious the client was feeling about the traumatic experiences and how difficult it was for her to talk about them. Using the structure on which the client and therapist had agreed, the client was able to spend the next several sessions discussing the previous traumatic experiences and the resulting changes in feelings about herself she had experienced. The dream was revisited and explored in greater detail when the client's anxiety was manageable and the work on the traumatic experiences was more developed. Using the steps of the model to have the client associate to each of the dream images and to interpret more deeply the meaning of the images further enhanced the work on resolving the trauma.

The following is another example of how discussing a dream allowed a client to open up an issue that she was unaware was surfacing. A client who was quite sophisticated about therapy brought up a dream in the early phase of therapy. She previously had long-term treatment with another therapist and had started therapy with me 3 months earlier. During that time, she had reviewed her past history but was focusing on current concerns in her life, which included getting started in her career and conflicts with her family of origin, with whom she had frequent contact, although they lived in another state. Although she told me about a history of sexual abuse, she had worked on this in previous therapy, and it was not the current focus of the work. The client told me about the following dream: She was painting the kitchen in her house when she broke through the wall and found a whole different kitchen on the other side. It was an old room that had not been open for years, smelled bad, and had standing water in it. The client was able to retell the dream in the first person. Using the DRAW (description, re-experiencing, associations, waking life triggers) method, she worked on the images of the kitchen, breaking through the wall, the old room, and the standing water. The client quickly jumped to a summary interpretation of the dream "opening a can of worms."

After stating the conclusion of the dream, the client went on to describe in detail an episode of sexual abuse by an uncle that occurred when she was 10. The client had previously described the same episode to a therapist who told her it probably never actually happened. In exploring the dream, the client reported that she felt it was important to tell me about the episode and to see how I would respond. I told the client that her description of the trauma and the types of details she remembered were consistent with other descriptions of trauma I had heard and with what is known about how traumatic memories are retained. In short, I told the client that I believed her. In reviewing the process, the client felt that the dream acted as a catalyst to tell me the story of the sexual abuse and to test how I would respond to it. She had begun to trust me but had some doubts as to whether I would respond to the report of sexual abuse as the other therapist had. We also explored what else in the client's waking life might be triggering feelings about sexual abuse as expressed in the dream. The client had recently found out that a used car she bought needed much more extensive work than she had expected, and she could not afford to get rid of it and buy a new one. This led to feelings about decisions she made and the feeling that she could never do things right, views of herself that she felt were connected to the sexual abuse.

Therapeutic work done during the first two stages of Hill's cognitive–experiential model of dream work, exploration and insight, activated the client's thoughts regarding her self-esteem and ability to master problems in her life. Several interconnecting issues for the client, such as concerns about making good decisions, feelings of lack of trust, and ways of responding to anxiety, had been elicited and were discussed during the next few therapeutic sessions. The dream provided a missing element, that of a lack of confidence in herself associated with the past history of sexual abuse. The dream was also important in allowing the client to test my response to the sexual abuse experiences and therefore was an important experience in building the therapeutic alliance. The action phase was not as important in regard to the sexual abuse, because more work needed to be done to achieve insight into the impact of the sexual abuse before action could be taken. However, action was needed to address the problems with the car. The client formulated a plan about confronting the previous owner and getting the work done.

TRANSFERENCE AND COUNTERTRANSFERENCE ISSUES

Of the types of new issues that may be introduced in therapy, feelings toward therapists are often the most difficult for clients to approach. Dream work can provide a vehicle for opening discussion of uncomfortable feelings and work on transference reactions. For example, I had to reschedule a client's weekly session several weeks in a row because of a family emergency. The client was gracious about the interruption and worked with me to reschedule sessions when possible. Because the client's schedule was very tight, several sessions were missed. Once the regular weekly sessions had resumed, the client reported a dream in which she had seen another therapist who had plenty of time and could schedule her sessions at times that were convenient for her. Using the exploration stage of the model, I asked the client to tell the dream in the first-person present tense as though she were currently experiencing the dream scene. Telling the dream this way elicited the client's feelings, and she was able to acknowledge that she was angry about the scheduling problems. This discussion led to further exploration of her difficulty expressing anger in many situations. The client acknowledged that although she was slightly aware of angry feelings, without the dream work she would not have been able to broach the topic of her anger directly with me.

Another client reported a dream in which I had done a beautiful painting and exhibited it in an art show. Again, using the exploration stage of the model, the client associated to the images of the beautiful painting and the art show. This elicited discussion of the client's idealization of me and her feeling that I can do many things well that she cannot do. The client was able to explore the transference reaction, which connected to her feelings about her mother, whom she viewed as much more competent and accomplished than herself. This discussion opened a new area of work for the client, who until then had resisted focusing on her relationship with her mother because she experienced a need to keep her positive views of her mother intact.

Another highly useful result of dream work is the synthesis of various aspects of an issue in therapy. In the following example, a transference dream brought together waking life events, internal dynamics, and aspects of the transference that had not yet been openly explored. This client had been exploring the difficulty she was having in organizing her home and dealing with her cousin who shared her home. She also had some understanding of a critical introject that was associated with her stepfather. She had been exploring triggers to patterns of thought in which she harshly criticized herself.

She reported a dream in which she temporarily moved into my home and that it was slightly messy and "lived in." In working on the dream with the exploration and insight stages of the model, she reported feeling relieved that I did not have a perfectly kept home, as she had imagined. She herself was struggling to keep order in her home and having difficulty doing so. She wanted help from her cousin but experienced the cousin as critical and expecting too much of her. The cousin's criticism mirrored her own intensely critical views of herself, which she had difficulty releasing. Her associations to living with me were that I would be more relaxed about her expectations of cleaning the house and far less critical of her. The image of the slightly messy house represented how she would like her house to look and symbolized a more relaxed, less critical attitude toward herself. The interpretation of the dream included the waking life aspects of dealing with the critical cousin, whom she could see embodied her own critical views of herself. She could see better ways to respond to the cousin based on the understanding that she was projecting her critical inner self onto him. Further work with the parts of self-interpretation helped the client to deepen her understanding of how her critical views of herself were related to her stepfather. In addition, the client could work with her fantasy about me to construct a more nurturing, reasonable set of expectations of herself.

Just as clients' feelings toward therapists are important to understand, so too can therapists' feelings and projections have a significant impact on the therapeutic process. Therapists can use the model to work with their own dreams that connect to feelings about clients and the issues being presented in therapy. For example, in the first meeting with a client, I found myself feeling extremely uncomfortable and actually wishing I could get up and leave. I was aware that the client's problem—her response to the departure of her last child for college—was something I would face in a few years, but I was not sure if that was the reason I was having such intense discomfort. I did not feel negatively toward the client, and I felt the concerns she had could be worked on in therapy. That evening, I had a dream in which my daughter and I were arguing about her curfew and she was shouting and crying. Although my daughter is a teenager, we rarely argue and shout, so the dream did not depict reality. However, as I associated to the dream image of arguing I was reminded of my own adolescence, in which there was considerable shouting and crying between my mother and myself. I realized that the dream represented my fears about how I would handle my daughter's increasing independence and eventual departure for college. Having worked on the dream, I became more consciously aware of how the client's issues elicited my own feelings and fears. At the next session, I was much more comfortable and more able to be fully focused on the client and her concerns.

Another therapist had the following dream about a client with whom she felt little progress was being made after several months of therapy. In the dream, the therapist was in a counseling session with the client and felt that it was going poorly, and she could not figure out what to do. The session was taking place in the kitchen of the house where the therapist grew up. The client talked on her cell phone to her boyfriend and handed the phone to the therapist to say hello to the boyfriend. The therapist felt put on the spot and waved away the phone. Later, the boyfriend was in the house, taking photos. The boyfriend wanted to take a photo of the therapist, who stood behind a clothesline with clothes on it so that only her head was showing. The therapist was puzzled about the dream and unsure about how to use the dream to improve the therapy. She decided to take the obvious message of the dream seriously and pay more attention to the role of the boyfriend in the client's life. She discussed with the client having the boyfriend come into a therapy session, and the client agreed. The meeting with the boyfriend alerted the therapist to ongoing problems with him that the client had not been able to discuss. Working on the relationship issues became a more productive focus in the therapy.

Another interesting aspect of the dream was that it took place in the therapist's childhood kitchen. As the therapist associated to that image, she became aware that the kitchen was the place where much of the arguing between her parents occurred. This led her to think that she may have been avoiding probing the client's relationship with her boyfriend too deeply because it connected her to distressing feelings about her parent's arguments. The image of hiding when the boyfriend wanted to take a picture of her also made her think she was hiding from issues about relationships, again because of distress about her early experiences with her parents. Work on the dream enabled the therapist to understand her own contribution to the therapeutic impasse and take a more active approach to working on the client's relationship issues.

Finally, a dream reported in the literature (Ladany et al., 1997) illustrates the usefulness of therapist dream work in understanding feelings toward clients. A therapist became aware of feeling sexual attraction to a client after the first session when she had the following dream. She dreamed of a fire that had not quite reached her house. She was trying to evacuate her family and dog. She opened the door and her client, who was dressed as a firefighter, had come to rescue them. In the dream, she felt relieved and attracted to the client, whom she thought of as a hero. The therapist interpreted the dream as sexual, because the fire connoted sexuality and passion to her. She felt disturbed by the dream, because it felt incestuous (she had previously been aware of having a maternal countertransference toward the client), and it suggested a reversal of roles in that the client rescued the therapist and took care of her needs. A therapist's ability to acknowledge and understand feelings toward clients is important so that he or she can avoid unconsciously acting on the feelings and keep the feelings from interfering with the therapeutic process. This dream clearly was useful in alerting the therapist to both her sexual and dependency feelings toward the client. Being aware of intense feelings toward a client allows the therapist to work with these feelings and to seek supervision or personal therapy if needed.

Transference and countertransference dreams provide useful information about feelings between therapists and clients. Dream work provides an opportunity to discuss feelings that clients may feel embarrassed or anxious about introducing and assists in understanding how a client's feelings toward the therapist are connected to the therapeutic issues. Similarly, dream work helps therapists understand emotional responses to clients that have the potential of disrupting their clinical effectiveness.

DREAMS THAT FACILITATE THERAPEUTIC PROCESS AND BEHAVIOR CHANGE

Once a client has identified a problem on which to work in therapy, and a therapeutic alliance has been established, dream work may fit into the therapeutic process in a variety of ways. For example, a client who had gained considerable insight and cognitive change through the course of the therapy was having difficulty changing her behavior. The client spontaneously reported a dream, the first dream she had brought into therapy. In the dream work, the exploration and insight phases were abbreviated, but the action phase of the work with the dream was crucial to the client in changing her behavior.

The client was a woman in her 40s whose husband had died of a rare brain cancer 1½ years before she began therapy. She came to therapy because she had been unable to go on with her life; had intense feelings of sadness and loss; and was avoiding socializing, even though she had an extensive network of friendships; and was feeling like there was something wrong with her. The feeling that something was wrong with her was connected to the fact that many of her friends had told her she should be over her grief by now. In the early weeks of therapy, the client retold the story of her spouse's cognitive and motor deterioration, the difficulty establishing his diagnosis, and especially the agonizing last few weeks of his life. The therapist worked on helping the client see her responses as part of a normal grief pattern commensurate to the enormous loss she suffered. As the client gradually came to see herself as responding normally, the issue of her need to avoid all social contact became the focus of the work. Some friends of the client were encouraging her to accompany them on a trip to California, and she felt that she could not go. Many issues were identified that contributed to her difficulty in resuming socializing, especially travel. A main theme was that her husband loved to travel, and she felt guilty that she had the opportunity to do something of which he was deprived. Two trips had been planned in advance, and both trips were canceled after her husband died. Another major concern for the client was that resuming a social life made her feel that she was leaving her husband behind. She expressed fear that she would forget him, although she rationally knew that this was impossible.

Although the issue was explored thoroughly, with the client apparently making cognitive shifts in her view of socializing, she continued to have difficulty changing her behavior. During one session she spontaneously reported a dream she had about her husband. In the dream, she saw her husband; he took her hand, and they levitated until they were in a beautiful garden. The light was very bright, and everything looked beautiful. Her husband said that he couldn't help her but that he loved her. The client's interpretation of the dream was that her husband wanted her to see what is beautiful in life but that he could not be with her and help her with her grief. In subsequent weeks, the client reported feeling less guilty about socializing and started seeing friends again. She was able to take the trip her friends had planned for her and enjoy her time away.

In this example, the dream interpretation process was abbreviated, because the work of the first two phases of dream interpretation had been addressed in the therapy. The goal of the exploration stage—activation of the thoughts, feelings, memories, and experiences about the problem—had been accomplished through discussion of the loss of her husband and her conflicts about resuming her social life. Insight into the meaning of her inability to resume her social life had also been gained through the therapeutic process. Translating insight into action was what the client was having difficulty with. In addition, the dream images were transparent, and the client's spontaneous interpretation clicked immediately for her. The interpretation fit perfectly with the changes she had been trying to make in therapy. Furthermore, the interpretation of the dream contained the prescription for action ("see what is beautiful in life"). The dream seemed to come at a time when the client was getting ready to take action as a result of the therapeutic process but was still resistant. The dream embodied the understanding she had achieved in therapy with the added component of permission from her deceased husband. As a consequence, she was able to take action and begin to resume her social life. In subsequent weeks, when the client again experienced guilt or uncertainty about socializing, referring back to the dream helped her to take action.

Another example of dream work's facilitating action is illustrated by the following vignette. A client who was chronically depressed had been working on preparing for retirement in 2 years. She had various artistic interests she wanted to pursue and had also considered starting a small business. She and her husband were considering buying a larger house, and she thought that more space would give her the opportunity to set up a work space for herself. One of the effects of the depression was that the client often felt blocked in planning for the future, indecisive, and unmotivated about what she really wanted to do when she retired. She also had difficulty letting go of past relationships and material objects associated with people about whom she cared. She liked the idea of the new house but was having difficulty detaching from her current home. She had many memories of entertaining her family there and in particular having her recently deceased mother at her house. She also felt guilty about getting such a spacious house, because her mother had always wanted a larger house but had never been able to afford one and died while still living in the house in which the client had grown up. As a consequence, the client was hesitant to allow herself to have the new, considerably larger house.

Work with two dreams during this time period helped the client to move ahead with her thinking about future work and with buying the larger house. In the first dream, she saw a figure dressed in white, moving through a wheat field, creating a path through the wheat as he moved. Her association to the person in white was that of a spiritual being, perhaps bearing a message from her mother. Spiritual life was very important to this client, and interpreting the dream in terms of a spiritual insight was quite meaningful to her. The image of the path through the wheat field meant to her that she would find her own path in the future and that it was time for her to be planning her path. The spiritual being signified to her that her mother would be happy about her moving ahead. She felt that her mother was giving her permission to have a bigger house than she had ever had. Having a sense of permission from her mother helped to diminish the client's guilt and move ahead with plans to buy the house.

The second dream consisted of a house that looked very much like the model house she and her husband were considering buying. The house was white and had large windows that let in a lot of light. The way the house in the dream looked was the way she wanted her new house to look. Dreaming of the house in this way seemed to help her accept her positive feelings about the new house. Both of these dreams contributed to the client's working through the conflicts preventing her from taking action on the house and focusing on interests she wanted to pursue.

In both of these dreams, the client gained insight into her thoughts, feelings, and internal dynamics associated with her problems through the process of the therapy, but she had difficulty taking action. The therapist addressed the dreams using both the insight and action stages of the model with the aim of motivating the client to use the insight gained to change her behavior.

An interesting example of a dream purposely being used to facilitate action came from a 40-year-old man who had done extensive work in therapy on his obsessional patterns. He was having difficulty deciding between two final candidates for a job in his department and worried that he had achieved less mastery of the obsessional processes than he believed had occurred in the course of the therapy. He learned from a friend a technique of "programming" dreams and decided to try to stimulate a dream about the two candidates. Before going to sleep, he focused on the candidates and the difficulty he was having with the decision. During the night, he had a dream in which he looked out of the front window of his house and saw that it was a perfect winter day with clear sky, puffy white snow, and bright light, but when he went to the back window of his house he saw that it was a beautiful summer day, with green grass, blooming flowers, and a blue sky. The dream left him very happy. His immediate interpretation of the dream was that the two candidates for the job were both superb. The one from Maine (winter) was "out in front," while the one from San Diego (summer) was in second place. He realized that because both candidates were so good, the decision was genuinely difficult, not associated with his obsessional patterns. He was able to make the decision to select the candidate from Maine, who subsequently performed in an outstanding manner.

Although this client had considerable insight into his obsessional patterns, he was having difficulty distinguishing between his internal dynamics and the actual difficulties of the decision facing him. The dream enabled him to understand the distinction and take action on the decision. The dream also validated his understanding of the progress he had made in therapy in changing his obsessional patterns. Next, I further explore the function of dreams as markers of progress.

DREAMS THAT SUMMARIZE PROGRESS

At times, a dream may function as a marker of progress made in psychotherapy. A man in his 40s who had been working on family-of-origin issues in therapy for several months reported the following dream: He was riding a bicycle with both of his adult brothers on the back. The dream clearly represented the feelings the client had about his role in the family and his relationship with his brothers. He commented about the dream, "that's how things used to be, but now they're different." The therapist's and the client's understanding of the dream was instantaneous. The dream image was used as a marker of the progress the client had made in understanding his role in the family dynamics and as a comment on the changes he had made in how he was interacting with his family in the present. In addition, the client had been able to look at his own personality dynamics of taking too much responsibility and taking over for others in other areas of his life, such as work and current family relationships. Referring to the dream in subsequent work helped the client to increase his awareness of his automatic tendency to take too much responsibility for others.

Clients often have several connected dreams that signify ongoing therapeutic process. Several dreams may be about the same theme, or the same or a similar dream may occur over and over again. The 23-year-old woman discussed earlier, whose dream about a monster signaled the need to work on a previously abusive relationship, was able to continue work on dreams as she worked through her feelings about the abuse. She had a series of dreams about being attacked by monsters while working on the issues. After a few months of work on the issues, as she was feeling that the issues were resolving, she dreamed that she was sexually abusing a male child. She was initially appalled about the image of herself in the dream but rationally knew that it did not fit her. As she described the image of the child, it became clear that the figure was actually a small version of the man she had a relationship with who had hurt her. Her association to the small figure was that she was now the "bigger" person who was hurting him. In the course of the therapy, she had been gradually feeling less scared and overwhelmed about the experiences and more in touch with her anger toward the former boyfriend. She was also gradually able to see herself as more in control and better able to say no and set limits with people who mistreated her. The dream images reflected her changed sense of herself as well as the angry feelings toward the former boyfriend that she was more able to experience.

Another illustration of how a series of dreams represents therapeutic progress is contained in the following example. A client came to therapy to work on her feelings of inadequacy about becoming a mother. She was in her early 30s, and she and her husband were ready to have a child, but she was having difficulty feeling emotionally ready. The therapy had focused on the client's conflictual relationship with her mother, who was emotionally labile and critical of her. The mother had relied on her to help her keep the house and care for her two younger brothers but was often angry at the client for not doing enough work or for not doing exactly what the mother wanted. The client felt that whatever she did for her mother was never enough and that she could never please her mother. The client feared that she would be an inadequate mother, just like her own mother, who was frequently depressed, angry, and overwhelmed. As the therapeutic work progressed, the client had a series of dreams about caring for a baby. In the dreams, she was bathing, feeding, or dressing a baby. In each dream she seemed to be more confident about knowing what needed to be done. While the client was having the dreams, she was working on resolving her angry feelings toward her mother and psychologically separating herself from her mother. She was developing her own identity as someone who was competent to care for a child. The client saw the dreams as a signal that she was feeling increasingly competent about being a mother. The interpretation stage of the model was most important for this client at both the waking life interpretation level and the inner personality dynamic level. The client interpreted the dreams as meaning that she was gaining more competence in the waking life issue of baby care and that she was working through her conflicts about her mother.

In the following example, a repetitive dream signaled difficulty in resolving an issue. As the client resolved the issue, the dream became less frequent and eventually disappeared. The client came to therapy because she was having persistent feelings of depression after the death of her closest friend of 20 years. The friend had died of cancer in her 40s after an agonizing deterioration during the last 6 months of her life. The client had been quite involved with the friend throughout the 4-year course of her illness, and in particular during the last 6 months, when the friend was bedridden. In therapy, the client discussed her relationship with her friend and how sad and alone she had felt since the friend died. She spent several weeks in therapy discussing many aspects of their friendship and how important the friend had been in her life. In spite of the discussions, she continued to have difficulty feeling that she had energy for her work or her family and was preoccupied with thoughts about the friend's death. She reported a dream that she had had repeatedly since the friend's death. In the dream, the friend was back to life in some way or another. Sometimes the friend was still dead but able to act alive again. In other dreams, the friend had come back from being dead and was again healthy in her regular life. The client felt the dreams symbolized her difficulty accepting her friend's death. While discussing the dreams, she revealed how out of control she felt as she watched the friend's physical deterioration. Reporting the dreams seemed to enable her to discuss her feelings of being out of control and her agony at not being able to do more to stop the progress of the cancer and help her friend survive. Her ability to face her feelings of powerlessness and discuss them with the therapist seemed to help her move further in the grief work. As the grief diminished, so did the dreams. The client felt that the decreasing frequency of the dreams signaled the increasing resolution of her grief and, in particular, her acceptance of her powerlessness over the cancer and the loss of her friend.

In these examples, dreams act as markers of progress in therapy, producing feedback to clients about changes in thoughts, attitudes, and behavior patterns that may still be evolving. Conversely, dreams may indicate a lack of progress or being stuck in a certain pattern that is not changing.

CONCLUSIONS

The Hill cognitive–experiential model of dream work provides a thorough guide to integrating dream work into ongoing psychotherapy. The model consists of three stages: exploration, insight, and action. Adapting the model to ongoing psychotherapy depends on selecting the appropriate stage of the model to interpret the particular type of dream reported and then using the dream work to accomplish the immediate goal of the therapy. For example, if a dream introduces a new problem or theme in the therapy, then the immediate goal of the therapy is to understand as much about the new problem as possible. Consequently, using the exploration stage of the model to work with the dream, the therapist facilitates thorough exploration of the client's thoughts, feelings, memories, and experiences about the new problem that are elicited by the dream. The insight stage of the model may be used if the client is ready for interpretation, or the therapist and client may do further work in the therapy process to understand the problem before developing insight. Finally, if understanding and insight have been accomplished through the therapy process, dream work done in the action stage helps clients translate insight into behavior change.

REFERENCES

Diemer, R., Lobell, L., Vivino, B., & Hill, C. E. (1996). A comparison of dream interpretation, event interpretation, and unstructured sessions in brief psychotherapy. *Journal of Counseling Psychology, 43,* 99–112.

Flowers, L. (1993). The dream interview method in a private outpatient psychotherapy practice. In G. Delaney (Ed.), *New directions in dream interpretation* (pp. 241–288). Albany: State University of New York Press.

Ladany, N., O'Brien, K. M., Hill, C. E., Melinkoff, D., Knox, S., & Peterson, D. (1997). Sexual attraction toward clients: A qualitative study of psychotherapy pre-doctoral interns. *Journal of Counseling Psychology, 44,* 413–424.

5
WORKING WITH DREAMS IN GROUPS

TERESA L. WONNELL

Dream interpretation in groups can be fun and energizing. What is already an intriguing process when done between two people becomes even more so when done among several or many people. The advantage to the dreamer of doing interpretation in a group is that the insights and perspectives of all group members are available, and so a layer of richness is added to the interpretation often beyond what is usually achieved during individual sessions. However, not only the dreamer benefits: Other group members also benefit because part of the process involves every person projecting his or her own thoughts and feelings onto the presented dream, and so it becomes personal and meaningful for all group members.

ADAPTING THE MODEL TO A GROUP FORMAT

In doing group dream interpretation using the Hill model, the therapist still uses the basic three-stage model, but one or two steps are added at each stage to take full advantage of the participation of each group member. The time needed for a full dream interpretation is therefore a little bit longer than what is usually needed for individual sessions, so groups should plan for at least 2 hours. The group's first task is to figure out who is going to present a dream. What works surprisingly well is for the group leader to simply ask whether anyone has a dream on which he or she would like to work. In my own experience, someone always responds affirmatively, even in groups whose members are not primarily interested in dreams, such as students in a basic counseling skills class. Even when more than one group member expresses an interest in presenting a dream, usually the group is able to work out who gets to present with little intervention by the group leader. One of the obvious advantages of an ongoing dream group is that every group member has a chance to work on a dream (or dreams) in depth.

Exploration Stage

The group leaders and group members facilitate the dreamer in the usual tasks of exploration, such as describing the dream images, reexperiencing the feelings, associating to each of the images, and making links to waking life. In addition, the group leader asks the group members to express their own associations to one or two of the images. The group leaders can offer associations as well, which is a helpful modeling process. One positive consequence of this additional step is that it tends to keep all group members active and involved during the session. Another consequence, which is more salient to the dreamer and the eventual interpretation, is that fresh perspectives on the dream and its images are offered.

It is very important to keep in mind that anything offered or suggested by other group members are projections of their own thoughts and feelings. The group leaders, therefore, may find it helpful to instruct group members to preface their associations and comments about the dream with the statement "If it were my dream…", because it reminds them, the dreamer, and other group members that what they say is in fact a projection and not a statement of fact about the dream or the dreamer. This way of handling projections and suggestions of group members was proposed by Montague Ullman, a psychiatrist well known for his work with dream groups (Ullman, 1987; Ullman & Zimmerman, 1979), and has been further reinforced by the work of Unitarian minister and dream worker Jeremy Taylor (Taylor, 1992).

Insight Stage

As with individual sessions, it is helpful to begin the insight stage by asking the dreamer to give his or her initial interpretation of the dream. This gives the group a good idea both of what level of interpretation to start with and how much more integration of dream images and feelings is needed to come up with a coherent and complete interpretation. One dreamer may respond that he or she still has no idea of what the dream means, whereas another dreamer may give a detailed interpretation. Even in the latter case, however, it is important to listen for elements of the dream that the dreamer may not have incorporated into his or her interpretation and to consider different levels of interpretation.

For the group leaders, facilitating the insight stage might feel more difficult than facilitating the exploration stage because the amount of structure is decreased, and the process is more "open." At the same time, it can be very creative and stimulating as group members and dreamer toss ideas back and forth. Again, group members can contribute by offering their interpretation as if the dream were their own. The dreamer, of course, has the freedom to decide which aspects of offered interpretations fit for her or him. One of the tasks of the group leader is to make sure that the dreamer's perspective is respected by other group members and that no one tries to force an interpretation on the dreamer, even when a group member feels strongly that his or her own interpretation is valid.

Action Stage

Group members and leaders can suggest how they might change the dream if it were their own and they can offer ideas for actions they might take. The major task, as in individual sessions, is to facilitate the dreamer in exploring action and in coming up with some kind of specific action idea, if possible. Again, one of the group leaders' tasks in this stage is to make sure that the dreamer has the space to choose his or her own action idea and is not pressured by another group member to adopt a particular idea. After the dreamer has formed an action idea, a good way for the group leader to end the session is to ask the dreamer how everything that was discussed during the session fits together.

CASE EXAMPLE

In the following example, the dreamer (D) was myself. The group members (GM1, GM2, and GM3) were graduate students in psychology, and the group leader (L) was a psychology professor. All were familiar with the Hill model of dream interpretation. This was a fairly small group, probably about the smallest number of people needed to make the process feasible, and although dream groups are often ongoing, this is an example of a group that met only one time.

Exploration Stage

> ***Dream:*** I'm in my mother's house near the water, in North Carolina. She is having an art exhibit; a lot of what is shown is her early stuff. It's really interesting to look around. Colors are very vibrant. I look closely

at all sorts of unfamiliar pieces. Somebody says that I should look at a certain sculpture, the first that she ever did, so I go looking for it. I identify it easily because it is quite different from a lot of her stuff. It is a stone sphinx, about 8 inches high with a scaly texture. On one flank is embedded an atomic clock (which looks like a regular watch dial) that my father had gotten for her. On the other flank, almost like a little memorial, is a gold bas-relief of a male scientist's head. The bottom of the sculpture says it was made in 1971, and has a name carved there as well.

L: What were your feelings in the dream, especially right now as you talk about it?

D: I dreamed this awhile ago, almost 5 years ago, but I still remember feeling very curious when I was in the dream. That's the main feeling. Right now as I think about it and try to go back into that experience, I still feel that sense of curiosity, really just as intense as it was then, and also some vibrancy and energy, but also some sadness when I think of my mother, who died 4 years ago. The sadness wasn't there originally. She was still alive when I had this dream.

L: So curiosity, and energy, and also sadness about your mother. That's certainly a mix of feelings. It sounds like your mother is a really important part of this dream, but before you tell us about her, I was wondering what your curiosity is about?

D: I'm so curious about what this sphinx represents! Where did it come from? Why on earth does it have an atomic clock on its leg? What does it mean that it was the first sculpture my mother ever did? She's not into sculpture, by the way, she's a painter, or was a painter, I should say.

GM1: I noticed that you just talked about your mother as if she were still alive, just then. Does this dream really bring her back for you? Was she herself in the dream?

D: Actually, she was not in the dream; neither she or my father were. There may have been a few other people milling around looking at the exhibit, but no one I knew, no one important to me. I don't really remember if there were other people or not. But yes, it's like her essential self, her artist self, is embodied in this dream, and when I think of the dream, it's like she's there.

GM1: Say more about your mom, and about your relationship with her. You said that her essential self was being an artist.

D: My mother was an artist first. She was very creative and expressive, artistically. But I think she had a hard time expressing herself in relationships. I really don't know how to describe our relationship. In some ways it was good, we had a close relationship. My aunts, her sisters, always talk about how close we were. But I also feel a lot of ambivalence about her. I was often irritated with her, and critical of her, maybe of some of her qualities that seemed to go along with being an artist. She could be impulsive, and sometimes self-centered. I often felt overshadowed by her, when I was with her, because she was so vital and energetic.

L: You have a lot of feelings about your mother. I wonder what you feel about her right now?

D: I miss her. In a way, it's still hard to believe that she's gone. My own daughter is 2 years old now, and I feel very sad when I think about how much my mom would have loved to be with her granddaughter, how I haven't been able to share being a mother with her and get her perspective and help. Also, I feel really glad that because she was an artist and I have so many pieces of her work, that in way she is still with me every day. I love her artwork, and it's all over my house.

GM2: It's wonderful to have an artist in the family! What is art, and what does it mean to you?

D: Art is expression; self-expression. My associations to it are it is energy, it is expression, it is nonverbal, a way of expressing without words, it is very personal and beautiful. And it just is itself; you don't argue with it like you do with words.

GM3: I'm really curious about that stone sphinx too. Can you describe it more?

D: Yeah, I've thought a lot of that sphinx. In the dream it was, not really scaly, but textured, like feathers were carved into the stone. Some sphinxes have wings, but the one in my dream did not. It was heavy, made of stone, about 8 inches high maybe. It was stone colored; it wasn't painted or anything. So it had the head of a person and the body of a lion. I'm looking down at it from the top. The atomic clock part was weird—I'm sure real ones don't look like watches!

GM1: What do you associate with the sphinx?

D: What comes to mind first is Egypt or Greece, and mystery, and old, very ancient. The words "the riddle of the sphinx." Mythology. I don't really know anything more about sphinxes.

GM3: You said it was made in 1971—what do you make of that year?

D: Well, because the dream is clearly about my mother and father, 1971 to me means something about their relationship. That was the year they separated, I think, although I'm not completely sure. The part I don't get is how this sphinx is, in my dream, the first thing my mom ever made. She was doing art long before that!

L: So there's no way it could really be the first thing she ever made. What do you make of that? Any associations?

D: Totally blanking on this one.

GM3: How old were you in 1971? What else was going on then that you remember?

D: I was, let's see, 7 years old, so probably in the second grade. As for what was going on in my life, that might be the summer that my dad, my sister, and I spent in Pennsylvania when my parents first separated, or it might be the first summer that my sister and I spent in Germany with my dad, because he moved over there for 2 years.

L: What about the atomic clock? Can you say more about that and your associations?

D: A really strong association to my dad. Of course, he gave it to my mom in the dream, but even so, I identify it with him because he is a scientist, a chemist, and at one time did work related to nuclear reactors. Atomic clocks are really super precise. So, science, precision, my father.

GM2: That's interesting—there's your mother the artist and your father the scientist, and they are kind of together in this one thing.

L: That's a great image. Why don't we go around and each talk about our own associations to the sphinx and the atomic clock, using the "if it were my dream" format. For me, if it were my dream, I would associate the stone sphinx with Egypt, with exotic things, perhaps pagan things. It does have this kind of religious quality about it, but it is definitely pre-Christian. The atomic clock, too, for me is about precision. Maybe a preoccupation with being precise, or being on time. That's something that's important to me, being on time.

D: That's true for me, too, I'm usually always on time, and very much a clock-watcher. I tend to be detail oriented.

GM1: For me, too, I associate the sphinx with riddles, and mysterious, and something old. And other mythical creatures, like griffins, the manticore; there's a couple of others. Something that is made up of two things, you know, the sphinx being part man, part lion. The atomic clock makes me think of something dangerous, like nuclear energy or nuclear bombs. Nuclear energy is really potent, and useful when held in control, but dangerous when out of control.

D: I kind of resonate to the idea that the sphinx represents two things, because of the way in the dream it is something formed by both my mother and my father. In some ways I really feel like

I am like both of my parents. I've followed my father's footsteps when it comes to science and education. He has a PhD, and now I'm working on mine. I'm studying psychology now, but I have a master's degree in engineering. On the other hand, my mother never went to college. But she's done all kinds of art and dance, and I like to dabble in art. I used to do calligraphy. And we shared a lot of interests, like in books and movies and music. So there is this blending of art and science.

GM2: I've read a lot about mythology, and what I remember about the sphinx is that it is connected to the story of Oedipus. Like, he was the first person to solve the riddle of the sphinx. That would make me wonder especially about my relationship to my parents when I was little. You know, the good old Oedipus complex.

D: I didn't know that the sphinx and Oedipus were connected. That's interesting. Doesn't really ring a bell, though.

GM3: Didn't you say something about there being a gold memorial on the other flank, a profile of a person's face?

D: Yes, a gold bas-relief of a scientist's head, a male scientist. I don't know who.

GM3: Memorial made me think of grief, of death, and of commemoration. Of something valuable, since it's made of gold. If I'd just lost my father, because of divorce or whatever, it would be about him.

L: If it were my dream, the male scientist's head makes me think of the musician's head that music teachers had when I was a kid. Like the bust of Beethoven or Mozart. Very pretentious. You have to be pretty famous before someone makes a bust of your head! It also reminds me of the death masks they used to make in Europe and ancient Rome. Now, as you are hearing all of these associations, does anything fit for you?

D: Yeah, a few things. Let's see if I can remember...somebody said that the atomic clock reminded them of nuclear energy, and that made me think of nuclear family, which this dream is about. My older sister isn't in it, but otherwise it's my nuclear family. And my dad could be unpredictable. He didn't get mad often, but when he did it was really big and scary, and also just out of the blue, unpredictable, so it connects with the nuclear bomb idea. Like his energy was usually contained, and precise, but not always. And I guess it is about grief and loss, that is what a memorial is all about. My parents divorcing, I mean. And also about how mysterious looking back at that time in my life is; it really does seem like a big riddle even now. I can only imagine how confusing it was then. I asked my mother once a few years ago how she and my dad told me and my sister about the divorce back when we were kids and it was all happening, and she said they never did sit down with us and explain anything.

L: That would seem pretty confusing to a child. I wonder if any of those feelings in the dream, especially the confusion, were going on in your waking life at the time you had the dream, or right now in your life.

D: Let's see, when I had the dream my husband and I had just returned from a trip to North Carolina to visit my mother and her new husband—she remarried less than a year before I had the dream. Her third marriage. What was confusing about that visit was navigating my place in her new relationship and continuing to build one with a new father, and at the same time trying to keep up an older relationship with the man she went out with for several years before she met her new husband, whom I really connected with—another artist, a sculptor, in fact, although he usually sculpted in wood and ceramic and not in stone. We actually found ourselves kind of sneaking around to visit him, since the new husband seemed to be upset that we still sought a relationship with this guy. I guess I was confused about my allegiances. And all these different father figures! Before visiting North Carolina, we had just come from visiting my real father, and stepmother.

L: Yeah, families can get pretty complicated and confusing! It is hard to figure out where you stand in all that. And what about right now in your life, what feels confusing?

D: The current picture about my family is a little less complicated, since my mother died, but I'm just as curious as ever about my early childhood, and the nature of my parent's relationship with each other and with me back then. Especially now that I have a few years of counseling under my belt. I have very few memories of that time, or at least the parts of it connected with my parents. Lots of kindergarten and school memories, but almost none of my parents interacting. So it's a big mystery, especially since it's a taboo area of conversation with my father. Or, if I ask him anything about it, he'll just say he doesn't know, or he doesn't remember.

L: That sounds kind of frustrating.

D: It is very frustrating. So I rarely ask.

Although exploration was going well and easily could have continued, more than an hour had already passed, and so in the interest of time, the group leader decided to have the group move on to the insight stage. The recommended steps of the Hill model were followed, in a flexible fashion. The steps of the DRAW acronym—Describe the dream image, Re-experience feelings, Associate to dream image, and Waking life connections to the dream image—were used in full for only a couple of images; for the majority of images, description and association were used without the other two steps. Group members still asked about waking life triggers even though the dream was not recent. Because the dream was several years old, it was difficult for me to remember clearly what was happening at that time, but even the general events I could remember seemed relevant.

The leader asked group members for associations only one time, but in practice this can happen more than once. As the dreamer, I found that some group members' personal associations seemed very pertinent and offered a new perspective for me, whereas other comments seemed irrelevant, although, as seen below, one group member's association that had seemed unconnected at the time it was offered turned out to be quite meaningful to me just a short time later.

Insight Stage

> L: We've done some good exploration here. Why don't we move on now to the insight stage. So what I'm going to do first is to ask what you think it means, right now, and then we'll try to elaborate on that, maybe look at some different levels of interpretation.
>
> D: Well, I do really feel that the sphinx represents me in the dream, or aspects of me at least, like my artistic side and my scientific side. When I dreamed this, I was just in my first year of graduate school in psychology and really trying on the psychologist hat for the first time, and psychology, or the practice of it anyway, feels pretty artistic to me. Or maybe going into it is a way of blending art and science, because the research side of it is using the scientific method, and the clinical side is art. So I get to be both, or have both.
>
> GM1: So it feels like a good thing to you? It sounds like a good combination.
>
> D: Yes, I think so, although especially that first year I had a lot of self-doubt about my ability to become a therapist. I really started out as a complete novice. I was much more comfortable in the scientist role, maybe not happy in it, but I knew the ropes, I had been good at my previous job in a physics environment. But I didn't feel like it was creative in a way that felt complete or holistic to me; I wasn't using my artistic side in that work. Some scientists can, but I wasn't doing that. A large reason I went into physics and engineering in the first place was because of my father's influence and my desire to connect with him and please him. Maybe that is where Oedipus comes in, come to think of it! That didn't ring a bell with me before, but

maybe there's something to that after all. How did he fit in with the sphinx again?

GM2: He solved the riddle of the sphinx; the sphinx was busy eating up people who couldn't solve it; but it wasn't a hard riddle. It goes "what walks on four legs in the morning, two legs in the afternoon, and three legs in the evening?" and the answer is man, who crawls as a baby, then walks on two legs, then in old age uses a cane.

L: So Oedipus, who isn't in your dream but is somehow connected to it, solves the riddle.

GM1: For me that might mean that my relationship with my father maybe is key to solving the riddle? What about the riddle itself; I wonder if that means anything?

D: Wow, I wish I could remember what time that atomic clock read! That would be pretty neat—was it morning, afternoon, or evening on the clock?

L: What comes to mind when you think of different possible times on the clock? What might that mean for you?

D: Let's see…what did you just say about Oedipus? (looks at GM1)

GM1: That maybe my relationship with my father is what is important here? In solving this riddle?

D: Right. And maybe there is a connection between that and the time and the riddle…like what's coming to my mind is that an early time on the clock would mean morning, the baby, or my relationship with my father in a child–parent fashion. And I think that in my study of physics and the hard sciences, I was in a very real sense doing that to please him, in a rather childlike way, and not doing it because I wanted to. Then at the time of the dream, I was more following my own likes and dislikes by changing my field of study to psychology. So I think the clock would read early afternoon, as I'm moving into a more adult relationship with my father. But I still feel like a child when I go and visit him and my stepmother! More so at the time of the dream than now, though.

GM2: (laughs) Me too! What is it about our parents? I feel like I would be in late morning in terms of how I feel when I go home. My mother still treats me like I'm a kid, which is really annoying, and then I get all sulky like I am one!

GM3: I experienced that too, but it did start to change once I became a parent myself. Actually in some ways it intensified at first, because my mother knew all about babies and I didn't, and it was easy to kind of let her take over at first because she spent a lot of time helping out over the first few months and telling me to do things a certain way. But as I gained confidence as a parent, I started to feel more equal to her and my dad—not completely; there's a tone of voice they use, or sometimes they ask me about what I'm really doing with my life, and I just automatically get defensive and feel like I've lost years of maturity!

D: Yes, it has changed somewhat since I've become a parent, too, but like you, there's still room for improvement.

L: You know, I have older kids now, and although I agree with what everyone has been saying about feeling like a child with their parents, because of course I have parents too and sometimes feel that way, I want to throw in my parental perspective. It's so hard to let your kids grow up. It was hard when they were little and starting school, and it's still hard now that they are so much more independent. I just want to protect them! I mean, I know I can't, but I do find myself making those remarks that make us all cringe when our parents say them! But now, I'm curious to find out now where people have gone with this dream. Let's go around and get everyone's interpretation as if this were your own dream.

GM1: For me, this dream would be about my mom and dad's relationship and the mystery of their breakup. I also think the Oedipus piece make sense in that I continued to live with my mother after the divorce and, in that sense, lost my dad and wanted him back. I'd also look at the scientific and artistic parts of the sculpture as representing the two parts of me that want to understand what happened. I want the logical cause-and-effect aspects of what happened to the relationship, and I'd want the intuitive/artistic or emotional explanation. Only by understanding what happened from both of those perspectives will I be able to feel content that I have solved the mystery.

GM3: If this were my dream, I think the idea of the atomic clock and the bas-relief statue of a scientist might reflect my grounding in psychology as a science. But the sphinx is such a mystical creature, so that part would be my interest in spirituality and other "unscientific" processes that I believe are very important. The fact that the scientist figure is male might reflect science as a male-dominated field for me. The more I think about it, it seems as though the sculpture is an integration for me of contrasts—a female artist creating something in a male-dominated field; the rational and the mystical coming together in one statue; a balance or integration that I am trying to find in my own life.

D: That is so true for me, too—the part of about having something rational and mystical in the same thing. Rationality versus art or spirituality or the emotional world is something I feel like I struggle with a lot.

GM3: Can you say more about your struggle?

D: I feel like I don't have a balance between the two—I go back and forth between rationality and a more emotional or intuitive way of thinking about things and dealing with things. When I deal with things too rationally, I feel cut off from things. But then I overcompensate and push away my rationality and try to just use my feelings or intuition and don't always make good decisions! And then I find myself drawn back toward science and precision and rational answers. I'm still looking for a good balance.

L: If this were my dream, I'd be surprised, because I'm so nonartistic that it would really make me wonder what was going on. I think it might have something to do at this point in my life with my feelings about my parents and death—time running out. My mother died a few years ago, and my father's getting quite old. I still feel like I haven't resolved a lot of issues about my feelings for them, and I think the dream relates to the tension I feel about my relationship with them.

GM2: For me, I'm trying to tie in the piece about the sphinx being the first sculpture your mom ever did. What that might mean. So if the sphinx represents you, I mean me, then that's something special. Because of the atomic clock, and the name on the bottom, maybe she made the sphinx *for* my father in some way. But if I'm the sphinx, this happened when I was already 7 years old. And I can't change, because I'm made of stone, so I'm sort of stuck in this role of being parts of both of my parents.

D: I really don't get that first-sculpture theme—although you're right, it does seem to mean something special. But to me it's part of the mystery.

L: So how does it all go together for you now? What does this dream mean to you?

D: For a short dream, it sure seems to mean a lot of different things, or at least have a whole bunch of different associations and layers to it. In essence, I think it has to do with how my childhood experiences have affected me and how they still affect me today, and my confusion about my relationships with my parents. There's something really positive about this dream, too. A riddle that has a solution, hopefully.

GM1: It's really colorful, your dream.

During the insight stage, the group touched on several levels of insight, including parts of self. As with exploration, the group could have continued productively in the insight stage for awhile longer. Given time constraints, however, the group moved on to the action stage.

Action Stage

L: Why don't we move on to the action stage now. How would you change this dream, if you could, first of all?

D: There'd be a signpost somewhere telling me what the sphinx means! Right there in the dream, part of the art exhibit. You know how the artist sometimes describes what a piece means, and it's posted right next to the art? Or better yet, my mother herself is there, and tells me about the sphinx. And I can ask her questions.

L: That might certainly solve the mystery, if you could talk to the artist! How might other people change the dream?

GM2: Maybe I'd add more people, coming to see this art exhibit, looking around and talking about the different pieces of artwork. Some could even be my own friends, people I trust who could talk to me about their impressions.

D: That would be kind of nice. There should be lots of people at art shows.

GM3: In terms of how I'd change the dream… I'd pick up the sculpture and find a small door on the bottom that contained instructions on how to solve the riddle and put this mystery to rest for myself.

GM1: And I'd change that scientist's head from a man's head into a woman's head!

GM3: Who would it be?

GM1: Oh, I don't know, maybe Marie Curie.

D: I'd make it into Mary Whiton Calkins—she was a student of William James, whom I really admire, and the first woman president of the American Psychological Association. She did a little research on dreams, which is why she comes to my mind.

L: Do any of these ideas, or what you came up with yourself, suggest something you could do, some kind of action?

D: Well, I would like to solve the riddle, and I think what we were talking about earlier might lead to that, about how my relationship with my father is something important here. I need to work on that relationship. We both tend to keep our distance, keep things comfortable but not very satisfying, at least not for me.

GM2: How might you work on that relationship?

D: I'd like to ask my dad questions about his marriage to my mom, find out some concrete facts, such as what year did they separate, and also get more of his perspective on their marriage itself, and why it didn't work out.

L: That sounds great. How do you see yourself doing this? What if your dad says he doesn't remember? I remember you said earlier he tends to sidestep questions like that.

D: Yeah, at least in person. Maybe it would work better to write him a letter. He expresses himself well in writing, and it would give him more time to think about my questions. The problem with writing a letter is for me it takes a lot of effort, and I'll probably want to say everything and make it really long, which means I'll be less inclined to finish…

GM1: So it feels kind of overwhelming?

D: Right—and I've started letters like this before and never finished them.

GM1: Maybe you can make this action plan into a smaller task, like writing a shorter letter and not trying to say everything, just starting things off. You want to give him a chance to respond, after all, and really get a dialogue going.

D: That's true.

L: Can you see yourself doing that?

D: I can see myself writing it and never mailing it!

L: We'll come back to that, but before that, what ideas does everyone have for action? What would your action plan be?

GM1: My action would be to explore more into my own comfort with ambiguity and contrasts between male and female, mystical and rational. Perhaps identifying different patterns within my life.

GM3: I would have to go through the action stage to know what my action plan is. The action stage itself would consist of figuring out what those instructions that I found in the bottom of the sphinx tell me to do to solve the riddle. And then I'd go and do that.

L: For my action plan, I need to do some deeper thinking about my parents. Maybe I need to write in a journal and dialogue with both parents about how I feel about them. To be honest, I'm not sure I'm ready to do that just yet, but I can feel a need to get settled about my feelings about them. I might not mail that letter either.

D: I don't want to write a letter and then not mail it—what's the point?

L: For me, just writing the letter would be healing, and a way to explore my own feelings about my parents in depth.

D: I don't know; I can't see that as particularly helpful.

GM2: What are your biggest obstacles to mailing it? Maybe you're a little anxious about taking that step?

D: Yeah, upsetting the apple cart.

L: Changing the family system?

D: Exactly.

GM1: What would be the benefits of mailing the letter? And the benefits of not mailing it?

D: Let's see…the benefits of not mailing it are obvious! I would feel less anxious, because our relationship would stay the same.

L: You'd know what to expect.

D: Right. And if I mailed it, maybe my relationship with my father, and with my stepmother for that matter, would become closer. And I might get that mystery solved! My curiosity satisfied.

GM3: You know, it sounds like you have two goals. One of them is to get more information about your parents' marriage, and the other is to work on your relationship with your father, and there's a little conflict between them.

D: Yeah, that's true, and now that you say it that way, I think one thing that is worrying me is that in the past, it seems like when I have tried to find out about their marriage, it always has created problems in my relationship with my father, and not been something that has brought us closer. I guess I'm worried that will happen again.

GM1: It feels like a big risk, then.

D: Right.

GM2: Maybe you could just pick one of those goals. Which one would you pick?

D: Hmm. I think finding out about my parent's marriage, because that sense of curiosity is so strong in the dream. Solving that mystery.

L: And how could you do that?

D: There are actually a lot of other people I could talk to, besides my father. There's my sister, of course, since she is older. There are a couple of old family friends who live in the area and who knew my parents before they divorced, and there's all my aunts and uncles. In fact, we are having a big family reunion this summer, so I will be seeing a lot of them soon. But to get the really basic facts about what happened and when it happened, I could ask my dad a couple of simple questions. Like what year did he move to Germany. That sort of thing.

L: Great, you have a lot of ideas. Try and come up with a specific action plan for this dream: maybe decide who you want to talk with, and plan to do it some time soon, maybe even this week.

D: Okay. Here's a good one. I ran into one of these old family friends just a week or two ago, in the grocery store. We get together maybe once or twice a year. I'm thinking of her because she has a really good memory. I mean, a *really* good one. And she came over to Germany to take care of me and my sister that first summer when my dad was living there. I could call her up.

GM1:   Awesome. What are friends for?

L: That's a great plan. When do you see yourself doing it?

D: I could do it this weekend, at least call and try to arrange a good time to talk!

Reflections on the Group Experience

    This session transcript is a great example of the structure and process of doing group dream work using the Hill model. All group members were actively involved and as a group offered a variety of associations and perspectives that helped me gain a good deal of new insight into the meaning of my dream. The action stage in this example went particularly well. The action plan that the group helped me to develop was not only relatively simple and concrete in concept but also very relevant to the dream and to my own personal life. It helped a lot to have the input of the group in formulating the plan, especially when one group member commented that I had two conflicting goals. That insight enabled me to move forward and pick an action with which I felt comfortable.

    This dream was one that I had thought about a lot and worked on by myself before bringing it to the dream group. I already knew before the session that the dream was about my confusion about my parents' relationship and that the sphinx represented me in some way and combined aspects of my mother and my father. The session helped me to develop these ideas and carry them further. One group member's association to Oedipus didn't fit for me at first, but later in the session I felt a flash of insight that did connect Oedipus with my relationship with my father. I also really liked how another group member talked about the dream being about a balance of the rational and the mystical or the intuitive. I had felt that tension in the dream but had not articulated it until this dream session.

During the dream work, group members jumped right in and were good at framing their associations and comments as projections, even when they did not strictly use the "If it were my dream" format. Of course, it should be remembered that all group members had worked with the Hill model before. When, however, a group has members who are unfamiliar with this model or other models of dream interpretation, it is not uncommon for group leaders to have to respectfully remind the group members to use the "If it were my dream" format. In this example, group members offered many creative and insightful associations, and one might be tempted to assume that group members who have experience doing dream interpretation would contribute associations of a higher quality than group members who do not have experience in dream interpretation. There is no research evidence either for or against this assumption, but in my own experience the quality of associations offered by individual group members seems to have more to do with interest in dreams and other individual characteristics rather than experience level.

RESEARCH

Falk and Hill (1995) investigated some of the benefits of group dream interpretation. It is interesting that this study is the only one so far carried out by Hill and her colleagues that has focused on groups, perhaps because several rather crucial methodological issues complicate group research (e.g., Kivlighan, Coleman, & Anderson, 2000). In the study, four dream interpretation groups with 5–7 members each were conducted with women who were recently separated or divorced. Falk and Hill reasoned that a group intervention that focused on dreams would be a practical approach, one that therapists can use with separated or divorcing women, because of the social support provided by the group format and because dreams tend to be more vivid during stressful events such as divorce (Cartwright, 1979).

One potential problem of conducting dream groups that focus on a specific theme, as was done in Falk and Hill's (1995) study, is that some of the dreams that are brought in might not be linked to the theme. Although that was an initial concern of the researchers, no problems arose. Many of the dreams that the women presented in the dream groups were obviously concerned with divorce and separation, as they contained images of estranged husbands and often dealt with themes of sadness, shame, and hurt. However, even though some dreams did not seem connected at the time of the initial presentation of the dream, the groups made the assumption that whatever dreams the women brought were related to separation or divorce and were always able to bring up meaningful divorce-related material when exploring the dream images thoroughly.

Each dream group met for 8 weeks and lasted for approximately 2 hours each time. Groups worked with one woman's dream in depth each week. One strength of Falk and Hill's (1995) study was that the women in the dream groups were compared with women in a wait-list control condition on measures of anxiety, depression, stress, self-esteem, and insight into their dreams. The results indicated that compared with the women in the wait-list control condition, the women who participated in the dream groups gained self-esteem and increased in their ability to interpret their own dreams. There were no differences in stress, depression, or anxiety levels, but because all of the women were relatively well functioning at the outset, there was not much room for improvement on these measures.

There are many more questions about working with dreams in groups that I would like to investigate, methodological difficulties notwithstanding. For example, given that dreams often contain very personal information about the dreamer, is the level of self-disclosure in the initial meeting of dream groups high relative to other groups, such as therapy process groups? Are process and outcome different for dream groups that proceed without designated leaders than for groups with leaders? Also, for groups with leaders, how are process and outcome different when leaders choose to offer associations and insights versus when they do not? What are the benefits and drawbacks of leaders' participation? I hope that other researchers will begin to investigate these or further questions about working with dreams in groups. There is a real need for quality research in this very exciting area.

REFERENCES

Cartwright, R. D. (1979). The nature and function of repetitive dreams: A survey and speculation. *Psychiatry, 42,* 131–137.

Falk, D. R., & Hill, C. E. (1995). The effectiveness of dream interpretation groups for women in a divorce transition. *Dreaming, 5,* 29–42.

Kivlighan, D. M., Coleman, M. N., & Anderson, D. C. (2000). Process, outcome, and methodology in group counseling research. In S. D. Brown & R. W. Lent (Eds.), *Handbook of counseling psychology* (3rd ed., pp. 767–796). New York: Wiley.

Taylor, J. (1992). *Where people fly and water runs uphill.* New York: Warner.

Ullman, M. (1987). The experiential dream group. In B. B. Wolman (Ed.), *Handbook of dreams* (pp. 407–423). New York: Van Nostrand Reinhold.

Ullman, M., & Zimmerman, N. (1979). *Working with dreams.* Los Angeles: Tarcher.

6

SELF-GUIDED METHODS FOR WORKING WITH DREAMS

JASON S. ZACK

Far more people use self-help than person-to-person professional help (Norcross, 2000), but why would somebody choose self-help over professional help? Understanding this phenomenon is important to help therapists guide consumers toward professional services and to optimally design self-guided interventions.

In this chapter I review the Hill cognitive–experiential model of dream work as it applies to self-guided methods of dream interpretation. First, I examine the nature of self-help—its allure and its effectiveness. Next, I address the relationship between self-help and dreaming. Then I discuss how the Hill model can be adapted for self-help use, in theory and practice. Finally, I review studies that involved self-guided use of the Hill model.

Seligman (1993) provided an informative and brief review of the history of the self-help movement. He explained that the culture of self-improvement is a relatively new phenomenon, inextricably connected to a general societal belief in personal control and freedom that did not generally exist before the 20th century. Today's U.S. consumers are convinced, not only by book covers but also by their own personal outlooks on the universe and beliefs in the human capacity to change, that nearly any problem can be remedied on one's own given the proper motivation.

Self-help methods are also valued for the privacy they offer (Fried & Schultis, 1995). Mental health care still has a considerable stigma attached to it. Self-guided techniques allow people to examine personal problems and learn how to make changes without anyone knowing about it (aside from the store clerk—and even that risk has disappeared with the advent of online booksellers). It is interesting to note that a recent trip to a major retail bookstore revealed that what was once called the *self-help* section is now labeled *self-improvement*, suggesting that "help" is still something one might be embarrassed to be seen seeking.

Self-help is also relatively more affordable and generally easier to access than is traditional professionally facilitated help (Fried & Schultis, 1995). Someone dabbling in dreams is more likely to pick up a $6 book or $30 computer program that can be reused indefinitely than to work with a professional who may or may not be helpful with one $100 session.

Overall, then, self-help is convenient, private, and inexpensive compared with professional help. But does it work?

BENEFITS OF SELF-HELP

Mental health professionals routinely assign self-help books to their clients to read in between sessions (Starker, 1988, 1989). There clearly is a widely held belief that self-help methods are valuable (beyond being convenient and affordable), and in fact the process has been termed *bibliotherapy*, lending it an additional air of credibility. The ability to access the wisdom and often well-written accounts of world-renowned experts is a self-evident benefit to clinicians and clients alike. Moreover, self-guided methods theoretically allow clients to take the treatment home with them and refer to the book when questions arise. Self-help books also often contain case studies that give hope to clients who feel alone and unusual as they struggle with their problems. Of course, I would be remiss to not mention that self-help has its critics, who have suggested that the often-exaggerated claims of self-help (e.g., on the covers of bestselling books) can actually make clients' problems worse (Ellis, 1993; Rosen, 1987), or that clients may be unlikely to use the self-guided methods properly and follow only the parts that they like. Ultimately, however, whether self-guided therapeutic methods are effective is an empirical question.

Fortunately, there is an ever-growing body of research devoted to assessing the efficacy of self-guided mental health treatment programs. Although most treatments examined are not the same ones to which consumers are exposed in popular books and in widespread clinical practice, the studies shed light on the extent to which one can expect self-guided treatments to be successful. In a meta-analytic review of self-administered treatment programs, Scogin, Bynum, Stephens, and Calhoon (1990) concluded that such programs are, in general, effective compared with no treatment. Because of study limitations, Scogin et al. felt unprepared to suggest that self-administered treatment programs were equivalent to therapist-guided programs, but they were confident in their assertion that self-help treatments "can be expected to benefit the consumer."

SELF-HELP AND DREAMING

Self-help books have been written on just about every topic imaginable. Santrock, Minnett, and Campbell (1994) reviewed more than 1,000 titles and provided a fairly comprehensive list via their chapter headings: Topics range from "Abuse and Recovery" to "Women's Issues" and everything in between. Dreams and dream interpretation, however, are conspicuously absent. Perhaps the authors did not consider dreams a legitimate mental health issue, or they, like many bookstores, mentally grouped dream interpretation with occult and mysticism but not psychological self-help.

Many consumer-oriented books do examine dreams in a professional manner, and not as windows to the spirit world or messages from angels. These books focus purely on using dreams as self-generated and extremely self-relevant narratives that can be tapped to help make positive life changes not unlike the goals espoused by most other self-help books. Some recent examples are *Inner Work*, by Johnson (1986); *Crisis Dreaming*, by Cartwright and Lamberg (1993); *Breakthrough Dreaming*, by Delaney (1991); and *Dream Power*, by Richmond (2001).

SELF-HELP AND THE HILL MODEL: CONCEPTUAL CONSIDERATIONS

Origins

Hill's cognitive–experiential model of dream work was originally intended for use only by therapists with formal training in helping skills. The title of Hill's (1996) original book, *Working With Dreams in Psychotherapy*, reveals its focus. Still, clients have always been encouraged to use the model on their own, and a manual for self-guided use was included in the original (1996) book. However, Hill and her colleagues generally advise clients and student trainees to avoid using the method on friends and relatives, just as would be advised for psychotherapy in general. This is sensible to some extent. After all, the model was developed on the basis of psychotherapy research, the model's stages are based on the tenets of three major psychotherapeutic orientations (humanistic, psychodynamic, and cognitive–behavioral for the exploration, insight, and action stages, respectively), and one of the aspects that sets the model apart is its professionally therapeutic stance. It does help to have a trained, psychologically minded facilitator guide the dreamer, offering suggestions and potential interpretations that may or may not fit the dreamer's experience, to get the best results from the model as originally presented. Nevertheless, a facilitator may not be a critical element for a successful and rewarding experience.

A Perfect Match

The Hill model appears particularly well suited for private dream work because of its structure, safety, and general approach. First, the model has a *simple structure*. It is very easy to teach, learn, and remember. Graduate students have been trained to use it in introductory theories courses. Undergraduate students have been taught the method in introductory helping skills classes. Nonprofessional dream enthusiasts quickly and eagerly learn the model at workshops and conferences such as those sponsored by the Association for the Study of Dreams. Clients are quick to grasp the methodology and underlying theory so that they might use the model at home, between therapy sessions.

Another benefit of the Hill model is that it is relatively *safe*. Unlike some other models of dream work (e.g., Johnson, 1986) that encourage dreamers to amplify feelings, which can sometimes be extremely negative and require professional intervention, the Hill model allows the dreamer to choose shallow or deep interpretations of the dream, depending on what feels comfortable for the dreamer.

Finally, the Hill model has a *nondirective* general approach; that is, even when a professional facilitator is working with the client, he or she is advised to exercise restraint in offering suggestions or interpretations on what the dream means for the dreamer. It is acceptable to offer a few interpretations, but this should always be done within a collaborative framework. One recommended way to do this is by taking the approach of "what it might mean to me if it were *my* dream." Thus, dreamers are given a great deal of autonomy in the model to begin with, so why not take it one step further and allow them complete control over the process?

There is, of course, a potential downside to self-guided dream work (or else there would be no reason to use therapists at all). When working alone on a dream, people are more likely to become defensive or blocked, putting limits on the amount of exploration and insight they might achieve (Heaton, Hill, Petersen, Rochlen, & Zack, 1998). A therapist can challenge resistance and encourage the client to move beyond preconceived ideas about the dream's meaning. Even if no specific input is given, a helpful facilitator can help clients look at their dreams in new ways. A one-sided exercise relies heavily on the participant's motivation and creativity. Still, the potential for self-exploration makes self-guided work a very worthwhile enterprise.

METHODS FOR SELF-GUIDED DREAM WORK USING THE HILL MODEL

Several self-help versions of the Hill cognitive–experiential model of dream work have been developed and studied empirically over the past several years. All models involve writing as a substitute for interpersonal communication. In a review of research on the therapeutic effect of writing about emotional experiences, Pennebaker (1997) reported that experimental paradigms have consistently shown positive outcomes from writing. In a variety of studies, participants who wrote about emotionally difficult experiences had, among other benefits, fewer physician visits, improved immune function, short-term drops in autonomic activity, long-term mood improvements, improvements in grades, and reduced work absenteeism. Although Pennebaker's work was not related to dreams and dream interpretation, his findings regarding the benefits of writing support the anticipation of gains made from writing about emotional dream experiences.

The positive effects of writing have not been linked to any particular personality variables, so many types of people may benefit from a self-guided written dream interpretation approach. Furthermore, actual or implied social feedback (the anticipation that others will review one's written material) has not been related to writing benefit, so it may not matter whether the dream work is kept private or revealed to a researcher or therapist. Smyth's (1996) meta-analysis of writing studies revealed that session length was unrelated to outcome, but length of treatment in days was related to outcome—that is, the longer the period of time over which the participant was required to write, the better the outcome. Hence, although single sessions of self-guided dream work may be helpful, several months worth of weekly dream work would be better.

Informed Journaling

Perhaps the simplest approach to self-guided dream work is to familiarize oneself with the method by reading about it (e.g., in this book) and then journal in an unstructured way, drawing on a new understanding of schematic change and what can be gained by exploring, interpreting, and generating action ideas. The dream enthusiast can even review his or her existing dream journals and do things like adding descriptions and associations to key images. Then the dreamer can consider all of the new information together to generate several types of interpretations, which may then be noted at the end of the dream entry. Delaney (1991) discussed similar methods of working with dreams in dream journals.

The Manual for Self-Guided Dream Interpretation

Hill, Heaton, and Peterson developed a 20-page self-help manual published as the Appendix of Hill's (1996) book (pp. 215–235). Although researchers (Heaton et al., 1998) studied the manual as a stand-alone intervention, it was published in a book for therapists. Thus, it can be assumed that it was originally intended for clients to use during or after a formal counseling treatment experience. The steps follow the same basic structure as the in-person model, except that the dreamer writes down what he or she would be expected to say in a typical face-to-face session. Unfortunately, the manual is relatively plain-looking and not very engaging, requiring tedious and repetitive writing of descriptions, associations, interpretations and action plans.

The Dream Toolbox

Because research participants said that Hill's (1996) self-help manual was less enjoyable than the therapist-led dream interpretation sessions, we wondered if a more dynamic and interactive self-led method for working with dreams would produce better outcomes and higher levels of client satisfaction. Hence, we developed a computerized version of the Hill method of dream interpretation.

Using a versatile, cross-platform database program called FileMaker Pro, we created the first version of The Dream Toolbox (Zack & Hill, 2001). We based the content of The Dream Toolbox primarily on the self-help manual. However, there are some key differences in form and function.

The current version of The Dream Toolbox (Version 1.06) begins with an opening screen and a brief description of the model and program authors. Then the user is presented with an index of any dreams entered so far. The number of dreams is limited only by the space on the user's hard drive where the program is stored. The index shows dream titles ("naming the dream" is an official part of the Hill model), the date the dream was entered, whether the dream has been interpreted yet, and buttons allowing the dreamer to delete data on the dream or to continue working with the dream where he or she left off. The dreamer can click on the title of the dream to review the entire process of the dream. The entire interface is pleasantly colorful and easy to read. There is a toolbar at the top of the screen that can be used to create data for a new dream, delete data for the current dream, reset the program, view general descriptive dream statistics (e.g., number of dreams, average number of words, average feeling scores, etc.), and generate a dream report for printout.

The user navigates through each stage using buttons at the bottom of the screen that permit movement back and forth as necessary, and the program will remember where the user left off if he or she has to stop in the middle of a session. In the exploration stage, the dreamer types in the dream and rates his or her feelings during and after the dream. He or she then identifies up to 10 images from the dream. The computer program asks for descriptions, associations, and waking life triggers for each image sequentially. One nice thing about the program as compared with the paper-and-pencil self-help manual is that associations and descriptions are automatically copied from earlier in the exploration stage and presented for the client's consideration when the time comes to identify waking life triggers and early life triggers.

In the insight stage, the dreamer is interactively prompted to generate an interpretation of the dream in terms of waking life or parts of self. The user writes an interpretation at the beginning and end of the interpretation stage for comparison purposes and to emphasize gains made in the stage. The computer encourages the user to use all of the images from the dream, offers a dialogue between conflicting parts of self, and prompts the user to consider additional interpretations.

Finally, in the action stage the dreamer is allowed to change the dream, identify analogous waking life changes, and develop action plans to effect those changes. The user is asked to title the dream and summarize the experience. Throughout the process, the computer presents the dreamer with open questions in a friendly and conversational tone, often addressing the participant by name.

During the development phase of The Dream Toolbox project, we conducted several test (beta) versions of the software and asked experienced and inexperienced individuals to evaluate it. The feedback was for the most part extremely positive, with users reporting that the process was engaging and helpful. The majority of the changes we made in subsequent versions involved wording changes.

The Dream Toolbox has a number of benefits. First, it is an improvement over the original self-help manual, because it is more engaging. Instead of a 20-page black-and-white booklet with blanks to fill in, often requiring the user to repeat earlier material, the computer version is colorful and dynamically presents already-entered text for use in later sections. It personalizes the process and maintains a warm emotional tone. Our hope was that the personal tone of the program would make the process more accessible and encourage people to voluntarily complete and become engaged in the process.

The structured self-guided methods of the self-guided manual and the Dream Toolbox are both good alternatives to therapist-led dream interpretation, because they are relatively inexpensive. This is especially appealing to clients who want to work with their dreams for self-improvement and cannot rely on insurance to pay for their work. Self-guided methods are also more convenient than therapist-led sessions because there are no time limits to the sessions. Dreamers can spend as much or as little time as they like, and there is no need to schedule sessions. Finally, the dreamer retains a written record of his or her work, which can be reviewed at any time, unlike therapist-led sessions, which are rarely recorded.

TIMING ISSUES

An interesting issue is the question of when to use self-guided dream interpretation methods. In general, there are three options: (a) The dreamer can do dream work completely on his or her own; (b) the dreamer can do dream work after doing it in a counseling setting and "learning the ropes," to continue personal growth and problem solving; or (c) the dreamer can do dream work between sessions in ongoing therapy, bringing in dreams and interpretations to review together with the therapist. Rosen (1987) strongly advocated for this last type of adjunctive use of self-help methods in the therapy context.

ETHICAL ISSUES FOR SELF-HELP DREAM WORK

It would be irresponsible to overlook some important ethical issues in discussing the self-guided approaches to the Hill model of working with dreams. First, it should be remembered that any human-change methodology comes with the risk that change for the worse is a possibility. Psychologists have an obligation to keep the consumer's safety first in their minds.

Pennebaker (1997) noted that, despite being generally helpful, writing about emotional experiences was difficult for certain people and that a number of research participants reported crying or being deeply upset by the experience. In a study examining the relationship between type of dream and outcome of single-session dream interpretation sessions, Zack and Hill (1998) found that the best outcomes came from dreams that were extremely pleasant (e.g., blissful flying), whereas the worst outcomes came from dreams that were extremely unpleasant (e.g., being physically abused). They concluded that extremely troubling dreams might be too difficult to work with properly in limited timeframe without substantial development of a working relationship with a professional therapist. Hence, one risk of promoting self-guided methods of dream interpretation using the Hill model is the possibility that the dreamer will be emotionally overwhelmed by the experience. Still, this seems to be an issue for only a few people and is not a general concern.

It is especially difficult to anticipate problems when working with dreams because of their cryptic nature. I have seen this occur sometimes in training groups when one member of the group volunteers a dream with which the group will practice. What can seem like an enjoyable and whimsical process at first can quickly become embarrassing at best, and painfully traumatic at worst. I am thankful that things have never gotten this bad in my own training sessions, but I have heard horror stories from reputable sources about amateur dream groups in other settings. Hence, I recommend that anyone using this (or any) approach to self-guided dream work be emotionally stable and relatively healthy from a psychological point of view. The dreamer should always know ahead of time whom he or she will contact in the event of a crisis. The best guidance of all is probably the simplest: Self-guided dream interpreters should stop if the process becomes too difficult or uncomfortable. This is a sign that professional assistance is probably warranted.

Another warning is one that has been repeated since the model's inception: Avoid using the model on others without additional training. It is fun to think about one's own dreams and, to the extent that it is helpful, it can also be tempting to turn to the dreams of others. This should not be done, because even though self-helpers can use the model relatively safely, its therapeutic stance makes interpersonal use problematic unless the interpreter has formal training in helping skills. For example, the model pushes the dreamer toward examining personal problems and developing positive action plans for change. Without a full understanding of helping skills, a lay dream interpreter can give extraordinarily bad advice and not honor the needs and boundaries of the dreamer.

RESEARCH ON SELF-HELP METHODS

The Hill model of dream interpretation is one of the most highly researched methods of working with dreams using clients and therapists. Unfortunately, there are relatively few studies of self-guided dream work.

Heaton et al. (1998) compared participants' ratings of gains made in therapist-facilitated and self-help (manual) versions of the Hill dream interpretation model. They reported that self-guided sessions generally lasted between 90 and 120 minutes—the same as the approximate time required by therapist-facilitated sessions. In the study, 25 volunteer clients completed both versions in random order and reported greater session depth, problem mastery, and insight from the therapist-facilitated condition. The therapist-facilitated sessions also yielded more model-specific gains from the exploration–insight and action parts of the process than did the self-guided sessions. Moreover, clients tended to prefer the therapist-facilitated sessions, claiming the self-help process was less engaging than the therapist-facilitated version. Although the self-help process was not as effective or enjoyable as the therapist-guided process, outcome ratings were comparable to normative scores for regular therapy sessions reported by Stiles et al. (1994). In the first formal study of The Dream Toolbox, Hill, Rochlen, Zack, McCready, and Dematatis (in press) studied 94 university students randomly assigned to a computer-led session or one of two therapist-led dream interpretation conditions. In one therapist-led condition, therapists were instructed to provide empathic listening and facilitate the process but to avoid additive input (e.g., interpretations). The other therapist-led condition involved a more active provision of interpretations. Session outcomes were compared in terms of session depth, mastery–insight, and model-specific gains. The results showed that there was very little difference between the two therapist-led conditions but that both were better in terms of a composite session outcome index than The Dream Toolbox condition. Still, the computerized version yielded outcome scores consistent with norms for regular single-sessions of counseling.

Hill et al. (in press) also reported a qualitative analysis of what participants liked most and least about The Dream Toolbox condition. In general, participants enjoyed doing associations and gaining insight. Overall, they liked the computer program, but some reported that the program was too long and repetitive (the research version of the software required that participants spend a minimum amount of time in each stage, to mimic the therapist-led conditions). Hill et al. (in press) were surprised to find that participants in the computer condition did not complain about other research procedures (e.g., completing measures) as much as did participants in the therapist-facilitated conditions, despite the fact that they followed exactly the same procedures. Perhaps filling out forms and answering questions just seemed like "more of the same" noncollaborative work. It is also interesting to note that one group of computer-condition participants reported enjoying working alone, whereas another reported preferring to work with a therapist.

It is unquestionable that different types of people are better suited for different interventions when it comes to deciding between self-guided and therapist-led dream interpretation. Research suggests that The Dream Toolbox computer program is best for people who like dreams and who enjoy working by themselves. People who do not remember or value their dreams and who prefer talking with another person about their dreams may not be good candidates for this type of work.

On the basis of this research, my colleagues and I plan to make future versions of The Dream Toolbox more interactive and provide the illusion of the computer program being more empathic. This is particularly important in light of the finding that therapist presence in the empathy condition was equally successful to the therapist input condition; that is, it may be necessary not or the computer to provide interpretations but merely to suggest that a real person is facilitating the process and listening empathically. As it stands, the technological platform of The Dream Toolbox may still be getting in the way for many clients; that is, they are too acutely aware that they are working with a computer. Some potential remedies that have been discussed include adding video clips of a counselor empathically asking questions, adding soft music, adding pictures of common dream images to help elicit associations, and so on. Another goal for future versions of The Dream Toolbox is the ability to offer helpful input based on dreams the user has previously entered. For example, the program might offer an association if an image had been recorded for a previous dream. The program might also come preloaded with a set of image–association pairs that it could use as suggestions, much as a counselor would do in a typical session:

- "You know, snow makes me think of coldness…"
- "For me, dogs represent companionship. What about you?"
- "If this were my dream, I think it might indicate that I was worried about something; how does that fit for you?"

One problem with this approach, however, is that it might encourage clients to grab onto easily accessible associations and avoid adding their own. Perhaps clients would have to explicitly ask for help if they were struggling, or associations could be offered only sporadically, as a therapist might do in a traditional dream interpretation session.

CASE STUDY

The case that follows (which is used with permission) is an illustration of self-guided dream work using The Dream Toolbox (from the Hill et al. [in press] study). The client was a 19-year-old male college student research volunteer earning credit for participation and unaware of the hypotheses of the study. The client had fairly good dream recall (he recalled dreaming just about every morning) and ability to remember having dreams (he had memorable dreams just about every night).

First, the client retold the dream in the first-person present tense. Words in boldface type in the dream text were selected by the client as elements to work with in the dream interpretation process.

> I'm **walking** outside through the **rain**; it's pouring, and I am getting **soaked**. I don't 100% **recognize** the area; however, I get the feeling it's our **old farm** … which my **family** owns. I run inside only to find myself surrounded by family members, the only one I can truly make out is my **uncle**. I'm feeling quite **smothered** for some reason, so I ask to go to the **bathroom**, which is quite elaborate. I then turn around only to find that my family members have **followed** me. I then wake up.

On a scale of 1 to 9 (1 = *low*), the client rated his feelings during the dream as a 3 in pleasure and a 2 in arousal. On awakening, he felt a 6 in pleasure and a 6 in arousal (i.e., happier and more aroused).

In the exploration stage, the client was first asked to describe the images in more detail. So, for example, *rain* led to the following description:

> Rain; it occurred rather suddenly, and viciously. Soaking me to the bone almost instantly, there was thunder and lightning as I recall as well.

After describing each image in sequence, the client associated to the images one by one, given prompts such as, "What does rain represent?", "What is rain?", "How does rain make you feel?", and "If I were from Mars, how would you describe rain?" In this case, the client's associations to rain were:

> When I think of rain, I think of stress, a disturbance in life; rain reminds me of the bad times, "dark clouds" in my life. Rain represents some bad times I have [had]. Rain is a source of water; a huge annoyance. I feel disturbed when I think of rain. If you were from Mars, I'd describe it as the water droplets that come from the clouds.

The client goes through this process with each image. For example, he described *bathroom* as follows:

> [The] bathroom seemed rather elaborate, like the toilet seemed more like a couch, and the curtains and area itself seemed a bit more pleasant.

The client also made the following associations about *bathroom*:

> A place to relieve myself; The bathroom reminds me of just a place where I go to relieve myself, sometimes an escape, a place where I just like to think.

All of the images were described and associated, and then the client entered the insight stage. First, he was prompted for an initial interpretation of the dream ("What do you think the dream means overall?"). In this case, the client's initial interpretation was:

> I think it has to do with the stress I've been having lately over a game. I like to have fun, be a free thinker, but I had felt a bit smothered as of late by the game I play, and wanted to escape it, yet stress followed me wherever I went. My family I don't know, other than that when I'm near them as of late, I feel like I want to get away from them, that there's something wrong with them, especially my father.

The client then had an opportunity to work with the dream on the level of how it relates to waking life and then how different parts of the dream represent different parts of the self. The client was ultimately able to make a new interpretation based on what he learned in the insight stage. In this case, the client developed the following interpretation:

> That I love my family, yet they don't give me the personal space I need whenever I'm in contact with them, that my father is a very controlling

individual, and that my uncle is in direct opposition to him. This stresses me out often[;] I try to fight it but rarely am able to win.

Thus, just from the exploration stage alone the client was able to see some basic metaphorical implications of the dream and its representation of him not being able to find refuge. Further work in the insight stage led the client to a deeper understanding of some personality features in himself and among the people with whom he interacts in his life.

Finally, on the basis of the previous two stages, the client moved to the action stage, in which he had a chance to identify potential changes in his life. In this case, the client decided that he needs to

> change the way my family treats me, as in older, more mature, able to make my own decisions, trust me more; have fun in the games I play, not to be stressed, and not to treat them as if they were like work, not act like they were a job, and be able to get away whenever I need to.

However, the program doesn't stop there. The client was then encouraged to develop specific, concrete action plans for implementing the desired change. In this case, the client decided that

> I will attempt to change it by sitting down and having a talk with them, without my father. After that is done I will try to put it as gently, and not bluntly, to him as possible what I think of the way he is treating me like; that I will stop leading in the game I play, though I like it, it puts too much of a burden on my shoulders and I stop having fun.

Thus, in the space of 1 hour and 14 minutes, the client moved from having a vague dream about being followed into the bathroom in the family farm, to understanding more about his frustrations with waking life stressors and family dynamics, to identifying a desire to improve his family relationships, to a specific action plan of how to bring up the problem with the troubling individuals. The client was quite satisfied with the session and gave an average score of 4.5 out of 5 on the Session Evaluation Scale (Hill & Kellems, 2002).

FUTURE RESEARCH

Much more research needs to examine self-guided dream work. It would be helpful to know if altering the protocol in different ways improves outcome. For example, how does placing time restrictions on the stages of the model change clients' reactions to a process the major values of which are flexibility and independence? Are there certain client personality variables that predict success in self-guided dream work? How does self-guided dream work compare with other self-help methods (e.g., some recent cognitive–behavioral approaches to automated psychotherapy; Cavanagh, Zack,

& Shapiro, in press)? Research is needed to determine whether certain individuals are better at doing daydream interpretation and informed journaling than others and how doing so compares with traditional dream work.

CONCLUSIONS

I hope this chapter inspires individuals to explore their dreams on their own, not through mere casual reflection but via the structured and effective model for working with dreams proposed by Hill. Clinicians might consider assigning dream work to their clients more often between sessions for later review. Finally, I hope that researchers will be intrigued by the many questions still left unanswered, inspired to develop new methods, and motivated to test these new methods empirically so that they can be fairly evaluated and adopted by dream professionals, clients, and enthusiasts.

REFERENCES

Cartwright, R. D., & Lamberg, L. (1993). *Crisis dreaming: Using your dreams to solve your problems*. New York: HarperCollins.

Cavanagh, K., Zack, J. S., & Shapiro, D. (in press). Empirically supported computerized psychotherapy. In R. Wooton & K. Anthony (Eds.), *Technology in counselling and psychotherapy: A practitioner's guide*. London: Palgrave.

Delaney, G. (1991). *Breakthrough dreaming*. New York: Bantam.

Ellis, A. (1993). The advantages and disadvantages of self-help therapy materials. *Professional Psychology: Research and Practice, 24*, 335–339.

Fried, S. B., & Schultis, G. A. (1995). *The best self-help and self-awareness books: A topic-by-topic guide to quality information*. Chicago: American Library Association.

Heaton, K. J., Hill, C. E., Petersen, D., Rochlen, A. B., & Zack, J. (1998). A comparison of therapist-facilitated and self-guided dream work sessions. *Journal of Counseling Psychology, 45*, 115–121.

Hill, C. E. (1996). *Working with dreams in psychotherapy*. New York: Guilford Press.

Hill, C. E., & Kellems, I. (2002). Development and use of the Helping Skills Measure to assess client perceptions of the effects of training and of helping skills in sessions. *Journal of Counseling Psychology, 49*, 264–272.

Hill, C. E., Rochlen, A. B., Zack, J. S., McCready, T., & Dematatis, A. (in press). Working with dreams using the Hill cognitive–experiential model: A comparison of computer-assisted, therapist empathy, and therapist empathy + input conditions. *Journal of Counseling Psychology*.

Johnson, R. (1986). *Inner work*. San Francisco: Harper & Row.

Norcross, J. C. (2000). Here comes the self-help revolution in mental health. *Psychotherapy: Theory, Research, Practice, Training, 37*, 370–377.

Pennebaker, J. W. (1997). Writing about emotional experiences as a therapeutic process. *Psychological Science, 8,* 162–166.

Richmond, C. (2001). *Dream power: How to use your night dreams to change your life.* New York: Simon & Schuster.

Rosen, G. (1987). Self-help treatment books and the commercialization of psychotherapy. *American Psychologist, 42,* 46–51.

Santrock, J. W., Minnett, A. M., & Campbell, B. D. (1994). *The authoritative guide to self-help books.* New York: Guilford Press.

Scogin, F., Bynum, J., Stephens, G., & Calhoon, S. (1990). Efficacy of self-administered treatment programs meta-analytic review. *Professional Psychology: Research and Practice, 21,* 42–47.

Seligman, M. E. P. (1993). *What you can change...And what you can't: The complete guide to successful self-improvement.* New York: Fawcett Columbine.

Smyth, J. M. (1996). Written emotional expression: Effect sizes, outcome types, and moderating variables. *Journal of Consulting and Clinical Psychology, 66,* 174–184.

Starker, S. (1988). Do-it-yourself therapy: The prescription of self-help books by psychologists. *Psychotherapy, 25,* 142–146.

Starker, S. (1989). *Oracle at the supermarket: The American preoccupation with self-help books.* New Brunswick, NJ: Transaction.

Stiles, W. B., Reynolds, S., Hardy, G. E., Rees, A., Barkham, M., & Shapiro, D. A. (1994). Evaluation and description of psychotherapy sessions by clients using the Session Evaluation Questionnaire and the Session Impacts Scale. *Journal of Counseling Psychology, 41,* 175–185.

Zack, J. S., & Hill, C. E. (1998). Predicting outcome of dream interpretation sessions by dream valence, dream arousal, attitudes toward dreams, and waking life stress. *Dreaming, 8,* 169–185.

Zack, J. S., & Hill, C. E. (2001). The Dream Toolbox (Version 1.06). (Available from J. S. Zack at jszack@mac.com)

7

INCORPORATING SPIRITUALITY INTO DREAM WORK

TIMOTHY L. DAVIS

Despite a consistent link between healthy spirituality and psychological well-being, only approximately one third of clinicians express personal competence in counseling clients regarding religious issues and matters of spirituality (Shafranske, 1996). Similarly, despite some encouraging evidence on the clinical use of dream interpretation, Mahrer (1990) suggested that only 10% to 15% of therapists work with dreams on more than a superficial level. Although the incidence of both dream interpretation and spiritual exploration is low, helping clients use their spiritual perspective within the dream interpretation process can help them access meaningful parts of their personality and enhance the therapeutic process (Davis & Hill, 2003).

The idea that dreams can be a source of spiritual insight is not a novel concept. Throughout history, dreams have been viewed as possible links to spiritual realms and sacred forces (Van de Castle, 1994; Wollmering, 1997). Virtually every religious tradition from antiquity to the present has sought spiritual guidance, divine revelation, and creative inspiration from dreams (Bulkeley, 1999). This point is illustrated by the 98 specific references to dreams and dreaming in the Old Testament (Wollmering, 1997). Doniger and Bulkeley (1993) noted that religion was the original field of dream study and that the earliest writings on dreams are primarily texts about their spiritual and religious significance. Given that dreams sometimes reflect deeply personal and sacred parts of peoples' lives (James, 1900/1958; Johnson, 1986; Jung, 1964), it seems likely that exploring clients' spiritual experiences and beliefs within dream interpretation may have some therapeutic benefit. The purpose of this chapter is to present a therapeutic approach to helping clients work with spiritual issues and concerns in their dreams.

Helping clients explore spiritual issues and concerns manifested in dreams seems justified by the empirical evidence of a positive relationship between mental health and spirituality. Spirituality has been associated with greater psychological well-being, more emotional adjustment, and higher marital satisfaction and with less depression; fewer suicides; less frequent substance abuse; and, in many cases, decreased anxiety (Bergin, 1983; Davis, Kerr, & Robinson Kurpius, in press; Gartner, Larson, & Allen, 1991; Glenn & Weaver, 1978; Koenig, Kvale, & Ferrel, 1988; Maton, 1989; Rogalski & Paisey, 1987). Therefore, helping clients explore and develop a healthy sense of spirituality in the context of dream interpretation may be conducive to psychological health.

Although many theoreticians have proposed an association between spiritual phenomena and dreams, I am not aware of any existing clinical model that provides clear guidelines for helping clients explore their dreams from the perspective of their spirituality. The approach that I describe is a modified version of the cognitive–experiential model of dream work (C. E. Hill, 1996; see also Introduction and chap. 1–3, this volume). In this chapter I provide a background for spirituality and dreams, explain the original model, review research on incorporating spirituality into the model, discuss the specific modifications for helping clients look for spiritual meaning in their dreams, and present a case example.

DEFINING SPIRITUALITY

For the purposes of this model, the term *spirituality* does not refer to specific religious practices or beliefs. Several authors have conceptualized spirituality as being closely related to transcendence (extending beyond human or material existence), without making specific reference to formal religious doctrine. For example, Ellison (1983) defined it existentially as "the capacity to find purpose and meaning beyond one's self and the immediate" (p. 338). Miller and Martin (1988) described spirituality more traditionally as the inner experience of "acknowledging a transcendent being, power, or reality greater than ourselves" (p. 200). In a biography of Jung, Jaffe (1970) described an overlap between spirituality and existentialism thus: "The experience of meaning depends on the awareness of a transcendental or spiritual reality that complements the empirical reality of life and together with it forms a whole" (p. 21).

For many individuals, spirituality overlaps with religion. Both can be understood as "a search for or experience of the sacred, as defined by the individual" (P. C. Hill & Hood, 1999, p. 1020). Furthermore, many people express their experience of the sacred in conventional religious terminology. Consistent with this conceptualization is the fact that 74% of people consider themselves to be both religious and spiritual (Zinnbauer et al., 1997).

Religiosity (in contrast to spirituality) connotes allegiance to a particular system of faith and worship, characterized by adherence to a set of sacred doctrines and behaviors or membership in a body of people who share similar beliefs about God, holy observance, and morality (*Webster's New World Dictionary of the American Language*, 1984). Religiosity adds an element of theological structure and formality not always present in spirituality.

In many cases, religiosity can provide a structure that is conducive to spirituality. In other cases, spiritual growth can be pursued outside the context of a religious framework. Therefore, for the purposes of this model, the client and therapist are by no means limited to explicitly religious or deistic conceptualizations of spirituality. Clients can find meaningful spiritual exploration in discussing existential issues such as purpose in life, mortality, postdeath experience, deep personal values, meaning in suffering, organization and creation of the universe, and ultimate truth, as well as more directly spiritual issues such as divine forces in one's life, transcendent reality (i.e., reality beyond the material universe), or reflection on specifically religious beliefs and practices. Therapists need to be open to hearing about clients' spiritual beliefs without imposing their own beliefs on them. This nonjudgmental stance is essential to encourage clients' open spiritual exploration.

SPIRITUALITY AND DREAMS

Although psychologists generally have been reluctant to consider possible spiritual aspects of dreams, some exceptions do exist. William James (1900/1958) philosophized that dreams may come from the nonrational part of the psyche that is the source of deep religious experience. Jung (1964) believed that dreams were linked to the spiritual life, even proposing the possibility that dreams are inspired by transcendental forces outside the dreamer, *somnia a Deo missa* (dreams sent by God):

> We are so captivated by and entangled in our subjective consciousness that we have forgotten the age-old fact that God speaks chiefly through dreams and visions ... If a theologian really believes in God, by what authority does he suggest that God is unable to speak through dreams? (pp. 92–93)

Jung elaborated on this assertion by explaining that prejudices, errors, and fantasies influence conscious life but that the unconscious is unencumbered by such distortions. This immunity to such psychic noise seems to be the basis for Jung's belief that the unconscious is receptive to spiritual communication. Perhaps the unconscious, finding expression in dreams, is the part of the psyche pure enough to hear the voice of a transcendent power. Although Jung theorized that dreams are multifaceted phenomena, which reflect both individual and universal influences, his consideration of divine presence in dreams was a unique perspective in the psychological study of dreams.

Bulkeley (1994, p. 21) proposed that all people's dreams have the potential for religious significance. Bulkeley (1999) suggested that dream interpretation can be enhanced by exploring both emotional and spiritual aspects of dreams, thereby promoting psychological integration and fostering spiritual and religious well-being.

Johnson (1986) suggested that existential concerns are archetypes residing in the spiritual realm of the collective unconscious. He concluded that this is an aspect of the psyche that must be revered and honored to attain psychological wholeness. In this sense, dream exploration can be a means of seeking spiritual integration.

Of course, whether dreams are influenced by a higher power or are inherently spiritual in nature is not known and cannot be empirically verified. However, no matter what the origin or function of dreams is, people can make use of them in terms of understanding more about themselves from a spiritual perspective.

CASE STUDY OF INCORPORATING SPIRITUALITY INTO DREAM WORK

When using the Hill cognitive–experiential model of dream work to explore spiritual aspects of dreams, the original three stages of the model remain fundamentally intact, with modifications made primarily to the Insight Stage. To help explicate the stages, I provide excerpts from a session with a client whom I call "Jessica."[1]

Exploration Stage

As described in chapter 1 of this book, the therapist starts the process by giving the client a brief overview of what to expect in the dream

---

[1]The session described in this chapter is based on a session conducted by Suzie Friedman, MS. Much of the dialogue has been condensed and modified to fit the chapter format and to illustrate the technique. I thank Suzie for her contribution as the therapist in this case study.

interpretation session, asking the client to tell the dream in the first-person present tense, asking the client to express how he or she felt during and after the dream, and exploring each major images sequentially using the DRAW acronym (description, re-experiencing, associations, waking life triggers).

C: One dream that I've had over and over again is really gross. I am standing in my house chewing many pieces of bubblegum. So many that I can hardly close my mouth. I start to gag, so I try to remove the gum from my mouth and it is stuck in my throat. So as I pull it out, it pulls on my throat and it is like I am pulling out my insides. I feel like I'm gagging and literally wake myself up so it will be over. I never get the gum out of my mouth in my dream.

T: Can you describe the bubblegum for me?

C: You know, the pink stuff. Little square pieces—like Bazooka Joe.

T: What did it feel like in your mouth? How does it taste?

C: At first it tasted fine. Good. Like bubblegum is supposed to taste. But for some reason, I keep putting more pieces in my mouth. Before I realize it I have so much crammed into my mouth that it is disgusting. Then it is a putridly—is that a word?—sweet taste. Almost like bubblegum-flavored syrup.

T: That does sound gross.

C: Yeah (laughing). But as I continue to try to chew it, it loses its flavor—just like bubblegum usually does. Then it turns into a sort of bland, flavorless clump in my mouth.

T: Next, tell me about the feelings you are having as you are chewing the gum. If you can, try to re-experience the feelings here with me. Tell me about the feelings as if you are going through the same experience here in this room.

C: At first I feel fine. I'm just standing there having some gum. But then as the wad swells in my mouth, I'm feeling frustrated with myself. I know that the more gum I put in my mouth the less I am enjoying it, but I kept doing it anyway.

T: You are doing great, but again, try to tell me about what you are feeling as if you are going through it right now.

C: Okay. I feel frustrated with myself, and I'm starting to feel panicked. I know I've got too much gum in my mouth, but now I can't do anything about it. I feel kind of scared now.

T: Out of control?

C: Yes. I feel out of control and mad at myself. I can't believe I did this to myself!

T: What is the first thing that comes to mind when you think about bubblegum?

C: Fun. Blowing bubbles. Childhood.

T: Keep going. What else?

C: Um, chewing. Sweet, but as you chew it, it loses its flavor. Pink.

T: Can you say a little more about pink? What do you associate with pink?

C: Feminine stuff. Little girls. Dolls. Playing house. Stuff like that.

T: Can you think of anything going on in your waking life that might have triggered the appearance of bubblegum in your dream?

C: Well, like I said, I've had this dream dozens of times.

T: Can you identify anything going on in your life that was common to the times you've had this dream?

C: I'm not sure. I think that I dream more when I am stressed. Come to think of it, I've probably felt more pressure at home when I've had this dream. You know, lots of stuff at home, with wifely and motherly activities. Sometimes I get a little overwhelmed.

T: Okay. And you said that you are standing in your house. Can you describe your house to me?

C: It is a two-story, red brick home. Three bedrooms. Actually, I wish it had four. Three bedrooms is a little crowded with five people living there.

T: What about the room you were standing in?

C: I think I was standing in the family room. It's probably the biggest room in the house ... and the messiest. It's usually where everyone hangs out when they're home.

T: How do you feel about being in the family room during the dream?

C: Fine. I didn't feel anything unusual until I started chewing the gum.

T: What things come to mind when you think of your family room?

C: In general, it is not the most relaxing place in the house. The kids are usually there, and their stuff is usually strewn all over.

T: What else comes to mind when you think of family rooms in general?

C: Well, it's literally the room for the family. It is where everyone lives. Loud. Hectic. Television. Noisy.

T: What about the "family" part of family room. What comes to mind when you think about your family?

C: Togetherness. Love. I really value family. But a lot of responsibility, too.

T: Can you say more about responsibility?

C: As a mom and wife, I have a lot to do. I'm a part-time stay-at-home mom, so I'm really busy with everything from carting the kids to soccer practices and recitals, cooking, daily chores like cleaning up the house and grocery shopping. Plus I work part time—two days a week—as a classroom assistant at the elementary school. Between that and taking care of everything at home, it's overwhelming sometimes.

T: Was there anything in your waking life at the time of the dream that might have triggered a dream about being in the family room?

C: Like I said before, I was probably busy with a lot of family-type mom stuff.

T: Next you said that you could hardly close your mouth. Can you describe that experience in more detail?

C: I was just cramming those pieces of gum into my mouth to the point where I could hardly chew. Even though my mouth was getting full, I kept putting more in.

T: What feelings are you experiencing when you couldn't close your mouth?

C: I remember my jaw muscles getting tired from trying to bite down.

T: So, physically, your jaws were tired. What were you feeling emotionally?

C: I was mad at myself for having been so self-indulgent. I also felt a little bit scared, because I couldn't close my mouth.

T: Does thinking of not being able to close your mouth bring up anything for you? Remind you of anything?

C: Lockjaw. Like when someone is so stunned that they can't close their mouth.

T: I'm also wondering about the phrase "can't keep her mouth shut." Does that wording bring up anything for you?

C: Yeah (appears slightly embarrassed). I've been accused of speaking out of turn. My husband and I sometimes have conversations about how we need to learn to keep out mouths shut when our teenager makes poor judgments. I know I'm a little overinvolved sometimes.

T: Is there anything in your waking life that might have precipitated a dream in which you keep putting so much in your mouth that you can't close it?

C: Not that I can think of. But the more we talked about what I was feeling emotionally when I could not close my mouth, the more I realized how similar those feelings are to what I feel in my everyday life—stressed, overwhelmed, and feeling sort of resentful about it.

T: Resentful?

C: Well, yeah. I don't like feeling so stretched all of the time. I want to be a good mom and wife, but sometimes I feel like my family takes what I do for granted.

T: And how does it make you feel when you are taken for granted?

C: It makes me mad. I don't mind doing what I do, but I'd like to have some help here and there. I'm always picking up after the kids and even my husband. Once in awhile I get aggravated.

T: In the dream you said that you are mad at yourself.

C: Yeah. That doesn't seem to fit.

T: Maybe we can come back to that.

Then the therapist inquires about the image of having something stuck in the throat.

T: Tell me more about the image of having the gum stuck in your throat.

C: It was like I was choking. Gagging. The wad of gum got too big for my mouth, but when I tried to get it out, it's like it was stuck.

T: Now I'd like for you to tell me what you are feeling in the dream when you realized that the gum was stuck in your throat.

C: I was scared. Panicked, really. I've never choked on something, but I think what I felt in this dream is probably what it feels like. Like I might die, and I'm helpless to do anything about it.

T: What is the first thing that comes to your mind when you think of choking?

C: You can't breathe. That it's life threatening.

T: What else?

C: Blue. You turn blue when you're choking. The Heimlich maneuver.

T: And tell me what the Heimlich maneuver does.

C: It's the procedure that someone does to pop out the thing you're choking on.

T: To remove the object that's blocking a person's airway—stopping her from breathing—so she doesn't suffocate.

C: Right.

T: Jessica, do you ever feel like you are suffocating—figuratively speaking?

C: Well, figuratively, yeah. Sometimes there's just so much going on in my life that it does feel sort of suffocating. I feel like I'm chronically at my limit.

T: Like you can't fit one more thing in or you'll gag?

C: Yes. You mean like how I felt in the dream?

T: Uh-huh.

C: So maybe there's a connection between how much I'm trying to cram into my real life and how much I'm trying to cram into my mouth in the dream?

T: Maybe there is. Let's talk more about that in a few minutes. Is there anything going on in your current waking life that might have caused you to dream about choking or having something stuck in you throat?

C: No. But I'm still thinking that maybe the times that I have this dream are the times when I feel the most stretched and overwhelmed.

T: In the last part of the dream you said that when you try to remove the gum from your mouth you felt like you were pulling your insides out. Can you describe that in more detail?

C: It feels like the gum is stuck to my throat and stomach. So when I try to pull it out it feels like I'm trying to pull my guts out. It feels like I'm getting sick, except worse. Like I'm about to gag up my whole stomach.

T: So you felt physically sick. What are you experiencing emotionally as you are tugging on the gum?

C: I was scared—really scared. I felt like I was in a horrible dilemma about whether to pull the gum and along with it my insides or leave it in and keep gagging. Ugh!

T: Does the idea of pulling your insides out remind you of anything?

C: It sounds like the phrase "pulling your hair out."

T: You mean like when someone is frustrated and they say, "I want to pull my hair out?"

C: Yes.

T: What else?

C: It reminds me of "gut wrenching." Like something that's painful is gut wrenching.

T: It sounds like you associate pulling your insides out with things that are frustrating and painful.

T: Was there anything going on in your waking life that might have triggered a dream about pulling your insides out?

C: (Laughing) Thankfully, no!

T: (Laughing) Yeah, thankfully no one is trying to do that to you in real life. What about anything in your waking life that might have triggered a dream about frustration or pain?

C: Well, frustration—yes. I get very frustrated with the fact that I'm always so busy—so stressed. And I get frustrated being underappreciated by my family.

T: That sounds emotionally sort of painful.

C: It is.

Insight Stage

To start the insight stage, the therapist should first work with the client to determine whether the client would like to understand the dream from the perspective of waking life, inner conflicts, experience of the dream, or spirituality. If one of the first three is chosen, the therapist can follow the regular model described in this book.

It is important to get the client's input on which level of interpretation he or she would like to use, especially when choosing a spiritual perspective. Using the spiritual perspective will not be productive for all clients. In fact, for clients who do not consider themselves to be "spiritual" people, the spiritual level of interpretation will probably not be helpful at all. The inclusion of the spiritual-inquiry substage within the insight stage is the most prominent modification to Hill's (1996) cognitive–experiential model of dream work. In this brief substage, the therapist works with the client to explore his or her spiritual belief system. By inviting the client to talk about what spirituality means to him or her personally, the therapist sets the groundwork for looking for spiritual significance in the dream. The spiritual-exploration substage can also be a useful intervention in and of itself. Because many clients (and therapists) perceive spirituality to be a taboo subject in therapy, inviting clients to discuss their spirituality can be a uniquely beneficial process. In introducing the spiritual-exploration substage, the therapist explains that they will temporarily depart from exploring the dream and spend 5–10 minutes talking about the client's sense of spirituality.

T: In a few minutes we are going to explore the meaning of your dream from your spiritual perspective. But first I'd like to ask you a little bit about some of your spiritual values. What does spirituality mean for you personally?"

C: Well, spirituality is important to me. Sometimes when I really start to struggle, going to God is the only thing that really grounds me and helps me regain perspective. Even when I'm not actively seeking God's help, somehow just knowing that there is a greater plan in place gives me comfort.

T: A greater plan?

C: To me it is helpful to know that all this stuff around me is not all that there is. I believe that there is a spiritual dimension of things that we can't see, hear, or even understand. But I believe that it's there. Things that seem random and chaotic—I don't believe that they are as random and chaotic as they seem.

T: It sounds like that children's song, "He's Got the Whole World in His Hands."

C: Yeah, it does. I think God has a plan for me, for everyone, but that plan is not plainly apparent. You sort of have to seek it out.

T: So how do *you* seek it out?

C: I think that you have to find quiet time—time alone to listen for a spiritual perspective on things. You know, time to talk to God about my problems and what's going on in my life, but I find that the best way for me to seek out God's perspective is to shut up and listen (laughs), which for me can be a little bit tough.

T: It sounds like taking that time to quietly listen is really important to you.

C: It is important to me, but as I'm sitting here talking about it I'm realizing that I rarely ever do it. I mean, I used to. But it seems like I just don't have time anymore. Here I am talking about the value of quiet spiritual time, and my life is anything but quiet. Actually, it is just the opposite. That kind of spiritually nourishing time got squeezed out of my life awhile back.

T: You mentioned earlier that you believe that God has a plan for you. Can you share with me a little bit about that plan?

C: I believe that plan includes my role as a mom and as someone who wants to do service—to help other people. But right now I feel at a loss to say much more. I feel out of touch with what that plan is.

Although Jessica was open to talking about her spirituality, other clients may not be as open to discussion of such a deeply personal topic, particularly in the early stages of the relationship. Other probes that therapists might use in helping clients explore their spirituality are: "What spiritual or religious tradition were you raised in?"; "Is that tradition still important to you?"; "How have your spiritual beliefs changed over time?"; "How would you describe your current spiritual beliefs or values?"; "What would you say are the ultimate principles, ideals, or values that guide your life?"; and "What do you believe to be sacred in your life?"

Once the therapist has gained an understanding of the client's spiritual viewpoint, he or she can introduce the idea of spiritual insight into the dream. First, the therapist offers the overall idea that dreams can be spiritual in nature. By explaining that experts from the fields of psychology and religion have theorized about the spiritual aspects of dreams, the therapist makes it safe and credible for the client to look for spiritual insight and direction in the dream. Second, the therapist explains that spiritual insight does not equate to religious insight; rather, spiritual insight encompasses a broader realm of life, including deep values, hopes, and beliefs, which need not be specifically religious in nature. Third, the therapist introduces the idea that dreams may be influenced by transcendental sources. The idea that dreams can serve as messages from powers outside the dreamer can be a particularly powerful idea for clients whose spirituality centers around a deity or omniscient force. Fourth, the therapist introduces the idea that dreams can reflect spiritual dynamics deep within the dreamer. By offering these four ideas to the client, the therapist not only establishes the idea that dreams can be spiritually meaningful but also gives the client some direction on where look for that meaning—either outside oneself or deep within.

> T: Now we are going to explore your dream from your own spiritual perspective. Some psychologists and theologians believe that dreams can be spiritual in nature—reflecting issues that go beyond our daily activities and touch on our deepest hopes, values, and beliefs. Some people also believe that dreams can provide guidance from sources outside the dreamer or from deeper levels within the dreamer—like the soul or the unconscious. What do you think your dream might mean from your own spiritual perspective?
>
> C: Well, my experience in the dream seemed so in contrast to what I value spiritually. I mean, the most important thing to me spiritually is quiet, peaceful time to reflect and listen to God. But in my dream I'm frustrated, stressed, and panicked. The more we talked about the dream the more I realized that those feelings are often what I feel during my waking life.
>
> T: You often feel frustrated and stressed.
>
> C: Yes. It's not that I don't enjoy being a mom. I do. That's important to me. It's just that I usually feel on overload. Like I just don't have time to pause for too long or something is going to get missed.
>
> T: So, spiritually you value peaceful time alone to experience God. But the pace of your life usually crowds out that quiet time.
>
> C: Right. I'm so busy tending to everything that is important in my life that I'm ignoring the thing that is probably most important.
>
> T: You look upset.

C: It just that I thought I was doing the things that are most important in my life. I love my family. I want to be good mom. I think it is personally and financially important for me to work part time outside of the home. But it just feels like too much. All of those things used to give me energy, but now I feel like a grease spot.

T: Now all of those things take more out of you than you have to give?

C: Yes. I feel pretty burnt out.

T: You know, it does sound similar to your experience of chewing that gum in your dream. At first it is flavorful and fun, but the longer you chew it, the more it becomes bland and flavorless.

C: That's true. I mean, again, at first all of those things in my life felt exciting. Exhilarating. But somewhere along the line they started feeling mundane.

T: They lost their flavor.

C: Right.

T: Jessica, in the dream you had some favorable associations to bubblegum—good memories of childhood, fun, blowing bubbles, playing house, dolls. What do you make of the fact that something representing good things to you ends up nearly choking you to death in your dream?

C: I don't know. Bubblegum to me is sort of emblematic of childhood.

T: What about the playing house and doll babies?

C: I used to love to play house. One year my dad made me this big wooden dollhouse. I just loved it! I would arrange my little dolls and pretend that this was really my house. I guess that was always one of my dreams as a child—to grow up and be a mom in my own house.

T: And that came true. Yet, in your dream the very thing that represents warm childhood hopes and memories ends up nearly choking you to death.

C: Yeah. All the things I have I've always wanted. But now that I have them, I feel overwhelmed.

T: Like too much of a good thing.

C: Right. And, you know, in the dream I'm the one who keeps sticking more bubblegum in my mouth. Even when I can hardly close my mouth anymore, I still try to fit more in.

T: So part of this you are doing to yourself?

C: Well, stepping back from things I can see that. Any one additional thing that I have tried to fit into my life—like volunteering on the school board—doesn't seem at the time like it would add too much stress to my life, but in totality my life is way too full.

T: So how does what you are telling me fit with the spiritual values you shared with me a few minutes ago?

C: Well, from the standpoint of the spiritual importance to me of my family and serving other people, I'm doing a lot of that. But in terms of my value on quiet time to pray and be alone with God—that's nonexistent.

T: So you're not getting something right now that is spiritually very important to you.

C: Yes, and I really miss that. When I used to take that spiritual time for myself, I felt like it was the one thing that helped me stay calm and keep my perspective.

The therapist can use the content of what the client shared in the spiritual-inquiry substage to broaden and deepen the client's interpretation of the dream. If the client jumps to a quick conclusion about what the dream might mean, the therapist can guide the client back to the content of the dream itself and encourage the client to incorporate parts of the dream that have not yet been assimilated into the interpretation. It can be particularly facilitative to remind the client of various associations that he or she made to dream images.

T: When you made associations to choking, you mentioned not being able to breathe. I wonder if your experience of choking in your dream might reflect your feeling that you can't breathe spiritually in your waking life.

C: That's right on. That's what it feels like—like I'm not getting what I need spiritually.

T: What's that like for you?

C: It feels like something is missing. I guess most of what I'm doing in my life feels on target with what is important to me. I mean, yeah, things are more hectic than I would like them to be, but it's like, "join the club." Whose life isn't? But when I'm getting what I need spiritually it seems to make everything else more manageable. It gives me a sense of peace that I haven't had in a long time.

T: So in the dream you are choking on something—something that is blocking your airway in a spiritual sense. What are you are choking on in real life?

C: Everything. Like I said earlier, I feel like I'm trying to fit too much in.

T: Like the bubblegum in your dream.

C: Right. I guess it is sort of like the bubblegum in that lots of the things I am trying to fit in are good. It's just that quantity of those things makes me feel like I'm choking.

T: All those things are choking out what is important to you spiritually—quiet time alone when you can reconnect with God and regain some perspective.

C: Yeah; I miss that.

For clients whose spirituality includes a concept of God, it can be powerful to revisit the idea of God communicating through dreams. Often this can deepen the session and provide a perspective on the dream not yet considered. However, it is important to ask about the client's beliefs regarding this possible dynamic before suggesting divine intervention in his or her dream.

T: I mentioned earlier that some people believe that dreams can provide guidance from outside ourselves—from God. How do you feel about that?

C: I guess that's possible. For me, I feel like I get the most spiritual guidance when I'm still and quiet. So, yeah, I could see getting that while I'm asleep.

T: So for you, right now, maybe when you're asleep is one of the few times that you're still long enough to receive some spiritual guidance.

C: Yeah, I think that's very possible.

T: Well, if that is the case, is there anything that you think God might be trying to say to you through this dream?

C: Just that I need to get back to what worked for me spiritually in the past. I didn't really realize how far away I've gotten from that. Maybe God is telling that I need to set some priorities in my life and make time for my own spiritual growth.

Toward the end of the insight stage, a large amount of material has usually been discussed, and the client and therapist may have considered many possible interpretations. To help the client sort out the material and consolidate what has been learned, the therapist can ask him or her to summarize the spiritual meaning of the dream.

T: How would you summarize what this dream means to you spiritually?

C: It's helped me see that I'm trying to fit too much into my life and that the result is that I'm really choking off my spiritual life. The more good stuff I try to cram in, the more I feel scattered and overwhelmed. I think it means that I need to step back and figure out how find time to feel more spiritually connected.

Action Stage

The purpose of the action stage is for therapists to help the client extend what he or she has learned during the previous stages and explore the possibility of making changes in his or her life. The action stage can begin with the therapist asking the client what changes she or he would like to make in the dream. Because the client created the dream initially, she or he can change it, too. Making changes in the dream is often a fun and creative way to get the client started in thinking about making specific changes in his or her life.

T: If you could change the dream in any way you wanted, how would you change it?

C: I wouldn't put so many pieces of gum in my mouth. I'd put just enough in to enjoy it. I'd blow some bubbles. Obviously, then I wouldn't feel scared—like I was choking.

T: So you'd have less in your mouth, but you'd enjoy it more.

C: Yea, I'd be chewing the gum, maybe even a lot of gum, but I'd be enjoying it. I wouldn't feel scared and overwhelmed. I'd still be able to breathe.

The next step involves bridging from making changes in the dream to making changes in the client's life. The therapist helps the client explore how changes in the dream parallel actual changes the client wants to make in his or her life.

T: So, how can "not putting so many pieces of bubblegum in your mouth" in your dream translate into a change that you can make in your waking life that could be beneficial to you?

C: I guess not trying to fit so much into my life. I guess a change that I could make would be to figure out what activities in my life are not important enough to me to allow them take time away from more important things.

T: More important things like what?

C: Like time to tend to myself spiritually. Quiet time when I can read, pray, or, you know, just sit quietly try to connect with God.

T: That sounds like it would be quite a contrast to your current life.

C: Yeah, I think that's why I need it so much. It's not just that I need to manage the pace of my life—I mean, I know that it is always going to be pretty hectic as long as I'm a mom. It's more that I need to put more of a priority on myself. I know that when I feel spiritually grounded, I feel like I have a framework for handling the rest of my life—even when the kids are fighting and the television is blaring—even the chaotic parts.

T: And how does putting aside spiritual-growth time help you do that?

C: It helps remind me of the stuff that is important to me—the spiritual principles that help me be the person I want to be.

T: What are some of those principles?

C: Like always trying to look for the best in other people. Recently I heard a reference to the scripture that says we are all made in the image of God. Just hearing that helped me to be more patient with people who usually annoy me. That concept sort of gave me a spiritual theme around which to conduct my life for the next few days. I like that. I also like that term you used, "spiritual-growth time."

T: Well, let's call it that, then. So what changes can you make in your life so that you actually get more spiritual-growth time?

C: I think that I just need to make that time a priority.

T: Sometimes setting a regular day and time when you are going to do something each week enhances the chances that you will get around to it.

C: That's a good idea. So maybe I could say that Tuesdays and Thursdays from 1:00–2:00—after I get home from working at the school—is my spiritual-growth time.

T: Right. And treat it like you would another appointment. If it is really a priority, then you don't allow other things to choke it out.

Finally, the therapist can ask the client to summarize what he or she learned from the dream and what he or she wants to do differently in life based on what was learned about the dream. This step can help the client sort through the large amount of material that has been discussed and clarify what he or she has learned.

T: As we wrap up, I'd like to have you summarize what you learned from the dream.

C: That I've lost any spiritual grounding. I've allowed the pace of my life and activities to choke out any sense of peace or meaningful connection with God. My spiritual life is important to me, but I haven't treated it like a priority. I think that getting back to putting aside time to work on my own spiritual development will not only help me spiritually but will also help me keep the other parts of my life in perspective.

FUTURE RESEARCH

Davis and Hill (2003) found that adding a spiritual component to Hill's (1996) cognitive–experiential model of dream work (see also Introduction and chap. 1–3, this volume) has therapeutic advantages for spiritually oriented clients. They compared a standard version of the cognitive–experiential model of dream work, in which clients explored their dreams from the perspective of events in their waking life, to a modified version of the model in which clients explored their dreams from the perspective of their spiritual beliefs. Fifty-one volunteer clients (all of whom were recruited from churches or considered themselves to be somewhat spiritual) completed two sessions of either waking life dream interpretation or two sessions of spiritual dream interpretation. Clients in both conditions increased general insight into their dreams and rated their sessions very favorably; however, clients in the spiritual condition experienced greater increases in existential well-being, which indicated that these clients had a more positive sense of life purpose and life satisfaction at the conclusion of their two sessions than clients in the waking life condition. Perhaps most impressive was the finding that the increase in existential well-being for clients in the spiritual condition was still present 1 month after they completed the second dream session. This finding was surprising given the brief nature of the intervention (two sessions). The results of Davis and Hill's study indicate that that helping spiritually oriented clients use their spiritual beliefs to explore and understand their dreams may be more therapeutically beneficial than nonspiritual approaches to dream work.

Future studies are needed to confirm Davis and Hill's (2003) findings. However, such studies should include a control condition consisting of spiritually attuned counseling that does not include dream interpretation. This will help answer the question of whether the benefits of spiritual dream interpretation in Davis and Hill's study were due to the blending together of dream interpretation and spiritual exploration or to the fact that spirituality was addressed at all.

Researchers need to continue studying the efficacy of dream interpretation as it relates to other dimensions of well-being. Davis and Hill (2003) appear to have made progress in identifying an appropriate instrument for measuring positive well-being: the Existential Well-Being subscale of the Spiritual Well-Being Scale (Ellison, 1983). However, researchers need to better understand the impact of spiritually based dream work on other dimensions of psychological well-being. One instrument that might be of interest to future researchers is the Psychological General Well-Being index (Dupuy, 1984).

Last, researchers should continue to investigate client spirituality and other trait characteristics that might influence the outcome of spiritual dream interpretation sessions. Future studies might include measures of religious experience (Hood, 1970), mystical orientation (Hood, 1975), and absorption or openness to experience (Tellegen & Atkinson, 1974).

CONCLUSIONS

Helping clients to assimilate their spiritual beliefs into an understanding of their dreams can be a therapeutically meaningful experience. Interpreting dreams from a spiritual perspective can help clients to access significant but underused parts of their psyches. The creative and often poetic nature of dreams provides a rich context for spiritual and religious exploration. The metaphors that often are present in dreams provide many dreamers with a language and framework for talking about their spiritual lives that may be otherwise lacking in their waking lives.

Given the empirical and anecdotal support for the benefits of incorporating spirituality into therapeutic treatment, it may be important for therapists to look for opportunities to explore spiritual concerns in therapy. Helping clients explore the spiritual relevance of their dreams provides such an opportunity.

REFERENCES

Bergin, A. E. (1983). Religiosity and mental health: A critical reevaluation and meta-analysis. *Professional Psychology: Research and Practice, 14,* 170–184.

Bulkeley, K. (1994). *The wilderness of dreams: Exploring the religious meanings of dreams in modern Western culture.* Albany: State University of New York Press.

Bulkeley, K (1999). *Visions of the night.* Albany: State University of New York Press.

Davis, T. L., & Hill, C. E. (2003). *Comparison of spiritual and waking life insight in the Hill cognitive–experiential model of dream interpretation.* Manuscript submitted for publication.

Davis, T. L., Kerr, B. A., & Robinson Kurpius, S. E. (in press). Meaning, purpose and religiosity in the lives of at-risk youth: The relationship between spirituality and anxiety. *Journal of Psychology and Theology, 31.*

Doniger, W., & Bulkeley, K. (1993). Why study dreams? A religious studies perspective. *Dreaming, 3,* 69–73.

Dupuy, H. (1984). The Psychological General Well Being (PGWB) index. In N. K. Wenger, M. E. Matterson, C. D. Furberg, & J. Elinson (Eds.), *Assessment of quality of life in clinical trials of cardiovascular therapies* (pp. 184–188). Greenwich, CT: Le Jacq.

Ellison, C. W. (1983). Spiritual well-being: Conceptualization and measurement. *Journal of Psychology and Theology, 11,* 330–340.

Gartner, J., Larson, D. B., & Allen, G. D. (1991). Religious commitment and mental health: A review of the empirical literature. *Journal of Psychology and Theology, 19,* 6–25.

Glenn, N. D., & Weaver, C. N., (1978). A multi-variate, multi-survey study of marital happiness. *Journal of Marriage and the Family, 40,* 269–282.

Hill, C. E. (1996). *Working with dreams in psychotherapy.* New York: Guilford Press.

Hill, P. C., & Hood, R. W. (1999). Affect, religion, and unconscious processes. *Journal of Personality, 67,* 1015–1046.

Hood, R. W. (1970). Religious orientation and the report of religious experience. *Journal for the Scientific Study of Religion, 9,* 285–291.

Hood, R. W. (1975). The construction and preliminary validation of a measure of reported mystical experience. *Journal for the Scientific Study of Religion, 14,* 29–41.

Jaffe, A. (1970). *The myth of meaning in the work of C. G. Jung.* London: Hodder & Stoughton.

James, W. (1958). *The varieties of religious experience.* New York: Mentor Books. (Original work published 1900)

Johnson, R. A. (1986). *Innerwork: Using dreams & active imagination for personal growth.* San Francisco: Harper & Row.

Jung, C. G. (1964). *Man and his symbols.* New York: Dell.

Koenig, H. G., Kvale, J. N., & Ferrel, C. (1988). Religion and well-being in later life. *The Gerontologist, 28,* 18–28.

Mahrer, A. R. (1990). *Dream work in psychotherapy and self-change.* New York: Norton.

Maton, K. I. (1989). The stress buffering role of spiritual support: Cross sectional and prospective investigations. *Journal for the Scientific Study of Religion, 28,* 310–323.

Miller, W. R., & Martin, J. E. (Eds.). (1988). *Behavior therapy and religion: Integrating spiritual and behavioral approaches to change.* Newbury Park, CA: Sage.

Rogalski, S., & Paisey, T. (1987). Neuroticism versus demographic variables as correlates of self-reported life satisfaction in a sample of older adults. *Personality and Individual Differences, 8,* 397–401.

Shafranske, E. P. (1996). Religious beliefs, affiliations, and practices of clinical psychologists. In E. P. Shafranske (Ed.), *Religion and the clinical practice of psychology* (pp. 149–162). Washington, DC: American Psychological Association.

Tellegen, A., & Atkinson, G. (1974). Openness to absorbing and self-altering experiences ("absorption"), a trait related to hypnotic susceptibility. *Journal of Abnormal Psychology, 83,* 268-277.

Van de Castle, R. L. (1994). *Our dreaming mind.* New York: Random House.

Webster's new world dictionary of the American language (2nd college ed.). (1984). New York: Simon & Schuster.

Wollmering, B. (1997). Dreams & spirituality: An historical perspective. *Dreamtime, 14*(2), 6–7.

Zinnbauer, B. J., Pargament, K. I., Cole, B., Rye, M. S., Butter, E. M., Belavich, T. G., et al. (1997). Religion and spirituality: Unfuzzying the fuzzy. *Journal for the Scientific Study of Religion, 36,* 549–564.

8

DREAMS OF THE BEREAVED

SHIRLEY A. HESS

Losing a loved one to death is an unavoidable experience for many individuals, and with this experience come normal grief reactions (e.g., Parkes, 2001; Rando, 1993; Sanders, 1999; Stroebe, Stroebe, Schut, & van den Bout, 1998; Worden, 2002). Affective reactions may include depression, anxiety, loneliness, guilt, and anger. Cognitive manifestations of grief may be depicted by disbelief, confusion, hallucinations, lowered self-esteem, and helplessness. Physiological and somatic reactions may include loss of appetite, sleep disturbance, fatigue, and somatic and physical complaints. Finally, behavioral manifestations can include social withdrawal, restlessness, and crying. Although many mental health professionals are well prepared to address these signs and symptoms in their work with bereaved individuals, they may not be as prepared to address another frequent occurrence: bereaved persons' dreams and nightmares related to the deceased.

Dreams of the bereaved typically are vivid and filled with emotion, and they affect the world of the dreamer in meaningful ways (Garfield, 1997). Often, clients may be startled, confused, comforted, or angered by these dream experiences and may not know that their dreams are normal.

Clients may believe they are "going crazy," "losing it," or "abnormal" when confronted with these dreams. Making the assumption that dreams are important, and asking bereaved clients about their dreams, gives clients permission to bring these experiences to counseling (Crook & Hill, in press) and may provide them a sense of relief and normalcy. Once clients feel validated in talking about their dreams, appropriately trained counselors can facilitate clients' understanding of their dreams.

This chapter provides counselors with the tools for working with bereaved clients' dreams by grounding the dreams in Worden's (2002) "tasks of mourning" with Hill's (1996) cognitive–experiential model of working with dreams. First, I introduce Worden's tasks, and then I discuss the concepts of grief work and dream work. Next, I present a dream representing each task and discuss them within the framework of Hill's model, which comprises three stages: (a) exploration, (b) insight, and (c) action.

Worden (2002) proposed that people experience four tasks of mourning in adapting to loss. The four tasks include (a) accepting the reality of the loss, (b) working through the pain of grief, (c) adjusting to the environment without the deceased, and (d) emotionally "relocating" the deceased and moving on with life. Many models of grief counseling describe phases (e.g., numbing, disorganization, reorganization) through which clients pass in the journey of healing (James & Cherry, 1988; Kubler-Ross, 1975; Parkes, 2001; Worden, 2002). Although Worden (2002) acknowledged the existence of these phases, he suggested that they are passive. He purported, in contrast, that *tasks* imply an active process by which bereaved persons can take action and counselors can intervene in the grief process. Because the death of a loved one leaves the bereaved feeling helpless and overwhelmed, viewing the grief process from the perspective of tasks to be completed gives the mourner hope that he or she can have some control in this process (Worden, 2002).

Worden (2002) likened this active process of completing tasks of mourning to *grief work* (Bowlby, 1980; Freud, 1917/1957), which is conceptualized as a cognitive process of confronting the loss, restructuring thoughts about the deceased and the loss experience, and adapting to life without the deceased (Stroebe, Hansson, Stroebe, & Schut, 2001). Grief work is analogous to the assimilation and accommodation process clients experience in dream work in which relevant schemas are activated by events of waking life, experiences are assimilated into existing schemas, and schemas are reorganized to accommodate the new information (Hill, 1996). Whereas talking about dreams can be cathartic for clients, actually working with the dreams can provide clients a powerfully rich experience of increased awareness and insight and can move the client to action. The dreams I describe in the sections that follow depict the tasks of mourning and were drawn from my work with bereaved clients or students. The names used in the dreams are pseudonyms.

TASK 1: ACCEPT THE REALITY OF THE LOSS

After the loss of a loved one, a bereaved person often may find him- or herself enacting "searching behavior" (Parkes, 2001). Such behaviors include calling out for the person, mistaking a person walking down the street for the lost loved one, hearing the deceased's voice, or unconsciously setting a place at the table for the deceased. Likewise, the bereaved individual may dream about the deceased loved one. In the Harvard Child Bereavement Study, participants who were grieving a sudden loss of a spouse reported dreaming about the deceased spouse during the first few months after the death (Worden, 1996). Worden (2002) suggested that dreams during this time may be the "mind's way of validating the reality of the death, through the sharp contrast that occurs when one awakes from such a dream" (p. 30).

The first task of mourning, then, is to help the bereaved individual realize that the deceased is really dead and will not be coming back, at least not in a physical form. During this time, bereaved individuals are also faced with a change in their *assumptive world*, that is, the world as they once knew it. Adjusting to this change is part of this task (Stroebe & Schut, 2001).

The following dream is of a 19-year-old woman, Jan, whose best friend, Sharon, had been killed in a car accident. Two months after Sharon's death, Jan sought counseling to deal with the sudden and devastating loss of her friend. They had been best friends throughout high school and roomed together their freshman year in college. Jan was feeling depressed, was having difficulty sleeping, and was experiencing feelings of guilt. Prior to the accident, Jan and Sharon had had a falling out. They had set up a date to talk about their relationship, but Sharon was killed before they could sort out the problem. This dream occurred after 1 month of counseling, 3 months after Sharon's death.

> ***Dream:*** I am floating on a cloud, and I see my friend, Sharon, floating above me. She is dressed in a white flowing gown. She looks like an angel. I reach for her and she is reaching for me, but there is a barrier between us. I can't see the barrier, but I know it is there. She drifts away and I can no longer see her. She is gone. I wake up. A part of me believes Sharon is not really dead. I feel very sad and upset that I can't touch her. I don't want her to be dead.

Exploration

Although Jan was surprised and happy to see Sharon floating above her, she experienced frustration and helplessness at not being able to connect with Sharon because of the barrier. On awaking, Jan felt sad and upset when the realization hit her that Sharon was dead.

Jan's associations to "floating" and "cloud" reflected freedom, peacefulness, a "sense of being in my own world," and "being out of sight." She also had the sensation of being unable to see clearly. When Jan talked about her associations to "friend," tears began to flow as she described the closeness and love she and Sharon had shared and the struggle that had recently dampened their relationship.

Jan saw Sharon as "above" her, better than her, and at a higher level. She imagined Sharon "floating around in heaven." The associations to "white flowing gown" and "angel" seemed to go together, representing a spiritual being, freedom, purity, and a transformation of some sort. The white flowing gown also reminded Jan of a bride, and the feeling she had of wanting to be united with Sharon.

The most troubling part of the dream occurred when both Jan and Sharon were reaching for each other and were unable to touch because of the barrier. Associations to "reaching" led to feelings of helplessness and panic at not being able to connect. "We were unable to reach each other. I felt so desperate to touch her, and I could sense that she desperately wanted to connect with me, almost like she wanted to pull me there with her." Jan couldn't see the barrier, the thing that kept them from reaching each other, but she knew it was there. She commented that she really didn't know what had happened to their relationship—"We just seemed to drift apart, just like in the dream. Something just went wrong, and we didn't get a chance to make it right again."

Insight

To Jan, the dream mirrored the relationship struggle, the "barrier" she and Sharon had experienced, as well as their attempt to reconnect with one another. One thing Jan noticed in the dream was that although both of them were reaching for each other, Sharon was the one who drifted away. Jan had made the call to Sharon to set up a time to try to work things out, and it was Sharon who left (died). Jan also came to realize that she felt abandoned by Sharon when Sharon "chose her boyfriend over me."

As Jan and I explored the dream, its meaning became obvious to Jan. She knew it was about "unfinished business" related to their relationship. Since Sharon's death, Jan had been plagued by feelings of guilt for letting the relationship remain unresolved and for allowing her unexpressed anger and hurt keep them apart. "Why was I so petty? I loved her, and now it's too late; she is gone." The painful realization of death's permanency hit Jan very hard.

Jan believed that the invisible, but felt, barrier was her inability to recognize and acknowledge the true intensity of the feelings she had for Sharon. "How ironic; I didn't talk with her about my feelings because I thought she would leave me, that she would not want to be my friend." There was some consolation in knowing that she and Sharon had agreed to reconnect. Jan believed that had the reunion occurred, they would have resolved, or at least talked about, what had happened in their relationship.

In addition to interpreting the dream from a framework of waking life and inner conflicts, Jan chose to work at a spiritual level. As discussed in chapter 7 of this volume, clients who are open to working at a spiritual level can experience significant comfort and relief. Jan's belief that Sharon knew of Jan's pain, that she wanted to connect with Jan, and that her spirit was present with Jan facilitated Jan's work in the action stage.

Action

Jan said that if she could have changed one thing in the dream, she and Sharon would have made a physical connection. Although she felt the intensity of the spiritual connection as her eyes met Sharon's in the dream, she wanted their hands to actually touch. Jan believed Sharon was in tune with her and knew the pain and hurt she was experiencing, yet Jan wanted the physical reassurance that she and Sharon were connected, that they had reconnected the relationship.

Jan thought that being able to touch in the dream symbolized the healing of the relationship. Because Jan believed that Sharon also wanted to reconnect, Jan was able to work on the relationship without Sharon's physical presence. Although the time they had set aside for reconciliation was not realized because of Sharon's death, Jan believed Sharon could hear her and could sense what Jan wanted to discuss with her. Jan decided to write a letter to Sharon and to bring it to the next therapy session. By reading and discussing the letter, Jan was able to address the many feelings she had about Sharon and their relationship. Jan also engaged in a two-chair dialogue that heightened the exploration of her feelings and enabled her to imagine what Sharon would have said to her. During the two-chair dialogue, Jan felt very close to Sharon, as if her spirit were present in the room. The experience was very healing for Jan.

Discussion

As an example of the first task of mourning, this dream illustrated the elusiveness and spirit form of the deceased. The dreamer reached for the loved one but was unable to touch or make contact with the deceased, reflecting a yearning to make a physical connection with the deceased. On awakening, the dreamer was upset when she realized the loved one was dead and that all hope of physically contacting the deceased was gone.

The goal in addressing dreams symbolizing Worden's (2002) first task is to allow the client to tell the dream and process his or her feelings surrounding the dream experience and the loss. Talking about the dream may lead to feelings connected to the way the loved one died, problems that existed in the relationship, the wish for the deceased to be alive, what the death means to the client, or what life is like now that the loved one is gone. As was evidenced by the processing of the above dream, Jan's action enabled her to work through some of the feelings about her relationship with Sharon and begin to heal from the loss.

TASK 2: WORK THROUGH THE PAIN OF THE GRIEF

Once a bereaved person has accepted the reality of the loss of a loved one, he or she also frequently experiences emotional and physical pain. For the bereaved person to progress through the process of mourning, he or she must acknowledge and work through the pain (Parkes, 2001; Worden, 2002). If such pain remains unacknowledged, "sooner or later, some of those who avoid all conscious grieving, break down—usually with some form of depression" (Bowlby, 1980, p. 158). If the bereaved avoid or suppress the pain in their waking lives, such feelings may confront the bereaved in their dreams, as illustrated in the next dream.

The following dream is that of an adult woman, Sally, whose mother died after a long illness a little over a year before the dream. Sally sought therapy 9 months after her mother's death because of major depression and a breakup of a significant relationship. Although Sally's dream was comforting on some level, aspects of the dream had a nightmare quality. As discussed in chapter 10 of this volume, it is important to help clients feel safe, supported, and in control as they re-experience a nightmare. It is fortunate that a trusting therapeutic relationship had been established with Sally; this facilitated exploration of her dream.

Sally had the dream the night before Mother's Day. This timing is certainly a reminder of how potent anniversaries and special days (e.g., holidays) are and how they can trigger lingering unresolved feelings and thoughts. This dream occurred about 4 months into therapy.

> **Dream:** I am in a funeral parlor, but it has a hallway shaped like a T, and my mother is in a casket. The casket is open and she is at the head of the T. I am standing over her, and she begins twitching like she did the day she died in the hospital. I turn away and slap my face. I can't believe this is happening. Then she yawns, and I say, "Mom, are you there?" Her eyes try to open, and as they do she says, "Yes, I'm here." She gets up and says, "I have to go." She disappears down the hallway through a door. I run down the hallway, through the door, but she is not there. I sit down on the floor and begin to sob. I can't stop crying. When I look down the hallway, my mother is in the casket, dead, like at the viewing and funeral. I feel myself withdraw. I can see and feel myself pulling away, fading out of sight like I did when I realized my mother was dying.

Sally felt disbelief that the tormenting hospital scene was being replayed in her dream. Although her mother died with her family around her, she had a "difficult death." It was comforting for Sally to hear her mother say, "I am here," but those words were offset by the casket and the twitching. Sally also expressed feeling upset and panicked throughout the dream. On awakening from the dream, she felt afraid, sad, and numb.

It was important to help Sally manage her anxiety while working with this dream, especially with the invasive image of her mother's "twitching." At times during the exploration process Sally's anxiety was monitored, and relaxation techniques were used to lessen the emotional intensity of the dream images (see chap. 10, this volume).

Exploration

The predominant associations related to being closed off, stifled, and restricted (i.e., casket; T—not being able to go left or right, restricted, or blocked) coincided with Sally's experience of feeling closed off from herself, shut down at times, feeling withdrawn, and trying to ward off the strong emotions. Sally also connected the "fading away" in the dream to her current state of "going inside myself," feeling depressed, "not present," and numb.

Another powerful image was that of her mother saying "I am here." Although there was some temporary comfort in the dream associated with these words, Sally was not comforted by the thought that her mother may be with her in some spiritual sense. "It's not enough for her to be here in a spiritual sense; I want her physical presence. And even in the dream, she leaves."

Sally noticed the confusion about whether her mother was dead or just asleep. She commented that she still could not believe her mother was dead, and often the only thing she saw when she thought of her mother was the awful way her mother died (i.e., mother's face twitching, struggle, gasping, and panic). Although her mother said, "I have to go," Sally continued to search for her, trying to catch up to her. The dream ended with her mother in the casket, dead, not awakening. When asked about the sobbing, Sally described the uncontrollable "breakdowns" she had been experiencing since her mother's death. She wished she could control the tears, but the sadness was overwhelming. Sally said she knew the grief process took time, but the pain was unbearable at times.

Insight

Sally's reactions to the feelings of sadness, coupled with panic, fear, and numbing, were analogous to how she was feeling in her waking life. She described feeling depressed and unfocused; not sleeping well; and experiencing alternating periods of intense emotion and feeling that she was distant, in another world. She related the panic and fear to having to confront the "gut-wrenching" awareness of her mother's impending death while she was in the hospital. There was a feeling of despair and unbelievable helplessness. The opportunity to talk with her mother about the things she wished she had said to her was gone; this awareness also brought a devastating sense of panic. Since her mother's death, she had been experiencing similar feelings of panic, despair, and helplessness. Sally also wondered whether the searching in the dream was symbolic of how disconnected from herself she had been feeling and how she had been trying to "recover [her] lost self."

Action

Sally had concerns about uncontrollable breakdowns. She wanted to have more control over when and how her grieving occurred. We talked about setting aside time during the day to allow the feelings to emerge in a safe place. Although she was uncertain whether this would help, she was willing to try to set some time aside each day. As discussed in chap. 10, relaxation and grounding techniques were reinforced to help Sally mange her "uncontrollable breakdowns" outside of therapy. She also decided to play some of her mother's favorite music, light a candle, and talk to her mother during this time. The thought of taking these actions seemed comforting to Sally.

When asked what she would change about the dream if she could, Sally said she wanted her mother to stay with her after she awakened and not "have to go." She also wished her mother were not twitching in the dream. Of course, she realized that to have these changes would mean her mother would be alive. We explored this further, and Sally related that she wanted her mother to stay around so she could talk with her. There was much left unsaid and unresolved in the relationship. We talked about the "unfinished business," and I introduced the empty-chair technique. Sally was open to us working with the technique during the next session. She also thought that it would be helpful to pull together pictures of her mother before her mother became ill, so she could implant those happier pictures in her mind rather than the horrible death scene. Sally was invited to bring some of the pictures of her mother to our next session. This form of imagery rehearsal (chap. 10, this volume) was used to help replace an aversive image with more positive images.

Discussion

Sally's dream depicted the fluidity of grief, as the dream contained characteristics of both Tasks 1 and 2. Sally was struggling to come to terms with not only the death of her mother and the meaning the loss has for her but also with how her mother died. The searching behavior, coupled with the ambivalence between her mother being dead or alive, clearly illustrated

Sally's struggle to accept the reality of her mother's death, which is typical of Task 1. Working with the dream images (e.g., casket, end of the dream) and talking about the reality of the loss helped to address Task 1.

Although she still had some disbelief that her mother was dead, amidst the searching, Sally's pain and grief could be seen. Sally's sobbing in the dream, and our discussion of the pain, agony, and despair she had been experiencing in her waking life, illustrated the move toward working through the pain of grief (Task 2). Playing her mother's favorite music, bringing in pictures of her mother, and talking to her mother helped Sally acknowledge both the reality of the loss and the emotions triggered by the loss. Altering the dream, working with the empty-chair activity during the session, and setting aside time to grieve during the day helped Sally complete Task 2 by facilitating the working through of the pain and guilt.

Other important issues addressed in the dream were those related to Sally's relationship with her mother (i.e., lingering feelings of guilt, lack of closure and feeling unresolved) as well as the signs and symptoms of depression. Such issues may have contributed to Sally's difficulty in adapting to the reality of her mother's death (Rando, 1993, Worden, 1996).

TASK 3: ADJUST TO THE ENVIRONMENT IN WHICH THE DECEASED IS MISSING

Worden (2002) described three areas of adjustment often encountered by grieving individuals. He identified these adjustment areas as

> (1) external adjustments—how the death affects one's everyday functioning in the world; (2) internal adjustments—how the death affects one's sense of self; and (3) spiritual adjustments—how the death affects one's beliefs, values, and assumptions about the world. (p. 32)

These adjustments vary according to the type of relationship the bereaved had with the deceased.

The following dream occurred 5 months after Ann's 29-year-old brother, Doug, died from cancer. She and many of the family members were with him when he died. Although he fought a courageous battle, "let go," and died peacefully, it was difficult and agonizing to lose her brother at such a young age. This dream was one of the many dreams Ann worked on during her therapy. She originally sought therapy for depression; at the time of the dream, Ann had been in therapy for 4 years.

> **Dream:** My brother and I are going canoeing somewhere in western Virginia. We are talking on the phone, not face to face. He is telling me that it's close to a place called Iron something and it's difficult to get to. He says it's very cold there—even though it's in the 90s here where I am; it will be very cold there, below 30. It's between two mountains. I'm

not convinced it will be as cold as he is saying. I say, "How could it be so much colder there when in all the surrounding areas, it is in the 90s?" I am concerned about what to bring on the trip. He says, "You'll be okay, just bring warm clothing." It also seems like I am looking at a map as he is describing where it is and how difficult it is to get there. I am glad to be going canoeing with my brother, but I am also confused about the temperature difference and wonder if I can make the trip if it will be so difficult to get there, even though he says I'll be okay.

Exploration

The thought of going on a "canoe trip" with her brother Doug brought Ann much joy, as the two of them took a day canoeing trip the summer before he died. She described this experience as an important time with her brother—a wonderful memory. She missed him and wished they could share more trips.

The "mountains" were significant, because Doug loved the mountains. Mountains to Ann meant peacefulness and challenge and reminded her of a spiritual journey "to the mountaintop." Also, she had been planning to attend a grief workshop in the beautiful mountains of western Virginia.

The issue of communication was prevalent in the dream with the images of "telephone" and "face to face." There was a connection but also a barrier. The communication was stifled in some ways, more detached, because they were not really with one another. Doug said the site was "difficult to get to," which implied a struggle, work, and no clear path, yet if Ann had a "map" she would be able to plan out the trip and find her way.

Temperature also seemed significant in that "cold" represented Ann's last experience of Doug's body: stone, detachment, and separation. Also, the temperature being below 30 reminded Ann that Doug had not yet reached the age of 30, and "in the 90s" represented oppression, thirst, and Doug's death occurring in the 1990s. Ann experienced her brother as having the characteristics associated with "warmth" and "warm clothing" (e.g., protection, supportive, friendly, gentle). This contrast of cold and warmth was symbolic of death and life.

Similarly, being "between two mountains" signified being between two worlds: life and death. Ann was reminded of the night her brother died and his ability to communicate what was happening for him in this in-between place. "In-between" also represented to Ann feeling stuck, indecisive, and unsure. In the dream, Ann doubted that the place Doug described was really that cold. She said that "Sometimes I don't really believe he is dead; it's hard to accept."

As she discussed the "in-between" connections, Ann described how she had been feeling lost, in the middle, between two worlds, trying to make the right decision, and not knowing which way to go. She had been feeling stuck, helpless, and confused as a result of her brother's death. Ann had also experienced herself withdrawing and feeling detached from others, the world, and her "self." She was not sure she had the confidence to pursue the things she needed—and, on some level, wanted—to pursue. She had been feeling fragile and confused.

Insight

Ann took very powerful messages from this dream, relaying how Doug had taught her that it was okay to let go of one's physical body (i.e., to not be trapped in what is not working) and to be free to go on to another level of living. "Just as he transcended the physical pain, the hurt, and went to a more peace-filled, contented existence, I am experiencing a similar, yet very different, transcendence." She described not having to be trapped in a past of suffering and painful experiences. She could transcend it all, move out of it, beyond it, and above it to a more peaceful and contented existence. She could be free to explore: "My soul has been set free—I'm finding my way to a new and better life."

Although she felt empowered by the dream, Ann described how the confusing map indicated that she wasn't sure how to get to this place of peacefulness. On further reflection, she said that she believed the message related to the map was that it was up to her to know how to get there but that it would be hard. "I just have to trust that I can find the way—the spiritual journey—it's unfolding, it's within me." It was meaningful that in the dream Doug told her she would be "okay," that she would find her way. Yet there was some doubt in the dream. Ann did not want to believe that Doug was dead, and she doubted she would ever see him again, yet she was aware that although she could not communicate with Doug in person (i.e., she spoke to him by telephone in the dream), she could still talk with him and connect with him in some way.

> Even though his physical body is cold, I can still reach him if I wear the right apparel. If I put on warmth—warmth reminds me of connection, a warm presence—I will find the way. There is no right way of getting there—no map—it's a struggle, but I'll know the right path. Intuitively, I'll know.

She also believed that the dream was telling her she could find her way in other areas as well, that she had the strength to push on and pursue the goals she had been questioning.

Action

When asked how she would change the dream, Ann responded by saying the map would not be as confusing. Even if the journey were difficult and a struggle, having a clear map would help. Yet it seemed to Ann that no one could provide her with a map; only she knew the direction. The way was within her and would become clearer to her if she were able to embrace the journey. As a result of this dream and her brother's message that she would be okay, she believed she could use his model of courage, "letting go," and his love, to move from "this stuck place."

As a result of her exploration of the dream, Ann decided to "go to the mountains," plant a tree in memory of her brother, and spend some time just "being with him" in this meaningful place. Ann also decided to give herself permission to walk, reflect, and absorb nature's healing energy.

Discussion

In this dream, the dreamer addressed the internal and spiritual adjustments that characterize Task 3. She was feeling ambivalent, uncertain, lost, and helpless. Worden (2002) referred to this type of internal adjustment as characterized by dealing with issues of self-efficacy. As a result of working on the dream, and especially through her brother's words of encouragement, Ann began to believe that she had the strength to face the journey; she would be able to find her way and get through and over the mountain.

In addition to internal adjustment, Ann's dream also addressed spiritual adjustment. Worden (2002) defined *spiritual adjustment* as finding meaning in the loss. Ann's life changed when her brother died: Her assumptive world was shaken, and she felt stuck on a path without direction. Ann found meaning in the message from the dream that encouraged her to transcend the pain and suffering, to move to a higher level of being, to accept the challenge with courage and reflection.

The metaphors present in the dream were powerful tools for Ann, as she reflected on the "journey to the mountain" and what that meant to her spiritually. Because mountains were one of her brother's favorite places, the meaning of the image was heightened by this connection to him. Similar to the discussion in chap. 7 of this volume, Ann's dream helped her address existential issues such as the spiritual dynamics within her life, transcendent reality, and deep meaningful personal values.

TASK 4: EMOTIONALLY RELOCATING THE DECEASED AND MOVING ON WITH LIFE

People who have lost a loved one to death know the struggle of adapting to the loss and "going on" after experiencing a loss. Worden (2002) stated that people do not give up the relationship; they "find an appropriate place for the dead in our emotional lives" (p. 36). The goal is to invest energy in new relationships and new roles, reconnect with old relationships, and pursue new goals that do not directly involve the deceased. It is important to discover how to keep the memories and influences of the deceased with one while going on with one's life, and to invest energy in the person one is without the deceased.

A graduate student, Brenda, agreed to discuss the following dream with me. The dream occurred a few months after Brenda's grandfather died unexpectedly. Brenda was 19 at the time of the dream. She lived in the Midwest, and her grandfather lived in the northwest United States. As a consequence, she saw him only once a year. Brenda was the first grandchild, so there was a strong connection between her and her grandfather: "He uplifted me." They had a close relationship even though they could not see one another frequently. The last time Brenda had seen her grandfather was at her high school graduation. Despite his health problems, he told the doctor that he was not going to miss his granddaughter's graduation. Brenda described the following dream.

> **Dream:** My parents are arguing, but I don't know what about. They never argue, so this is very unusual. I am there with them, but it's like I am observing because they don't sense I am there or acknowledge my presence. I am upset by their arguing. The next thing I notice is that I'm in a movie theater, standing in the back. I am thinking about my parents arguing and I'm feeling upset. I notice that my grandfather is sitting there in the movie theater—he turns toward me. I am surprised and shocked, but happy. I am sitting there with him, in the row behind him. We are talking, and I am telling him about school and how I am doing. He says, "It will be okay." I tell him that I miss him and give him a hug. His presence is very real. When I wake up, I have to jar myself back to reality.

After the dream, Brenda felt confused, because the dream "felt so real. I felt like I had spoken to my grandfather in a spiritual sense. I felt very much at peace." Other emotions included feeling upset earlier in the dream when her parents were arguing. She felt frustrated because she couldn't help.

Exploration

One of the parts of the dream that stood out for Brenda was her parents "arguing" in the dream. Brenda said it was unusual for her parents to argue, yell, or fight. She "couldn't believe it" was happening. When her parents were arguing, she felt "not seen/noticed," which she associated to feeling frustrated, sad, helpless, alone, and transparent, similar to how she was feeling after her grandfather's death. The next part of the dream took place in a "movie theater," which represented "escape," "quiet," "calm," "relaxing," and "anonymous" to Brenda. She was "sitting in the back," which highlighted the bigness of the theater and that "so much [was] in front of me." Brenda described how in her waking life she realized that there was so much ahead of her but that she didn't know exactly what it would be. When her grandfather remarked that "it will be okay," she said it made her realize that everything would be okay because he was there and "he will take care of me; I will be okay."

Insight

Brenda described what was happening in her life during the time between her grandfather's death and the dream. Two weeks after Brenda's grandfather died, her brother's best friend was killed. Soon after the two losses, Brenda had to return to college. It was hard for her to believe that she was actually back in school after everything that had happened. She was very worried about her brother. Brenda remembered walking down the street, crying, and asking her grandfather to take care of her brother. At that moment, she felt like he was there and that he would take care of her brother. During this time, she poured herself into work. Also, she did not feel safe being alone, so she spent as much time with other people as she could. She felt lost, unsure of herself, alone, and in the dark. She wasn't sure where she was headed.

In addition to a feeling of being lost, the dream reflected Brenda's feelings of passivity and helplessness. As she talked about the beginning of the dream, she sometimes wondered whether her parents were "truly happy." Her parents arguing was unusual and unexpected, and she felt helpless to intervene. She also felt like an observer, removed from the scene, and at a distance. She likened this to how she was feeling distanced from herself, far away from home, and not able to intervene to help her brother. Because Brenda didn't allow others to know the pain she was experiencing, she felt unnoticed and transparent, as if others were just looking through her. She also connected to the feelings of anger and frustration. She was angry that her grandfather died and that her brother had to endure this devastating loss. Both events were unexpected, happened so close to one another, and left her feeling alone.

Although part of the dream exemplified Brenda's waking life experiences of disconnectedness, Brenda also experienced the dream as a "supernatural connection." The peace that came over her as a result of the dream was comforting. After she talked with her grandfather about what was happening in her life, he told her "it will be okay." This was a very powerful message to Brenda that was evidenced by the subsequent absence of her grandfather in her dreams. Brenda thought that because she believed she was going to be okay, she didn't need to see him. In fact, she felt closer to him now than when he was alive, because she knew he would always be with her.

Action

As a result of her encounter with her grandfather in the dream, Brenda decided it was time to "look at the future and begin to tackle the things I am struggling with;" she could now go on with her life. She now had a direction and the energy to pursue it. She began to believe that she would be okay, because her grandfather was going to be with her.

Brenda said that if she could have changed the dream in some way, she would have had more time in the movie theater with her grandfather. To Brenda, movie theaters represented an escape from the stress, a time to reflect and think, and a place of quiet and calm. She felt a need to make time for the symbolic representation of the "movie theater." She decided to give herself time for quiet and reflection, which she thought would assist her in moving on with her life and pursuing the path that was becoming clearer to her. She now had some sense of direction and decided to take steps to address her struggles.

Extending her time in the movie theater also meant more time with her grandfather. Brenda longed for the comfort and physical closeness she experienced when she was talking with him and hugging him, yet she was very clear that the effect of the dream was that she didn't need the physical presence because "I sense, feel—I know his presence will always be a part of me."

Discussion

Prior to this dream, Brenda was struggling with issues related to Task 3, particularly in the areas of external adjustments (i.e., she was having difficulty functioning effectively in the environment) and internal adjustments (she was experiencing a diminished sense of self). As a result of the dream, Brenda began to tackle Task 4. She began to feel increased self-efficacy and believed she was going to make it along this path because she now had a place for her grandfather (i.e., he would be with her). She moved forward and began developing a new sense of self.

RESEARCH

Much of the empirical research about bereavement and dreams is descriptive in nature and has investigated the themes of the dreams of bereaved individuals. Only two studies dealing with loss have used the Hill model of dream interpretation. Falk and Hill (1995) explored the effectiveness of dream interpretation groups for women experiencing transition due to divorce. In another study, Hill et al. (2000) compared the efficacy of therapy that focused on dreams with therapy that followed a structured three-stage approach. Fourteen clients with troubling dreams and a recent loss of a loved one participated in brief structured therapy. Although 8 of the 14 clients discussed a loss due to death, the results were reported by condition, not by type of loss. These two studies found that dream interpretation led to high levels of insight and depth (quality).

Given these findings, of interest would be a study designed similarly to Hill et al.'s (2000), in which the efficacy of "traditional" therapy is compared with therapy focusing on dreams and the loss is identified as death of a loved one. Also, a powerful and supportive resource for people grieving the death of a loved one is a bereavement group. Does the use of dream work in a group setting strengthen the cohesiveness of the group, provide normalization of dream experiences, and allow the members to benefit from each other's exploration of dreams? Given the power of bereavement dreams, might such a group experience provide increased insight, self-understanding, and movement toward action? Finally, might research reveal that the gains of group work are more apparent when dreams are used as the focus rather than when traditional group work is done?

CONCLUSIONS

As can be seen by the examples in this chapter that illustrate Worden's (2002) tasks of grief, exploring dreams is a powerful tool in helping bereaved clients heal from their losses. I have found that clients want to share their dreams, particularly after the death of a loved one. Often these dreams are seen as gifts from the deceased, and even dreams of suffering and pain can provide important messages for the dreamer. Because the attachment to the deceased is broken through death, clients typically yearn for the attachment to be reconnected. Dreams of the deceased keep that connection in place, at least until the bereaved individual can move through the four tasks and find a way to remember the deceased without needing his or her physical presence of the loved one.

REFERENCES

Bowlby, J. (1980). *Attachment and loss: Vol. 3. Loss, sadness, and depression.* New York: Basic Books.

Crook, R. E. & Hill, C. E. (2003). Client reactions to working with dreams in therapy. Manuscript in preparation.

Falk, D., & Hill, C. E. (1995). The effectiveness of dream interpretation groups for women undergoing a divorce transition. *Dreaming, 5,* 29–42.

Freud, S. (1957). Mourning and melancholia. In *The standard edition of the complete works of Sigmund Freud* (Vol. 14, pp. 239–260). London: Hogarth. (Original work published 1917)

Garfield, P. (1997). *The dream messenger: How dreams of the departed bring healing gifts.* New York: Simon & Schuster.

Hill, C. E. (1996). *Working with dreams in psychotherapy.* New York: Guilford Press.

Hill, C. E., Zack, J. S., Wonnell, T. L., Hoffman, M. A., Rochlen, A. B., Goldberg, J. L., et al. (2000). Structured brief therapy with a focus on dreams or loss for clients with troubling dreams and recent loss. *Journal of Counseling Psychology, 47*, 90–101.

James, J. W. & Cherry, F. (1988). *The grief recovery handbook.* New York: Harper & Row.

Kubler-Ross, E. (1975). *The final stage of growth.* New York: Simon & Schuster.

Parkes, C. M. (2001). *Bereavement: Studies of grief in adult life* (3rd ed.). Philadelphia: Taylor & Francis.

Rando, T. A. (1993). *Treatment of complicated mourning.* Champaign, IL: Research Press.

Sanders, C. (1999). *Grief, the mourning after: Dealing with adult bereavement* (2nd ed.). New York: Wiley.

Stroebe, M. S., Hansson, R. O., Stroebe, W., & Schut, H. (2001). Introduction: Concepts and issues in contemporary research on bereavement. In M. Stroebe, R. Hansson, W. Stroebe, & H. Schut (Eds.), *Handbook of bereavement research* (pp. 3–22). Washington, DC: American Psychological Association.

Stroebe, M., & Schut, H. (2001). Models of coping with bereavement: A review. In M. Stroebe, R. Hansson, W. Stroebe, & H. Schut (Eds.), *Handbook of bereavement research* (pp. 375–404). Washington, DC: American Psychological Association.

Stroebe, M., Stroebe, W., Schut, H., & van den Bout, J. (1998). Bereavement. In H. Friedman, N. Adler, & R. D. Parke (Eds.), *Encyclopedia of mental health* (pp. 235–246). San Diego, CA: Academic Press.

Worden, J. W. (1996). *Children and grief: When a parent dies.* New York: Guilford Press.

Worden, J. W. (2002). *Grief counseling and grief therapy* (3rd ed.). New York: Springer.

9

USING DREAMS TO WORK WITH MALE CLIENTS

AARON B. ROCHLEN

The challenges of intervening therapeutically with male clients or prospective male clients has been well documented in the literature (Brooks & Good, 2001). Although different perspectives have been expressed, the majority of authors in this area have described the characteristics associated with interest and successful engagement in psychotherapy (including being emotionally expressive, intimate, etc.) as being in contrast with the values of the male culture and norms (Good, Gilbert, & Scher, 1990; O'Neil, 1981; Robertson & Fitzgerald, 1992; Wilcox & Forrest, 1992). This lack of fit between the culture of masculinity and the culture of therapy has frequently been described as presenting several challenges for counselors who work with male clients. It is not surprising, then, that men have also been found to underuse psychological services and have correspondingly more negative attitudes toward therapy compared with women (Fischer & Farina, 1995; Good et al., 1990; Robertson & Fitzgerald, 1992; Zeldow & Greenberg, 1980).

With regard to dreams and dream work in particular, significantly less research on men has been initiated, but several general gender differences with parallels to the psychotherapy literature have emerged. First, research has shown that men recall their dreams considerably less often than women (Cowen & Levin, 1995) and have less positive attitudes toward dreams (Robbins & Tanck, 1988). Second, researchers have documented content differences between men and women's dreams (Van de Castle, 1994). For example, compared with women, men's dreams have significantly more aggression, anxiety, and achievement outcomes. Women typically report dreams that have more female characters, friendly interactions, food references, and themes of internal pressure (Hall & Domhoff, 1963; Howard, 1979; Winget, Kramer, & Whitman, 1972).

Yet although gender differences in dream recall, attitude, and content have been investigated, considerably less is known about the process and outcome of conducting dream work with men versus women (see Hill & Goates, 2003). More information in this area could be useful not only to clinicians who apply the Hill cognitive–experiential model of dream work to male clients but also to researchers. Thus, in this chapter I integrate my own clinical and research experiences working with male clients with the literature on men and counseling to provide a description of the challenges, benefits, and common themes that may emerge in regard to working with men and dreams.

To meet these objectives, I describe segments of a dream brought into a single session of dream interpretation by Mel (a pseudonym), a 20-year-old Lebanese American college sophomore from a predominately middle-class, suburban town. This dream interpretation session was conducted as part of a recent study comparing computer- versus therapist-facilitated approaches to working with the Hill model (Hill, Rochlen, Zack, McCready, & Dematatis, in press). The therapist in this case, Tracy (also a pseudonym), was a 26-year-old female doctoral student. At the end of each of the three sections corresponding to the stages of the model (exploration, insight, and action), I provide a commentary on the interaction and a summary of the rest of the client–therapist dialogue. Permission from both therapist and client to reprint this dialogue has been received. Slight modifications in the transcript have been made.

> **Dream:** I'm walking down the street, and I see a convenience store. As I'm opening this unusually large door, I notice that the store sells Lebanese food. I'm walking around being very confused about what exactly it is that I'm looking for—yet it's clear that I'm looking for something. Suddenly, I'm waiting in line at the cash register with nothing to buy. A guy that I don't recognize starts pushing me from behind—telling me to get out of his way as he was in line first. At first I ask him to excuse himself, but he keeps pushing—harder and harder. I can feel the bruises building up on my spine. I realize that I need to fight back immediately, but as I'm trying to punch him back I notice I can't move my arms—they are just swaying with the momentum of my body as I'm trying to punch him. I feel embarrassed as the people in the store are laughing at me.

Finally, I regain my feelings in my arm, but before I can fight back, I wake up. I'm relieved to know it was only a dream.

EXPLORATION STAGE

T: Mel, how did you feel upon waking up from the dream?

C: What do you mean? I said I was relieved it was just a dream.

T: Any other feelings?

C: Not really, maybe a little frustrated I wasn't able to beat the guy up.

T: Okay, so a little frustration. Now, let's walk through some of these images using the DRAW acronym [Description, Re-experiencing, Associations, Waking life triggers] that I had discussed earlier. Let's start off with the scene of you walking down the street and seeing a convenience store. First, just describe this a little more for me.

C: It just looked like a regular street. It had four lanes, no traffic. Each lane was approximately 15 feet or so in width. The convenience store looked like a 7-Eleven, but it just had the word "convenience" written on the top of it. I walked directly from the street to the front door.

T: Can you give me a better sense of what it felt like as you were walking down the street and saw the convenience store? Maybe try and visualize it right now and get into the feelings and what your mind set was.

C: You know this isn't easy for me.

T: I know this is hard—but give it a shot. Often it is helpful to the process of learning from the dream to really try and get into the feelings and emotions.

C: Well, I know I felt kind of clueless walking around the street—I wasn't with my usual group of friends, which seemed a little disappointing I guess. I was very relieved to see the convenience store. I guess it helped to distract me away from what I was thinking.

T: Let's associate to some of these beginning images. I want you to tell me what you think of when I mention a street.

C: I think of all of the streets that I cross on my way to school.

T: And what is a street? What is it used for?

C: It's a slab of flat concrete used by vehicles and people to travel from one place to another.

T: Anything else?

C: Not really.

T: And did this particular street or the feelings that you described remind you of anything? Anything in your waking life that this seemed to reflect or represent for you?

C: I can't think of anything right now. It seemed like a normal street, and the feelings that I described didn't really seem particularly representative of anything at this point.

T: Well, let's try something else on one of the other images—the convenience store, as this seemed central to the dream. Pretend I was from Mars; describe to me precisely what a convenience store is and what it's used for.

C: I'd say that it is a place that people go to get things that they need. They tend to be centrally located. Often, with things in a convenience store, people aren't thrilled with the prices or the range of things to select from. But the location tends to be really nice and accessible. That's why they call it convenience, I guess.

T: Now, can you tell me if you've ever had an experience of walking into someplace that you went to for convenience, where you had purchased something despite not being thrilled with the selection or quality?

C: Are you asking if I've ever been to a convenience store? If so, yes. I buy deodorant, beer, and chips all the time by myself.

T: Okay. But let's try to think in a different way about the association that you had to convenience stores. For example, can you try to think of another situation you have been in where you did something just because it was convenient, but were not necessarily happy with the selection or even what you had purchased?

C: Well, hearing you say that again, it does make me think of a girl I was involved with my freshman year. I used to go up to her room all of the time. And honestly, it was just a matter of convenience, and I know that at times it was really hard for me to spend time with her. She ended up being very hurt when I broke up with her. I don't think I handled the whole thing very well.

Summary of the Remainder of the Exploration Stage

In the rest of the exploration stage, Mel was able to provide more detail and associations to many of the other dream images. Of particular importance were the scenes in which Mel was walking around aimlessly in the store and when he was being pushed by another man. When asked about his associations to walking around aimlessly, he said that it seemed very similar to his process of selecting a career. He has never been sure of what he has wanted to do professionally and somehow "fell into" a dual major in English and history. Mel described being pushed by another man while waiting in line as similar to the sense of competitiveness that men often have with each other. In addition, Mel provided a relevant association to the part of the dream in which he was unable to move his arms. He described this as a sense of feeling hopeless and without defense. Mel said that in situations similar to this he feels vulnerable to the insults and critiques of others (as in the dream, when others in the store were laughing at him). Finally, Mel provided associations to the "Lebanese food" that he described as being "unusual" and not "fitting in" with what seemed logical to be sold in an American convenience store. Through his associations and connections to waking life, Mel revealed that his mother is Lebanese and is heavily influenced by traditional Lebanese cultural values.

Commentary on Exploration Stage

Although the above segment from the exploration stage is brief, many challenges that could potentially emerge with other male clients can be noted. First, at several points the client was reluctant and resistant to the entire process of working with his dream. For example, at one point Mel openly expressed his annoyance with being asked about his feelings. Challenges in working with male clients could be due to a number of factors. First, authors have discussed the "culture" of therapy as being antithetical to the basic rules or codes of masculinity (Campbell, 1996; Meth, Pasick, & Gordon, 1990; Scher, 1981; Wilcox & Forrest, 1992). In other words, the characteristics associated with interest and successful engagement in psychotherapy (including being emotionally expressive, open, intimate, and comfortable with self-disclosure) stand in contrast with the values of the male culture (e.g., solving problems without the help of others, avoiding intimacy, refraining from expressing emotions).

This lack of congruence between the culture of a therapy session and men's typical values has relevance for working with men in dream interpretation. In the exploration stage, the therapist needs to encourage the client to reexperience the most salient components of the dream, elaborate on the details, and maintain an open and curious approach as to the client's thoughts and feelings about the dream and the dreamer. However, therapists also need to respect the difficulties and resistances that may emerge for the client without being overly challenging. One approach for reducing a client's resistance may include explaining why exploring feelings and other skills and techniques is important. With time, skeptical clients will ideally be more willing and able to express their emotions.

The second not-atypical challenge that can be observed in the above dialogue is Mel's concrete responses and the difficulty he seemed to have with responding to more abstract, metaphorical questions. For example, when asked to describe the function of a street, Mel provided an appropriate but concrete (no pun intended) response (e.g., a piece of concrete used as a means for vehicle transportation). This response clearly presents challenges in finding a meaningful personal association for therapists of all skill levels. In addition, it would not be inappropriate for the therapist to model what type of associations might be useful for the dream interpretation process. Rochlen, Ligiero, Hill, and Heaton (1999) found some evidence for the effectiveness of practicing the skills associated with the dream interpretation process for clients with low levels of dream recall and negative attitudes toward dreams.

Finally, Mel's difficulty with connecting the restated associations to meaningful waking life material should be noted. The therapist asked him about the familiarity of an experience of going somewhere that was convenient but not necessarily the "right place." Although rich for a meaningful association, Mel responded by saying that he uses convenience stores to "buy beer and chips." This response may reflect Mel's difficulty in thinking in more abstract terms. As a result, therapists should probe further when a client initially responds to a task with a very literal response.

INSIGHT STAGE

The beginning of the insight stage with Mel proceeded as follows.

T: So Mel, based on what we have explored already, can you put together a preliminary interpretation of what this dream means for you?

C: Well, I told you earlier, I'm not a big believer in this stuff. But if I had to put something together I'd have to say that it's reflecting my general character or personality. I like to go to convenience stores when at times I should really be taking my time to shop around for the best price. I like to find quick solutions to things even when I don't know what I'm looking for.

T: I think I'm following you on some of this. But can you tell me precisely how you are connecting that interpretation to the actual content of the dream and your earlier responses?

C: Well, in the dream I'm in this convenience store, and I do tend to go to places or hang out with people just because they are convenient and not necessarily because it is in my best interest. I like things that are done quick and easy. But sometimes that gets me in trouble. In the dream I end up getting my ass kicked in front of everyone else. Also, as I stated earlier, I'm not much of a fighter. I'm also not great at arguing myself out of situations. I think my hands being paralyzed represents this conflict. I'm not sure if this all fits or not—but if I had to give you a response this is what it would be.

C: Maybe it also has something to do with me floundering around in my career.

T: Mel, I think that's a great start. But I'm wondering if we can't try to work together to extend upon the initial interpretation. I'd like to work with you in looking at some of the interactions in the dream that happened between you and the characters.

C: Okay.

T: Earlier, you associated to the part of the dream where you were fighting with the other male customer as being a competition or a race to the register. In associating to the register, you said "where the money is stashed" and where you go to "pay for what you deserve and have worked hard for." Are there any instances in your life where you feel this competition with other men?

C: Well, I guess in my career this might be true. My friends and I are pretty competitive about what we will end up doing professionally. And I think there is a lot of pressure placed on me, and maybe other guys to make a lot of money and be successful. But right now, I'm struggling in some of my classes and am feeling the pressure to do a lot better.

T: That makes a lot of sense. In the dream you are literally struggling to fight back and have another guy who is trying to sneak ahead of you in line. I can sense that struggle you are talking about.

C: It's not that bad, but I guess it's there.

Summary of the Remainder of the Insight Stage

In the remainder of the insight stage, Mel was able to make several connections between the dream's content, associations, and his waking life that significantly extended his initial interpretation. Perhaps of greatest significance for him was the identification of an internal struggle between wanting to take the easy way out and putting in the effort and commitment necessary to make more productive decisions. Mel was able to connect much of this conflict to his early developmental years, when he identified a split between his overachieving mother, who adjusted to multiple life demands, and his father, whom he described as lazy and complacent.

Commentary on Insight Stage

In this beginning segment of the insight stage one can again see the emergence of several dynamics not atypical of dream work with other male clients. First, Mel's initial interpretation has themes that have personal relevance but seem to be a bit "loose." Mel was able to connect the dream to what seems to be his accurate style of looking for the easy solution in both his personal and professional lives. In addition, he was able to identify a parallel between his dream and waking life in that this style of convenience tends to lead to a number of problems for him.

Yet, it appears that a considerable amount of "missing data" or information for the dream has not yet been incorporated into the interpretation. First, Mel's manner of interpreting his dream seems to parallel his style of relating and behaving in the dream. His initial interpretation seems to be legitimate, yet a bit rushed and convenient. Second, his initial interpretation seems devoid of a significant emotional component. The difficulty with accessing and talking about emotions has been a source of considerable writing in men's counseling literature. For example, Levant (2001) coined the term *normative male alexithymia* to account for the common occurrence in men of alexithymia in mild to moderate form. Alexithymia was originally described by Sifneos (1967) and Krystal (1982) as being a condition characterized by severe emotional constriction encountered most often with men with an array of other psychiatric disorders, including drug dependence, posttraumatic stress disorder, and other psychosomatic disorders. Levant noted, however, that many men without debilitating disorders may have pronounced difficulty with recognizing and verbalizing their emotions.

A critical question in trying to move a session toward a deeper more emotional level involves considering the extent to which a therapist should provide his or her own ideas or should challenge the client. A central assumption of the Hill model of dream interpretation is that the dreamer needs to come to an understanding of the significance of the dream, as this cannot be provided by the therapist (Hill, 1996; Hill & Goates, 2003; Hill & Rochlen, 2002). Yet, for clients who may be skeptical of working with dreams, or who have difficulty working at a more emotional level, it seems inherently useful for therapists to not ignore their own intuition in generating possible interpretations. Of course, this should be done cautiously so that the therapist is not providing the final interpretation. If done effectively, however, therapist-generated interpretations can be particularly effective in facilitating clients' consideration of additional interpretations and understanding that dreams can have multiple meanings.

Another consideration for therapists working with male clients is to recognize common themes that may emerge when working with men. O'Neil's (1981; O'Neil, Helms, Gable, Laurence, & Wrightsman, 1986) model of gender role conflict, which describes the restrictive and conflictive components associated with the masculine male role identity, seems particularly promising for this purpose. O'Neil originally defined *gender role conflict* as a psychological state that occurs when rigid, sexist, or restrictive gender roles result in restriction of human potential, devaluation, or violation of self or others. Four dimensions to the gender role conflict construct have emerged. The *success, power, and competition* dimension pertains to the extent to which a man places importance on achievement, authority, control, and competition for material and personal gain. The *restrictive emotionality* dimension pertains to difficulty with emotional self-disclosure and expressiveness. The *restrictive affectionate behavior among men* dimension involves discomfort with emotional and physical closeness with other men. Finally, the *conflict between work and family relations* dimension pertains to the degree to which a man expresses distress due to difficulty in balancing work or school with personal and family responsibilities. Because these areas of a man's life may create or coexist with psychological distress (see O'Neil, Good, & Holmes, 1995, for a complete review), it is logical that these themes may surface in men's dreams.

Several of these gender role conflict dimensions can be identified in Mel's dream. For example, if one looks exclusively at the dream content, one sees that Mel is competing with the other man in the dream to be "first in line." This may represent possible struggles with achievement, competition, and fears of making it to the top. Second, I have already discussed examples of Mel's difficulty expressing feelings; this emerged both in the dream and when he shared his ambivalence about discussing his emotions with the therapist. Finally, based on Mel's association between walking aimlessly about in the store with his quest to find an appropriate career, themes pertaining to conflict surrounding work and school relations may be emerging. References pertaining to career identify, career indecision, and struggles with career satisfaction are not uncommon given the importance that men attach to career choice and related success (Rochlen, 2001; Skovholt, 1990; Zunker, 1994).

ACTION STAGE

T: Mel, if you could make any changes to this dream, what would they be?

C: I guess I would like to have my best friend Darren with me on the street. He is great with making sure I make good decisions.

T: Good; what else?

C: Well, I think this time I would skip the convenience store altogether. I would run to the quality department store on the other side of town. Once there, I would be sure about what I wanted to purchase. Not sure what that would be right now. But in the dream I'm sure I would know. And if I did see that guy, that was trying to sneak in front of me in line—I think I would want to kick his ass.

T: Really?

C: Well, yeah, I think that's what I would want to do. But I guess the better move would be to more effectively communicate to this guy to wait his turn. And then we will all be able to get what we want at the store.

T: Nice job. Now, I want to read back some of the changes you suggested making in the dream. I'm going to paraphrase things a bit. And I want you to just think about whether any of the things I am suggesting represent or parallel actual changes that you would like to make in your life. Am I clear with this?

C: Sure.

T: I noted the following changes. You would like to have someone with you who helps you make good decisions; you want to pass a place of convenience and go to a better, more high quality store; you want to be certain as to what you are purchasing; and you want to be able to effectively communicate with someone who was competitive with you. Which of those do you feel accurately represents changes you want to make in your life?

C: Well, the one that makes the most sense, at least initially, is passing by the convenience store. Like my dad, I tend to do things that are convenient or easy. Both in my relationships and in school this has not always been the best move for me.

T: Anything else that fits?

C: I would also say that I really do want to know what I'm looking for—and not walk around aimlessly as I was doing through the dream. This fits in several areas of my life, but especially in my career. Right now, I have no idea what kind of career fits with my education. I also feel the pressure to pick a career that is going to make a lot of money.

T: Nice work. Now, in the remainder of the time together today, let's really take a look at precisely how you can make some of these changes in your life.

Summary of the Remainder of the Action Stage

In the remainder of the action stage, the therapist and Mel identified other areas of Mel's life that he would like to change and considered ways he could meet those objectives. Ideas generated from the work in the action stage include visiting the campus career center to learn more about careers available to him, taking more time in his schedule to prioritize his values regarding his relationships, and practicing being more emotionally expressive to his parents and friends.

Commentary on Action Stage

Compared with the earlier stages, Mel seemed to have greater ease and expressed the least resistance in transitioning to the goals and objectives of the action stage. After some initial encouragement from the therapist, Mel was able to provide several changes to the dream and connect these changes to realistic considerations for changes in his waking life.

Although untested empirically, this tendency to find the action stage easier or perhaps more helpful than the earlier stages may be true for other men working with the Hill model. First, by the end of the third stage of the model male clients may feel more comfortable working with the therapist. In the sample dialogue presented earlier, Mel's defenses seemed to have subsided, perhaps because of this rapport as well as because he learned that several pieces of the dream seemed to make sense. Second, the action stage might be easier for male clients because it is considerably more directive and behaviorally oriented than the exploration and insight stages (Hill, 1996). Research conducted on a range of different types of counseling services has indicated that men prefer more structured, directive approaches to therapy over more open-ended, affective styles (Good & Sherrod, 2001; Robertson & Fitzgerald, 1992; Rochlen & O'Brien, 2002; Wisch, Mahalik, Hayes, & Nutt, 1995). Thus, it may be that men seem to work best in the action stage because of this directiveness. It is possible that men may like the focus on concrete behavioral changes, as this style provides a tangible focus of what precisely needs to be addressed in counseling.

It is important for therapists to recognize whether their client is overly focused on action to the exclusion of integrating the insights gained in the earlier phases of the model. In describing the action stage, Hill (chap. 3, this volume) cautioned that action without insight is often misdirected, does not remedy the problem, and may be built on faulty assumptions.

GENDER DYNAMICS

Another consideration in conducting dream work with male clients is the gender dynamics of the therapeutic relationship. Researchers have identified several possible barriers and benefits relevant to male client–male therapist and male client–female therapist dyads (Heppner & Gonzales, 1987; Johnson, 2001; Scher, 2001). In regard to male–male counseling dyads, authors have suggested that clients may have a heightened sense of shame and humiliation in opening up to another man as well as an inherent sense of competitiveness and difficulty in establishing trust and compassion. Possible advantages to a male–male counseling dyad include the male therapist appropriately modeling the expression of affect for clients and an increased ability for the male therapist to understand the challenges associated with the male role.

In regard to the male client–female therapist dyad, authors have discussed the challenges that may be presented by the reversal in power dynamics (i.e., with the female therapist being in a position of "power"), flirtatiousness or sexual tension in the counseling relationship, and the difficulty men may experience being emotional or vulnerable in front of a woman. Possible benefits associated with male–female counseling dyads include an improved capacity for connection, more support, and increased likelihood of male emotional expression (Carlson, 1987; Johnson, 2001).

Although yet untested empirically, therapists should consider these themes as they emerge in the process of dream work. Moreover, therapists should be aware of their own attitudes toward working with male clients and be able to provide therapy in a flexible manner to meet the needs and preferences of male clients.

FUTURE RESEARCH

As alluded to earlier, very little research has examined the unique considerations relevant to conducting dream work with male clients. The majority of the studies that have examined gender differences have demonstrated an equivalent and relatively high ability of both sexes to generate insight, self-understanding, and relative action plans based on participating in dream interpretation (Hill, Diemer, Hess, Hillyer, & Seeman, 1993; Hill et al., 2001; Hill et al., in press; Zack & Hill, 1998). However, in a study of heterosexual couples who worked with their dreams with a trained therapist, men seemed to benefit less from the process than did women (Kolchakian & Hill, 2002). In particular, female partners who received dream interpretation had greater improvements in relationship well-being, insight, and gains than female partners in the wait list condition. However, no differences emerged on these variables between men who participated in dream interpretation and male wait list control participants. In addition, a recent dream work outcome study showed that female clients demonstrated significantly more insight into their dreams from participating in a dream interpretation session than did male clients (Hill et al., in press).

Hence, at this point the research appears to be mixed in terms of whether most men have any significant advantages or disadvantages based on participating in dream work as compared with female clients. Future research should address within-group differences in studying male clients in the dream work process. Promising variables that may predict the types of men who may best benefit from dream interpretation include psychological-mindedness, gender role identity, openness to new experiences, intimacy, and need for closure. Also, further research should examine alterations in the actual technique or structure by which the Hill model of dream interpretation is conducted by different types of clients. For example, men may benefit from practice and explanation of the skills associated with dream interpretation. In addition, male clients may work best with more behaviorally oriented counselors; this has been suggested in several different studies (Rochlen & O'Brien, 2002; Wisch et al., 1995).

REFERENCES

Brooks, G. R., & Good, G. E. (2001). *The new handbook of psychotherapy and counseling with men*. San Francisco: Jossey-Bass.

Campbell, J. L. (1996). Traditional men in therapy: Obstacles and recommendations. *Journal of Psychological Practice, 2*, 40–45.

Carlson, N. L. (1987). Woman therapist: Male client. In M. Scher, M. Stevens, G. Good, & G. A. Eichenfield (Eds.), *Handbook of counseling and psychotherapy with men* (pp. 39–50). Newbury Park, CA: Sage.

Cowen, D., & Levin, R. (1995). The use of the Hartmann Boundary Questionnaire with an adolescent population. *Dreaming, 5*, 105–114.

Fischer, E. H., & Farina, A. (1995). Attitudes toward seeking professional psychological help: A shortened form and considerations for research. *Journal of College Student Development, 36*, 368–373.

Good, G. E., Gilbert, L. A., & Scher, M. (1990). Gender aware therapy: A synthesis of feminist therapy and knowledge about gender. *Journal of Counseling and Development, 68*, 376–380.

Good, G. E., & Sherrod, N. B. (2001). Men's problems and effective treatments: Theory and empirical support. In G. R. Brooks & G. E. Good (Eds.), *The new handbook of psychotherapy and counseling with men* (pp. 22–40). San Francisco: Jossey–Bass.

Hall, C., & Domhoff, B. (1963). A ubiquitous sex difference in dreams. *Journal of Personality and Social Psychology, 46*, 1109–1117.

Heppner, P. P., & Gonzales, D. S. (1987). Men counseling men. In M. Scher, M. Stevens, G. Good, & G. Eichenfield (Eds.), *Handbook of counseling and psychotherapy with men* (pp. 30–38). Beverly Hills, CA: Sage.

Hill, C. E. (1996). *Working with dreams in psychotherapy*. New York: Guilford Press.

Hill, C. E., Diemer, R., Hess, S., Hillyer, A., & Seeman, R. (1993). Are the effects of dream interpretation on session quality, insight, and emotions due to the dream itself, to projection, or to the interpretation process? *Dreaming, 3*, 269–280.

Hill, C. E., & Goates, M. K. (2003). Research on the Hill cognitive–experiential dream model. In C. E. Hill (Ed.) *Dream Work in Therapy: Facilitating Exploration, Insight, and Action*. (pp. 245–288). Washington DC: American Psychological Association.

Hill, C. E., Kelley, F. A., Davis, T. L., Crook, R. E., Maldonado, L. E., Turkson, M. A., Wonnell, T. L., Suthakaren, V., Zack, J. S., Rochlen, A. B., Kolchakian, M. R., & Codrington, J. N. (2001). Predictors of outcome of dream interpretation sessions: Volunteer client characteristics, dream characteristics, and type of interpretation. *Dreaming, 11*, 53–72.

Hill, C. E., & Rochlen, A. B. (2002). The Hill cognitive–experiential model of dream interpretation. *Journal of Cognitive Psychotherapy, 16*, 75–89.

Hill, C. E., Rochlen, A. B., Zack, J. S., McCready, T., & Dematatis, A. (in press). Working with dreams using the Hill cognitive–experiential model: A comparison of computer-assisted, therapist empathy, and therapist empathy + input conditions. *Journal of Counseling Psychology*.

Howard, M. (1979). Manifest dream content of adolescents. (Doctoral dissertation, Iowa State University, 1979) *Dissertation Abstracts International, 39,* 8–13: 4103.

Johnson, N. G. (2001). Women helping men: Strengths of and barriers to women therapists working with men clients. In G. R. Brooks & G. E. Good (Eds.), *The new handbook of psychotherapy and counseling with men* (pp. 696–718). San Francisco: Jossey-Bass.

Kolchakian, M. R., & Hill, C. E. (2002). Dream interpretation with heterosexual dating couples. *Dreaming, 12,* 1–16.

Krystal, H. (1982). Alexithymia and the effectiveness of psychoanalytic treatment. *International Journal of Psychoanalytic Psychotherapy, 9,* 353–378.

Levant, R. F. (2001). Desperately seeking language: Understanding, assessing, and treating normative male alexithymia. In G. R. Brooks & G. E. Good (Eds.), *The new handbook of psychotherapy and counseling with men* (pp. 424–443). San Francisco: Jossey-Bass.

Meth, R. L, Pasick, R. S., & Gordon, B. (1990). *Men in therapy: The challenge of change*. New York: Guilford Press.

O'Neil, J. M. (1981). Patterns of gender role conflict and strain: Sexism and fear of femininity in men's lives. *Personnel and Guidance Journal, 60,* 203–210.

O'Neil, J. M., Good, G. E., & Holmes, S. (1995). Fifteen years of theory and research on men's gender role conflict: New paradigms for empirical research. In R. Levant & W. Pollack (Eds.), *The new psychology of men* (pp. 164–206). New York: Basic Books.

O'Neil, J. M., Helms, B. J., Gable, R. K., Laurence, D., & Wrightsman, L. S. (1986). Gender-Role Conflict Scale: College men's fear of femininity. *Sex Roles, 14,* 335–350.

Robbins, P. R., & Tanck, R. H. (1988). Interest in dreams and dream recall. *Perceptual & Motor Skills, 66,* 291–294.

Robertson, J. M., & Fitzgerald, L. F. (1992). Overcoming the masculine mystique: Preferences for alternative forms of assistance among men who avoid counseling. *Journal of Counseling Psychology, 39,* 240–246.

Rochlen, A. B. (2001). Men and career counseling: New perspectives and directions for clinicians and administrators. *The Texas Psychologist, 52,* 18–23.

Rochlen, A. B., & O'Brien, K. M. (2002). The relation of male gender role conflict and attitudes toward career counseling to interest in and preferences for career counseling styles. *Psychology of Men and Masculinity, 3,* 9–21.

Rochlen, A. B., Ligiero, D. P., Hill, C. E., & Heaton, K. J. (1999). Effects of training in dream recall and dream interpretation skills on dream recall, attitudes, and dream interpretation outcome. *Journal of Counseling Psychology, 46,* 27–34.

Scher, M. (1981). Men in hiding: A challenge for the counselor. *Personnel and Guidance Journal, 60,* 199–202.

Scher, M. (2001). Male therapist, male client: Reflections on critical dynamics. In G. R. Brooks & G. E. Good (Eds.), *The new handbook of psychotherapy and counseling with men* (pp. 719–734). San Francisco: Jossey–Bass.

Sifneos, P. E. (1967). Clinical observations on some patients suffering from a variety of psychosomatic diseases. In *Proceedings of the Seventh European Conference on Psychosomatic Research*. Basel, Switzerland: Kargel.

Skovholt, T. M. (1990). Career themes in counseling and psychotherapy with men. In D. Moore & F. Leafgren (Eds.), *Problem solving strategies and interventions for men in conflict* (pp. 39–53). Alexandria, VA: American Association for Counseling and Development.

Van de Castle, R. L. (1994). *Our dreaming mind*. New York: Random House.

Wilcox, D. W., & Forrest, L. (1992). The problems of men and counseling: Gender bias or gender truth? *Journal of Mental Health Counseling, 14,* 291–303.

Winget, C., Kramer, M., & Whitman, R. (1972). The relationship of socioeconomic status and race to dream content. *Psychophysiology, 7,* 325–326.

Wisch, A. F., Mahalik, J. R., Hayes, J. A., & Nutt, E. A. (1995). The impact of gender role conflict and counseling technique on psychological help-seeking in men. *Sex Roles, 33,* 77–89.

Zack, J. S., & Hill, C. E. (1998). Predicting outcome of dream interpretation sessions by dream valence, dream arousal, attitudes toward dreams, and waking life stress. *Dreaming, 8,* 169–185.

Zeldow, P. B., & Greenberg, R. P. (1980). Who goes where: Sex-role differences in psychological and medical help-seeking. *Journal of Personality Assessment, 44,* 433–435.

Zunker, V. G. (1994). *Career counseling: Applied concepts of life planning*. Pacific Grove, CA: Brooks/Cole.

10

WORKING WITH NIGHTMARES

KRISTIN J. HEATON

The experience of dreaming can be powerful and impacting, especially when the dream comes in the form of a nightmare. The powerful nature of the nightmare is clearly reflected in its content, which can expose the dreamer's most persistent concerns and deeply rooted fears (e.g., fear of failure, abandonment, helplessness) or even replay disturbing events from waking life (see Cartwright & Lamberg, 1992; Hartmann, 1984; Krakow et al., 2002; Robbins & Houshi, 1983). Nightmares are intense, frightening experience that disrupt sleep and leave the dreamer in a heightened state of physiological arousal and emotional discomfort. Common reactions on awakening from a nightmare include increased heart and respiratory rates, sweating, sharpened attention, fear, anger, panic, or feeling helpless or out of control. For many people, this initial response subsides quickly. However, research has suggested that adverse reactions to nightmares—including disorientation, confusion, anxiety, fear of sleep, and general agitation—could persist for hours, days, or even weeks (Krakow, Kellner, Pathak, & Lambert, 1995; Madrid, Marquez, Nguyen, & Hicks, 1999; Vielhauer & Zimering, 1997; Zadra & Donderi, 2000). The disruptive effects of nightmares appear to be exacerbated by their frequency or chronicity (or both), with progressively severe consequences associated with more frequent or chronic nightmares.

In fact, research has reported insomnia, chronic fatigue, compromised immune function, impaired psychosocial and interpersonal functioning, depression, and occasionally substance abuse in adults who have frequent nightmares (see Hartmann, 1984; Kramer, Schoen, & Kinney, 1984; Kuhne, Nohner, & Baraga, 1986; Madrid et al., 1999; van der Kolk & Fisler, 1993; Zadra & Donderi, 2000).

Given the potentially deleterious impact of nightmares on human health and well-being, it is perhaps fortunate that most healthy adults (roughly 76%–86%) typically experience only one nightmare each year (see Belicki & Belicki, 1982; Janson et al., 1995; Levin, 1994; Nielsen & Zadra, 2000; Wood & Bootzin, 1990). Nightmares are typically more frequent in children, with 1 in every 4 children experiencing at least one nightmare each week (Pagel, 2000). However, epidemiological research has suggested that between 8% and 29% of adults experience nightmares on a monthly basis, and 1% to 6% of adults report nightmares occurring weekly (see Belicki & Belicki, 1982; Janson et al., 1995; Levin, 1994; Nielsen & Zadra, 2000; Wood & Bootzin, 1990). In addition, approximately 10% to 50% of children between the ages of 3 and 5 reportedly have nightmares of sufficient frequency and intensity to cause their parents concern (American Psychiatric Association, 1994; Pagel, 2000; Terr, 1987).

Although the precise etiology of frequent or chronic nightmares is not clearly understood, some factors contributing to the problem have been identified. These include use of certain medications or narcotics (e.g., barbiturates, certain antidepressants, beta blockers) and withdrawal from REM-suppressing drugs (e.g., ethanol, benzodiazepines, barbiturates; Pagel, 2000). Some research has also identified certain personality traits common to people who experience chronic nightmares (see Hartmann, 1984), including fluid personal boundaries, creativity, sensitivity, defenselessness, and openness to experience. Hartmann (1984) characterized such traits collectively as reflecting "thin" mental boundaries. Nightmare frequency also has been noted to increase during periods of unusual stress (Hartmann, 1984) or with the onset of medical or psychiatric disturbances, such as depression (Cartwright, Young, Mercer, & Bears, 1998), schizophrenia-spectrum disorders (Levin, 1998), and temporal lobe epilepsy (Solms, 1997). Finally, nightmares have also been reported after traumatic events in waking life. In fact, nearly 65% to 79% of people diagnosed with posttraumatic stress disorder (PTSD) report problems related to frequent nightmares (DeFazio, 1975; Krakow, Tandberg, Scriggins, & Barey, 1995; Schreuder, van Egmond, Kleijn, & Visser, 1998).

In general, nightmares fall into one of two broad categories: (a) nonrecurrent (unique each time it occurs) or (b) recurrent (with at least part of the nightmare repeated over time). Evidence from sleep laboratory studies and other research has suggested that both recurrent and nonrecurrent nightmares tend to occur late in the sleep cycle, often during REM sleep, and are generally characterized by the absence of gross motor movements (see Hartmann, 1984; Hobson, 1988; Solms, 1997). However, nightmares have been reported during non-REM sleep across the entire sleep cycle, particularly for nightmares that occur after traumatic waking life experiences (e.g., Hartmann, 1984; Ross et al., 1994b). Some recurrent nightmares also have been associated with movements of large muscle groups, especially in people diagnosed with PTSD (e.g., Ross et al., 1994a) and REM behavior sleep disorder (e.g., Olson, Boeve, & Silber, 2000).

Recurrent nightmares are relatively common, with nearly 60% of students in one college sample reporting at least one recurrent nightmare in their lifetimes (Robbins & Houshi, 1983). Although evidence exists that recurrent nightmares can begin at any time in a person's life, many begin in childhood and often portray the dreamer as being chased or threatened by unknown people, monsters, or animals (see Hartmann, 1984; Robbins & Tanck, 1992). Nightmares that follow traumatic life events are a particularly virulent form of recurrent nightmare, graphically and precisely re-enacting the traumatic experience over time. These posttraumatic nightmares can occur repeatedly in a given sleep period (contingent on the dreamer's ability to return to sleep) and can persist decades after the actual traumatic event (Cartwright & Lamberg, 1992; Hartmann, 1984; Karon & Widener, 1997). Although posttraumatic nightmares vary considerably with regard to their duration, frequency, and the exactness with which the traumatic event is re-enacted, they tend to gradually lose their intensity and similarity to the traumatic event as the trauma survivor navigates through the process of recovery (Cartwright & Lamberg, 1992; Hartmann, 1998b).

During the past 20 years, interest in nightmare research and treatment has grown considerably. This is likely due, in part, to a deeper awareness of the adverse impact of physical and psychological trauma on human health and well-being and the close association between nightmares and traumatic life events. This interest has resulted in a growing body of literature describing several nightmare-focused treatment methods and providing evidence for the importance of addressing nightmares directly in therapy. Treatment approaches that address nightmares, either as a discrete entity or as a symptom of a specific disorder, have been developed primarily from psychoanalytic–psychodynamic, behavioral, and cognitive–behavioral perspectives. However, most empirical investigations of nightmare-focused treatments have emerged from the cognitive–behavioral literature and have involved imagery rehearsal (e.g., Krakow et al., 2001), eye-movement desensitization and reprocessing (e.g., Silver, Brooks, & Obenchain, 1995), and other exposure-based treatments (e.g., Burgess, Gill, & Marks, 1998).

Another method of working with dreams in therapy, the Hill cognitive–experiential approach, has received considerable empirical attention over the last 10 years (see chap. 12, this volume). Although this method has been used with a wide variety of dreams, research has only begun to document its use specifically with nightmares. In addition to examining the effectiveness of the Hill method for working with nightmares, this research is also exploring the impact of client arousal on the outcome of nightmare-focused sessions (Heaton, 2002). Further research is needed to compare the Hill method with other nightmare-focused treatments, to investigate the appropriateness of this approach for working with different types of nightmares (e.g., recurrent, nonrecurrent, chronic, acute) and different client populations (e.g., children, clients with PTSD). Research is also needed to explore the use of this treatment approach as part of ongoing therapy or as a self-guided treatment.

In this chapter I outline and describe recent work that has applied the Hill method to nightmare-focused treatment. In this work, a *nightmare* is defined as a dream that leads to an abrupt awakening from sleep (partial or full arousal), accompanied by *intense* negative feelings (e.g., fear, terror, anger, horror), elevated cardiac and respiratory rates, sweating, and other signs of sympathetic nervous system arousal. According to this definition, nightmares are true dreams in that the dreamer is able to recall the content of his or her nightmare, typically with some detail. This definition also differentiates nightmares from anxiety dreams or other unpleasant dreams by the intensity of emotional arousal they produce in the dreamer and the disruption of sleep.

WORKING WITH NIGHTMARES USING THE HILL COGNITIVE–EXPERIENTIAL APPROACH

The goals of dream work using the Hill approach are the same for all clients, regardless of the valence (pleasantness) of their dreams. These goals include collaborating with clients to develop a deeper, more complete understanding of the dream or nightmare, helping clients use this understanding to inform and clarify problems in their daily lives, and helping clients use what they have learned about the dream or nightmare and themselves to develop clear, realistic plans for cognitive or behavioral change.

In the case of nightmares, clinical experience indicates that the pace of work tends to be slower and is met with greater client resistance and emotional distress than when working with more pleasant dreams. Research has suggested that nightmares have been associated with central conflicts and fears or traumatic events in the dreamer's life (see Hartmann, 1998a; Kramer, 1991). Directly confronting these painful issues through nightmare work might be met with considerable resistance because of the client's fear of losing emotional control, fear of discovering something unwanted or uncomfortable about him- or herself, or feeling unprepared for change. Clients might also withhold important information about themselves or their nightmares, either in an effort to protect their therapist from being traumatized or because they fear that their therapist will be unable to manage the terrifying content of the nightmare or the intensity of the client's emotional reactions to it.

The inherent flexibility of the Hill approach makes this model well suited to working with nightmares in therapy. In our work with nightmares, my colleagues and I (a) incorporate several techniques from the trauma literature (e.g., imagery rehearsal, grounding) into the treatment process, (b) explore a single nightmare in two or more sessions, (c) allow a full 90 minutes for each session, and (d) complete the full three-stage model in each session. We believe that by using the Hill method in this manner, therapists enable clients to work with their nightmares in a safe and manageable way, develop a sense of mastery over their nightmares, and have time to create and refine plans for using new insights and understandings to effect meaningful change in their lives.

In this chapter, I describe three sessions of nightmare-focused treatment in which the Hill method was used, offering examples and dialogue from actual treatment sessions involving a single nightmare. To preserve the anonymity of the client and therapist in these examples, identifying details have been removed or altered. The first session of this model presents a basic guideline for establishing the groundwork needed to engage in effective nightmare work using the Hill method. The primary goals of this session, which apply to stand-alone and ongoing treatment alike, are to (a) establish a sense of safety and trust within the therapeutic relationship, (b) familiarize the client with the goals and process of nightmare work, and (c) develop sufficient understanding of the client's personal history before delving into the specific details of the nightmare. The second and third sessions described in this example are devoted to therapists' and their clients' exploring one nightmare using all three stages of the Hill approach in each session. In my experience, I have found that at least two sessions are needed to adequately explore and process any given nightmare, regardless of whether this model is applied to a stand-alone treatment or used within the context of ongoing therapy.

Session 1

A great deal of courage and trust are required for clients to share and confront their nightmares in a therapeutic setting. For this reason, I recommend that therapists set aside some time to help their clients adequately prepare for the upcoming work. This can be achieved, in part, by working to create an environment in which the client feels safe, supported, and in control and to develop rapport and trust within the therapeutic relationship. The collaborative, empathic stance emphasized by the Hill method is well suited to this goal, as it helps to foster trust, communicates a sense of shared goals, and reinforces the client's sense of personal control. Safety and trust are further reinforced through up-front communication about confidentiality, the limits of this confidentiality, and the client's access to an effective social support network. Clients who fear traumatizing or harming their therapist by sharing personal material of a disturbing nature might also be reassured by disclosure of the therapist's own network of professional support (e.g., supervisory relationships, institutional backup). Recognizing that nightmare work can be quite difficult for the therapist as well as the client, I recommend that therapists pay close attention to issues of self-care. Therapists who regularly engage in nightmare work are strongly encouraged to regularly access their own personal and professional support networks. I also suggest that therapists allow themselves time and space to care for their own reactions to potentially traumatizing material.

Preparation for nightmare work also includes developing an accurate picture of the client's personal history. This not only provides important context for the work to come but also communicates the therapist's interest in and focus on the client as a whole person. In addition to the client background information that is typically acquired (e.g., medical, psychiatric, family, educational, occupational, social history), therapists should gather specific information pertaining to the *onset of nightmares* (age of onset, precipitating events), *nightmare frequency* (changes in frequency and highest, lowest, and current frequency), *nightmare intensity* (physiological and emotional reactions during and after nightmare; changes in intensity over time; ability to return to sleep; coping strategies used following nightmare), *presence of sleep disorders* (e.g., sleep apnea, insomnia, somnambulism, night terrors, REM behavior sleep disorder), and *treatments sought for nightmares* (e.g. pharmacological, individual or group treatment, self-help).

Finally, therapists are encouraged to help clients prepare for nightmare work by providing them with a brief overview of the Hill approach and the underlying rationale for using this method to explore nightmares. Therapists might begin by describing potential benefits to exploring nightmares across multiple sessions. For example, this approach allows clients an opportunity to explore different images and themes within and across nightmares and to develop and refine effective plans for taking action in their lives. It is hoped that by using this approach, clients will develop a deeper understanding of themselves and their nightmares as well as acquire a new tool for exploring future dreams and nightmares on their own.

In addition to the potential benefits to exploring nightmares in therapy, clients should be cautioned that as they begin to confront and challenge the issues underlying their nightmares, they might experience an exacerbation of nightmare frequency or severity. This experience can be quite distressing and demoralizing, occurring precisely at a time when clients are seeking to reduce nightmare occurence, and can undermine client's confidence in the therapeutic process. Throughout treatment, it is important that therapists check in with their clients about any changes in nightmare intensity or frequency and work with clients to manage any adverse emotional reactions that may accompany such changes.

Session 2

The process of working with a specific nightmare begins only after the client has had an opportunity to prepare for this work. The therapist might begin the session by reviewing with the client the treatment process and therapeutic goals, and checking in with the client about any concerns or questions he or she might have, including concerns about changes in nightmare frequency or severity.

Exploration (approximately 35 minutes)

The primary goal of the exploration stage is to build a well-integrated, accurate schema of the nightmare experience through a deconstruction of the nightmare, image by image. By repeatedly linking the client's associations, feelings, and waking life triggers to the nightmare, connections between the nightmare and issues or problems in the client's waking life are developed and strengthened in a guided and thoughtful manner. To facilitate the present-focused nature of this work, clients should be encouraged to retell their nightmare in the present tense using detailed descriptions (images, feelings, other sensations) in an effort to immediately reexperience the nightmare as fully as possible. However, the goal of reexperiencing is not catharsis, as this can exacerbate client's feelings of being emotionally stalled or stuck in the nightmare and could leave some clients feeling overwhelmed or retraumatized. In this stage the idea is to reexperience the nightmare in a safe, contained setting, exploring the emotional and cognitive content of the nightmare while helping the client maintain a sense of control. Therapists can facilitate this process by helping clients pace their exploration and disclosure of difficult material in a way that feels safe and comfortable. Therapists can also help clients maintain a sense of control and safety by checking in with them about their level of anxiety or arousal throughout treatment and using relaxation or other tools to reestablish comfortable levels of arousal when necessary. For some clients, maintaining a sense of safety and control might involve openly addressing cultural expectations regarding emotional expression, normalizing the process of emotional exploration, and inviting the client to share only as much as he or she feels comfortable. It may also be necessary to postpone exploration of certain images or reroute lines of exploration in the interest of helping clients maintain control of their emotional experiencing.

In the following example, Frank, a 45-year-old, Caucasian, noncombat veteran in ongoing psychotherapy, presents a nightmare he experienced a week before his eighth therapy session.

Dream: I am at the ocean, walking along the shore, and I hear some people crying out for help. I look around—I can't see anyone. The voices are becoming more frantic. I run down the beach toward a lighthouse and suddenly spot a bright orange rescue raft about 300 to 400 yards out. I can see four soldiers, all men in Army combat fatigues, holding onto the raft for dear life. The raft is taking on a lot of water and is beginning to buckle. I yell at them to swim to shore. Then I notice that each man is lashed with thick rope to a cement block. The raft takes on more water, and its sides begin to collapse. The men are no longer yelling, they just stare at me. One by one, they slide into the water and disappear. I can't move or even yell. I wake up in a cold sweat, breathing hard.

After Frank completes his narrative, the therapist works with him to explore the nightmare.

T: Tell me more about how you felt while you were actually having this nightmare.

C: Frantic. I could hear them yelling, but I couldn't find them. When I did see them, I felt, like, queasy. They were soldiers. They were smart enough to know how to get to shore—it wasn't that far. Something was wrong.

T: So you felt frantic, uneasy—something wasn't right. Anything else?

C: When they went into the water, I couldn't move. They just sank. I wanted to throw up.

T: What did you do after waking up?

C: I went to the kitchen. I was shaky. I didn't want to see those eyes again.

T: The soldiers' eyes bothered you. Did you go back to sleep?

C: Yeah, about 3 hours later.

T: And now? How do you feel after having just retold this nightmare?

C: Just a little uneasy. I don't want to think about those eyes, though.

Frank acknowledged feeling terrified when he first experienced this nightmare. However, it was his feelings of helplessness and paralysis in the nightmare that were reflected in a more concrete sense by his muted affective response during the re-exposure. Some clients may become overwhelmed by their emotions, whereas some others might use numbing, avoidance, or dissociation (or some combination of these) to disengage from the nightmare work and return to a more manageable emotional state. Although these defensive postures serve a valuable, protective function over time, they also prevent the client from fully engaging in the therapeutic process. Gestalt techniques such as "staying with" a particular emotion, using empty-chair dialogue exercises, or attending to nonverbal behaviors and language usage (e.g., *cannot* vs. *will not*) can help clients identify, clarify, and confront their thoughts and feelings.

T: I know that it may be difficult for you, but I would like to go back to the soldier's eyes for a moment. Those eyes bother you. Can you say more about how those eyes make you feel?

C: They're eerie. Like they're drilling holes into me.

T: They feel intense, drilling right through you. What else do they feel like?

C: It's like they are dead—no life, no feeling in them.

T: They are cold, dead eyes. They unnerve you. Have you felt something like this before in your waking life?

C: You know, I feel this way when I am with my son in the hospital. The tests he has to go through, the hospital rooms, those doctors and their tools and drugs. They feel cold and dead to me. They don't care about him. It's a mystery, and they're just excited to be detectives.

Once Frank's affective responses to the nightmare have been explored and elaborated, the therapist guides Frank toward selecting several images (approximately 5–7) from the nightmare to examine more closely. The process of selecting images is by no means a prescribed one. Images might be selected for their perceived importance to the overall meaning of the nightmare or for the client's emotional response (strong or minimal) to each. Although it is generally preferable in this approach to stay with the emotional content of the nightmare rather than following the exact sequencing of images and events, exploring highly arousing images could prove to be too overwhelming for some clients and could leave others feeling retraumatized. Thus, focusing on less arousing images initially serves the dual purpose of helping the client maintain a sense of safety and control while allowing the therapist time to assess the client's readiness to confront more difficult nightmare content.

T: Let's start by selecting some of the images from your nightmare to look at more closely. Which images strike you as particularly intriguing or important?

C: Let's see. I think the soldiers, the life raft, the lighthouse…um, I'm not sure…

T: What about staring, the soldiers staring at you?

C: I guess. [begins to shift weight in chair, clears throat]

T: Thinking about those eyes bothers you, doesn't it? You seem anxious right now.

C: I just don't like them staring at me like that.

Reexposure to a nightmare can be quite overwhelming for many clients. Therapists might find it helpful to use quantitative language to communicate with clients about their level of anxiety or emotional discomfort. One such tool is the Subjective Units of Discomfort Scale (SUD; Wolpe, 1985). Using this scale, clients assign a number from 0 to 11 (0 = *neutral feelings/no anxiety*, 11 = *highest level of anxiety possible*) to describe how anxious they feel. Clients who report high levels of anxiety (exceeding 8) may benefit from relaxation (deep breathing, progressive muscular relaxation) or grounding exercises to help them focus on the present, reduce tension and anxiety, and eventually reengage in the treatment process. Grounding has proven to be an especially useful technique for helping clients disengage from escalating tension and emotions and refocus on the present. According to this strategy, clients direct their full attention to an object in their immediate environment (e.g., chair) and, with eyes open, mentally explore the object in detail, noting such qualities as touch, temperature, texture, movement, color, sounds, smells, and so forth.

After selecting several images, Frank and the therapist used the DRAW steps (Describe image, Re-experience feelings, Associate to image, Waking life triggers) to explore each image in detail.

T: Tell me more about the ocean in the nightmare. Paint a picture of it for me.

C: Well…it swallows the horizon. It's enormous. So blue it's almost black—dark. The air feels heavy, thick, too, like it's part of the ocean.

T: How does this ocean make you feel?

C: I feel heavy in the pit of my stomach.

T: When else have you felt this way?

C: When I'm nervous about something, I guess.

T: So this heavy feeling could also be nervousness—foreboding, like the air and ocean.

C: Yeah. I think this ocean makes me nervous, maybe a little afraid.

T: What is an ocean?

C: Big. Dangerous—like an accident waiting to happen.

T: Does anything else pop into your head when you think of "ocean"?

C: When I was about 10, I was swimming and got caught in the undertow. It pulled me way out. I was screaming, and no one heard me.

T: That must have been terrifying. To struggle and struggle; you have no control.

C: That was the first time in my life I felt totally out of control—and alone.

T: And now, the ocean is still a frightening place?

C: It scares the hell out of me. I never went to the beach with my kids—it drove me insane to watch them play in the water.

T: What do you think might be going on in your life now that resembles these thoughts and feelings you have about the ocean—feeling out of control, afraid, dark—foreboding?

C: I don't know, my son. He's sick. He's been through all sorts of tests, and the doctors still don't know what's going on. There is nothing I can do—just watch and wait.

After all selected images have been explored using the DRAW approach, the therapist then retold Frank's nightmare, inserting his associations, descriptions, and links to waking life throughout as appropriate.

T: You are at the ocean, walking along the shore. This ocean is horizon-swallowing, dark, foreboding, and the air around you feels think and heavy. This ocean is dangerous and brings to mind being caught in the undertow as a kid, alone and out of control…

Insight (approximately 20 minutes)

Once the nightmare has been deconstructed into its component images and explored in detail, the therapist and client can begin the process of reconstructing it with new meanings, understandings, and connections to waking life. However, it is easy to feel overwhelmed by the enormity and adverse nature of the nightmare experience. Clients can sometimes become mired down by their own fear and frustration, reaching unrealistic, superficial, overly concrete or simplistic impressions about the nightmare's meaning. Clients also might selectively attend to the least arousing nightmare images in an effort to protect themselves from becoming overwhelmed. In addition, the vast collection of details, feelings, associations, and links to waking life developed through exploration can leave the client with a sense of information-overload. The goal of the insight stage is to help clients move beyond this "stuck" feeling, bring clarity and structure to the details, and gain new insight and understanding into the nightmare. First, it is helpful to gain a sense of where the client is at in terms of his or her understanding of the nightmare.

T: We've had a chance to explore this nightmare in more detail. If you were to put all this material together, what would you say your nightmare means to you at this moment?

C: I think it means I'm worried about my son.

Given Frank's disclosure of his son's unexplained illness, this interpretation certainly seems plausible, albeit somewhat simplistic and superficial. At this point, the therapist's job is to gently challenge the client's interpretation in a supportive and respectful manner. The therapist might encourage Frank to further explore issues in his waking life in an attempt to help Frank better understand or articulate his concerns for his son. As an alternative, the therapist might help Frank to explore nightmare images as reflecting different aspects of his own personality and internal sense of self. After developing new insights and understandings into the nightmare, the therapist might explore how these new insights compare with Frank's initial understanding of the nightmare.

T: It does seem like you are really worried about your son. The heavy, foreboding sky and the dangerous ocean in the nightmare seem to reflect this worry and uncertainty that you feel. One interesting thing about nightmares is that they can reflect many different concerns at the same time. I wonder if your nightmare is reflecting other concerns in your life now?

C: Like what?

T: Well, if we were to look at this nightmare as reflecting different parts of your own personality, what part of you might resemble the life raft?

C: [Pauses. Sighs.] I guess the part that tries to hold things together.

T: In what way do you hold things together?

C: Well, there's a lot of chaos in the family about my son. Everyone expects me to take control like I always do—go to all the appointments, listen to the doctors, make all the decisions. Sometimes I feel like…[tears welling up in his eyes]…I can't talk about this…

T: It's a lot of pressure being the one everyone looks to for support and strength. Earlier you mentioned those cement blocks were like a burden. What part of you feels tied to a block now, feels burdened?

C: All of me. [Looks down and shakes his head.]

T: People have so many expectations of you, you have all the responsibility, you're in control. What if you can't control this—what if the raft sinks?

C: (Looks startled.) I can't let it sink, you understand? [Fighting tears]

> T: But you feel the burden nonetheless. It's weighing you down, and your raft *is* sinking, and the occupants, those brave, naïve soldiers as you described them, are just sitting there looking at you. You said earlier that those eyes looking at you were like an "accusation." If those eyes are a part of you, inside of you, what might you be accusing yourself of?
>
> C: [Pause.] I'm a failure. I'm not good enough or strong enough to hold it together. If I don't hold it together, I'll lose them all.

Once new insights and understandings have been developed and explored, the therapist asks Frank to summarize his current understanding of the nightmare, integrating material from both the exploration and insight stages.

> T: So now, looking back at all we've talked about, what does this nightmare say to you? What meaning does it have for your life?
>
> C: It says I feel like I'm losing control and I'm afraid that I can't hold the pieces of my life together. That I feel helpless to protect my son from this unknown thing that's after him. I'm afraid of failing my family—of losing them all.

Action (approximately 25 minutes)

For Frank, arriving at a deeper level of insight into his nightmare was the first step in clarifying his own inner conflicts and fears. The next step is to explore how these insights could be used to effect meaningful, useful change in his life. This step is a particularly difficult aspect of nightmare work, because taking action also means confronting intense fears and conflicts that clients often work hard to avoid and have failed to overcome. Clients may need considerable support, guidance, and structure to help them stay focused on the present, address resistance when encountered, and work through the process of change in a manner that is safe and manageable. The action stage is initiated when the therapist asks Frank how he might change his behavior or role in the nightmare given his new understanding of it. At this point, emphasis is placed directly on personal change.

> C: I think I would find a boat, drive out to the raft, cut the ropes off the cement blocks, and let the soldiers climb into my boat.

Next, the therapist explores with Frank how to translate these changes in fantasy to actual changes in his waking life. Gestalt techniques are useful in helping clients uncover particular areas for taking action and exploring areas of resistance to action. For some clients who view their nightmares as a source of creative expression and inspiration and who are resistant to change based on this view, exploring new ways to use the nightmare creatively can be a valid and useful endeavor.

T: So you would get rid of those cement block burdens. What small changes could you make in your life now to help ease the everyday burdens you feel?

C: I guess I could use some help getting my son back and forth to the hospital; that's a lot of time. But it's really hard. I don't ask for help.

After identifying a waking life issue that Frank wished to change, the therapist works with Frank to examine his concerns about this change using gestalt techniques to clarify the resistance (e.g., staying with specific feelings, open-chair dialogue, projecting).

T: I am struck by the similarity between what you just said ("I don't ask for help") and the soldiers sitting quietly, staring at you as they slip into the water. Let's suppose the part of you that doesn't ask for help is sitting right here, in this chair (across from the client). I'd like you to talk with that person about asking for help.

The therapist then helps Frank to develop a clear, manageable plan for asking a family member for help with his son. The therapist uses role playing with Frank to practice the action plan and then uses an imagery rehearsal exercise (see Krakow, Kellner, Neidhardt, Pathak, & Lambert, 1992) to develop and reinforce positive imagery around the task of asking for and receiving help. In brief, this technique involves having the client imagine a difficult situation (e.g., losing control when asking for help) and rate his or her level of anxiety associated with that situation using SUD ratings. Then the client is asked to create and write down a positive image to replace this difficult imagery (e.g., staying calm and in control while asking his or her spouse for help), holding the new image in mind until his or her rated level of anxiety is reduced to a SUD rating of 1 or 2. Imagery rehearsal also can be used to replace adverse nightmare images with more positive imagery, allowing the client to experience successful control over his or her nightmare and emotional reactions to it.

The therapist then asks Frank to summarize his action plan and explores with Frank any concerns he might have with implementing the plan (perceived barriers, handling "failure" or setbacks, gauging success). The therapist encourages Frank to continue working on the nightmare between sessions and to practice the imagery rehearsal exercise several times at home before asking for help. In assigning homework, the therapist gauges Frank's ability to manage the emotional reactions he may have to the exercises outside of therapy. As a safeguard, Frank and the therapist work out a plan for managing difficult emotions outside of therapy, including the use of relaxation and grounding, and the therapist reminds Frank to make use of his safety network if he feels unsafe at any time.

Session 3

The primary goals of the second nightmare treatment session are (a) to continue the re-exposure to the nightmare in a safe, controlled environment and (b) to further develop and refine both the client's understanding of the nightmare and his or her plans for action based on this understanding. The session itself proceeds in much the same manner as the first session.

Exploration Stage (approximately 35 minutes)

At the outset of this session, the therapist checks in with Frank about any changes in his sleep patterns or nightmares and any concerns or questions he might have. She then asks Frank to briefly retell the nightmare in the present tense, including any new details that he might have recalled since the last session. Next, the therapist works with Frank to select several images (5–7) to explore in more depth. Some images (e.g., ocean, raft) are selected because of their rich emotional significance to Frank's waking life and because it seems as though there is more to explore with these images. Other images (e.g., the shore, unable to move) are selected because they had not been addressed in the previous session. As in the previous session, the therapist uses the DRAW sequence with each image to elicit any new feelings, associations, or waking life triggers that Frank can identify.

T: In our last session, you described the ocean as dark, dangerous, heavy. What else can you tell me about this ocean?

C: It's rough, but not real big waves. It smells really salty, too. Unusually salty.

T: What feelings do you have about this rough, briny-smelling ocean?

C: I feel, well, like I'm looking over my shoulder—paranoid, I guess.

T: Like danger is lurking.

C: Yes, not just dangerous, but like it's after me.

T: Does anything else come to mind when you think about this ocean now?

C: I was thinking that it is really unpredictable—calm one minute, *The Perfect Storm* the next.

T: Have you thought of any more ways in which the ocean or any aspect of the ocean reflect things going on in your waking life now?

C: Actually, two nights ago I was sitting with my son in the hospital and I remembered what we had talked about last week. I started to think that the ocean is in control, not us. It can kill you in a second, or give you food the next.

After this second pass through Frank's nightmare, the therapist retells the nightmare, inserting the newly acquired associations, descriptions, and links to waking life where appropriate.

Insight Stage (approximately 20 minutes)

As in the first session, the therapist initiates the insight stage by asking Frank to describe his current understanding of the nightmare. Given that time has passed between sessions, the therapist focuses on comparing this new understanding with insights or understandings gained during the previous session. She then explores with Frank new ways of looking at the nightmare. In this session, the therapist uses a different interpretive approach than in the previous session. However, there are no hard and fast rules about which approach to select, because the decision should be based on the flow of the discussion and the material acquired through exploration.

> T: In the last session, we explored the nightmare as it related to different parts of yourself. This time, using the images we've just discussed, how might this nightmare reflect what's going on in your life now?
>
> C: I think it means I'm not in control. That's what bothers me. The ocean, the raft, it's telling me that I can't control this like I control everything else.

Frank and the therapist then consider how this current understanding is similar to or differs from Frank's previous understanding.

> T: In the previous session, you said the nightmare reflected your fears of failing and losing your family. How does this understanding compare to your feelings about the nightmare now?
>
> C: I'm starting to see how I control things and people. I don't want to ask for help, because then I'm not the one in control. I was blaming other people for not helping, but it's really me who won't let them help.
>
> T: Are you surprised by anything you learned this time around with the nightmare?
>
> C: I guess I'm surprised by how hard it is for me to admit I'm not in control.

Finally, the therapist asks Frank to summarize his understanding of the nightmare, integrating the material that has been covered in both the current and previous session.

Action Stage (approximately 25 minutes)

Repeated exposure to and support with action plans can help clients gain a greater sense of control and mastery over the action itself. In this second session, the therapist explores with Frank his experience in carrying out the action plan from the previous session. The therapist also explores any barriers Frank encountered with implementing his plan and his overall feelings about the action.

> T: Last week we explored ways of asking your wife for help in taking your son to his appointments. Were you able to put those plans into action?
>
> C: Yeah, I did the imagining thing on Monday and Tuesday and then asked my wife to take him to his appointment on Wednesday.
>
> T: Did she do it?
>
> C: Yes, she did.
>
> T: What was it like for you to ask her?
>
> C: She didn't want to, but I told her I just couldn't do it. I made up some excuse.
>
> T: That's great that you were able to practice the imaging exercise and to then ask your wife for help. It must have been difficult, but you took that first step. It sounds like it didn't go quite the way you had expected, though.
>
> C: No, I shouldn't have had to lie.
>
> T: You've spent a lifetime learning to be in control and now you're letting some of that control go. It will take time and effort—give yourself a break. You took a really big step, and now we can work on ways to make it easier for you to ask without feeling like you need to make up an excuse.

As the session draws to a close, Frank expresses his surprise that working with his nightmare would lead to issues as powerful and rich as his need for control and the factors underlying his inability to ask for help. The therapist encourages Frank to continue exploring this and other nightmares using the model of nightmare work practiced in their sessions. To facilitate this effort, the therapist recommends that Frank keep a journal close to his bed in which to record any dreams and nightmares recalled on awakening. Frank is also encouraged to practice the skills he developed for managing his anxiety and other adverse reactions to his nightmares outside of treatment and to work with the therapist during future sessions to refine and enhance these skills as needed. The therapist invites Frank to bring additional dreams or nightmares into future sessions at his discretion. Finally, the therapist works with Frank to begin laying out plans for using the information and issues generated by their exploration of the nightmare in their continuing work together.

CONCLUSIONS

The model of nightmare work described in this chapter is yet another example of how the Hill approach can be easily adapted to fit diverse client needs. In my experience, this method can facilitate exploration of nightmares in a manner that emphasizes client control and safety while fostering a deeper understanding of the nightmare and its relevance to the client's waking life. I believe that this approach, when used within a supportive therapeutic environment, will provide clients the time needed to address and perhaps overcome their resistance to exploring the nightmare and its associated waking life concerns. I also feel that this approach can provide important opportunities for clients to develop insights into their nightmares and to use feedback and experiences outside of therapy to further revise, refine, and enhance plans for change. This extended support is especially useful for clients who struggle to incorporate changes in thinking or behavior into their newly developed understanding of the nightmare experience.

REFERENCES

American Psychiatric Association. (1994). *Diagnostic and statistical manual of mental disorders* (4th ed.). Washington, DC: Author.

Belicki, D., & Belicki, K. (1982). Nightmares in a university population. *Sleep Research, 11,* 116.

Burgess, M., Gill, M., & Marks, I. (1998). Postal self-exposure treatment of recurrent nightmares. *British Journal of Psychiatry, 172,* 257–262.

Cartwright, R. D., & Lamberg, L. (1992). *Crisis dreaming: Using your dreams to solve your problems.* New York: HarperCollins.

Cartwright, R., Young, M., Mercer, P., & Bears, M. (1998). Role of REM sleep and dream variables in prediction of remission from depression. *Psychiatry Research, 80,* 249–255.

DeFazio, V. (1975). The Vietnam era veteran: Psychological problems. *Journal of Contemporary Psychotherapy, 7,* 9–15.

Hartmann, E. (1984). *The nightmare: The psychology and biology of terrifying dreams.* New York: Basic Books.

Hartmann, E. (1998a). *Dreams and nightmares: The new theory on the origin and meaning of dreams.* New York: Plenum Trade.

Hartmann, E. (1998b). Nightmares after trauma as paradigm for all dreams: A new approach to the nature and functions of dreaming. *Psychiatry, 61,* 223–238.

Heaton, K. J. (2002). *An investigation of nightmare-focused treatment using the Hill method of dream work.* Unpublished doctoral dissertation, University of Maryland, College Park.

Hobson, J. (1988). *The dreaming brain.* New York: Basic Books.

Janson, C., Gislason, T., De Backer, W., Plaschke, P., Bjornsson, E., Hetta, J., et al. (1995). Prevalence of sleep disturbances among young adults in three European countries. *Sleep, 18,* 589–597.

Karon, B. P., & Widener, A. J. (1997). Repressed memories and World War II: Lest we forget! *Professional Psychology: Research and Practice, 28,* 338–340.

Krakow, B., Hollifield, M., Johnston, L., Koss, M., Schrader, R., Warner, T. D., et al. (2001). Imagery rehearsal therapy for chronic nightmares in sexual assault survivors with posttraumatic stress disorder: A randomized controlled trial. *Journal of the American Medical Association, 286,* 537–545.

Krakow, B., Kellner, R., Neidhardt, J., Pathak, D., & Lambert, L. (1992). Imagery rehearsal treatment of chronic nightmares with a thirty month follow-up. *Journal of Behavior Therapy and Experimental Psychiatry, 24,* 325–330.

Krakow, B., Kellner, R., Pathak, D., & Lambert, L. (1995). Imagery rehearsal treatment for chronic nightmares. *Behaviour Research & Therapy, 33,* 837–843.

Krakow, B., Melendez, D. C., Johnston, L. G., Clark, J. O., Santana, E. M., Warner, T. D., Hollifield, M. A., Schrader, R., Sisley, B. N., & Lee, S. A. (2002). Sleep dynamic therapy for Cerro Grande fire evacuees with posttraumatic stress symptoms: A preliminary report. *Journal of Clinical Psychiatry, 63,* 673–684.

Krakow, B., Tandberg, D., Scriggins, L., & Barey, M. (1995). A controlled comparison of self-rated sleep complaints in acute and chronic nightmare sufferers. *Journal of Nervous and Mental Disease, 183,* 623–627.

Kramer, M. (1991). The nightmare: A failure in dream function. *Dreaming, 1,* 277–285.

Kramer, M., Schoen, L. S., & Kinney, L. (1984). Psychological and behavioral features of disturbed dreamers. *Psychiatric Journal of the University of Ottawa, 9,* 102–106.

Kuhne, A., Nohner, W., & Baraga, E. (1986). Efficacy of chemical dependency treatment as a function of combat in Vietnam. *Journal of Substance Abuse Treatment, 3,* 191–194.

Levin, R. (1994). Sleep and dreaming characteristics of frequent nightmare subjects in a university population. *Dreaming, 4,* 127–137.

Levin, R. (1998). Nightmares and schizotypy. *Psychiatry, 61,* 206–216.

Madrid, S., Marquez, H., Nguyen, T. T., & Hicks, R. A. (1999). Nightmare distress and stress-related health problems. *Perceptual & Motor Skills, 89,* 114–115.

Nielsen, T., & Zadra, A. (2000). Dreaming disorders in principles and practices in sleep medicine. In M. Kryger, T. Roth, & W. Dement (Eds.), *Principles and practices of sleep medicine* (3rd ed., pp. 753–771). Philadelphia: W. B. Saunders.

Olson, E., Boeve, B., & Silber, M. (2000). Rapid eye movement sleep behavior disorder: Demographic, clinical and laboratory findings in 93 cases. *Brain, 123,* 331.

Pagel, J. (2000). Nightmares and disorders of dreaming. *American Family Physician, 61,* 2037–2042, 2044.

Robbins, P., & Houshi, F. (1983). Some observations on recurrent dreams. *Bulletin of the Menninger Clinic, 47,* 262–265.

Robbins, P., & Tanck, R. (1992). A comparison of recurrent dreams reported from childhood and recent recurrent dreams. *Imagination, Cognition, and Personality, 11*, 259–262.

Ross, R., Ball, W., Dinges, D., Kribbs, N., Morrison, A., Silver, S., & Mulvaney, F. (1994a). Motor dysfunction during sleep in posttraumatic stress disorder. *Sleep, 17*, 723–732.

Ross, R., Ball, W. A., Dinges, D. F., Kribbs, N. B., Morrison, A. R., Silver, S. M., & Mulvaney, F. D. (1994b). Rapid eye movement sleep disturbance in posttraumatic stress disorder. *Biological Psychiatry, 35*, 195–202.

Schreuder, B. J., van Egmond, M., Kleijn, W. C., & Visser, A. T. (1998). Daily reports of posttraumatic nightmares and anxiety dreams in Dutch war victims. *Journal of Anxiety Disorders, 12*, 511–524.

Silver, S. M., Brooks, A., & Obenchain, J. (1995). Treatment of Vietnam War veterans with PTSD: A comparison of eye movement desensitization and reprocessing, biofeedback, and relaxation training. *Journal of Traumatic Stress, 8*, 337–342.

Solms, M. (1997). *The neuropsychology of dreams*. Mahwah, NJ: Erlbaum.

Terr, L. (1987). Nightmares in children. In C. Guilleminault (Ed.), *Sleep and its disorders in children* (pp. 231–242). New York: Raven.

van der Kolk, B. A., & Fisler, R. E. (1993). Biological basis of posttraumatic stress disorder. *Psychiatric Clinics of North America, 20*, 417–432.

Vielhauer, M. J., & Zimering, R. T. (1997, November). *Characteristics of recurrent, combat-related nightmares in veterans with PTSD*. Paper presented at the 13th annual meeting of the International Society for Traumatic Stress Studies, Montreal, Québec, Canada.

Wolpe, J. (1985). *The practice of behaviour therapy* (3rd ed.). New York: Pergamon Press.

Wood, J., & Bootzin, R. (1990). The prevalence of nightmares and their independence from anxiety. *Journal of Abnormal Psychology, 99*, 64–68.

Zadra, A., & Donderi, D. C. (2000). Nightmares and bad dreams: Their prevalence and relationship to well-being. *Journal of Abnormal Psychology, 109*, 273–281.

III

TRAINING AND RESEARCH ON THE HILL COGNITIVE–EXPERIENTIAL DREAM MODEL

11

TRAINING THERAPISTS TO WORK WITH DREAMS IN THERAPY

RACHEL E. CROOK

In this chapter I describe some ideas about how to train therapists in using the Hill cognitive–experiential dream model. One impetus for this chapter was research indicating that a sizable portion of clients (15%–70%) bring dreams into therapy, but therapists do not always know how to work with dreams beyond listening to the client (Crook & Hill, 2003). Training therapists, therefore, about how to work with clients' dreams seems important. The ideas for training presented in this chapter have come from my experiences being trained by Clara E. Hill, conducting several training workshops on my own, and discussing the ideas for how to conduct training with Dr. Hill.

The first part of the chapter focuses on preparing for the training session; I discuss fundamental considerations, such as the amount of time allotted for the training, the knowledge and skill levels of the participants, the goal of the training, and the use of reading materials before the training. In the second part of the chapter I describe the actual training through didactic and experiential approaches. For both the didactic and experiential portions of the training, I discuss issues that I have encountered in conducting training, and a sample format is presented. At the end of the chapter, I discuss current and future research on training therapists in dream work. Throughout the chapter, I use the term *trainer* to refer to the individual leading the workshop or training session and use *participants* to refer to those who are attending the training. To give this chapter a first-hand account flavor, I have also included comments and reactions from therapists and graduate students trained in the cognitive–experiential model.

PREPARATION FOR TRAINING

There are a variety of settings and contexts in which training in dream work can be done; possibilities range from a workshop at a professional conference to a graduate psychotherapy seminar. The training may be anywhere from 90 minutes to a full-day workshop. The participants to be trained vary as well, from seasoned professional clinicians with expertise in working with dreams to untested graduate students eager to learn new skills. The goal of the training can also differ. On the one hand, the goal may be to examine one aspect of the Hill cognitive–experiential model for research purposes, in which case the training may emphasize close adherence to the model. On the other hand, the goal may be to introduce clinicians to another way of working with dreams and thus encourage the participants to try out parts of the model and incorporate these parts into their existing methods of working with dreams. Hence, trainers should be sensitive to the time, participants, and goals of the training when planning for and conducting a training session.

Time

Although the time for training varies depending on the setting, I have generally found that a 4.5-hour training session is sufficient for participants to become familiar with the three-stage model if therapists are already skilled in basic therapeutic techniques. The first 1.5 hours are typically a didactic explanation of the assumptions of the model, the theoretical background of each stage, the steps associated with each stage, and the relevant research findings. During the second 1.5 hours, the participants have a chance to practice the model in a group format with the trainer acting as a coach during the dream facilitation. The final portion of the training is typically a 1.5-hour experiential session during which the participants are paired with another training participant or with a volunteer client to have an opportunity go through the complete model. It can be difficult to fit both the didactic and the experiential portions into one training session, so trainers will want to monitor the time closely to present the complete model and give participants a chance to practice.

Participants

The number of participants is another matter of concern for trainers. I have generally found that as the sole trainer, it is difficult to have more than 15 participants in the training session because people may feel too vulnerable to tell a dream, and others may feel too exposed when practicing the model in front of the group. I usually ask participants before the training to have a dream ready that they would feel comfortable sharing or to role-play a client's dream and situation. Larger groups can be accommodated if the trainer has assistants who can separate the participants into smaller groups to practice the model in a group format. Being aware of the skill and knowledge levels of the participants is another important consideration. For therapists who are more experienced and have expertise in basic therapy skills prior to this training, trainers can devote less attention to the types of skills that are appropriate at each stage of the model and perhaps more time on understanding the model and incorporating dream work into ongoing therapy. However, when training graduate student therapists to work with the model, it has been my experience that students often need more instruction in the types of interventions that are appropriate for each stage (e.g., reflection of feeling and restatement in the exploration stage; interpretation in the insight stage; and direct guidance in the action stage) than more experienced clinicians. Because the model is somewhat structured and easy to follow, therapists in training usually grasp the concepts fairly quickly. According to Stoltenberg's (1981) counselor complexity model, an optimal training and supervision environment for beginning counselors includes structure and autonomy. Thus, the experiential portion seems particularly helpful to students as they practice the model and have opportunities to give and receive feedback.

Reading

Depending on the setting of the training, trainers may want to consider sending or giving participants some reading about the model before the training. Part I of this book would be useful to orient participants to the model. By using readings, the trainer offers another learning avenue to participants who may be less aurally oriented. One participant noted that "the readings were useful, right to the point." Another participant mentioned that the readings "got the model in my head, then from there, I just needed to work on applying the model, thinking on my feet and making good clinical decisions." The didactic portion of the training, in my experience, seems to make more sense for participants after they have read about the model. Hence, including reading in the training tends to reinforce the presentation of the model during the didactic portion.

Qualifications of the Trainer

A final important point to discuss is who might be qualified to conduct training in the cognitive–experiential model. I suggest that trainers first familiarize themselves with the model by attending a training session and by reading Part I of this book. Second, prospective trainers should practice using the cognitive–experiential model with clients and seek supervision, if necessary, from someone who is more experienced in the model. A third recommended step is to colead training sessions with a more experienced trainer.

DIDACTIC PORTION

Training in the model usually begins with some time (usually 90 minutes) devoted to presenting (or, if pretraining readings were distributed, reviewing) the assumptions and the stages of the model. During the didactic portion, I try to engage all participants by asking them to introduce themselves and encouraging participants to share their own experiences in working on dreams. Similarly, although it is important to present the model thoroughly, it does not have to be done in a rote manner. Trainers may want to spice up the training by offering clinical examples at different stages, generating discussions, and encouraging questions. In addition, to help participants understand the model, trainers may want to offer handouts of the presentation or an outline of the model (see outline in Appendix A).

Participants typically enjoy the didactic portion because it gives them a chance to learn about an approach to working with dreams and allows them an opportunity to ask questions. For example, a therapist in training reported that the didactic portion was very helpful because he was just beginning to learn the helping skills associated with each stage. Another therapist in training noted that the didactic portion was "fun and engaging."

To help illustrate what a training session may look like, in the next section I offer a sample transcript for the didactic portion of dream training. At the end of each stage, I offer some thoughts on that particular stage of the model and comment on critical issues that might arise at that point in the training. Trainers may, of course, modify the didactic portion or develop their own way of presenting the cognitive–experiential model of dream work.

SAMPLE TRAINING PRESENTATION

The following sample training presentation is presented from the point of view of the trainer.

Introduction

Today, I'm going to present a cognitive–experiential model of dream work developed by Clara Hill and her colleagues. We'll first learn a little about why it can be important to work with dreams in therapy. Next, I will give an overview of the model, the different stages in the model, as well as the theoretical underpinnings of each stage. We will also work through a dream together as a group, and you will have a chance to be paired up with another participant to practice the model, so start thinking about a dream that you might be willing to work on. Please feel free to ask any questions or make comments throughout this training session. I'd like to begin by asking each of you to introduce yourselves and say what you think about dreams and working with dreams in therapy. [Encourage each participant to share some thoughts about dreams.]

Why Work With Dreams?

There are several reasons why therapists may want to work with clients' dreams in therapy. One is that we all dream, and so dreaming is a major part of our experience. Physiological findings about dreaming indicate that 60%–90% of people who are awakened from rapid eye movement (REM) sleep can recall their dreams. People who are REM-sleep deprived (and thus perhaps dream deprived) perform worse on creative-thinking and problem-solving tasks than do non-REM sleep deprived people. Furthermore, it appears that REM sleep increases when learning is taking place, suggesting that REM sleep helps people incorporate new learning. So, in fact, it seems that it does help to "sleep on it" (Hill, 1996, pp. 12–13).

A second reason for working with clients' dreams is that people often have troubling dreams that influence their waking lives. Research on trauma survivors indicates that survivors may have nightmares about the traumatic event (Kilpatrick et al., 1998). Similarly, anxious clients often have dreams about anxiety-provoking situations. Finally, working with dreams is a means of navigating around clients' defenses and quickly getting to clients' core issues, a kind of "back door" to deeper issues. In this way, dream work can be a helpful component of brief psychotherapy.

Effectiveness of Dream Work

Unlike other approaches to working with clients' dreams, the Hill (1996) model has been rigorously researched. Seventeen studies have been conducted on the Hill (1996) model, and the model has been shown to be effective in single sessions, brief individual therapy, group therapy, and couples therapy. One consistent finding across the studies is that clients who have positive attitudes toward dreams also have positive outcomes of dream sessions. Dream work also leads to higher ratings of insight, depth, and working alliance than regular therapy sessions (see chap. 12, this volume).

Goals for Training

There are two goals for the training today: (a) to help you understand the philosophy underlying the model and (b) to practice using the model several times. We'll practice the model first as a group, and then you will split into pairs.

Assumptions of the Cognitive–Experiential Model

To help you understand the philosophy underlying the cognitive–experiential model, I will outline the model's assumptions. One assumption is that dreams reflect waking life. Another assumption is that the meaning of dreams is personal. In other words, because of my personal experiences with dogs, an image of a dog in my dream may have a very different meaning for me than it does for another dreamer. A third assumption is that the process of working on a client's dream should be collaborative in that the therapist facilitates the client's exploration and understanding of the dream. Hence, the therapist does not give the client the interpretation and is not the expert on what the dream means. However, therapists should have expertise in basic helping skills and therapeutic techniques (see Hill & O'Brien, 1999). A final assumption is that because dreams involve cognitive, emotional, and behavioral components, dream work also needs to target those three areas.

Stages of the Model

There are three stages of the model. The first stage is exploration and is based on client-centered/humanistic theory. We assume that the client has a meaning for the dream but needs support to find that meaning through the facilitative conditions (e.g., empathy, warmth, and genuineness) that a therapist provides. The goal of the exploration stage is to stimulate the client's cognitive schemas so that the experiences, memories, thoughts, and feelings that propelled the dream are activated. After the exploration stage, the therapist and client work together to understand the meaning of the dream in the insight stage. The next stage, insight, is based on psychodynamic theory, and the main goal is to understand the meaning of the dream at one of a number of levels (e.g., experience, waking life, inner personality dynamics). The final stage, action, is based on behavioral theory. In the action stage, the therapist helps the client translate insights gained from working on the dream into exploring changes in the waking life.

Exploration Stage

Before beginning the exploration stage, it is helpful to give the client a brief overview of what you will be doing in the session. A therapist could say something like,

Today we'll have 50 minutes to talk about one of your dreams. There are three stages in this process: first, we'll talk about the different images in the dream, and I'll ask you to describe them in greater detail and inquire about the associations you have to those images. Then, we'll move into the insight stage, in which we'll work together to come up with a meaning for the dream that fits for you. The last stage is the action stage, when we will see how you might want to continue to work on this dream or perhaps make some changes in your life. Do you have any questions?

At this point, I often ask the client whether it would be okay for me to jot down a few notes during the session.

The therapist then begins the exploration stage. The first step of the exploration stage is to ask the client to retell the dream in the first person and in the present tense as if he or she were experiencing the dream in the session. As a therapist, even though the dream may seem bizarre or disturbing, you will want to suspend judgment of the dream until you know the meaning for the dreamer. Also, you do not have to know the meaning of the dream immediately, even if the client seems to expect it. Explain to the client that by working through the stages, he or she will have an opportunity to gain a richer understanding of the dream. As the client is telling the dream, it is helpful to write down the images as they appear (e.g., horse, walking, sky). The next step is to sequentially explore 5 to 10 dream images with the client using description, reexperiencing, associations, and waking life (DRAW) triggers.

First, the therapist asks the client to describe the dream image in greater detail by asking the client to paint a picture of the image verbally, for example, "what does the dog look like; what kind of collar is he wearing?" The therapist then encourages the dreamer to re-experience feelings about each image in the dream: "How are you feeling at this moment in the dream?" The third step is to ask the dreamer for any associations he or she may have to the dream image. The therapist can help the client make associations to dream images by asking questions such as "What is a dog?", "What's the first thing that comes to your mind when you think of a dog?", and "What memories do you have of a dog?" The fourth step is to ask for waking life triggers for each dream image ("What's going on now in your waking life that reminds you of this image?). The therapist goes through each of the DRAW steps for one image and then moves on to the next image, spending about 5 minutes on each image. Before moving on to the insight stage, the therapist retells the dream using the descriptions and associations generated from the exploration stage. Because the exploration stage is the foundation for the insight and action stages, it is important that therapists do not hurry through this stage. A good gauge is to spend no more than half the time allotted for a dream session in the exploration stage.

Before continuing with the sample training session, I want to highlight some issues and participants' reactions to the exploration stage. Something that I have found helpful to get participants involved during the didactic portion is to have each participant associate to a common image when I introduce the DRAW steps. In general, most surveyed participants reported that the steps of the exploration stage were easy to grasp and use. One therapist in training noted that learning the exploration stage was "fairly easy, because all I had to remember were the DRAW steps for each image."

It is also important to remind participants that it is not necessary to go through the DRAW steps for each image in a rote manner. One participant reported that "sometimes the client has already addressed one of these parts [DRAW] while talking about another; it can feel rote and repetitive to go through each one for every image." Another aspect of the exploration stage that many participants found challenging was how to do a thorough exploration of the dream images in a timely manner. One participant noted that because "the exploration stage is the foundation for the rest of the stages, it is difficult not to spend a lot of time exploring dream images." To ensure that all stages of the model are covered, the trainer should encourage training participants to spend no more than half the allotted dream session time in exploration before moving on to insight and action.

The Insight Stage

To introduce the insight stage, the therapist first asks the client for an initial understanding of the dream. At this point, the therapist should respect what the client thinks about the dream, allow the client to integrate information from the exploration stage, and listen for parts of the dream that the client ignores. The therapist then collaborates with the client to construct understanding at one of several levels of insight. After the client finds a meaning that fits for the dream, the therapist asks the client to summarize the meaning of the dream.

Dream as an experience in and of itself (experiential). This level looks at what it means for a client to live through an experience in a dream. As an example, I had a client who was expecting her first baby, and she brought in a dream about giving birth. As a result of focusing on the dream as an experience in and of itself, she felt confident that having gone through the delivery in a dream, she would be able to do it in waking life. In looking at a client's dream from this perspective, the dream really does not need to be "interpreted." Instead, the dream needs to be understood for what it is so that the dreamer can more fully understand the extent of his or her fears and desires. The therapist may ask the client to share what it was like to solve the world's problems, attend one's own funeral, or be a secret agent. This approach seems particularly appropriate when clients bring dreams in that are very vivid and arousing or contain scenarios in which the client might like to be engaged or fears being engaged.

Dream as reflecting waking life. Another way of looking at dream images is as though they reflect waking life concerns. This is the level that clients tend to think of when they look for a dream's meaning; for example, what is going on in my life now that triggered this dream? In approaching the dream as reflecting waking life, it is important to remember that the dream images can be metaphors to portray feelings. The image of cabinets floating in the air, for example, may reflect the dreamer's feelings of uncertainty and lack of grounding in making an important decision. Likewise, the inability to find the room in which one is to take a final exam may reflect the dreamer's concerns about being evaluated in his or her present occupation. In addition to current concerns, the waking life level of insight can include thoughts and feelings about the past and future. In this approach, the waking life triggers from the exploration stage can be particularly helpful in finding meaning in the dream. This approach seems most appropriate for dreams that mimic waking life closely.

Dreams as reflecting inner personality dynamics. A third way of approaching the dream in the insight stage is by examining the dream as reflecting inner personality dynamics. Although there are doubtless many ways to understand dreams using this approach, I'll mention three ways: parts of self, complexes, and spiritual–existential concerns. This approach seems most appropriate for dreams that are metaphoric, symbolic, or abstract.

One way to examine the dream as reflecting inner personality dynamics is to think of each dream image as representing parts of the dreamer. The dream images may, for example, be projections of the dreamer's inner conflicts. Alternatively, as Perls (1969) suggested, dream images are projections of the self. By exploring what the images represent and how the images interact in the dream, the dreamer comes to a greater understanding of how the different parts of self interact. Similarly, Jungians propose that dream images represent the dreamer's archetypal parts of self (e.g., persona, anima, animus, shadow, trickster, etc.) For example, one client presented a dream in which she was being chased by man and she had locked herself into a house with many windows. She could never hide from the man because he could always see her in the windows. As a result of focusing on the dream as representing parts of self, she came to an understanding of the thin veneer that she shows to the world (windows) and that her anger (man) can always find her.

A second way to examine the dream as reflecting inner personality dynamics is to think of the dream as representing personality or inner conflicts, such as the classical Oedipal or Electra conflict, the desire to individuate from parents, or the recycling of maladaptive interpersonal patterns. In using this approach, therapists should not just give a standard symbolic interpretation (e.g., all trees are phalluses) but should help the dreamer become aware of deep-seated personality conflicts.

A third way to examine the dream as reflecting inner personality dynamics is to think of the dream as representing the dreamer's relationship with a higher power or the dreamer's concerns about existential issues (e.g., meaning of life, freedom, isolation, death). For example, a client presented a dream in which she was playing the organ but was not able to play louder, no matter how hard she pressed on the keys. Through the use of a spiritual approach to dreams, she began to feel that by relying on her own understanding and power, she was not able to appreciate life fully (playing louder) and needed assistance from a higher power.

Choosing among levels. So, how do you decide which level to choose? One factor to consider is the type of dream. As I mentioned earlier, vivid dreams that reflect experiences out of the ordinary for the client seem most appropriate for the experiential level. Dreams that reflect normal waking life experiences are often appropriate for the waking life level. Finally, dreams that are filled with artistic and metaphorical components seem suitable for the inner-dynamics level.

Another factor to consider in choosing a level is to assess the level to which clients are drawn in their initial understanding of the dream. As I mentioned previously, most people think of dreams as reflecting waking life. So, it makes sense to collaborate with the client first to understand the dream on that level. However, some clients may be willing to experiment further in the insight stage. It is important for therapists to present a plausible rationale for looking at another level of interpretation. I usually introduce the parts-of-self approach by saying something like:

> There are several different theories about how to interpret dreams. One theory is that each image in the dream represents a part of yourself and that by figuring out what each image means, and how they interact in the dream, it will help us to understand more how you might be feeling about different parts of yourself. What do you think about trying out this approach in looking at your dream?

A third factor to consider is if you, as the therapist, have a guess about the meaning of the dream and hence feel that one level of interpretation would be more helpful than others. For example, if the client has mentioned spiritual issues during the exploration stage, it seems reasonable to use the spiritual level.

Thoughts about training in the insight stage. The insight stage of the model is less structured than the exploration and action stages and thus seems more difficult for both trainers and participants. Most surveyed participants have indicated that the insight stage was more difficult to learn and use than the exploration stage. One trainer reported that it was more difficult for her to train participants in the insight stage because "so much depends on where the clients are, and therapists have to rely more on their own sense of how things fit together." A participant noted that she did not learn several parts of the insight stage (e.g., the meaning of the dream as an experience, related to spiritual issues, or reflecting relationship concerns) and felt that the training was rushed through the insight and action stages. Hence, trainers should allow enough time during the didactic portion to thoroughly explain the different levels of the insight stage and offer clinical examples. One participant felt that a demonstration of the model, "especially with regard to the insight stage," would be helpful.

Although the insight stage may be the most difficult to learn or teach, it can also be the most creative and exciting time for therapist and client (and trainer). One technique that I have used is to present a sample dream at the insight stage of the training and ask participants how they might hypothesize about interpretations at each of the levels. This allows participants an opportunity to begin practicing and orienting to the model. Another participant called the insight stage the "most fun" stage of the model. Finally, participants have reported that having different levels to collaborate on a meaning for the dream with clients was particularly useful, "because one level may be tremendously meaningful to a client, while the other just [doesn't] feel as relevant." Trainers, therefore, should encourage participants to use their clinical judgment in deciding which level to collaborate on a dream meaning for the client.

Exploring the Action Stage

The purpose of the action stage is to help clients carry over what they have learned in the exploration and insight stages into thinking about changes they might want to make in waking life. Remember, as therapists, we do not have much control over whether our clients complete their action plans. Instead, we can help clients articulate their intentions to carry out the plans. So, in the action stage, therapists are kind of like coaches or consultants to facilitate clients' exploration of action. There are three steps of the action stage: changing the dream, translating changes into waking life, and summarizing the action plan. It is important not to cut the action stage short, so plan ahead to leave enough time (usually about 15–20 minutes) to complete the action stage.

Changing the dream in fantasy. You can begin the action stage by asking the client how he or she would change the dream. The idea behind this question is that because the dreamer initially created the dream, he or she can change it as well. By taking responsibility for making changes in the dream, clients may begin thinking about taking responsibility for changes in waking life. Another benefit of asking clients how they would change the dream is that it gives therapists a glimpse into how ready the client is to change. If the client acts helpless and does not seem willing to change the dream, then he or she is probably not ready to make waking life changes. It is important to remember that not all clients feel comfortable changing a dream—in these cases, therapists may ask clients to imagine a sequel to the dream, or move directly to behavioral change. Alternatively, if a client seems stuck about changing the dream, I might suggest to the client how I would change the dream if it were mine. Similar to the insight stage, therapists should be aware of parts of the dream that the client ignores in the action stage. Discussing the omission with the client might necessitate cycling back to the insight stage. (The trainer should remind participants that cycling back and forth between stages is normal.)

Changing bad dreams. A specific application about changing dreams in the action stage is when clients have troubling dreams or nightmares. The idea here is to help clients change nightmares while in progress, that is, while they are sleeping. Some of you may have heard of *lucid dreaming*—the notion that one can become aware that one is dreaming and control some aspects of the dream. Using the concept of lucid dreaming, therapists can focus on two steps. First, teach the client in session to visualize the nightmare and stop it before it becomes too terrifying. Then, teach the client to change the nightmare into something more pleasant by inserting a positive image into the dream. Practice the change a few times in the session until the client seems confident that he or she can implement the change at the crucial time in the nightmare. Follow up with the client to discuss any difficulties in applying the procedure, and modify as needed. Another method is to suggest that the client befriend the terrifying image. (This might be especially helpful with young children.)

Translating changes to waking life. Asking clients how they would change the dream in fantasy is kind of a precursor, or warm-up to the next step of the action stage: bridging changes in the dream to changes in the client's waking life. Sometimes, possible changes in waking life are readily apparent after going through the stages; other times, changes in the dream do not translate easily into changes in waking life. Thus, you might want to first help hesitant clients assess the advantages and disadvantages of changing. For some clients, change may be more frightening than the familiar, if unsatisfactory and unpleasant, situation or feeling. If the client does not want to change, therapists should be respectful of the client's decision. If the client does want to change, there are several kinds of action he or she can take. I'll discuss three today: behavioral changes, rituals, and continued work on the dream.

Behavioral changes. If my client wanted to change her behavior in a dream to be a great orator, I might help the client improve her communication skills and practice specific situations in which the client could be clearer in her communication. Clients often know how they want to change but lack the necessary skills to do so. By using behavioral techniques such as reinforcement and feedback, we can help clients learn how to change their behavior. Even if the dream is not recent, you may still work on changes in current life. I assume that the client still remembers the dream because of some unresolved issue; therefore, I assess what might be going on in the client's current waking life that made her or him think about this dream, and work from there. Again, as in the insight stage, when therapists offer possible interpretations, in the action stage therapists can offer tentative suggestions for change.

Rituals. Another possible change in waking life is for the client to honor the dream or the work on the dream through some kind of ritual or symbolic act. I have used this step if the client is resistant to making waking life changes or if the dream does not seem conducive to specific behavioral change. Rituals that some clients have used include the following: a client purchased a picture of whales to remind her of her own gentle nature, and a client built a quiet spot in her garden like a spot she had seen in her dream.

Continued work on the dream. A third kind of action is to help the client continue to work on the dream. Because session time is often limited, and because therapists want to help clients acquire skills to work with dreams on their own, homework assignments for continued work on the dream can be helpful. I have encouraged clients to write the dream down, to continue thinking about the insights gained in the dream session, to keep a dream journal, and to use the self-help manual in Hill's (1996) book. Alternatively, clients who enjoy drawing, dancing, or music might use those modalities for continuing to work on the dream and exploring new insights into the dream.

Summarizing the action plan. The final step of the action stage, after exploring action, changing the dream, and using an action plan to translate changes into waking life, is to ask the clients to summarize what they learned from the dream and what they want to do differently in their lives based on the insights gained from the dream. As part of this process, I often ask clients to come up with a title for the dream that helps them remember the significance of the dream. Some examples of titles include "The Chase," "Remembering the Baby in Me," and "Distressing National Events Indicate Hidden Anxiety With Religious Expectations."

Thoughts about training in the action stage. Participants have typically felt that the action stage was easier to learn than the insight stage and more difficult to learn than the exploration stage. Participants also reported that time was a factor in learning the steps of the action stage. For instance, one therapist noted that the presentation of the action stage in the didactic part was rushed because time was running out. Similarly, a trainer reported that she found it challenging to describe and discuss the action stage in the brief time allotted. Trainers, therefore, should allow enough time to thoroughly present each stage of the model and answer any questions participants have about each stage.

Trainers should also recognize that therapists may have different beliefs about whether to encourage action or change in clients. One trainer noted that the action stage is usually the most difficult part for her to teach, because participants can be reluctant to push action with some clients or think that action means making the client do something, even though the action stage in reality tends to be more an exploration of action. Similarly, participants, depending on their theoretical approaches to therapy, may be unfamiliar or uncomfortable with the idea of developing an action plan. One participant reported that he was not used to "action stuff" in counseling. Trainers, therefore, should be clear in the didactic portion that the goal of the action stage is to help clients think about changes they might want to make in waking life rather than instituting waking life changes (see chap. 3, this volume). Likewise, trainers may want to remind participants to be sensitive to the client's readiness to change (Prochaska, DiClemente, & Norcross, 1992).

Experiential Portion

The second portion of the training is an experiential portion in which participants have an opportunity to practice the model. This can be done in a number of ways at the discretion of the trainer. I have found that working on a dream in a group setting is a good way to show participants how the model fits together and to encourage involvement from the training participants (see chap. 5, this volume, which addresses group dream work).

What I typically do is have the participants lead the dream work so that I can be the coach. I first ask whether someone is willing to be the dream client. After the dream is told, we write the images on the board and pick 5 to 6 images. Then, we go around and the first participant asks for a description (D) of the first image. The second participant asks for feelings (R) of the first image, the third participant asks the dreamer for associations to the same image (A), and the next participant inquires about waking life triggers (W). I give the participants gentle feedback or offer suggestions as they practice doing the exploration steps. We then go on to the second image, and so forth, through the 5 to 6 images. During this part of the experiential portion, I encourage participants to try out each part of the DRAW steps and ask me any questions about the exploration stage. One participant then summarizes the exploration stage.

In the insight stage, one participant asks the dreamer for an initial interpretation of the dream. Several participants then offer an interpretation and allow the dreamer an opportunity to respond and then work with the dreamer to explore and expand the interpretation. Then a participant asks the dreamer to summarize what the dreamer has learned from the insight stage.

In the action stage, one participant asks the dreamer to change the dream, and another participant asks the dreamer to bridge those changes to waking life. We continue in the action stage by having a participant ask about continuing to work with the dream. If there is time, the trainer might ask two or three people what they might do if the dream were their own. Finally, a participant asks the dreamer to summarize what the dreamer learned about the process and the dream.

As a trainer, I try to be very conscious of the time so that we can move through each stage in a timely manner. I also act as a coach in case a participant gets stuck in a stage or step of the model. I might suggest an interpretation or action during the appropriate stage to serve as a model to the participants, but my primary goal is to encourage participants to try out the model.

Another way to practice in a group format is to use a sample dream (such as the one presented below). Some groups—for example, a cohort of graduate students, or colleagues in a counseling center—may not feel comfortable sharing a dream in front of their colleagues or supervisors, so using a sample dream is a good way to ensure that participants have a chance to practice under the trainer's watchful eye. When using a sample dream, participants will still be able to practice the steps, but they will take turns being the dreamer at the different stages. For example, one participant may be the dreamer for the exploration stage and respond to the other participants' DRAW inquiries. Another participant takes on the role of the dreamer in the insight stage in order to give everyone a chance to practice offering interpretations at different levels and exploring what fits for the dreamer if it were his or her dream. In the action stage, a third participant acts as the dreamer, and the other participants help the dreamer explore action and changing the dream.

> **Dream:** My family and I are at a huge picnic with lots of people we don't know. All of a sudden, everyone starts running up this hill. I can't tell where they are going, but they seem very excited. I want to go and see what's up there, but my family lags behind, picking up all our picnic things. By the time we get to the top of the hill, we see a spaceship taking off. Everyone waves to us. I feel sad that we missed the spaceship.

When the group includes all therapists, another way of practicing the dream model is to have a participant role play a client who recently brought a dream into a session. I have used this approach with a cohort of graduate students, and the role play seemed to work well in giving participants an opportunity to practice the model. However, it might be difficult for participants to remember the dream or related information about the client, or to put themselves in the role of the client. Having several ways of approaching a group dream work exercise allows the trainer some flexibility in case no one is willing to share a dream or if the dreamer turns out to be kind of a dud. In the latter case—when the participant who volunteers to share a dream is fairly dull, boring, or reluctant to disclose information—then the experiential portion suffers. If this situation arises, in the insight stage the trainer can redirect some of the focus from the dreamer to other members by asking participants to give an interpretation of the dream as if it were their own dream. Then, during the action stage, participants suggest actions as if it were their dream. A cautionary note about group dream work is in order before moving to the dyad training. Although trainers will want to be aware of the needs of the dreamer/volunteer participant and assess whether the experience might be too overwhelming or disclosing for the dreamer, the purpose of the group experiential portion is to allow participants an opportunity to practice the stages of the model. If the dreamer seems to be having some reactions to the group dream work, then the trainer can intervene (as described earlier in this paragraph) by redirecting the focus of attention from the dreamer to each of the participants. This allows the dreamer a chance to compose him- or herself and the other participants to continue practicing their skills.

Suggestions for Dyad Training

After the participants go through a group dream work exercise, trainers can divide participants into pairs to practice the complete model (or the trainer can ask for volunteer clients). I also typically give participants cheat sheets with the steps of the model as they practice. It is helpful to have the trainer be available during the experiential portion to answer any questions, offer suggestions, and so forth. The trainer should keep in mind that monitoring the sessions can be somewhat challenging, especially if there are many dyads of participants practicing the model. One trainer noted that it was difficult to "bounce back and forth between participants and give good feedback" during the experiential portion, so she had participants audiotape their practice session, and she provided written feedback. Alternatively, trainers could have assistants who are trained in the model available as consultants during the experiential portion. After all participants in the dyads have had an opportunity to work through the model, everyone can meet back together as a large group to discuss their experiences. I have found that people are very willing to share about difficulties they encountered in implementing the model and are relieved to hear that other participants had similar struggles. I typically ask about participants' experience as both the therapist and the dreamer, so that therapists may become aware of what their clients may be feeling at different stages of the model. I end the training by encouraging participants to try out their new skills when appropriate with clients. Figure 11.1 illustrates half-day and full-day training agendas.

Participants' Reactions to the Experiential Portion of Training

Most of the individuals surveyed on training in the Hill model have agreed that "the best way to learn the model is to just do some sessions." One participant noted that he

> particularly liked the part that involved doing a group interpretation in training. It was really cool to be able to watch the trainer modeling some very good clinical skills rather than just practicing on one another without getting to see a really experienced person at work.

Typical Training Agenda

Half-day training
- 8:30–8:45 am: Introductions
- 8:45–10:15 am: Didactic portion
- 10:15–10:30 am: Break
- 10:30–12:00 pm: Group dream work
- 12:00–12:30 pm: Group debriefing/feedback

Full-day training
- 8:30–8:45 am: Introductions
- 8:45–10:15 am: Didactic portion
- 10:15–10:30 am: Break
- 10:30–12:00 pm: Group dream work
- 12:00–1:00 pm: Lunch
- 1:00–4:00 pm: Dyad training (each person presents a dream)
- 4:00–4:30 pm: Group debriefing/feedback

Figure 11.1. Full- and half-day agendas for dyad training.

One participant noted that the experiential portion was "somewhat helpful, though I think you can learn some different things having a session with a classmate versus a real client. Still, practicing the model and flow of the session was important." Another participant reported that "the best way to learn is through practice." Similarly, a participant reported that she could not imagine not doing a practice part: "It was helpful when I got stuck to get ideas on how to overcome an obstacle. With one practice client, I was stuck, and the trainer suggested a gestalt intervention, which helped." By practicing the model, participants were able to "cement" the information learned in the didactic portion of the training.

RESEARCH ON TRAINING

Although there is not much research on training participants in the cognitive–experiential model, I close this chapter with some interesting research findings that might be interesting to explore in further empirical investigations. For instance, Crook and Hill (in press) found that therapists with more positive attitudes toward dreams were more likely to engage in all types of dream activities with clients. Attitudes toward dreams was measured by the Attitude Toward Dreams—Revised scale (ATD–R; Hill et al., 2001), a 9-item self-report measure of a person's attitudes about dreams. Participants responded to all items on a 5-point Likert scale (5 = *high*). A question arises, then, as to whether attitudinal change in therapists is possible.

In some additional analyses of Hill et al.'s (in press) study, some possible answers to this question may be found. Hill et al. showed that ATD–R scores for 15 therapists who were trained for the first time in the Hill model increased from 3.96 (SD = 0.70) before training to 4.23 (SD = 0.64) after participating in training and seeing clients for the study, $t(13)$ = 3.42, $p < .01$. In contrast, ATD–R scores did not change significantly (pretraining M = 4.37, SD = 0.41; posttraining M = 4.25, SD = 0.51) for the 14 therapists who had previous experience with the Hill model.

It is interesting to compare the data from the Hill et al. (in press) analyses of changes that therapists make to the mean of 3.88 ($SD = 0.83$) for the ATD–R of 129 practicing therapists collected by Crook and Hill (in press). If one uses an effect size (ES) analysis, no difference emerges between Hill et al.'s therapists before training and those in Crook and Hill's sample (ES = .10), but there was a difference between Crook and Hill's sample and posttests for both therapists trained for the first time (ES = .48) and therapists with some experience (ES = .55). Hence, therapists who obtained training and practice in the Hill model thought that dreams were more valuable after training than they did before training.

These results offer a tantalizing glimpse of the dynamic relationship between training, attitudes toward dreams, and use of dream work in therapy. It appears that therapists had more positive attitudes toward dreams after receiving training in dreamwork. Future researchers, therefore, could investigate the effect of training in dream work on the use of dream work in therapy and whether therapists' attitudes toward dreams is a mediating variable.

Another area that needs further research is the relative helpfulness of the didactic and experiential portions of the dream training. In an informal survey, most participants reported that both portions were helpful in learning the model. However, some participants indicated that the didactic portion was not as helpful as the experiential portion in understanding how to use the model. It is possible that people with certain learning or processing styles may benefit from different approaches to training.

Similarly, characteristics of trainers could influence how people learn and implement the cognitive–experiential model. Social influence theory (Barak & LaCrosse, 1975) suggests that the perceived attractiveness, trustworthiness, and expertise of trainers could influence participants. Perhaps participants who perceive the trainer as having desired characteristics are more likely to use the dream model in their clinical work than participants who do not have such perceptions.

A final area of research focuses on examining the effects of training in dream work on therapists' work with clients in private practice. Conducting training workshops in the cognitive–experiential model and then tracking the frequency with which participants use the model in their work with clients is an exciting prospect. In addition to assessing the frequency of dream work in therapy, researchers could also examine the effects of training on the therapeutic alliance and treatment outcome.

REFERENCES

Barak, A., & LaCrosse, M. B. (1975). Multidimensional perception of counselor behavior. *Journal of Counseling Psychology, 22,* 471–476.

Crook, R. E., & Hill, C. E. (2003, June). Working with clients' dreams in psychotherapy. *Dreaming*.

Hill, C. E. (1996). *Working with dreams in psychotherapy*. New York: Guilford Press.

Hill, C. E., Kelley, F. A., Davis, T. L., Crook, R. E., Maldonado, L. E., Turkson, M. A., et al. (2001). Characteristics and type of interpretation. *Dreaming, 11*, 53–72.

Hill, C. E., & O'Brien, K. M. (1999). *Helping skills: Facilitating exploration, insight, and action*. Washington, DC: American Psychological Association.

Hill, C. E., Rochlen, A. B., Zack, J. S., McCready, T., & Dematatis, A. (in press). Working with dreams: A comparison of computer-assisted, therapist empathy, and therapist empathy and input sessions. *Journal of Counseling Psychology*.

Kilpatrick, D. G., Resnick, H. S., Freedy, J. R., Pelcovitz, D., Resick, P., Roth, S., and & der Kolk, B. (1998). Post-traumatic stress disorder field trial: Evaluation of the PTSD construct-criteria A through E. In T. A. Widiger & A. J. Frances (Eds.), *DSM–IV sourcebook* (pp. 803–846). Washington, DC: American Psychiatric Press.

Perls, F. (1969). Gestalt therapy verbatim. New York: Bantam.

Prochaska, J. O., DiClemente, C. C., & Norcross, J. C. (1992). In search of how people change: Applications to addictive behaviors. *American Psychologist, 47*, 1102–1114.

Stoltenberg, C. (1981). Approaching supervision from a developmental perspective: The counselor complexity model. *Journal of Counseling Psychology, 28*, 59–65.

12
RESEARCH ON THE HILL COGNITIVE–EXPERIENTIAL DREAM MODEL

CLARA E. HILL AND MELISSA K. GOATES

Empirical evidence is needed to establish the effectiveness of the cognitive–experiential model of dream work, especially given the paucity of research on any method for working with dreams. Outside of our own research, we have found fewer than a handful of studies on dream work. In this chapter, we review the 19 studies that we and our colleagues have conducted on the Hill model of dream work[1] (see Table 12.1 for a review of each study). Although our journey in conducting the studies was by no means linear, we try to present the findings in a logically consistent manner. We first review

---

[1]Because the focus of this book is on the Hill dream model, we do not review the few studies on other models of working with dreams or nightmares (Dahlenburg, Christensen, & Moore, 1996; Krakow et al., 2001; Shuttleworth-Jordan & Saayman, 1989; Webb & Fagan, 1993). Similarly, we do not review studies on changes in dreams as a result of a variety of types of therapy (Bergin, 1970; Bishay, 1985; Breger et al., 1971; Carlson, 1986; Cavenar & Sullivan, 1978; Cavior & Deutsch, 1975; Cellucci & Lawrence, 1978; Glucksman, 1988; Greer & Silverman, 1967; Haynes & Mooney, 1975; Hendricks & Cartwright, 1978; Kellner et al., 1992; Marks, 1978; Maultsby & Gram, 1974; Melstrom & Cartwright, 1983; Miller & DiPilato, 1983; Silverman & Greer, 1968; Warner, 1983). See Hill (1996) and Van de Castle (1994) for reviews of this research.

TABLE 12.1
Summaries of Empirical Studies on the Process and Outcome of Studies Using the Hill Dream Model

Study	Clients	Therapists	Design	Treatment length	Results
Cogar & Hill (1992)	67 undergraduate students who got course credit.	6 graduate students, 2 PhD. All did readings, attended 2-hr workshop, and were supervised.	Compared dream work + dream monitoring, dream monitoring, and wait list control.	Six 1-hr individual dream sessions in Condition 1 using a precursor to Hill model.	No pre–post differences on GSI or self-esteem for Condition 1 (ES = −0.14 and 0.00). No differences among 3 conditions on GSI or self-esteem.
Hill, Diemer, Hess, Hillyer, & Seeman (1993)	60 undergraduate students who got course credit.	4 graduate students, 1 PhD. All had dream seminar, practice with model, and were supervised.	Compared work on own dream, another's dream as if own, and own troubling event.	One 60–90 min individual session.	Own dream condition better than other dream or event condition on Depth Scale and MIS, but no differences on positive and negative emotions.
Falk & Hill (1995)	34 adult women recently separated or divorced. No incentive for participation.	8 graduate students. 1st-timers did readings and attended a 6-hr workshop. All were supervised.	Compared dream group vs. wait list control. 4 groups, each with 4–6 members and 2 coleaders.	Eight 2-hr group sessions; 1 dream per session, with everyone projecting onto the dream.	Pre–post changes in dream insight, BDI, and IES (ES = 0.80, −0.45, −0.26) but not on BAI or self-esteem (ES = 0.02, 0.14) for dream clients. Dream group changed more than control on self-esteem and dream insight.
Diemer, Lobell, Vivino, & Hill (1996)	25 adults who were at least moderately distressed and remembered dreams. No incentives given for participation.	20 graduate students, 3 PhD. 1st-timers did readings and attended a 6-hr workshop. All were supervised.	Within-subject analysis of 2 dream sessions using Hill model vs. 2 event sessions.	Within 12 sessions of individual therapy, clients received 2 dream sessions, 2 event sessions, and 8 unstructured sessions.	Postsession outcome: no differences among types of sessions. Treatment outcome: pre–post changes on GSI, IIP, and dream insight (ES = −1.23, −0.75, 0.69). Cognitive complexity in 2nd dream session predicted session and treatment outcome.

Study	Participants	Design	Sessions	Results
Hill, Diemer, & Heaton (1997)	336 undergraduate students got course credit for completing measures. 65 volunteered for and participated in dream sessions for no additional credit.	8 graduate students and 1 PhD therapist. 1st-timers did readings and attended a 4-hr workshop. All were supervised.	Predicted who volunteered for dream sessions and who benefited from dream sessions. Analyzed most and least helpful aspects.	One 60–90 min individual dream session.	Volunteers for dream sessions had positive attitudes toward dreams, high dream recall, high openness, high absorption, and were more often women. Those who gained the most from dream sessions had recorded fewer dreams. Insight, waking life links, and therapist's input were cited as most helpful aspects.
Heaton, Hill, Petersen, Rochlen, & Zack (1998)	25 undergraduate students who received no incentive for participation.	8 graduate students. 1st-timers did readings and 10 hr of training, including 3 practice sessions. All were supervised.	Within-subjects comparison of therapist-facilitated dream sessions vs. self-guided dream sessions.	One 60–90 min individual therapist-facilitated session and one 60–90 min self-guided session.	Clients rated therapist-facilitated higher than self-guided on Depth Scale, SIS—Understanding, MIS, Exploration–Insight (EI) Gains, and Action Gains. At follow-up, clients rated therapist-facilitated higher than self-guided, and 88% preferred therapist-facilitated.
Heaton, Hill, Hess, Hoffman, & Leotta (1998)	1 distressed undergraduate students who received no incentive for participation.	1 experienced graduate student who was supervised.	Charted changes in assimilation across 20 sessions of therapy involving 12 dream sessions.	20 sessions of individual therapy: 5 recurrent dream sessions, 7 nonrecurrent dream sessions, 8 unstructured sessions.	Pre–post improvements on GSI, IIP, and dream insight. Maintained changes on GSI and IIP but not dream insight at follow-up. Client and therapist rated depth higher for dream sessions than unstructured sessions. Assimilation increased over therapy, mostly in recurrent-dream sessions.
Zack & Hill (1998)	38 undergraduate students who got course credit.	12 graduate students. 1st-timers did readings, attended 7-hr workshop, and practiced with a volunteer client.	Predicted outcome from dream valence, dream arousal, waking life stress, and attitudes toward dreams	One 60–90 min individual dream session.	Outcome was predicted by dream valence and attitudes toward dreams.

continues

TABLE 12.1 (Continued)

Study	Clients	Therapists	Design	Treatment length	Results
Hill, Nakayama, & Wonnell (1998)	51 undergraduate students who got course credit.	16 graduate students; all experienced with model. All trained in condition for 1 hr.	Compared description, association, and combination for exploring images.	One 20–40 min individual dream session focusing only on the exploration stage.	Association condition had higher EI Gains than description condition. No differences on depth, cognitive complexity, dream insight, or action ideas from dream.
Rochlen, Ligiero, Hill, & Heaton (1999)	42 undergraduate students with below-average attitudes toward dreams and dream recall who participated for course credit.	14 graduate students. 1st-timers did readings, attended a 7-hr workshop, and practiced with volunteer client.	Compared training to improve recall and attitudes, training to build dream work skills, and control.	Two 1-hr group training sessions followed by one 60–90 min individual dream session.	No significant differences among conditions in posttraining dream recall, attitudes toward dreams, or session outcome, but small to medium ESs indicated better outcome for skills than recall/attitudes condition in dream session.
Hill et al. (2000)	14 distressed adults who had troubling dreams and a recent loss.	9 experienced graduate students who did readings, attended 2-hr workshop on loss, and practiced with 2 volunteer clients.	Compared therapy focused on dreams vs. therapy focused on loss.	Eight to eleven 1-hr individual sessions. At least 5 (including the 1st session) involved dream or event work.	Dream clients rated session outcome higher, got involved more quickly in therapy, gained more dream insight, and kept fewer secrets but gained less insight about effects of past and loss and liked therapist guidance more than clients in loss condition.
Wonnell & Hill (2000)	43 undergraduate students who got course credit.	22 graduate students. All did readings, attended an 8-hr workshop focusing on the 2 conditions.	Compared all 3 stages of Hill model vs. Hill model without action stage.	One 60–90 min individual dream session.	Action stage > no action stage on SIS–Problem-Solving and action ideas, but no differences for depth, EI Gains, or Action Gains.

Hill et al. (2001)	105 undergraduate students who got course credit.	11 graduate students, 1 PhD. All in dream seminar, had experience with model, and were supervised.	Compared waking life vs. parts-of-self interpretations in insight stage; predicted outcome.	One 60–90 min individual session.	No differences between waking life and parts-of-self conditions. Clients who had positive attitudes toward dreams and pleasant dreams had better session outcome.
Kolchakian & Hill (2002)	40 male and 40 female undergraduate students in dating relationships. Usually at least 1 person in couple got course credit for participating.	17 graduate students, experienced in model, attended 4-hr workshop on couples dream work and practiced with volunteer couple.	Compared dream work with wait list. After waiting, wait list participants got sessions. Compared outcome for men vs. women and for own vs. partner's dream.	Two 90–120 min sessions; each person presented a dream for one session.	Women in dream sessions improved more in relationship well-being and dream insight than control. No differences between treatment and control for men. Women gained more from dream sessions (GDI) than did men. No differences on GDI for own dream vs. other dream.
Hill, Rochlen, Zack, McCready, & Dematatis (in press)	94 undergraduate students who got course credit.	25 graduate students, 4 PhD. 1st-timers did readings, attended 7-hr workshop, and practiced with a volunteer client. All were supervised.	Compared computer-assisted, therapist empathy, and therapist empathy + input conditions. Predicted outcome of 3 conditions. Analyzed most- and least-liked aspects.	One 60–90 min individual session.	Therapist conditions better than computer for session evaluation, no difference on dream insight, therapist empathy condition best for action ideas. At follow-up, therapist empathy input condition better than therapist empathy which was better than the computer on session evaluation.
Davis & Hill (in preparation)	51 spiritually oriented adults who got no incentive for participating.	29 graduate students, 1 MA, 1 PhD. 1st timers did readings, workshop, practice. Spiritual therapists did readings and workshop.	Compared waking life vs. spiritual interpretations in insight stage.	Two 90–120 min sessions.	Spiritual insight into dream and existential well-being increased pre–post for spiritual condition but not for waking life condition. No differences on session outcome index or overall insight.

continues

TABLE 12.1 (Continued)

Study	Clients	Therapists	Design	Treatment length	Results
Crook & Hill (in press)	N/A	129 practicing therapists randomly selected from American Psychological Association Division 42.	Survey about techniques for dream work and likelihood for doing dream work with different types of clients.	N/A	Therapists listen, connect dream to waking life, ask clients to describe images, and collaborate on interpretations. Don't interpret regarding relationship, unconscious, spirituality, or archetypes; mention working with dreams or explain how work with dreams; ask client to change dreams or life. Therapists likely to work with dreams if client has troubling dreams or is psychologically minded but not if client is psychotic or schizophrenic.
Wonnell & Hill (2002)	30 adults who got no incentive for participating.	24 graduate students, 4 interns, 2 PhDs. All did readings, workshop, practice.	Predicted intention to act and implementation of action from client involvement in action stage, difficulty of action plan, and therapist skills in action stage. Described components used in action stage.	Two 75–90 min sessions.	Intention was predicted by client involvement, difficulty of action plan, and therapist skills. Implementation was predicted by client involvement and difficulty of action plan. Therapists mostly defined the plan but also changed dream, developed strategy, and supported and reinforced.

Note. ES = effect size; GSI = Global Severity Index of the Symptom Checklist–90; MIS = Mastery Insight Scale; BDI = Beck Depression Inventory; IES = Impact of Events Scale; BAI = Beck Anxiety Inventory; IIP = Inventory of Interpersonal Problems; SIS = Session Impacts Scale; GDI = Gains From Dream Interpretation; PTSD = posttraumatic stress disorder.

the outcome of working with dreams to determine whether dream work is effective, and then we examine research on who volunteers for dream work, who benefits from dream work, the influence of therapists, the influence of client involvement, and the effectiveness of components of the model. Finally, we discuss several methodological issues involved in conducting research in this area and conclude with directions for future research. We hope that this review illuminates what we currently know and encourages others to get involved and do research on dream work.

IS DREAM WORK EFFECTIVE?

We review the outcome of dream work both at the session level and in terms of pre–post treatment changes. Session-level outcome involves evaluations immediately after the sessions. We look at, perceived gains made during sessions and the therapeutic alliance in sessions. In contrast, treatment outcome involves longer term changes (e.g., in symptomatology and interpersonal functioning) that occur as a result of dream work.

Session-Level Assessments of Outcome

Comparisons With Published Norms

One way to investigate the effects of dream work is to compare the session outcome for dream work with published norms for regular therapy. To do this, we used the Depth Scale of the Session Evaluation Questionnaire (SEQ; Stiles & Snow, 1984) because this measure has been used frequently as an index of session quality in psychotherapy research and because we have used it in many of our dream studies. Stiles and Snow developed the SEQ to assess session impact, which they considered to be a mediator between what happens in the session (process) and changes over time as a result of therapy (outcome). *Depth*, which is one of four subscales of the SEQ, refers "to a session's perceived power and value" (Stiles & Snow, 1984, p. 3) and is measured on a 7-point scale, with higher scores representing more depth.[2] We found that depth scores were significantly higher in the 12 dream studies

---

[2]The Depth Scale includes 5 bipolar items (deep–shallow, valuable–worthless, full–empty, powerful–weak, and special–ordinary) rated on a 7-point scale; high scores reflect high depth. In a sample of 942 sessions with 72 clients (primarily undergraduate and graduate students and a few community residents) and 17 therapists (graduate students in clinical psychology using a variety of theoretical orientations) at a psychology department clinic, Stiles and Snow (1984) reported average client-rated depth of 5.06 (SD = 1.00) and average therapist-rated depth of 4.62 (SD = 1.08). In a sample of 2,412 sessions of 218 adult clients from the community with 8 experienced therapists providing psychodynamic–interpersonal and cognitive–behavioral therapy, Stiles et al. (1994) reported average client-rated depth of 5.16 (SD = 0.91).

than in regular therapy (see Table 12.2).[3] Although the samples were somewhat different, and the number of sessions ranged from 1 to 20, the results are very consistent in that every dream study had higher ratings than regular therapy. Similarly, client ratings of gains in understanding across dream and regular sessions, using the Session Impacts Scale—Understanding subscale (SIS–U; Elliott & Wexler, 1994),[4] were significantly higher for five dream studies (see Table 12.2) than for regular therapy.[5] In contrast, even when differences were in the same direction, therapists did not rate depth significantly higher in dream studies than in regular therapy (see Table 12.2).[6] We can also conclude, then, that clients (but not therapists) perceived that sessions were deeper and that they gained more understanding in dream sessions than in regular therapy.

Comparisons Within Studies

Another way to address the effects of dream sessions is to compare dream work with other interventions within the same study in which clients are randomly assigned to condition (which controls for many confounding effects). Hill, Diemer, Hess, Hillyer, and Seeman (1993) compared clients working with their own dream, someone else's dream, or a recent troubling event in a single session. They speculated that if dreams are meaningful reflections of unconscious or waking conflicts, then working with one's own dream ought to be superior to the other two conditions in terms of session outcome. However, if people create meaning out of meaningless symbols, and thus the projection process is the key mechanism of change, then working on someone else's dream as if it were one's own should be just as effective as working with one's own dream in terms of session outcome. Finally, if the structured approach of carefully exploring each image and then constructing meaning and figuring out what to do differently is the key ingredient, then using the model to work with a recent troubling event (e.g., irrational anger at a spouse) should be just as effective as the other two conditions, because the same three-stage model was used in all conditions. Results indicated that

---

[3] One-sample t tests, which involved a comparison of the set of studies against a criterion study, were used to test differences. The average of 6.19 (SD = 0.29) for depth in the 12 dream studies is significantly higher than the average score of 5.06 (SD = 1.00) for regular therapy in Stiles and Snow's (1984) study, $t(11) = 3.71, p < .01$, and 5.16 (SD = 0.91) in Stiles et al.'s (1994) study, $t(11) = 3.25, p < .01$ (see Table 12.2).
[4] The SIS–U is a 3-item subscale (with a 5-point scale on which 5 = *high*) that measures amount of insight into self, insight into others, and awareness.
[5] Using a one-sample t test, we found that the mean client-rated SIS–U for five dream studies (M = 3.67, SD = 0.16) was significantly higher than the average (M = 2.60, SD = 1.05) in Stiles et al.'s (1994) study, $t(4) = 12.33, p < .001$ (see Table 12.2).
[6] A one-sample t test revealed that the average therapist-rated depth score for four dream studies of 5.32 (SD = 0.48) was not significantly higher than the standardized score of 4.62 (SD = 1.08) for regular therapy (Stiles & Snow, 1984), $t(3) = 1.75, p < .20$.

TABLE 12.2
Comparison of Effect Sizes for Client-Rated Session Evaluation Questionnaire—Depth Subscale (SEQ–Depth) and Session Impacts Scale—Understanding Subscale (SIS–U) and Therapist-Rated SEQ–Depth in Dream Work Sessions as Compared to Regular Therapy Sessions

Study	N	No. sess[a]	Sample type[b]	Client scores							Therapist scores		
				SEQ–Depth			SIS–U			SEQ–Depth		
				M	SD	Standard[c]	M	SD	Standard[c]	M	SD	Standard[c]
Hill et al. (1993)	20	1/1	1	6.16	0.87	7.08						
Diemer et al. (1996)	25	2/12	2	6.18	0.74	8.35	3.76	0.85	4.42	5.46	0.68	8.03
Hill, Diemer, & Heaton (1997)	65	1/1	3	6.18	0.82	7.54	3.83	0.96	3.99	5.33	0.96	5.55
Zack & Hill (1998)	38	1/1	1	5.86	0.97	6.04	3.54	0.84	4.21			
Heaton, Hill, Petersen, et al. (1998)	25	1/2	3	6.43	0.41	15.68	3.75	0.87	4.31			
Heaton, Hill, Hess, et al. (1998)	1	12/20	4	6.80	0.34	20.00						
Rochlen et al. (1999)	42	1/1	5	5.72	0.79	7.24	3.45	0.94	3.67	5.78	0.57	10.14
Wonnell & Hill (2000)	20	1/1	1	6.17	0.91	6.78				4.69	1.34	3.50
Hill et al. (2000)	7	5/8–11	6	6.49	0.40	16.23						
Hill et al. (2001)	105	1/1	1	6.07	0.81	7.49						
Davis & Hill (in prep)	51	2/2	7	6.23	0.76	8.20						
Hill et al. (in press)	55	1/1	1	5.98	0.66	9.06						

[a]Number of dream sessions/number of total sessions.
[b]1 = one-time-only dream sessions with undergraduate psychology students who received course credit for participating but self-selected into this particular study; 2 = adult clients who volunteered for this study and received no compensation and received 2 dream sessions within 12 sessions of therapy; 3 = one-time-only dream sessions with undergraduate students who volunteered for this study and received no compensation; 4 = 12 sessions of dream work within 20 sessions of regular therapy with 1 undergraduate student who volunteered for this study and received no compensation; 5 = one-time-only dream sessions with undergraduate students who were below-average in attitudes toward dreams and dream recall and who received course credit for participating but self-selected into this particular study; 6 = adult clients who volunteered for this study and received no compensation and received at least 5 dream sessions within 8–11 sessions of regular therapy; 7 = spiritual adult clients who volunteered for this study and received no compensation and received 2 dream sessions. Only those clients within each study who received the full therapist-guided Hill model of dream work for one of their own dreams were included.
[c]Standardized score = M / SD.

clients who worked with their own dreams rated depth and insight higher than did clients in the other two conditions, although no differences were found among conditions for client-rated positive and negative emotions. These results provide some evidence that the effectiveness of dream work is due at least partly to dreams and that dream work is more helpful than some other types of interventions.

In Diemer, Lobell, Vivino, and Hill's (1996) study, all clients received 2 dream sessions, 2 event sessions (i.e., in which the focus was on a recent troubling event), and 8 regular (i.e., no predetermined focus) sessions within 12 sessions of therapy (order of dream and event sessions was counterbalanced). No differences were found among the three types of sessions in client-rated or therapist-rated depth, insight, and working alliance, suggesting that working with dreams was no more effective than focusing on troubling events or other issues. However, there may have been a ceiling effect given that scores were extremely high for all three types of sessions (> 6 on a 7-point scale), suggesting that it may have been difficult to detect differences among types of sessions. Furthermore, a spillover effect might have occurred, such that the benefits of dream sessions spilled over into ratings of other sessions. This last alternative hypothesis is compelling given that ratings of unstructured sessions were much higher than those that have been reported for regular therapy (Stiles et al., 1994; Stiles & Snow, 1984).

In a 20-session case study, Heaton, Hill, Hess, et al. (1998) found that both client-rated and therapist-rated depth scores were higher for dream sessions (that focused on both recurrent and nonrecurrent dreams) than for unstructured sessions.[7] Similar to Diemer et al.'s (1996) study, this study involved a within-subject design but found differences between conditions, casting some doubt on the ceiling effects and spillover hypotheses.

In Hill et al.'s (2000) study, clients were selected because they were having troubling dreams and had sustained recent losses. They were then assigned either to brief therapy (9–11 sessions) that focused either on dreams or loss. Dramatic differences between the dream-focused and loss-focused conditions were found for session outcomes. Figure 12.1 shows that clients in the dream condition rated session outcome (a composite of the Depth scale, Working Alliance Inventory [WAI-S; Tracey & Kokotovic, 1989]; Mastery–Insight Scale [MIS; Kolden, 1991], and Gains From Dream Interpretation [GDI; Heaton, Hill, Petersen, et al., 1998] scales) high at the beginning of therapy, and their ratings stayed high throughout therapy, whereas ratings for clients in the loss condition started low and increased over therapy but never reached the same level as clients in the dream condition. Figure 12.2

---

[7]The average client-rated Depth score for the recurrent and nonrecurrent dream sessions was 6.79 (SD = 0.34), whereas the average for the unstructured sessions was 6.17 (SD = 0.57), which is a large effect size (1.51). The average therapist-rated Depth score for recurrent and nonreccurent dream sessions was 5.76 (SD = 0.57), whereas the average for the unstructured sessions was 4.83 (SD = 0.53), which is a large effect size.

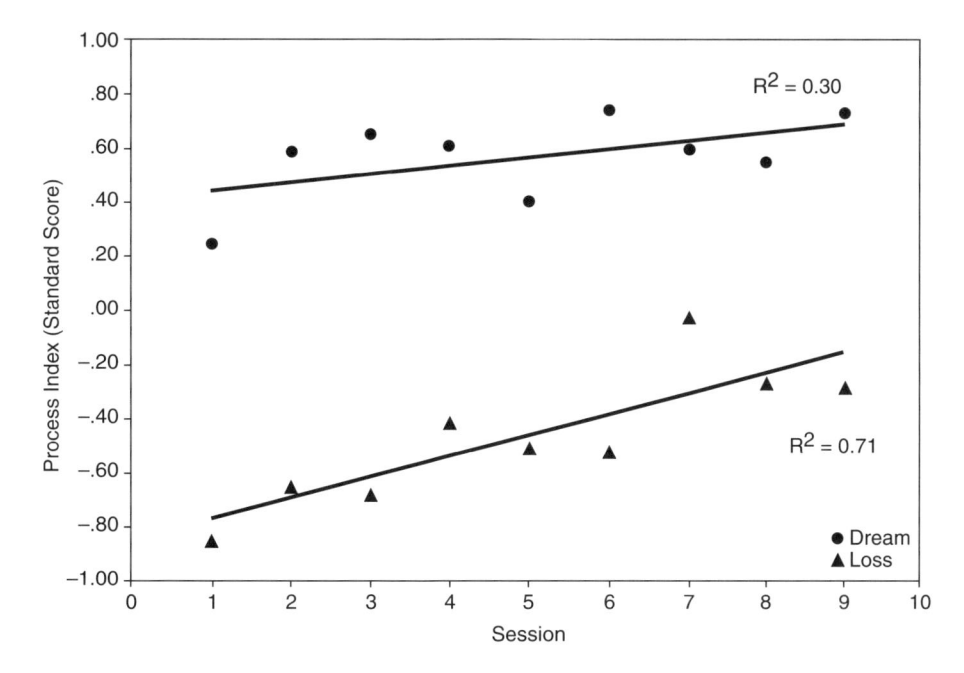

Figure 12.1. Changes in the composite client-rated process index (composite of Working Alliance Inventory–Short Form, Session Evaluation Questionnaire–Depth subscale, Mastery–Insight Scale. Exploration/Insight Gains, and Action Gains) over time for dream and loss conditions. From "Structured Brief Therapy With a Focus on Dreams or Loss for Clients with Troubling Dreams and Recent Losses," by C. E. Hill, et al., 2000, *Journal of Counseling Psychology*, *47*, p. 95. Copyright © 2000 by the American Psychological Association. Reprinted with permission.

shows that dream condition therapists rated the working alliance higher at the beginning of therapy, but loss condition therapists increased to the same level as dream condition therapists by the end of therapy. Given that the two conditions used the same model, these results suggest that the focus on dreams adds something above and beyond the structure of the model.

Three of the four studies that have compared a focus on dreams with other foci within the same study found evidence for the effectiveness of working with dreams in terms of session outcome. It is notable that these effects were found for single sessions of dream work as well as for dream work conducted within brief therapy.

Summary of Session-Level Assessments of Outcome

In comparisons to normative data, clients (but not therapists) rated depth higher and perceived themselves as gaining more understanding from dream sessions than from regular sessions. Furthermore, when dream sessions were compared with other foci within the same studies, three of four studies found higher session-level ratings for dream sessions than non-dream sessions. Hence, these results suggest that clients evaluate dream sessions as more effective than regular therapy.

Treatment Outcome

We tested for changes as a result of treatment in the six studies that involved more than one session of treatment.[8] The most consistent changes have been on ratings of insight into dreams. The method used for obtaining insight ratings involves two steps: First, clients write an interpretation of the same dream before and after dream work, and then the paired interpretations

---

[8]As is often done in meta-analyses, we excluded the Cogar and Hill (1992) study from this meta-analysis because it was our first study of the model and was completed before the model was well developed, we did not define for therapists exactly what they should do in sessions, and we did not check for adherence to the model.

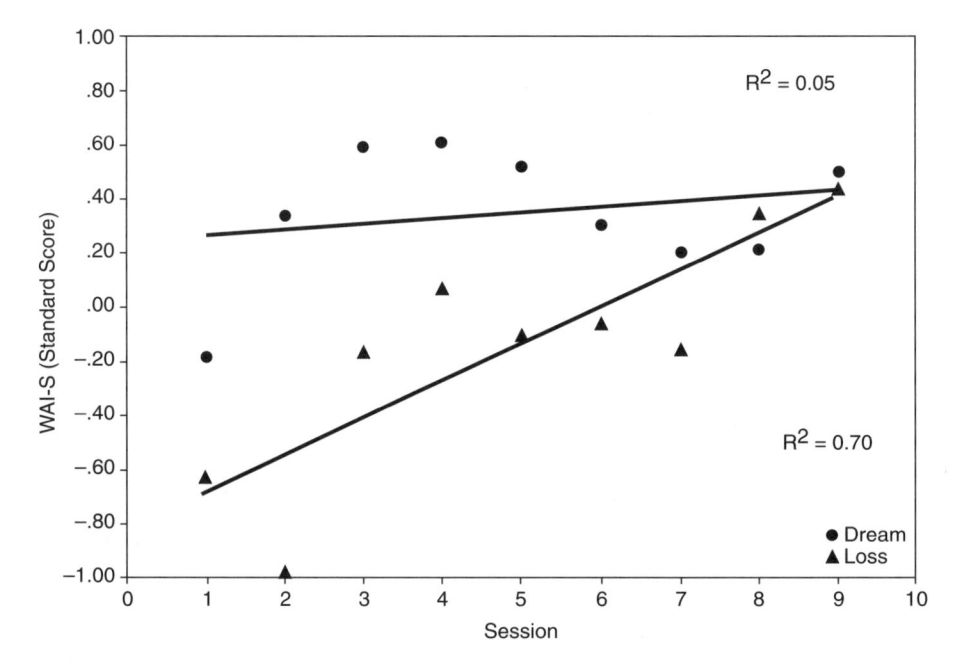

Figure 12.2. Changes in therapist ratings of the working alliance over time for dream and loss conditions. From "Structured Brief Therapy With a Focus on Dreams or Loss for Clients with Troubling Dreams and Recent Losses," by C. E. Hill, et al., 2000, *Journal of Counseling Psychology, 47*, p. 96. Copyright © 2000 by the American Psychological Association. Reprinted with permission.

are rated by trained judges on a 9-point insight scale[9] (9 = *high*), without judges knowing which interpretations were written at pre- or posttreatment. Effect sizes[10] (ESs) for gains in overall insight ranged from 0.06 to 1.64,[11] with an average ES of 0.74 for all samples (individual, group, couples) and an average ES of 1.06 for individual sessions. These results suggest that clients gained considerable insight into their dreams, particularly in individual sessions.

Attempts have also been made to investigate more specific types of insight. Kolchakian and Hill (2002) rated insight into the partner's dream and insight into the relationship, and Davis and Hill (2003) rated spiritual insight. The results suggest that clients gained the most insight into whatever was the focus of sessions.[12] Hence, when the relationship was the focus, clients gained more insight into the relationship than into their own or their partner's dream. Similarly, clients gained more spiritual insight when spirituality was the focus than when it was not the focus of the insight stage.

Another way of assessing change as a result of treatment is to assess changes in in-session behaviors. More specifically, Heaton, Hill, Hess, et al. (1998) studied changes in assimilation for a successful 20-session case of therapy with a dissociative client who had recurrent dreams. They used the Assimilation of Problematic Experiences Scale (Stiles, Meshot, Anderson, & Sloan, 1992), which maps the progress of client change in incorporating a problematic experience into his or her broader network of schemas. Stiles et al. (1992) hypothesized that problematic experiences progress from being initially warded off from conscious awareness, to being vaguely acknowledged, to being articulated clearly, to gaining insight, and then to problem solving in successful therapy. In Heaton, Hill, Hess, et al.'s (1998) study,

---

[9]*Insight* was defined as "Client expresses an understanding of something about himself or herself and can articulate patterns or reasons for behaviors, thoughts, or feelings. Insight usually involves an 'aha' experience, in which the client perceives self and world in a new way. The client takes appropriate responsibility rather than blaming others, using 'shoulds' imposed from the outside world, or rationalizing" (Hill et al., 1992, pp. 548–549).

[10]Effect size was determined using Cohen's $d = M_{post} - M_{pre} / SD_{average\ of\ pre\ +\ post}$. To interpret the results, consider that a large effect is >.80, a medium effect is between .50 and .79, and a small effect is between .20 and .49 (Cohen, 1988).

[11]The effect size was .07 for men and .06 for women in two dream sessions with dating couples (Kolchakian & Hill, 2002), .69 for 12-session individual therapy including 2 dream sessions (Diemer et al., 1996), .80 for dream groups (Falk & Hill, 1995), .90 for 2 individual dream sessions focused on waking life interpretations, .99 for 2 individual dream sessions focused on spiritual interpretations (Davis & Hill, 2003), and 1.64 for a case in which a client received 20 sessions of therapy including 12 sessions of dream work (Heaton, Hill, Hess, et al., 1998).

[12]In Kolchakian and Hill's study of dating couples, the effect size for gains in insight into a partner's dream was .01 for both men and women, and that for gains in insight into the relationship was .24 for men and .53 for women. In the Davis and Hill study comparing spiritual and waking life interpretations in the insight stage, ES for gains in spiritual insight was 1.20 for the spiritual condition but was –.04 for the waking life condition.

assimilation increased modestly over treatment, with more changes occurring during the five sessions working on recurrent dreams than in the eight sessions working on nonrecurrent dreams or the seven unstructured sessions. Furthermore, although not reported in the published article, the authors also rated the level of anxiety and personal involvement (using scales published by Breger, Hunter, & Lane, 1971) in the written dreams reported by the client after every four sessions of therapy (dreams were rated in a random order by trained judges). In these dreams, rated anxiety steadily decreased (from 4.17 to 1.00 on a 7-point scale), and personal involvement steadily increased (from 2.17 to 3.92 on a 7-point scale) over the course of therapy.

Pre–post change has also been assessed using a number of standardized measures typically used to assess outcome in psychotherapy research.[13] Small to medium ESs have been found for decreases in symptomatology and impact of the traumatic event and for increases in interpersonal functioning and perspective taking. In addition, a medium ES was found for existential well-being when the focus of the insight stage was spiritual.

Only two studies have compared dream work participants to wait list controls, which is important to control for confounding effects (e.g., of history). Evidence for treatment effects was found for increases in self-esteem and dream insight for group dream therapy (Falk & Hill, 1995). Furthermore, changes were found in relationship well-being, rated dream insight, and gains from dream interpretation for women in couples dream therapy (Kolchakian & Hill, 2002).[14]

---

[13]Using the Global Severity Index of the Symptom Checklist 90, Diemer et al. (1996) found a large effect (–1.23), and Hill et al. (2000) found a small effect (–.33), indicating decreases in symptomatology. For the Outcome Questionnaire, Wonnell and Hill (2002) found a small effect (–.35), indicating decreases in symptomatology. On the Inventory of Interpersonal Problems, Diemer et al. (1996) found a medium effect (–.75), but Hill et al. (2000) did not find an effect, indicating mixed evidence for changes in interpersonal functioning. For the Impact of Event Scale, both Hill et al. (2000) and Falk and Hill (1995) found small effects (–.42 and –.26, respectively), suggesting improvement in reactions to a specific traumatic event. For the Beck Depression Inventory, Falk and Hill (1995) found a small effect (–.45), indicating decreases in depression. For Existential Well-Being, Davis and Hill (2003) found a medium effect size (.60) for two sessions of spiritually focused dream work but no effect (.00) for two sessions of waking life focused dream work. For Other Dyadic Perspective Taking, Kolchakian and Hill (2002) found a small effect for men (.33) but none for women (.17), suggesting that men increased in their ability to take their partner's perspective. No effects were found on the Beck Anxiety Inventory, Rosenberg Self-Esteem Scale, Dyadic Adjustment Scale, Primary Communications Inventory, and Self Dyadic Perspective Scale (Falk & Hill, 1995; Kolchakian & Hill, 2002).

[14]In Falk and Hill's (1995) study, women in a dream group benefited more than women on a wait list control on the Rosenberg Self-Esteem Scale and ratings of dream insight into their dreams, but there were no differences on the Beck Anxiety Inventory, the Beck Depression Inventory, or the Impact of Events Scale. In Kolchakian and Hill's (2002) study of dating couples, female partners in the dream condition improved more in relationship well-being (a composite of scores on the Dyadic Adjustment Scale, Primary Communication Inventory, Other Dyadic Perspective Taking, Self Dyadic Perspective Taking), insight into their dreams, and gains from dream interpretation than female partners in the wait list control condition, whereas no differences were found for the male partners between the dream and wait list condition.

Finally, we recently developed a rating scale to assess the quality of action ideas[15] to assess gains made during the action stage of the Hill model (Hill, Nakayama, & Wonnell, 1998). Wonnell and Hill (2000) found that clients who received the action stage had higher-rated quality of action plans than those who did not receive the action stage. Although we have not assessed pre–post changes with this measure, we would guess that clients would be likely to show changes on this measure similar to those with insight ratings, because action is a target of treatment.

Summary of Treatment Outcome

The most robust treatment outcome has been insight into dreams, which makes sense given that insight is a major target of the Hill dream model. Promising results in one study were found for changes on the Assimilation of Problematic Experiences Scale, dream anxiety, personal involvement in dreams, and quality of action plans, although these need to be replicated. Modest effects have been found on measures of symptomatology and interpersonal functioning, which also makes sense given that these constructs are not the direct targets of dream work. Changes in existential well-being and spiritual insight occurred only when spirituality was the focus of the sessions, and changes in relationship insight occurred only when the relationship was the focus of sessions.

WHO VOLUNTEERS FOR DREAM WORK?

In Hill, Diemer, and Heaton's (1997) study, undergraduate psychology students received course credit for completing a number of personality measures and keeping a diary of their dreams for 2 weeks. At the end of this task, they were asked whether they would be interested in participating in a dream interpretation session, although it was emphasized that they would receive no compensation for their participation. Of the 336 students who completed the first part of the study, 109 (32%) volunteered for dream sessions, and 65 (19%) actually participated the next semester. (No differences on personality measures were found between the 44 who volunteered but did not participate and the 65 who volunteered and participated.)

Female students were more likely to volunteer to participate in dream sessions than were men. Furthermore, students were more likely to volunteer

---

[15]Clients are asked to write a response to the following question: "Based on this dream, what changes would you like to make in your current life, and how would you go about making these changes?" The quality of the intended action is assessed by trained judges using a 9-point Likert scale (1 = *no action*, 9 = *high action*). Quality of intended action is assessed in terms of the relationship of the written action ideas to the dream (whether the action ideas seem connected to the dream), the number of ideas expressed, whether the ideas are clear and detailed, and whether it would be possible to carry out the ideas.

if they had positive attitudes toward dreams, were high in absorption (i.e., emotionally responsive to engaging in sights and sounds, think in images, become absorbed in vivid and compelling recollections and imaginings, and experience episodes of expanded awareness and other altered states), were more open to their experiences, and had higher estimated levels of dream recall. Variables that did not predict who volunteered to participate in dream sessions were average hours of sleep per night, neuroticism, extraversion, agreeableness, conscientiousness, vividness or visual imagery, and dream recall as assessed through diaries. So, volunteers appeared to be different from nonvolunteers. It is clear that not everyone is attracted to working with their dreams.

WHO IS MOST LIKELY TO BENEFIT FROM DREAM WORK?

In our clinical experience, we have noted that some people gain a lot from dream work, whereas others do not. These differences intrigued us and made us wonder whether we could predict who benefits from dream work. We have investigated a number of client self-report variables: psychological-mindedness, attitudes toward dreams, dream recall, demographic characteristics, and characteristics of the dream. We also surveyed therapists about which clients they thought were most suited for dream work.

Client Psychological-Mindedness

Psychological-mindedness has been described as a cognitive understanding of psychological issues and an ability to experience one's inner life and share others' feelings (Farber, 1989). Because the Hill dream model emphasizes both cognitive and affective understanding, we hypothesized that more psychologically minded clients would benefit more from dream work than less psychologically minded clients.

Indeed, therapists have reported to us anecdotally that they prefer to work with psychologically minded clients. Put more empirically, practicing therapists in Crook and Hill's (in press) survey reported that they would be very likely to do dream work with psychologically minded clients and less likely to dream work with non-psychologically minded clients. Furthermore, client psychological-mindedness was cited as a factor that facilitated implementing the action stage by 25% of therapists (Wonnell & Hill, 2000).

To date, however, the hypothesis that client psychological-mindedness is related to better outcome has not been verified statistically when we used client self-report measures of psychological-mindedness (the Private Self-Consciousness Scale, Fenigstein, Scheier, & Buss, 1975; Psychological Mindedness Scale, Conte, Plutchik, Jung, Picard, & Karasu, 1990; NEO–Five Factor Inventory Openness Scale, Costa & McCrae, 1992; Need for

Cognition Scale, Cacioppo, Petty, & Kao, 1984) and client-rated session or treatment outcome. Thus, it would appear that psychological-mindedness is not related to outcome when both are measured from the client's perspective. We should note, however, that these psychological-mindedness measures were not typically related to each other or to therapist ratings of client insight (Diemer et al., 1996), which raises questions about their validity. Trained observers might be able to provide more valid assessments of psychological-mindedness because they could be trained in the specific definition and manifestations of psychological-mindedness (e.g., Piper, Joyce, McCallum, Azim, & Ogrodniczuk, 2002).

Taken together, these studies suggest that therapists prefer working with psychologically minded clients but that client-rated psychological-mindedness does not make any difference in client-reported outcome of dream sessions. It might be more difficult and less fun for therapists to do dream work with less psychologically minded people, but it appears that clients who are not psychologically minded view themselves as profiting as much from dream work as their more psychologically minded counterparts.

Client Attitudes Toward Dreams

In early studies, we noted anecdotally that some clients who had poor attitudes about dreams did not seem to benefit from dream work. For example, one older male client who likened dream work to palm reading thought that dream work was a waste of his time; it is not surprising, then, that he did not benefit from dream work. Hence, we developed the Attitudes Toward Dreams (ATD)[16] measure (see Appendix B) to see whether it would predict outcome.

As mentioned earlier, clients who volunteered for dream work had more positive attitudes toward dreams, but dream attitudes were not related to client-rated or therapist-rated session outcome (ESs = .02 and .19, respectively) for those who participated in sessions (Hill et al., 1997). The restricted range of attitudes (i.e. all had positive attitudes) among participants may have precluded the finding of a significant relationship.

Two other studies (Hill et al., 2001; Zack & Hill, 1998) have been conducted that had a wider range of scores (both involved introductory psychology students who participated for course credit and so included people who valued and did not value dreams). In these studies, client attitudes were

---

[16]The ATD measure was first developed for the Heaton, Hill, Petersen, et al. (1998) study. It has been revised several times. The most recent version (Hill et al., 2001) includes 9 items using 5-point Likert scales (5 = *positive attitudes*), such as "I value my dreams," "I believe that dreams are one of the most important ways to understand myself," and "Dreams have no meaning." The ATD was positively related to the NEO Openness Scale, Need for Cognition Scale, estimated dream recall, and diary dream recall (Hill et al., 1997, 2001), so it seems to reflect a general openness and ability to remember dreams.

related to client-rated session outcome, such that clients with more positive attitudes toward dreams had better outcomes than students with negative attitudes.[17]

Finally, because socialization is an important part of the therapy process, we were interested in whether clients with negative attitudes toward dreams could benefit from training prior to sessions. Hence, in Rochlen, Ligiero, Hill, and Heaton's (1999) study, volunteer clients with below-average attitudes toward dreams and dream recall were assigned to 2 hours of training in one of three conditions: (a) focus on improving dream recall (i.e., volunteers were taught about the benefits of attending to dreams and provided suggestions for increasing recall), (b) focus on skills needed for dream work (i.e., volunteers were taught how to associate, make connections to waking life, identify themes or meanings in dreams, and identify areas for change in life), or (c) a control condition that focused on different approaches to counseling (i.e., volunteers viewed and discussed video excerpts of individual, marriage, family, and group counseling as well as excerpts of psychoanalytic, humanistic, and cognitive–behavioral counseling). After training, participants received a single dream session. Participants in the skills condition gained more from dream sessions than did participants in the other two conditions.

Attitudes toward dreams seem like a possible predictor of outcome when the range of attitudes is wide. Attitudes are not likely to predict outcome when clients volunteer for no incentive, because they are already likely to have positive attitudes. Furthermore, there is some preliminary evidence that training improves outcome.

Client Dream Recall

Clients must remember dreams to be able to participate in a dream session, so we wondered whether dream recall is a predictor of outcome. Hill et al. (1997) assessed dream recall in two ways. First, they obtained an estimate of recall by asking participants "During the last 2 weeks, immediately upon waking up in the morning, how often could you recall dreaming?" and "How often do you have dreams you remember?" They provided several alternatives for participants to check for each item and then summed the scores on the two items, because they were highly related (.72). Second, they asked clients to keep a diary for 2 weeks, writing down their dreams as

---

[17]In Zack and Hill's (1998) study, the effect size was .24 between ATD–R and a composite outcome index (combined scores on MIS, Depth, SIS–U, EI Gains, and Action Gains), but the nonlinear relationship was a better fit for the data. The best outcomes were obtained with clients who had moderate attitudes, whereas poorer outcomes were obtained with clients with low or high attitudes. These results were provocative but tentative given the small sample ($N = 38$). In a larger sample, Hill et al. (2001) found a linear relationship (ES = .40) between ATD–R and client-rated session outcome (composite of Depth, MIS, EI Gains).

soon as they awoke in the morning. No memory of dreaming was assigned a 1, recall of dreaming with no details was assigned a 2, and recall and written details were assigned a 3. The average score across the 14 nights was used as the indicator of dream recall.

Hill et al. (1997) found that estimated dream recall predicted who volunteered for dream sessions (higher recall was associated with volunteering) but that diary recall predicted client-rated and therapist-rated outcome (higher recall was associated with worse outcome). Hence, although correlated moderately (.52), these two different measures of dream recall clearly assess somewhat different things.

The findings about dream recall are somewhat conflicting. After reflecting on these findings, we realized that clients do not have to have high dream recall to participate in dream sessions; they need only recall one dream on which they are willing to work. If they do not remember any dreams—or, perhaps more important, do not value their dreams—they do not volunteer to participate. Hence, attitudes toward dreams is probably more important than dream recall for predicting participation and outcome of dream work.

Demographic Variables

Gender Effects

In studies of individual dream work (Hill et al., 1993, 2001; Hill, Rochlen, Zack, McCready, & Dematatis, in press; Zack & Hill, 1998), no gender differences have been found on session outcome. Hill et al. (in press) found that female participants had higher ratings of insight into their dreams than did male participants. Moreover, in Kolchakian and Hill's (2002) study of dream work with dating couples, women reported that they gained more from sessions than did men. Kolchakian and Hill suggested that men and women may adhere more to gender role stereotype interactions in couples work than in individual work (e.g., women discuss feelings, men solve problems). It would be interesting to include gender roles measures in future studies involving couples (see chap. 9, this volume).

Race–Ethnicity Effects

In three studies (Hill et al., 2001, in press; Zack & Hill, 1998), no differences were found among racial–ethnic groups on any measures. It may be, however, that other race–ethnicity effects would be found on other measures. For example, Kim, Atkinson, and Umemoto (2001) suggested that Asian American clients with high Asian values prefer therapists to be directive, so it seems likely that, in comparison to traditional Asian American clients, they would prefer therapists to be more active and directive in dream sessions.

Characteristics of Dreams

If dreams are indeed important stimuli, what about them leads to successful outcome? We have looked at a number of possibilities: valence, recency, vividness, arousal, and distortion.

Valence of dreams. Three studies, all involving single sessions with undergraduate clients, investigated the influence of the valence of dreams (i.e., positivity or pleasantness vs. negativity) on session outcome. Zack and Hill (1998) found a nonlinear relationship between dream valence and a session outcome index, such that the best session outcomes were attained with dreams that were moderately unpleasant or extremely pleasant, whereas the worst session outcomes were attained with dreams that were moderately pleasant or extremely unpleasant. With a much larger sample (105 vs. 38), Hill et al. (2001) found a significant linear (but not nonlinear) relationship between dream valence and session outcome, $r(103) = .33$, $p < .001$, such that session outcomes were best for positive dreams. Hill et al. (in press), however, found no relationship of any type between dream valence and session outcome. The inconsistency across studies is perplexing and points to an important area for further investigation. It may be that the therapy relationship mediates the effects of dream valence. Clients may be willing to explore positive dreams with any therapist but may be willing to explore negative dreams only when they trust their therapists.

Recency of dreams. In Wonnell and Hill's (2000) study, therapists reported that it was more difficult to work with older dreams in the action stage, and older dreams were associated with poorer client-rated gains in exploration–insight. However, client-reported recency of the dream did not predict client-rated session outcome (combined scores on Depth, Mastery–Insight, and Exploration–Insight Gains scales) or dream insight change in Hill et al.'s (2001) study. Salience of the dream to the client is probably more important than recency. Clients sometimes bring in dreams from years ago that they really want to understand, whereas they may not be as interested in working on recent dreams.

Vividness of dreams. Because the Hill model involves exploring images in great detail, we expected that clients would have a better outcome when they presented vivid dreams. Contrary to prediction, Hill et al. (2001) found that judge-rated vividness (i.e., vivid, clear, distinct, strong, intense vs. not vivid, vague, unclear, indistinct) was not related to outcome. Ratings, however, were high ($M = 6.76$, $SD = 1.93$ on a 9-point scale on which $9 = high$), which suggests that clients presented only dreams that were vivid. The restricted range of scores may have made it difficult to obtain significant relationships among vividness and outcome variables.

Arousal of dreams. Similarly, we thought that clients would have a better outcome when they presented arousing dreams. Contrary to prediction, Zack and Hill (1998) found that client-rated dream arousal (i.e., ratings on bipolar adjectives of stimulated–relaxed, excited–calm, frenzied–sluggish, jittery–dull, wide awake–sleepy, and aroused–unaroused) was not related to outcome. Ratings, however, were high ($M = 6.43$, $SD = 1.16$, on a 9-point scale on which 9 = *high*), which suggests that clients presented only dreams that were arousing. Again, the restricted range may have prevented a finding of significance.

Distortion of dreams. We thought that dreams directly linked to actual waking life events would be suitable for waking life interpretation, because the translation would be so apparent. In contrast, we thought that dreams that were discrepant from waking life would be more suitable to deeper levels of interpretation because they would not be so obviously representative of waking life events. However, in Hill et al.'s (2001) study, judge-rated distortion level (i.e., the degree to which people or objects in the dream appeared or behaved in ways that would seem uncommon in waking life) did not predict how much the clients benefited from either waking life or parts-of-self interpretations.

Summary of dream characteristics. Characteristics of dreams do not appear to be consistently good predictors of session or treatment outcome. It appears that clients can profit from working with pleasant, old dreams as much as from working with negative, recent, vivid, arousing, distorted dreams. White-Lewis (2002) wrote a compelling article about how people can gain a lot from working with trivial dreams, so it may be more the client's willingness to become involved in the dream work than the type of dream that matters. We should note, however, that these results could be an artifact of the research methodology used. In all the studies reviewed in this chapter, clients chose which dreams they brought into sessions. They may have brought in dreams that were at least somewhat important rather than the whole range of dreams (which harkens back to the findings for attitudes for dreams being significant only when we had the whole range of scores). To test this hypothesis more fairly, researchers would need to manipulate the type of dream by asking clients, for example, to bring in trivial or important dreams.

Therapist Perspective on Who Is Likely to Benefit From Dream Work

In a survey of 129 practicing therapists, Crook and Hill (in press) found that therapists were very likely to work with dreams with two clusters of clients: (a) clients who presented troubling or recurrent dreams or nightmares or who had posttraumatic stress disorder and (b) clients who were psychologically minded, interested in learning about and working with their dreams, and healthy and seeking growth. They were moderately likely to work with dreams when clients were adjustment disordered, in long-term therapy, depressed/anxious, presenting dreams as a way of avoiding important life issues, presenting pleasant dreams, at an impasse in therapy, personality disordered, or presenting substance abuse problems. They were not likely to do dream work with clients who were schizophrenic, psychotic, or not psychologically minded. Hence, therapists had clear internal guidelines, presumably based on clinical experience, for when it is potentially fruitful to work with dreams.

Summary of Predictors of Outcome

The only variable that has been replicated across studies as a predictor of outcome is attitudes toward dreams, and that was only when there was a wide range of scores. It appears that clients must value their dreams or else they will not benefit from dream work. Likewise, therapists indicated that they were likely to work with clients who valued their dreams. These results point to the importance of assessing attitudes and perhaps educating clients about the benefits of working with dreams.

Variables that had seemed promising as predictors of outcome (e.g., dream recall, psychological-mindedness, dream characteristics, demographic variables) were not consistently predictive of outcome. Moreover, a number of other client variables did not predict outcome: client openness (Diemer et al., 1996; Hill et al., 1997); neuroticism, extroversion, agreeableness, conscientiousness, vividness of visual imagery, hours of sleep per night, anxiety before sleep (Hill et al., 1997); visualization–verbalization (Cogar & Hill, 1992); and stress level (Zack & Hill, 1998). Perhaps these findings are good news because they suggest that therapists can do dream work with any clients who are willing to work with their dreams.

Other variables could be examined. Of particular interest is the severity of client disturbance, as suggested in Crook and Hill's (in press) survey of practicing therapists and in the psychotherapy literature (Beutler, Harwood, Alimohamed, & Malik, 2002). Another possible variable is *reactance*, or a predisposition to resist external influence (the opposite of openness; Beutler, Moleiro, & Talebi, 2002; Dowd, Milne, & Wise, 1991). It may be that what we are picking up with low attitudes to dreams or low recall is a more characterological resistance to influence. Finally, willingness to disclose to a stranger might be relevant (Kahn & Hessling, 2001). Because dreams can lead quickly to deep feelings, a lack of willingness to disclose might make it difficult for clients to become involved in sessions.

DO THERAPISTS MATTER?

In response to an open-ended question about what they liked about their dream sessions, one thing clients mentioned frequently was liking another person's input regarding their dreams (Hill et al., 1997). These results intrigued us, given the burgeoning self-help movement (Scogin, Bynum, Stephens, & Calhoon, 1990) and the large number of people who keep dream journals and work with dreams on their own. Hence, we have conducted two studies comparing therapist-facilitated and self-guided dream sessions.

In the first study (Heaton, Hill, Petersen, et al., 1998), clients participated in one session of self-guided dream work and one session of therapist-facilitated dream work. Clients gained more from and preferred therapist-facilitated sessions to self-help sessions. Some of the clients in the self-help condition, though, told us that the writing was tedious and boring and that they had a hard time getting involved.

We speculated that using a computer program to go through the model would be more engaging than the paper-and-pencil manual, so we developed The Dream Toolbox (see chap. 6, this volume), an interactive computer program that guides users through the steps of the model. We then compared a computer-assisted condition to two therapist-facilitated conditions, using single sessions of dream work. In the first therapist condition (empathy), therapists used open questions, restatements, and reflections of feelings to guide participants through the three stages. In the second therapist condition (empathy + input), therapists used the empathy interventions plus at least one interpretation in the insight stage and one action suggestion in the action stage. We discovered that clients had better session-level outcome (depth, session evaluation, exploration–insight gains, action gains) for the two therapist-facilitated conditions than for the computer-assisted condition, equal levels of rated insight into their dreams across the three conditions, and better action ideas in the empathy condition than in the other two conditions.

There was a small subgroup of participants in the computer condition who liked working by themselves (10%) and a small subgroup of participants in the empathy condition who did not like talking to a stranger (12%). Likewise, there was a subgroup of participants in the computer condition who would rather have worked with a therapist (23%) and a subgroup of participants in the two therapist conditions who really liked working with their therapists (21% and 24%). These results suggest that therapists matter more for some people than for others.

Most clients preferred to work with a therapist in trying to understand their dreams, although a small subgroup preferred working alone. It is important to note, though, that both the paper-and-pencil manual and the computer program were as effective as regular therapy, just not as effective as therapist-facilitated dream sessions.

DOES CLIENT INVOLVEMENT MATTER?

It seems obvious that clients need to be involved in the process for dream work to be helpful. Hill and Williams (2000) indicated that *client involvement* is a generic term indicating that the client is actively and productively involved in the tasks of therapy. In the psychotherapy literature, client involvement has most often been assessed through judges' ratings of experiencing, progress, assimilation, and cognitive complexity.

The psychotherapy literature indicates that clients who are more involved in their sessions have better outcomes than those with less involvement (Gomes-Schwartz, 1978) and that more involved clients have better session evaluations as rated by both therapists and clients (Eugster & Wampold, 1996). Bohart and Tallman (1999) estimated that 70% of change in therapy is due to clients. They suggested that therapy offers clients the opportunity for self-healing and that clients take advantage of whatever therapists offer to help them work through and resolve their problems.

When therapists were questioned about factors that contributed to the ease or difficulty of doing the action stage, they frequently mentioned that it was easier when clients were actively involved in sessions (Wonnell & Hill, 2000). In Falk and Hill's (1995) study of dream groups, however, client involvement (a composite of self-ratings, therapist ratings, and other group member ratings) was not related to treatment outcome. These findings are puzzling, but perhaps involvement is less relevant for dream groups than for individual or group therapy because dream groups focus on working to understand a particular person's dream rather than on the group process. It may be more involvement in the dream work is more relevant than involvement in the group.

In Wonnell and Hill's (2002) study of the action stage, judges rated the amount of client involvement, which was defined as amount of energy invested in the action stage, as manifested by the client's verbal and nonverbal activity, expression of affect, degree of initiative, and willingness to engage in the therapeutic process. Client involvement predicted client intention to implement action as well as actual implementation of action (accounting for 32% and 15% of the variance, respectively).

The cognitive complexity of the dialogue is another way to operationalize client involvement. In Diemer et al.'s (1996) study, judges' ratings of five scales of cognitive complexity (depth, elaborativeness, personal orientation, clarity, and conclusion orientation) were combined to form a composite cognitive-complexity score. This composite score was positively related to client and therapist judgments of insight gained, working alliance, and depth.

All three studies of individual dream work found positive relationships between client involvement and outcome, although one study of group dream work did not find a significant relationship. Further work (as was begun by Wonnell & Hill, 2002) needs to be done on defining and measuring client involvement in the specific tasks of dream work (e.g., involvement in the exploration, insight, and action stages).

COMPONENTS OF THE MODEL

Up to this point, we have discussed research on the model as a whole. Of course, however, the model has a number of components. We need to know the efficacy of the various components so that we can build a better model. We have tried three strategies to get at the effectiveness of the various components. First, we asked clients what they liked most and least in dream sessions. Second, we experimentally manipulated various components of the model. Finally, we asked practicing therapists to tell us what components of dream models (not just the Hill model) they are most likely to use with clients.

Qualitative Analyses of Most and Least Helpful Aspects of Dream Sessions

Table 12.3 shows the most and least helpful things that clients mentioned in three different studies (Hill et al., 1997, 2000, in press). Clients mentioned more helpful than unhelpful things, suggesting overall satisfaction. In addition, the unhelpful aspects were more diverse and difficult to cluster than the helpful components, suggesting that clients were not as consistent in the things they disliked as in the things they liked.

A summary of Table 12.3 indicates that clients in all three studies mentioned something positive about insight or interpretations, suggesting that one of the most helpful aspects of dream work is working on insight. In at least two of the studies, participants also mentioned associations, links to waking life, catharsis, getting an objective perspective, and liking the therapist. It is interesting that there were fewer references to action (changing the dream, making changes in waking life, learning new skills) being helpful, either because clients do not think these activities are important or because they were not as salient as exploration and insight activities. Another explanation for the lack of mentioning of action activities is the lower amount of time spent in action during dream sessions (see Wonnell & Hill, 2002).

Experimental Manipulations of Model Components

Exploration Stage

Hill, Nakayama, and Wonnell (1998) studied the impact of description and association in the exploration stage using three conditions: (a) description only, (b) association only, or (c) a combination of description and association. Results indicated that clients reported significantly more exploration–insight gains from the association condition than from the description condition, but there were no differences on client-rated session quality, judges' ratings of client cognitive complexity of client dialogue, judges'

TABLE 12.3
Helpful and Unhelpful Components of Dream Work

Study	Most helpful component	Least helpful component
Hill et al. (1997)	Gaining awareness, insight, understanding, meaning, explanation (55%). Linking dream to waking life (31%). Hearing new input or perspective (15%). Associations or symbolism (14%). Experiencing feelings or catharsis (9%). Ideas for changing dream or life (6%).	Some aspect of insight stage (parts of self interpretation, that therapist gave interpretation before client gave one, did not agree with therapist interpretation; 25%). Some aspect of exploration stage (figuring out what images meant, associations; 12%). Some aspect of action stage (therapist was too pushy, therapist did not give enough advice; 8%).
Hill et al. (2000)	Therapist was likeable/facilitative (general). Focus on dreams (typical). Interpretations (typical). Structure (typical). Guidance or suggestions (variant). Restatement or reflection of feelings (variant). Asking client to change dream (variant).	Negative perceptions of therapist or therapy (variant). Wanted a different focus (variant). Client problems interfered with progress (variant). Wanted to know more about therapist (variant).
Hill et al. (in press)	Gaining awareness and insight (36%, 44%, 55%). Making links to waking life (5%, 36%, 7%). Associating to dream images (28%, 16%, 14%). Overall method (28%, 8%, 14%). Liked therapist (3%, 24%, 21%). Catharsis (0%, 16%, 10%). Objective perspective (0%, 8%, 14%). Working by themselves (10%, 0%, 0%). Ideas for changing dream or life (3%, 8%, 3%).	Session was too long (31%, 16%, 7%). Something about computer program (31%, 0%, 0%). Nothing mentioned (15%, 16%, 28%). Wanted person instead of computer (26%, 0%, 0%). Repetitiveness (23%, 4%, 10%). Something about research (0%, 20%, 17%). Getting into feelings (3%, 12%, 7%). Talking to a stranger (0%, 12%, 3%). Perceived therapist mistake (0%, 12%, 7%). Did not value dream work (0%, 0%, 10%). Overall method (8%, 0%, 3%).

Note. In Hill et al.'s (1997) study, clients were asked to indicate in writing what they found most and least helpful about their dream interpretation session. Categories of responses were developed from the data, and each response was then assigned to one of the categories.

In Hill et al.'s (2000) study, clients were interviewed after the end of brief therapy. Using consensual qualitative research (Hill, Thompson, & Williams, 1997), categories were developed and responses placed into those categories. In the table, *general* means that all clients reported this response; *typical* means that more than half of the clients reported this response; and *variant* means that less than half of the clients reported this response. Note that client responses from another condition in this study (loss-focused therapy) are not presented here because they were not related to dream work.

In Hill et al.'s (in press) study, clients were asked to indicate in writing the most and least helpful aspects of their dream interpretation session. As with Hill et al.'s (1997) study, categories were developed based on the data, and then trained judges placed each response into one of the categories. The numbers after the components refer to the three conditions in Hill et al.'s (in press) study: (a) clients who used a computer program, (b) clients who worked with a client-centered therapist, and (c) clients who worked with a therapist who provided input in the form of one or two interpretations and suggestions for action.

ratings of insight in dreams, or judges' ratings of the quality of action ideas. Hence, associations were more helpful in terms of exploration and insight gains, but they were not more helpful on a number of other dimensions.

Insight Stage

A comparison of waking life and parts-of-self interpretations in the insight stage revealed no significant differences in terms of client-rated session process and outcome (Hill et al., 2001). Furthermore, both types of interpretation were equally effective with different types of clients and different types of dreams. A comparison of waking life and spiritual interpretations in the insight stage revealed no differences in nonspiritual outcomes (depth and general insight into dreams), but spiritual insight and existential well-being increased only for the spiritual condition and not for the waking life condition (Davis & Hill, 2003).

In the study described earlier, Hill et al. (in press) tested the impact of interpretations and suggestions for action in the insight and action stages. Results indicated better client-rated session-level outcome (depth, session evaluation, exploration–insight gains, action gains) for the two therapist-facilitated conditions than the computer-assisted condition, no differences in judged insight into dreams among conditions, the best action ideas in the empathy condition, and better 2-week follow-up client ratings for the empathy + input condition than for the other two conditions. Furthermore, in open-ended comments, some clients (14%) mentioned liking the objective perspective in the empathy + input condition. These results suggest that empathy, interpretations, and action suggestions were all valuable contributors to outcome. It is interesting that it did not make much difference immediately if therapists provided interpretations and action suggestions, but these interventions seemed to have had a lingering effect. Note that therapists in this study typically used only one or two interpretations or action suggestions per session, and these results might not generalize when therapists use more than that or when they do not use these interventions in a collaborative manner. Future research needs to separate interpretations and suggestions for action, because these two interventions might have very different effects.

Action Stage

Wonnell and Hill (2000) compared a condition including only the exploration and insight stages with another condition including all three stages (exploration, insight, and action). No differences were found for client-rated session depth or insight ratings, but clients who went through all three stages rated sessions higher on problem solving and were judged as having better action ideas (Wonnell & Hill, 2000). Furthermore, the action stage was easier for therapists to do when the dream was recent; the client was involved and psychologically minded; the therapist was experienced, confident, and comfortable with the action stage; and the goals of the exploration and insight stages had been attained.

Wonnell and Hill (2002) investigated what therapists actually did in the action stage and found that all therapists worked at least somewhat to define an action plan, about two thirds worked on changing the dream, about one third developed a strategy to implement the action, and about one third supported or reinforced the client for action. Furthermore, they found that client involvement, therapist skills in implementing the action stage, and the difficulty of the action plan predicted client intention to act at the end of the session and actual implementation of the action plan following the session.

Future Work on Components of the Three Stages

We need to know how much time should be spent in the exploration stage prior to moving to the insight stage, how many images need to be covered, and how to handle long dreams. In regard to the insight stage, we need to know more about what level of interpretation to use (e.g., experience, waking life, inner personality conflicts), when to offer interpretations versus when to encourage clients to come up with their own interpretations, and the importance of accuracy of interpretations. In regard to the action stage, we need to know more about when to use the various interventions in the action stage (e.g., changing the dream, bridging changes to waking life, suggesting rituals, and assigning homework) and how much to offer action suggestions versus encouraging clients to come up with their own action ideas. It is important to continue investigating the effects of components of the model, and we need to keep revising the model as we gather more empirical evidence about the components.

Therapists' Report on Components of the Model Used in Therapy

Another way to assess the helpfulness of components of the model is to ask therapists which components they use in actual therapy. In Crook and Hill's (in press) survey, 129 therapists in private practice reported which techniques they used to work with dreams. They indicated that they most often listened, explored connections to waking life, asked clients to describe images in greater detail, and collaborated to construct interpretations. In contrast, they seldom interpreted dreams in terms of the therapy relationship, unconscious wishes, spiritual terms, or archetypes. They also seldom interpreted the dream for the client, suggested changes that could be made based on dream learning, mentioned that they were willing to work with dreams, explained how they worked with dreams, helped clients try to change dreams, or asked clients to act out different parts of dreams. In essence, then, they used mostly exploration and collaborative insight techniques but did not use deep dynamic interpretations or action techniques. It is particularly noteworthy that they did not mention to clients that they were willing to work with dreams or explain how they worked with dreams. Crook (2003), in an extension of the findings of this survey, found that cognitive–behavioral therapists had received less training in working with dreams, felt less competence in and affinity for dream work, and engaged in fewer of all the dream activities than psychoanalytic or eclectic therapists.

Summary of Components

We have found some evidence for the efficacy for the components of all three stages. Clients seem to especially value insight, associations, links to waking life, catharsis, getting an objective perspective, and therapist participation. It appears that the action stage is not needed to achieve insight but is needed to get to problem solving and action ideas. Furthermore, therapists in practice used a few exploration skills and collaborative insight skills but seldom used action skills (perhaps because of minimal training in working with dreams).

Researchers need to investigate how therapists approach dream work with different types of clients because therapists probably modify what they do (even within the confines of adhering to the model) to match the needs of different types of clients. For example, therapists may give more interpretations to clients who either cannot come up with their own interpretations or to clients who seem particularly eager to brainstorm about the meaning of their dreams, whereas they may not give many, if any, interpretations to clients who are convinced that they know the meaning of the dream.

SUMMARY OF RESEARCH FINDINGS

We have evidence from both session and treatment outcome that dream work is effective:

- Clients rated dream sessions high on depth, working alliance, and insight.
- Clients made consistent gains in understanding their dreams, with more modest changes in symptomatology and interpersonal functioning.

There were four predictors of success in dream work:

1. Clients who have positive attitudes toward dreams volunteer more for and profit more from dream work.
2. Clients seem to prefer and benefit more from working with therapists than from working with dreams by themselves.
3. Clients need to be actively involved in dream work to profit from it.
4. All the components of the Hill model seem to be helpful.

METHODOLOGICAL ISSUES

We focus in this section on methodological issues that must be considered in conducting and evaluating research on dream work. Specifically, we discuss issues related to clients, therapists, adherence to the model, length of treatment, modality of treatment, measures, and investigator allegiance to the model. Note that some of these issues are similar to those in psychotherapy research (Hill & Lambert, in press).

Clients

We have primarily used as clients undergraduate students who participate for course credit. These clients become deeply involved in the dream work, and we presented evidence earlier in the chapter that they rate sessions deeper than typical therapy. However, because they were not clients who sought therapy, we needed to examine the influence of client characteristics on the results.

We first examined client motivation for participating in studies involving single sessions of dream work (see Table 12.2). We used the Depth Scale for this evaluation because we have used it in many studies. The average depth score for studies with students who participated for credit was significantly lower than the depth scores for studies involving undergraduate students who volunteered for the experience without course credit.[18] Thus, clients who participated in dream studies without compensation (and hence were probably motivated for self-growth) rated sessions as more beneficial than those who participated as a course requirement (and hence were not necessarily motivated for self-growth). In another study, Hill et al. (1997) found that undergraduates who volunteered for dream sessions for no credit were more likely than nonvolunteers to be women, to have positive attitudes toward dreams, to have higher estimated dream recall, to be more open, and to be higher in absorption (i.e., have a capacity for restructuring one's phenomenal field). These results suggest that client motivation makes a difference in the outcome of dream sessions and that a biased sample of people volunteer to work on their dreams if no compensation is involved.

In a comparison of nine studies involving undergraduate students (a combination of those who received course credit and those who did not) and three studies involving adults from the community, no studies were

---

[18]The average score of 6.05 ($SD = 0.13$) for five studies (Hill et al., 1993, 2001, in press; Wonnell & Hill, 2000; Zack & Hill, 1998) with students who participated for credit was significantly lower on an independent-samples t test than the score of 6.47 ($SD = 0.31$) for three studies (Heaton, Hill, Hess, et al., 1998; Heaton, Hill, Petersen, et al., 1998; Hill et al., 1997) involving undergraduate students who volunteered for the experience without course credit, $t(6) = -2.76, p < .05$. Note that Rochlen et al.'s (1999) study was not included in this comparison because participants were selected only if they had low dream recall and low attitudes toward dreams, whereas all the other studies included anyone who volunteered.

found on Depth scores.[19] We can tentatively conclude that age of participants (undergraduate student vs. adult from the community) does not influence depth scores.

These results suggest that level of motivation is important, but age is not. Of course, we must remind readers that all the clients in these studies have been volunteers (i.e., clients who responded to recruiting efforts) and not clients who sought out therapy. We need to determine whether clients who volunteer for dream work in therapy are different from clients who do not want to work with dreams in therapy. Furthermore, we need to investigate the effects of the model with other samples, such as children, elderly clients, medically ill clients, and dying clients.

Therapists

For the most part, we have used graduate students as therapists because we have more access to them than to practicing therapists. Furthermore, from our perspective, our graduate students are ideal therapists because they have been through helping skills training and so are easy to train in this model. They are not typically locked into a theoretical orientation and are willing to learn and use the model as required for participation in studies. However, the question can be raised about the influence of therapist characteristics on the results.

Wonnell and Hill (2000) found some evidence for the effects of overall therapist experience level on client-rated depth, although therapist experience with the model and belief in the model were not significantly correlated with any of the outcome variables. Moreover, no significant correlations were found between therapist experience level and any client- or therapist-rated outcome variables in several other studies (Diemer et al., 1996; Hill et al., 1993, 1997, 2001, in press; Zack & Hill, 1998).

Another way to examine differences among therapists is to enter therapists into regression equations as dummy variables (essentially pitting each therapist against all the others) predicting outcome variables. In most studies (e.g., Davis & Hill, 2003; Hill et al., 2001, in press; Wonnell & Hill, 2002; Zack & Hill, 1998), we have not found differences among therapists, although Kolchakian and Hill (2002) did find differences and had to adjust for therapist differences by centering scores across clients (i.e., subtracting the therapists' mean for each variable from the individual client's score for that variable).

When the author of a study served as a therapist, we tested whether his or her scores were different from other therapists. In several studies in which one of the coauthors served as a therapist (Davis & Hill, 2003; Hill et al.,

---

[19]No difference was found between nine studies involving undergraduate students ($M = 6.15$, $SD = 0.32$) and three studies of adults from the community ($M = 6.30$, $SD = 0.17$), $t(10) = 0.76$, $p = .47$.

1993, 1997, 2001, in press; Kolchakian & Hill, 2002; Wonnell & Hill, 2000, 2002), their outcomes were no better or worse than those of other therapists. Therefore, it appears to be okay for authors to serve as therapists (which is sometimes necessary to get enough therapists), but researchers must make sure to test for differences between authors and other therapists. Of course, when knowledge of the hypotheses might bias the data, authors should not serve as therapists.

For this chapter, we went back to the data from Hill et al.'s (in press) study to examine the influence of other therapist characteristics because we had a large sample of 29 therapists with a range of experience (from students with just one practicum to a person 27 years post PhD). No significant correlations were found between any of the therapist characteristics (age, attitude toward dreams, dream recall, years of overall experience, number of sessions conducted using the Hill model, psychodynamic orientation, humanistic orientation, cognitive–behavioral orientation, belief in the Hill model, feelings of competence using the Hill model) and any of the session outcome variables. These results suggest that therapist characteristics were not associated with outcome. Of course, we must note that all therapists in these studies have been trained carefully, and we have thrown out data from analyses when therapists did not adhere strictly to the protocols (so that we could have a cleaner test of the hypotheses). So perhaps the best statement is that trained therapists who adhere to the model have equivalent outcomes. Similarly, a review of several studies of brief therapy by Crits-Christoph et al. (1991) found minimal effects for therapists who had been trained in treatment manuals, although these researchers did find some effects of experience level.

We were also interested in whether some therapists were more drawn to the model than others, so we correlated belief in the model with a number of variables in Hill et al.'s (in press) data set. Belief in the Hill model was significantly correlated with feelings of competence in using the Hill model, dream recall, number of sessions in which the model was used, a humanistic orientation, and posttraining attitudes toward dreams. So, therapists were more likely to believe in the model if they valued their dreams, were humanistic in orientation, and had some experience with the model.

Few differences in outcome were found among trained therapists. These results suggest that it is acceptable to use therapists of any experience level as long as they are well trained. However, researchers need to test for differences among therapists and adjust data when differences are found (cf. Kolchakian & Hill, 2002).

Therapist Adherence to the Model

To have confidence that we are testing the Hill model as it is proposed, we must know that therapists are adhering to the model. We have most often assessed adherence using therapist self-ratings of how completely and how well they do the exploration, insight, and action stages (using 9-point scales on which 9 = *high*). See Appendix D for a therapist-rated adherence measure. We initially asked separate questions about "how completely" and "how well" the stages were completed but found high correlations (.52, .76, and .83 for the exploration, insight, and action stages, respectively; Hill et al., 1997), and so we now combine the two questions into one. Across several studies of individual dream work (Davis & Hill, 2003; Hill et al., 1997, 2001; Rochlen et al., 1999; Wonnell & Hill, 2000, 2002; Zack & Hill, 1998), therapist-rated adherence ranged from 7.25 to 8.12 for the exploration stage ($M = 7.50$, $SD = 1.23$), 6.47–7.81 for the insight stage ($M = 7.18$, $SD = 1.21$), and 6.08–7.30 for the action stage ($M = 6.64$, $SD = 1.41$).[20]

We typically drop sessions in which therapists rate themselves low on the adherence ratings. Our criterion has been that therapists must rate themselves at least a 4 or 5 on 9-point scales (9 = *high*) on at least two of the three stages (under the rationale that it is not always appropriate to do all three stages, so there needs to be some flexibility) to be retained in the study. Across several studies (Davis & Hill, 2003; Heaton, Hill, Petersen, et al., 1998; Kolchakian & Hill, 2002; Rochlen et al., 1999; Wonnell & Hill, 2000; Zack & Hill, 1998), we had to drop 5 of 230 sessions (2%). We recommend that researchers use the slightly more stringent criteria of 5 on the 9-point scale for at least two of the three stages. We also recommend that researchers check to make sure that therapist adherence ratings for each stage fall within the range of adherence scores presented above.

Heaton, Hill, Petersen, et al. (1998) attempted to develop a judge-rated adherence measure. They created several items about the various activities in the exploration, insight, and action stages and asked judges to rate the overall quality of therapist performance in each stage. Despite many hours of training and practice, however, they never were able to obtain high reliability among judges for the individual activities. The best explanation is that trained therapists did what they were supposed to do, resulting in minimal variance in ratings. The authors eventually reported only the overall ratings for each stage (using questions parallel to those completed by therapists). The correlations between the therapists and judges were .68, .52, and .40 for the three stages, respectively, indicating only modest agreement across perspectives. Therapists and judges probably used different criteria for judging adherence (perhaps confusing adherence and competence). Given the difficulty and the amount of time required to have trained observers rate entire sessions, we have since used only therapists' ratings of adherence to each stage.

---

[20]The t tests indicated no significant differences in therapist adherence between the exploration and insight stages, $t(10) = 0.43$, $p = .68$; marginal differences between the exploration and action stages, $t(10) = 2.03$, $p = .07$; and marginal differences between the insight and action stages, $t(10) = 1.94$, $p = .08$.

However, there are problems with the rating scales for therapist adherence. First, the adherence questions are very global (e.g., "How completely and well did you do the exploration stage?"), and therapists might lump too many activities together in their ratings. Perhaps we should ask therapists more specifically how much they adhered to the steps of the model (e.g., "How completely and how well did you do associations?") Second, adherence ratings are confounded with client responsiveness, in that therapists can adhere to the model only if clients are involved and respond appropriately. We can ask about specific activities within stages, but it will be difficult to resolve the confound between therapist adherence and client responsiveness.

On a more simple level, we have also had judges evaluate on a yes–no basis whether therapists adhered to the appropriate condition when comparing more than one condition. For example, in the Hill et al. (2001) study, therapists listened to the insight stage and determined whether therapists were using waking life or parts-of-self interpretations. Assessing adherence in this manner is very straightforward and yields high interjudge reliability.

Furthermore, because adherence is not necessarily the same as competence, we need to assess competence in using the model. We have reported data only for therapist-perceived competence in Zack and Hill's (1998) study but did not report correlations between ratings of adherence and competence.

Some attempt has been made to assess adherence and competence, primarily from the therapist's perspective. We need to continue working on developing valid and reliable measures of these constructs.

Length and Modality of Treatment

Our studies have ranged from 1 to 20 sessions, so one might wonder about the influence of number of sessions. A comparison of studies indicates that number of sessions had minimal influence on session outcome.[21]

Length of sessions has ranged from 35 to 150 minutes, although most sessions last about 60 to 90 minutes.[22] However, length of sessions was not

---

[21]Standardized scores for client-rated depth were 8.53 for six studies of single dream sessions, 8.20 for one study with 2 dream sessions, and 11.71 for three studies with 8 to 20 sessions of brief therapy (see Table 12.2 for more data on the studies). The t tests comparing the three sets of studies were not significant: first versus second set, $t(4) = 0.75$, $p < .49$; second versus third set, $t(3) = 0.84$, $p < .49$; first versus third set, $t(7) = 0.88$, $p < .41$.

[22]Wonnell and Hill (2000) indicated that sessions ranged from 50 to 100 minutes ($M = 73.55$, $SD = 13.34$), and Hill et al. (2001) reported that sessions ranged from 35 to 145 minutes ($M = 73.42$, $SD = 18.01$). In Hill et al.'s (in press) study, the computer condition average 88.49 ($SD = 25.74$) minutes, the therapist empathy condition averaged 70.96 ($SD = 15.80$) minutes, and the empathy + input condition averaged 69.14 ($SD = 16.53$) minutes. In the Wonnell and Hill (2000) and Hill et al. (2001) studies, length of sessions was not related to any outcome measures.

related to any outcome measures. Client and therapist talkativeness vary greatly, so client involvement may be more important than session length.

In terms of modality, most of our studies have involved individual therapy. Although we have conducted one study of group dream work (Falk & Hill, 1995) and one study of couples dream work (Kolchakian & Hill, 2002), we did not use the same outcome measures for these nonindividual studies as we did for the individual studies, so we cannot compare across modalities. Furthermore, the dream model was modified somewhat for each of the modalities, which also makes comparisons across modalities more complicated. However, the outcomes for the two nonindividual studies were positive, suggesting that groups and couples are promising modalities for dream work. It would be interesting to compare participants' experiences in individual, group, and couples dream work.

Measures

Client-Rated Session-Level Measures

Three measures have been imported from psychotherapy research to assess client overall perceptions of dream sessions: the Depth Scale of the SEQ (Stiles & Snow, 1984), the WAI-S (Tracey & Kokotovic, 1989), and the Session Evaluation Scale (SES; Hill & Kellems, 2002). A major concern with all scales is a ceiling effect given that scores were very high (i.e., > 6 on a 7-point scale for the Depth Scale and WAI-S, > 4 on a 5-point scale for the SES). It seems to be difficult to get a range of scores, which was probably exacerbated by dropping sessions in which therapists did not adhere to the model.

Furthermore, the Depth scale and the SES are general measures of session quality, and the WAI-S is a general measure of the alliance, but none are dream-specific measures. In our first study (Cogar & Hill, 1992), clients told us that the major gains they made from dream work were in understanding their dreams. Hence, we started using the Understanding subscale from the SIS and the MIS (which we extended from a 3-point rating scale to a 5-point rating scale) to assess insight. In addition, to be more responsive to what clients gain specifically from dream sessions, we developed the GDI (Heaton, Hill, Petersen, et al., 1998) from answers to open-ended questions in Hill et al.'s (1997) study about what clients found most helpful in dream sessions. The GDI assesses exploration–insight gains, action gains, and experiential gains (although this last scale involves only 2 items and hence has not been used as often as the other two scales). Note that *gains* refers to what the client got from sessions rather than to changes made in life outside of sessions. Unfortunately, ratings are still very high on the GDI, so the ceiling effect problem has not been solved. The GDI is reprinted in Appendix C.

Given that several session outcome measures have been used, we investigated the relationship among measures. Moderately high intercorrelations ranging from .42 to .88 (typically between .60 and .70) have been found among the client self-report measures (Depth, WAI-S, SES, SIS–U, MIS, Exploration–Insight [EI] Gains, Action Gains). Because of these high correlations and potential problems with multicollinearity in the data analyses, the session-level measures have sometimes been combined into composite session outcome indexes, which had high internal consistency estimates.[23] The high correlations and internal consistency estimates of the outcome indexes indicate that the measures assess similar constructs, perhaps because they all involve client self-report. Clients valued sessions in which they perceived a strong therapeutic relationship and made gains in understanding and action. In other words, there may be a global "good guy" factor at work, making it hard to distinguish client perceptions of specific gains from dream work from the overall quality of the session.

We suggest that future researchers use at least one of the client self-report session-level measures (Depth, SES, MIS, SIS–U, EI Gains, Action Gains). There is no empirical guide to suggest which measure is best, but we lean more toward the GDI because it is was developed specifically for dream work. If more than one client self-report measure is used, researchers should check for intercorrelations and combine scores if highly correlated.

Therapist-Rated Session-Level Measures

We have assessed therapists' perceptions of the overall quality of dream sessions using the Depth, SIS–U, and MIS scales. However, we have been concerned about using therapist reports for evaluating the model because therapists are not good judges of what clients gain (although they can evaluate their own experiences in sessions). This view is consistent with the pervasive lack of correlation between perspectives in psychotherapy research (see Hill & Lambert, in press). Furthermore, we have been concerned that therapists may be biased because they may want to prove that their interventions are valuable. Hence, although therapists provide an important perspective on their experience in dream sessions, we caution researchers about relying on the therapist perspective for the outcome of dream work. We prefer and recommend the use of client perspective given that the client is the consumer of the services.

Judges' Ratings of Outcome Variables

We developed rating scales to be used by trained judges to rate client level of insight into interpretations of dreams as well as the quality of action ideas based on their dreams. After relatively brief training (usually about 2 hours), we have obtained high interjudge reliability (range:

---

[23]Internal consistency was .78 for Depth, SIS–U, and MIS in Hill et al.'s (1997) study; .83 for Depth, SIS–U, MIS, EI Gains, Action Gains, and Experiential Gains in Zack and Hill's (1998) study; .89 for WAI-S, Depth, MIS, EI Gains, Action Gains in Hill et al.'s (2000) study; .79 for Depth, MIS, and EI Gains in Hill et al.'s (2001) study, and .84 for Depth, SES, EI Gains, Action Gains in Hill et al.'s (in press) study.

.88–.97) for insight with 2 to 5 judges and high interjudge reliability (range: .93–.96) for action ideas with 3 to 5 judges in several studies, suggesting that it is relatively easy to do these ratings. Future researchers need only use three judges as long as these judges can grasp the constructs. We recommend that future researchers train their judges using established ratings to ensure that they are measuring the same constructs as we did.

Ratings of dream insight and quality of action ideas were not highly related to each other (correlations ranged from .14 to .41) or to client self-report session-level measures (correlations ranged from .13 to .47). Hence, ratings of insight and quality of action ideas are distinct from each other and from client self-report measures. We suggest that researchers use ratings of both insight and action ideas, because these represent targets of dream sessions and are behavioral estimates (and perhaps less subject to a global "good guy" bias) of what clients gained from dream work.

On the basis of our experiences with the insight and action ideas ratings, however, we suggest some modifications to the procedures. The written responses lack the depth and richness of insights and action ideas discussed in sessions. After a 90- to 120-minute session in which they just talked about the interpretations and action ideas, clients often become annoyed at having to write it all out. In other research, we have found that clients respond better to interviewers than having to respond in writing, so we suggest that trained interviewers naïve to any experimental manipulations use a standard protocol to ask clients for an interpretation and action ideas for the dream. Transcribed client statements would then be rated by trained judges. An alternative method would be to have therapists use standard probes to ask for interpretations at the end of the insight stage and action plans at the end of the action stage.

It also makes sense to look for changes in judge-rated content or emotion of dreams. Such ratings were used in Heaton, Hill, Hess, et al.'s (1998) study, and they have been used in other studies (Bergin, 1970; Bishay, 1985; Breger et al., 1971; Carlson, 1986; Cavenar & Sullivan, 1978; Cavior & Deutsch, 1975; Cellucci & Lawrence, 1978; Glucksman, 1988; Greer & Silverman, 1967; Haynes & Mooney, 1975; Hendricks & Cartwright, 1978; Kellner, Neidhardt, Krakow, & Pathak, 1992; Marks, 1978; Maultsby & Gram, 1974; Melstrom & Cartwright, 1983; Miller & DiPilato, 1983; Silverman & Greer, 1968; Warner, 1983). If we assume that dreams change as a result of treatment, it is obvious that we should assess dreams more often, especially when treatment involves more than a single session. More work needs to be done, though, to standardize what to assess in the dreams.

Client-Rated Treatment Outcome Measures

A number of measures have been used to assess treatment outcome, but most have shown only modest changes as a result of multiple dream sessions.

Perhaps the problem here is that changes in symptomatology, interpersonal functioning, or well-being are not necessarily the targets of dream sessions. Individualized measures of change, such as Target Complaints (Battle et al., 1965) or Goal Attainment Scaling (Kiresuk & Sherman, 1968), could solve some of the problems by assessing only these changes relevant to the client. Unfortunately, however, clients may not be aware of what is causing the troubling dreams until after sessions, making pre–post assessment difficult.

We suggest that researchers rely more on dream-specific measures (changes in insight and action ideas for dreams, changes in dream anxiety and personal involvement in dreams, attitudes toward dreams) than on more general measures of symptomatology and interpersonal functioning given that these might not even be the focus of dream work. Furthermore, research needs to be study the relationship among dream-specific variables, session outcome, and treatment outcome. It may be that change in the distal variables (treatment outcome) is mediated by dream-specific changes and session outcome. For example, positive session outcome and changes in insight and action may lead to valuing of sessions and changes in behaviors, which in turn leads to changes in symptomatology, interpersonal functioning, and well-being. Specifically, then, we need to examine how clients use insight and action ideas after sessions.

Generalizability of Results

All of the studies of the Hill model have been conducted at the University of Maryland. Furthermore, the first author (Clara E. Hill) has monitored the training and data collection in all the studies. Other trainers will not be as intimately involved with the model as she is. To prove that the model is portable, we need other researchers not affiliated with us to do studies on the Hill model.

FUTURE RESEARCH AND CONCLUSIONS

An exciting area for future research is to study the effects of dream work within the context of ongoing therapy. How should therapists introduce the topic of dream work? How should therapists modify the model to fit the needs of different types of clients? How should therapists work with people from other cultures who have different beliefs about dreams? How can therapists modify the model to fit a 50-minute session? Can therapists teach clients to use the model on their own to speed up the work of therapy?

The use of self-help methods of dream work also merits further study. Can we improve the computer program to make it more desirable for clients? Would it work for therapists to do a dream session with a client and then use The Dream Toolbox (the computer program) to continue working with their dreams? We also need to learn more about which types of clients are likely to benefit from using the computer program.

The Hill dream model also needs to be compared with other dream models (e.g., Freudian, Jungian, Gestalt) as well as with other expressive, creative therapeutic techniques (e.g., art therapy techniques, gestalt techniques, projective testing). Results of such studies could shed light on what it is about dream work that makes it effective.

Another exciting area for future research would be to chart the cognitive changes that occur during successful dream work, a task that seems possible with improvements in cognitive psychology. We have speculated that dreams are puzzling because they do not fit into existing cognitive schema and that the task of dream work is to help the person change his or her cognitive schema to integrate dreams. Charting what these changes look like would be very interesting, especially for recurrent dreams and nightmares.

Studies could also be conducted to determine whether we can change attitudes toward dreams so that more people become more open to dream work. Researchers could follow up on Rochlen et al.'s (1999) study to determine whether more or different training would be more effective. In particular, people who might not otherwise volunteer could be persuaded that dream work might be beneficial. Educational efforts might also be aimed at the public for large-scale efforts to change attitudes toward dreams.

We hope that provision of this updated cognitive–experiential dream work model and accompanying research findings will encourage more therapists to begin to use dream work in therapy. Dream work does seem to be effective, so it would be useful for therapists to know when and how to use it. Furthermore, we hope that more researchers will begin to study this and other models of dream work so that we can improve the delivery of dream work and discover more about its uses. We are optimistic about the possibilities of this model to help people understand their dreams and make changes in their lives. We invite other researchers to join us in the journey to understand more about this and other dream models.

REFERENCES

Battle, C. G., Imber, S. D., Hoehn-Saric, R., Stone, A. R., Nash, E. R., & Frank, J. D. (1965). Target complaints as criterion of improvement. *American Journal of Psychotherapy, 20,* 184–192.

Bergin, A. E. (1970). A note on dream changes following desensitization. *Behavior Therapy, 1,* 70.

Beutler, L. E., Harwood, T. M., Alimohamed, S., & Malik, M. (2002). Functional impairment and coping style. In J. C. Norcross (Ed.), *Psychotherapy relationships that work: Therapist contributions and responsiveness to patients* (pp. 145–174). Oxford, England: Oxford University Press.

Beutler, L. E., Moleiro, C. M., & Talebi, H. (2002). Resistance. In J. C. Norcross (Ed.), *Psychotherapy relationships that work: Therapist contributions and responsiveness to patients* (pp. 129–144). Oxford, England: Oxford University Press.

Bishay, N. (1985). Therapeutic manipulation of nightmares and the manipulation of neuroses. *British Journal of Psychiatry, 146,* 67–70.

Bohart, A. C., & Tallman, K. (1999). *How clients make therapy work: The process of active self-healing.* Washington, DC: American Psychological Association.

Breger, L., Hunter, I., & Lane, R. (1971). The effect of stress on dreams (Monograph 27). *Psychological Issues, 7*(3), 1–214.

Cacioppo, J. T., Petty, R. E., & Kao, C. F. (1984). The need for cognition. *Journal of Personality and Social Psychology, 42,* 116–131.

Carlson, R. (1986). After analysis: A study of transference dreams following treatment. *Journal of Consulting and Clinical Psychology, 54,* 246–252.

Cavenar, J. O., & Sullivan, J. (1978). A recurrent dream as a precipitant. *American Journal of Psychiatry, 135,* 378–379.

Cavior, N., & Deutsch, A. (1975). Systematic desensitization to reduce dream induced anxiety. *Journal of Nervous and Mental Disease, 161,* 433–435.

Cellucci, A., & Lawrence, P. (1978). The efficacy of systematic desensitization in reducing nightmares. *Journal of Behavior Therapy and Experimental Psychiatry, 9,* 109–114.

Cogar, M. M., & Hill, C. E. (1992). Examining the effects of brief individual dream interpretation. *Dreaming, 2,* 239–248.

Cohen, J. (1988). *Statistical power analysis for the behavioral sciences* (2nd ed.). Hillsdale, NJ: Erlbaum.

Conte, H. R., Plutchik, R., Jung, B. B., Picard, S., & Karasu, T. B. (1990). Psychological mindedness as a predictor of psychotherapy outcome: A preliminary report. *Comprehensive Psychiatry, 31,* 426–431.

Costa, P. T., Jr., & McCrae, R. R. (1992). *Revised NEO-Personality Inventory (NEO-PI-R) and NEO Five-Factor Inventory (NEO-FFI): Professional manual.* Odessa, FL: Psychological Assessment Resources.

Crits-Christoph, P., Baranackie, K., Kurcias, J. S., Beck, A. T., Carroll, K., Perry, K., et al. (1991). Meta-analysis of therapist effects in psychotherapy outcome studies. *Psychotherapy Research, 1,* 81–91.

Crook, R. E. (2003). A comparison of cognitive, psychodynamic, and eclectic therapists' attitudes and practices in working with dreams in psychotherapy. In R. I. Rosner, W. J. Lyddon, & A. Freeman (Eds.), *Cognitive therapy and dreams.* New York: Springer.

Crook, R. E., & Hill, C. E. (in press). Therapists' attitudes toward working with dreams in therapy. *Dreaming.*

Dahlenburg, R., Christensen, O. J., & Moore, J. C. (1996). The effect of group dreamwork on spiritual well-being. *Journal of Psychology and Theology, 24,* 54–61.

Davis, T. L., & Hill, C. E. (2003). *Comparison of spiritual and waking life interpretations in the Hill cognitive–experiential model of dream interpretation*. Manuscript in preparation.

Diemer, R., Lobell, L., Vivino, B., & Hill, C. E. (1996). A comparison of dream interpretation, event interpretation, and unstructured sessions in brief psychotherapy. *Journal of Counseling Psychology, 43*, 99–112.

Dowd, E. T., Milne, C. R., & Wise, S. L. (1991). The Therapeutic Reactance Scale: A measure of psychological resistance. *Journal of Counseling and Development, 69*, 541–545.

Elliott, R., & Wexler, M. M. (1994). Measuring the impact of sessions in process–experiential therapy of depression: The Session Impacts Scale. *Journal of Counseling Psychology, 41*, 166–174.

Eugster, S. L., & Wampold, B. E. (1996). Systematic effects of participant role on evaluation of the psychotherapy session. *Journal of Consulting and Clinical Psychology, 64*, 1020–1028.

Falk, D. R., & Hill, C. E. (1995). The effectiveness of dream interpretation groups for women in a divorce transition. *Dreaming, 5*, 29–42.

Farber, B. A. (1989). Psychological mindedness: Can there be too much of a good thing? *Psychotherapy: Theory, Research, Practice, and Training, 26(2)*, 90.

Fenigstein, A., Scheier, M. F., & Buss, A. H. (1975). Public and private self-consciousness: Assessment and theory. *Journal of Consulting and Clinical Psychology, 43*, 522–527.

Glucksman, M. L. (1988). The use of successive dreams to facilitate and document change during treatment. *Journal of the American Academy of Psychoanalysis, 16*, 47–69.

Gomes-Schwartz, B. (1978). Effective ingredients in psychotherapy: Prediction of outcome from process variables. *Journal of Consulting and Clinical Psychology, 46*, 1023–1035.

Greer, J. H., & Silverman, I. (1967). Treatment of recurrent nightmare by behavior modification procedures: A case study. *Journal of Abnormal Psychology, 72*, 188–190.

Haynes, S., & Mooney, D. (1975). Nightmares: Etiological, theoretical, and behavioral considerations. *Psychological Records, 25*, 225–236.

Heaton, K. J., Hill, C. E., Hess, S., Hoffman, M. A., & Leotta, C. (1998). Assimilation in therapy involving interpretation of recurrent and nonrecurrent dreams. *Psychotherapy, 35*, 147–162.

Heaton, K. J., Hill, C. E., Petersen, D. A., Rochlen, A. B., & Zack, J. S. (1998). A comparison of therapist-facilitated and self-guided dream interpretation sessions. *Journal of Counseling Psychology, 45*, 115–122.

Hendricks, M., & Cartwright, R. D. (1978). Experiencing levels in dreams: An individual difference variable. *Psychotherapy: Theory, Research, and Practice, 15*, 292–298.

Hill, C. E. (1996). *Working with dreams in psychotherapy*. New York: Guilford Press.

Hill, C. E., Corbett, M. M., Kanitz, B., Rios, P., Lightsey, R., & Gomez, M. (1992). Client behavior in counseling and psychotherapy sessions: Development of a pantheoretical measure. *Journal of Counseling Psychology, 39*, 539–549.

Hill, C. E., Diemer, R., & Heaton, K. J. (1997). Dream interpretation sessions: Who volunteers, who benefits, and what volunteer clients view as most and least helpful. *Journal of Counseling Psychology, 44*, 53–62.

Hill, C. E., Diemer, R., Hess, S., Hillyer, A., & Seeman, R. (1993). Are the effects of dream interpretation on session quality, insight, and emotions due to the dream itself, to projection, or to the interpretation process? *Dreaming, 3*, 211–222.

Hill, C. E., & Kellems, I. S. (2002). Development and use of the Helping Skills Measure to assess client perceptions of the effects of training and of helping skills in sessions. *Journal of Counseling Psychology, 49*, 264–272.

Hill, C. E., Kelley, F. A., Davis, T. L., Crook, R. E., Maldonado, L. E., Turkson, M. A., et al. (2001). Predictors of outcome of dream interpretation sessions: Volunteer client characteristics, dream characteristics, and type of interpretation. *Dreaming, 11*, 53–72.

Hill, C. E., & Lambert, M. J. (in press). Assessing psychotherapy outcomes and processes. In M. J. Lambert (Ed.), *Bergin and Garfield's handbook of psychotherapy and behavior change* (5th ed., pp. 84–135). New York: Wiley.

Hill, C. E., Nakayama, E., & Wonnell, T. (1998). A comparison of description, association, and combined description/association in exploring dream images. *Dreaming, 8*, 1–13.

Hill, C. E., Rochlen, A. B., Zack, J. S., McCready, T., & Dematatis, A. (in press). Working with dreams using the Hill cognitive–experiential model: A comparison of computer-assisted, therapist empathy, and therapist empathy + input conditions. *Journal of Counseling Psychology*.

Hill, C. E., Thompson, B. J., & Williams, E. N. (1997). A guide to conducting consensual qualitative research. *The Counseling Psychologist, 25*, 517–572.

Hill, C. E., & Williams, E. N. (2000). The process of individual therapy. In R. W. Lent & S. D. Brown (Eds.), *Handbook of counseling psychology* (pp. 670–710). New York: Wiley.

Hill, C. E., Zack, J., Wonnell, T., Hoffman, M. A., Rochlen, A., Goldberg, J., et al. (2000). Structured brief therapy with a focus on dreams or loss for clients with troubling dreams and recent losses. *Journal of Counseling Psychology, 47*, 90–101.

Kahn, J. H., & Hessling, R. M. (2001). Measuring the tendency to conceal versus disclose psychological distress. *Journal of Social and Clinical Psychology, 20*, 41–65.

Kellner, R., Neidhardt, J., Krakow, B., & Pathak, D. (1992). Changes in chronic nightmares after one session of desensitization or rehearsal instructions. *American Journal of Psychiatry, 149*, 659–663.

Kim, B. S. K., Atkinson, D. R., & Umemoto, D. (2001). Asian cultural values and the counseling process: Current knowledge and directions for future research. *Counseling Psychologist, 29*, 570–603.

Kiresuk, T. J., & Sherman, R. E. (1968). Goal attainment scaling: A general method for evaluating comprehensive community mental health programs. *Community Mental Health Journal, 4,* 443–453.

Kolchakian, M. R., & Hill, C. E. (2002). Working with unmarried couples with dreams. *Dreaming, 12,* 1–16.

Kolden, G. C. (1991). The generic model of psychotherapy: An empirical investigation of patterns of process and outcome relationships. *Psychotherapy Research, 1,* 62–73.

Krakow, B., Hollifted, M., Johnston, L., Koss, M., Schrader, R., Warner, T. D., et al. (2001). Imagery rehearsal therapy for chronic nightmares in sexual assault survivors with posttraumatic stress disorder: A randomized controlled trial. *Journal of the American Medical Association, 286,* 537–545.

Marks, I. (1978). Rehearsal relief of a nightmare. *British Journal of Psychiatry, 133,* 461–465.

Maultsby, M. C., Jr., & Gram, J. M. (1974). Dream changes following successful rational behavior therapy. *Rational Living, 9,* 30–33.

Melstrom, M. A., & Cartwright, R. D. (1983). Effects of successful vs. unsuccessful psychotherapy outcome on some dream dimensions. *Psychiatry, 46,* 51–65.

Miller, W., & DiPilato, M. (1983). Treatment of nightmares via relaxation and desensitization: A controlled evaluation. *Journal of Consulting and Clinical Psychology, 2,* 870–877.

Piper, W. E., Joyce, A. S., McCallum, M., Azim, H. F., & Ogrodniczuk, J. S. (2002). *Interpretive and supportive psychotherapies: Matching therapy and patient personality.* Washington, DC: American Psychological Association.

Rochlen, A. B., Ligiero, D. P., Hill, C. E., & Heaton, K. J. (1999). Effects of training in dream recall and dream interpretation skills on dream recall, attitudes, and dream interpretation outcome. *Journal of Counseling Psychology, 46,* 27–34.

Scogin, F., Bynum, J., Stephens, G., & Calhoon, S. (1990). Efficacy of self-administered programs: Meta-analytic review. *Professional Psychology: Research and Practice, 21,* 42–47.

Shuttleworth-Jordan, A. B. & Saayman, G. S. (1989). Differential effects of alternative strategies on psychotherapeutic process in group dream work. *Psychotherapy, 26,* 514–519.

Silverman, I., & Greer, J. H. (1968). The elimination of recurrent nightmare by desensitization of a related phobia. *Behavior Research and Therapy, 6,* 109–111.

Stiles, W. B., Meshot, C. M., Anderson, T. M., & Sloan, W. W., Jr. (1992). Assimilation of problematic experiences: The case of John Jones. *Psychotherapy Research, 2,* 81–101.

Stiles, W. B., Reynolds, S., Hardy, G. E., Rees, A., Barkham, M., & Shapiro, D. A. (1994). Evaluation and description of psychotherapy sessions by clients using the Session Evaluation Questionnaire and the Session Impacts Scale. *Journal of Counseling Psychology, 41,* 175–185.

Stiles, W. B., & Snow, J. S. (1984). Dimensions of psychotherapy session impact across sessions and across clients. *Journal of Counseling Psychology, 31,* 3–12.

Tracey, T. J., & Kokotivic, A. M. (1989). Factor structure of the working alliance inventory. *Psychological Assessment, 1*, 207–210.

Van de Castle, R. L. (1994). *The dreaming mind.* New York: Ballantine.

Warner, S. L. (1983) Can psychoanalytic treatment change dreams? *Journal of the American Academy of Psychoanalysts, 11*, 299–316.

Webb, D. E., & Fagan, J. (1993). The impact of dream interpretation using psychological kinesiology on the frequency of recurring dreams. *Psychotherapy and Psychosomatics, 59*, 203–208.

White-Lewis, J. (2002). In defense of little dreams. *Dreamtime, 18*(4), 4–7.

Wonnell, T., & Hill, C. E. (2000). The effects of including the action stage in dream interpretation. *Journal of Counseling Psychology, 47*, 372–379.

Wonnell, T., & Hill, C. E. (2002, June). *The action stage and predictors of action in dream interpretation.* Paper presented at the annual meeting of the Society for Psychotherapy Research, Santa Barbara, CA.

Zack, J. S., & Hill, C. E. (1998). Predicting dream interpretation outcome by attitudes, stress, and emotion. *Dreaming, 8*, 169–185.

APPENDIX A

STEPS OF THE DREAM INTERPRETATION MODEL

I. Exploration Stage
   A. Explain three-stage model briefly
   B. Have client retell dream in first-person present tense
   C. Have client explore overall feelings (and determine when dream occurred if not apparent)
   D. Explore 5–10 major images sequentially using DRAW acronym
      a. **D**escribe
      b. **R**eexperience feelings
      c. **A**ssociate
      d. **W**aking life triggers
   E. Summarize exploration process (optional)

II. Insight Stage
   A. Ask client for initial understanding of the meaning of the dream
   B. Collaborate with client to construct a meaning of the dream
      1. Experience
      2. Waking life
      3. Inner personality dynamics
         a. Parts of self
         b. Conflicts originating in childhood
         c. Spiritual/existential
   C. Ask client to summarize insights about meaning of dream

III. Action Stage
   A. Ask client to change the dream or create a sequel
      1. In fantasy
      2. During sleep
   B. Coach client about making changes in waking life
      1. Specific behavioral change
      2. Ritual to honor the dream
      3. Continued working with dreams
   C. Ask client to summarize action plan (can include asking for title of dream)

APPENDIX B

ATTITUDES TOWARD DREAMS SCALE

Instructions: Mark the response that best describes you.

1. I believe that dreams are one of the most important ways to understand myself.	Agree 5	4	3	2	Disagree 1
2. I do not pay any attention to my own dreams.	Agree 1	2	3	4	Disagree 5
3. Dreams have meaning.	Agree 5	4	3	2	Disagree 1
4. Dreams are too confused to have any meaning to me.	Agree 1	2	3	4	Disagree 5
5. I dislike speculations about the meaning of dreams.	Agree 1	2	3	4	Disagree 5
6. I value my dreams.	Agree 5	4	3	2	Disagree 1
7. Practical everyday life is too important to me to pay attention to my dreams.	Agree 1	2	3	4	Disagree 5
8. How often have you speculated about the possible meaning of one of your dreams?	Never 1	2	3	4	Often 5
9. Do you have any beliefs or theories about the meaning of dreams?	Yes 5	4	3	2	No 1
					TOTAL

The Attitude Toward Dreams Scale (ATD) was originally constructed by Hill, Thompson, and Williams (1997) by combining items from Cernovsky (1984) and Robbins and Tanck (1988) and creating one item. A factor analysis on the 11 items yielded a single factor accounting for 36% of the variance with all items loading above .40 and an internal consistency alpha of .79. In Hill et al.'s (1997) study, the ATD was related positively to the NEO Openness Scale (Costa & McCrae, 1992), estimated dream recall, and diary dream recall. The ATD also predicted whether participants volunteered for dream interpretation sessions, providing some evidence of validity.

For the Hill et al. (2001) study, the ATD was revised so that all items used 5-point scales, the wording of half of the items was reversed so that all items were not scored in the same direction, and 1 new item was added. On the basis of a preliminary examination, 3 items that did not correlate highly with the total score were dropped. A factor analysis on the revised 9-item measure found a single factor (eigenvalue = 4.60) that accounted for 51% of the variance, with all items loading .50 or higher. Internal consistency was .88, 2-week test–retest reliability was .92, and the correlation between the original ATD and the ATD-R was .91. Scores are determined by summing the ratings (after reversing the negatively worded items) and dividing by the total number of items.

REFERENCES

Cernovsky, Z. Z. (1984). Dream recall and dream attitudes. *Perceptual and Motor Skills, 58*, 911–914.

Costa, P. T., Jr., & McCrae, R. R. (1992). *Revised NEO-Personality Inventory (NEO-PI-R) and NEO Five-Factor Inventory (NEO-FFI): Professional manual.* Odessa, FL: Psychological Assessment Resources.

Hill, C. E., Diemer, R., & Heaton, K. J. (1997). Dream interpretation sessions: Who volunteers, who benefits, and what volunteer clients view as most and least helpful. *Journal of Counseling Psychology, 44*, 53–62.

Hill, C. E., Kelley, F. A., Davis, T. L., Crook, R. E., Maldonado, L. E., Turkson, M. A., et al. (2001). Predictors of outcome of dream interpretation sessions: Volunteer client characteristics, dream characteristics, and type of interpretation. *Dreaming, 11*, 53–72.

Hill, C. E., Thompson, B. J., & Williams, E. N. (1997). A guide to conducting consensual qualitative research. *The Counseling Psychologist, 25*, 517–572.

Robbins, P. R., & Tanck, R. H. (1988). Interest in dreams and dream recall. *Perceptual and Motor Skills, 66*, 291–294.

APPENDIX C

GAINS FROM DREAM INTERPRETATION MEASURE

Instructions: We are interested in hearing exactly what you gained from participating in this session. Please think about each question carefully and answer as honestly as possible. Circle the number that best describes your response.

	Disagree Strongly				Neutral			Agree Strongly	
1. I was able to explore my dream thoroughly during the session.	1	2	3	4	5	6	7	8	9
2. I learned more about what this dream meant for me personally during the session.	1	2	3	4	5	6	7	8	9
3. During the session, I was able to re-experience the feelings I had in my dream.	1	2	3	4	5	6	7	8	9
4. Because of the session, I have more of a sense that I can change my dreams when they are frightening or bad.	1	2	3	4	5	6	7	8	9
5. I got ideas during the session for how to change some aspect(s) of myself or my life.	1	2	3	4	5	6	7	8	9
6. I learned more from the session about how past events influence my present behavior.	1	2	3	4	5	6	7	8	9
7. I learned more about issues in my waking life from working with the dream.	1	2	3	4	5	6	7	8	9

	Disagree Strongly				Neutral			Agree Strongly	
8. I felt like I was very involved in working with this dream during this session.	1	2	3	4	5	6	7	8	9
9. I felt like I was actually reliving the dream during this session.	1	2	3	4	5	6	7	8	9
10. I learned a new way of thinking about myself and my problems.	1	2	3	4	5	6	7	8	9
11. I will use things that I learned in this dream interpretation in my life.	1	2	3	4	5	6	7	8	9
12. I learned things that I would not have thought of on my own.	1	2	3	4	5	6	7	8	9
13. I was able to make some connections between images in my dream and issues in my waking life that I had not previously considered.	1	2	3	4	5	6	7	8	9
14. I felt reassured about myself or my dream after this session.	1	2	3	4	5	6	7	8	9

Note. The three subscales identified through factor analyses are Exploration–Insight Gains (items 1, 2, 6, 7, 12, 13; $\alpha = .83$), Action Gains (Items 4, 5, 10, 11, 14; $\alpha = .82$), and Experiential Gains (Items 3 and 9; $\alpha = .79$). From "A Comparison of Therapist-faciliated and Self-guided Dream Interpretation Sessions," by K. J. Heaton, C. E. Hill, D. A. Petersen, A. B. Rochlen, & J. S. Zack, 1998, *Journal of Counseling Psychology, 45*, p. 122. Copyright © 1998 by the American Psychological Association. Reprinted with permission.

APPENDIX D

THERAPIST-RATED ADHERENCE MEASURE

Instructions: Respond to the following questions about how much you were able to do the following steps and stages of the Hill Dream Model with this client during this particular session. Please note that your ability to do each of these steps or stages is a function of both your skills and the client's readiness, so please answer as honestly as possible about what actually occurred in the session. Please circle the best response.

	Low								High
How completely and how well did you do the exploration stage?	1	2	3	4	5	6	7	8	9
How completely and well did you do the step of gathering descriptions for several images?	1	2	3	4	5	6	7	8	9
How completely and well did you do the step of reexperiencing for several images?	1	2	3	4	5	6	7	8	9
How completely and well did you do the step of associations to several images?	1	2	3	4	5	6	7	8	9
How completely and well did you do the step of gathering waking life triggers of several images?	1	2	3	4	5	6	7	8	9

	Low								High
How completely and how well did you do the insight stage?	1	2	3	4	5	6	7	8	9
How completely and how well were you able to work on the level of experience?	1	2	3	4	5	6	7	8	9
How completely and how well were you able to work on the level of waking life?	1	2	3	4	5	6	7	8	9
How completely and how well were you able to work on the level of inner dynamics?	1	2	3	4	5	6	7	8	9
How completely and how well did you do the action stage?	1	2	3	4	5	6	7	8	9
How completely and well did you do the step about changing the dream step?	1	2	3	4	5	6	7	8	9
How completely and well did you do the step about making changes in waking life?	1	2	3	4	5	6	7	8	9
How completely and how well did you do the entire model?	1	2	3	4	5	6	7	8	9

INDEX

Accepting the reality of the loss (task 1), 171–174
Accuracy, determining, 60–61
Actions
   dictating vs. exploring, 86
   examples of, 86–93
Action stage, 8–9, 71–93
   changing the dream in, 72–79
   client summarization of, 85–86, 237
   of grief work, 173, 176, 179–180, 182–183
   group, 117
   of nightmare work, 215–216, 218–219
   in ongoing psychotherapy, 102
   purpose of, 71
   research about, 259, 268
   in spirituality case study, 164–165
   thoughts about doing, 86–87, 237–238
   training therapists about, 235–238
   and waking life changes, 79–85
Adherence Measure, Therapist-Rated, 295–296
Adjusting to the environment in which the deceased is missing (task 3), 177–180
Adults, nightmares of, 204
Alarm clocks, 101
Alexithymia, 194
Antidepressants, 204
Anxiety
   and bereavement, 175
   in exploration stage, 29
   and nightmares, 206, 209, 219
   in ongoing psychotherapy, 99, 100
   and therapist training, 229
Arousal (of dreams), 264–265
Aserinsky, E., ix
Asian Americans, 263
Assertiveness training, 81
Assessment (of dream work), 251–259
   session-level outcome, 251–256
   treatment outcome, 256–259
Assimilation of Problematic Experiences Scale, 257, 259
Association for the Study of Dreams, x, xiv

Associations (with images), 29–34
   definition of, 32
   extended, 30–32
   and grief, 172
   methods for eliciting, 32–34
   and spirituality, 162
Assumptive world, 171
ATD–R. *See* Attitudes Toward Dreams–Revised scale
ATDS (Attitudes Toward Dreams Scale), 261
Atkinson, D. R., 263
Attitudes Toward Dreams Scale (ATDS), 261, 291–292
Attitude toward dreams, client's, 45, 261–262, 266

Barbiturates, 204
Behavioral changes, 75
   and ongoing psychotherapy, 102, 108–111
   specific, 80–83
   training therapists about, 236–237
Behavioral theory, 9
Benson, H., 76
Bereavement. *See* Grief work
Bereavement groups, 184
Beta blockers, 204
Bibliotherapy, 134
Bohart, A. C., 268
Brainstorming, 8, 42
Breakthrough Dreaming (G. Delaney), 135
Breathing exercises, 29
Bulkeley, K., 150, 152
Bynum, J., 135

Calhoon, S., 135
Campbell, B. D., 135
Cartwright, R. D., 135
Change(s)
   benefits/drawbacks of, 80
   human capacity for, 134
   in waking life, 79–85, 236

Changing the dream, 72–79
    in fantasy, 73–76, 235–236
    of nightmares, 76–79, 236
Childhood experiences, 54–56
Children, nightmares of, 78, 204
Client-centered therapy, 7, 21, 38, 72, 80
Client characteristics, 98–99
Client(s), 260–266
    attitudes toward dreams of, 45, 261–262
    demographics variables of, 263–266
    dream recall in, 100–101, 262–263
    education of, about dream work, 100
    identification of, for dream work, 98–99
    initial dream interpretation by, 42–48
    involvement of, 21, 27, 267–268
    level of functioning of, 43
    level of understanding of the dream by, 43–45
    psychological-mindedness of, 260–261
    as term, 10
    therapist perspective on, 265–266
    valuing perspective of, 42
Cogar, M. M., xiii, 246
Cognition, 5
Cognitive complexity, 268
Cognitive–experiential method. *See* Hill cognitive–experiential dream model
Cognitively complex, 98
Collaboration, 4–5, 7–9, 41–42, 207, 230
Collective unconscious, 152
Competition, 55, 194–195
Computer software, 84, 138–140, 142–143, 267
Concrete thinkers, 99
Confidentiality, 208
Conflicts
    personal, 51, 59, 232
    work and family, 195
Content analysis methods, x
Content (of nightmares), 203
Control
    personal, 133, 176
    sense of, 209
Countertransference issues, 106–108
Courage, 207
Creativity, 204
Crisis Dreaming (R. D. Cartwright and L. Lamberg), 135
Crook, R. E., 241–242, 250, 260, 265, 266
Cultural interpretations, 59
Curiosity, 38, 100, 101

Davis, T. L., 166, 249, 257
Defenselessness, 204
Delaney, G., 32, 135, 138
Dematatis, A., 142, 249
Depression, 43, 204
Depressive symptoms, 99
Depth, 251–253
Description, re-experiencing, associations, waking life triggers (DRAW), 8, 25–36
    example of steps in, 35–36
    in spirituality case study, 153
    in therapist training, 231–232, 238
Description (of image), 25–26
Diary, 262–263
Diemer, R., 246, 247, 252, 254, 259
Distortion (of dreams), 265
Domhoff, G. W., x
Doniger, W., 149–150
DRAW. *See* Description, re-experiencing, associations, waking life triggers
Dream helpers, 73
Dreaming, x
Dream Interpretation Model. *See* Hill cognitive–experiential dream model
Dream interpretation (term), 10
Dream journals, 84
Dream Power (C. Richmond), 135
Dream recall, 100–101, 219, 262–263
Dream(s)
    changing the, 72–79
    characteristics of, 264–265
    continued work on the, 237
    determining when, occurred, 23–24
    emotional climate of the, 23–24
    length of, 22
    real vs. made-up, 23
    recency of, 22–23
    retelling, 20–23
    timing of, 24
Dream Time, x
Dream Toolbox, 138–140, 142–143, 267
Dream work, x–xii
    effectiveness of, 229, 251–259
    reasons for doing, 229
    as term, 10
    value of, 45

Education, client, 100
Effect size (ES), 242, 257, 258

Electra conflict, 54–55, 232
Ellison, C. W., 150
Emotionally relocating the deceased (task 4), 180–183
Emotions, 5
Empathy, 7–9, 207
Empowerment, 5
Empty-chair technique, 28, 176, 211
Environment
   of safety, 207
   in which the deceased is missing, 177–180
ES. *See* Effect size
Ethical issues, 140–141
Ethnicity, 263
Existential fears, 56
Existential Well-Being subscale of the Spiritual Well-Being Scale, 166
Experience(s)
   childhood, 54–56
   dream as, 49–50, 232
   individual, 4
   past, 51
   personal, 230
Experiential interpretations, 57
Explaining the model to client, 20
Exploration stage, 7–8, 19–39
   eliciting overall feelings/determining when dream occurred in, 23–24
   explaining the model to client in, 20
   of grief work, 171–172, 175, 178–179, 181–182
   group, 116
   of images, 24–36
   of nightmare work, 209–213, 217–218
   in ongoing psychotherapy, 101–102
   retelling the dream in, 20–23
   in spirituality case study, 152–158
   summarization of the, 36–37
   thoughts about doing the, 38–39
   training therapists about, 230–232
Exposure-based treatments, 205
Extended associations, 30–32
Eye contact, 21
Eye-movement desensitization, 205

Falk, D. R., 131–132, 183, 246, 268
Fantasy, 73–76, 235–236
Faraday, A., 50
Fears, existential, 56
Feelings
   eliciting overall, 23–24
   metaphors to portray, 50
   re-experiencing, 27–29
FileMaker Pro, 138
First-person present tense, 20
Fluid personal boundaries, 204
Focus, 38–39, 101
Freedom, personal, 133
Frequency (of nightmares), 208
Freud, Sigmund, ix, 10, 54
Freudian associations, 29–30
Freudian interpretation, 58
Functioning level (of client), 43

Gains, 293–294
Gains from Dream Interpretation (GDI), 254, 293–294
GDI. *See* Gains from Dream Interpretation
Gender, 194–195, 263
Gestalt exercises, 28, 211, 215, 216
Gestalt therapists, 52
Gifts, dreams as, 76
God, dreams sent by, 151, 163
Grief
   dreams of, 169–170
   reactions to, 169
Grief work, 169–184
   accepting the reality of the loss, 171–174
   action stage of, 173, 176, 179–180, 182–183
   adjusting to the environment in which the deceased is missing in, 177–180
   benefits of, 170
   discussion in, 173–174, 176–177, 180, 183
   emotionally relocating the deceased/ moving on with life in, 180–183
   exploration stage of, 171–172, 175, 178–179, 181–182
   insight stage of, 172–173, 175–176, 179, 182
   in ongoing psychotherapy, 108–109, 112–113
   research on, 183–184
   and tasks of mourning, 170–183
   working through the pain of the grief in, 174–177
Gross motor movements, 205
Grounding exercises, 29, 176, 212
Groups, 115–132, 268

adapting the model to, 115–117
case example of, 117–131
dream work in, 23, 239–240
reflections on, 130–131
research about, 131–132

Hall, C., x
Hartmann, E., 204
Harvard Child Bereavement Study, 171
Heaton, K. J., 138, 141, 192, 247, 248, 254, 257, 259, 262
Hess, S., 246, 247, 252, 254, 257
Hill, C. E., x–xii, 131–132, 135–136, 138, 140, 142, 166, 183, 192, 225, 229, 237, 241–242, 246–250, 252, 254, 257, 259, 260, 262–266, 268, 270
Hill cognitive–experiential dream model, xi
action stage of, 8–9, 71–93
adaptation of, to groups, 115–117
adaptations of, to ongoing psychotherapy, 101–102
assumptions of the, 4–6, 230
cognitive component of, 6–7
experiential component of, 7
exploration stage of, 7–8, 19–39
extensions of, 97–220
insight stage of, 8, 41–67
and nightmares, 205–207
in ongoing psychotherapy, 97
overview of, 19–93
self-help using, 135–140
steps of, 289–290
structure of, 136
theoretical foundation of the, 6–9
three stages of, 6–9
Hillyer, A., 246, 252
Hoffman, M. A., 247
Homework, 83
Hysteria, 43

Imagery rehearsal, 205, 216
Images
definition of, 24
description of, 25–26
educating clients about dream, 100
exploration of, 24–36
notes about, 21
selection of, 25–26

waking life triggers to, 34–35
Individual experiences, 4
Informed journaling, 137–138
Initial assessment, 99
Initial dream interpretation, 42–48
example of working with, 45–48
and functioning level of client, 43
and interpretation level client is drawn to, 45
and understanding of dream by client, 43–45
and valuing of client perspective, 42
Inner conflicts, 58, 232
Inner personality dynamics, 52–59, 232–233
Inner Work (R. Johnson), 135
Insight stage, 8, 41–67
client's initial dream interpretation in, 42–48
client summarization of dream understanding in, 66
example of, 61–65
expanding on client's initial understanding of dream, 48–59
of grief work, 172–173, 175–176, 179, 182
group, 116–117
of nightmare work, 213–215, 218
in ongoing psychotherapy, 102
in spirituality case study, 158–164
thoughts about doing, 59–61, 234–235
training therapists about, 232–235
Intensity (of nightmares), 208
Interactive computer software program, 84, 138–140
Interpretation
client's level of, 45, 158
initial dream. *See* Initial dream interpretation
as term, 10
Involvement (of client), 21, 27, 267–268

James, W., 151
Johnson, R., 135
Johnson, R. A., 152
Journaling, 137–138, 219
Journals, 84
Jung, C. G., ix, 30, 150, 151–152
Jungian interpretation, 58, 232
Jungian theorists, 9, 52

Kim, B. S. K., 263
Kleitman, N., ix
Kolchakian, M. R., 249, 257, 263
Kyrstal, H., 194

Lamberg, L., 135
Language usage, 211
Length (of dreams), 22
Leotta, C., 247
Levant, R. F, 194
Level of functioning (of client), 43
Level of interpretation (by client), 45, 158
Level of understanding of the dream, client's, 43–45
Ligiero, D. P., 192, 248, 262
Listening, 42, 44, 60, 86
Lobell, L., 246, 254

Mahrer, A. R., 149
Making friends (with terrifying image), 78
Male clients, 187–198
    action stage used with, 195–197
    exploration stage used with, 189–192
    future research on, 198
    and gender dynamics, 197–198
    insight stage used with, 192–195
Manual for self-guided dream interpretation, 138
Markers of progress, 111–113
Martin, J. E., 150
Mastery–Insight Scale (MIS), 254, 255
McCready, T., 142, 249
Medications, 204
Memories, image-related, 33
Messages, dreams as, 76, 160, 182
Metaphors, 50, 51, 99, 100
Methodological issues, 274–282
    clients, 274–275
    generalizability of results, 282
    length/modality of treatment, 278–279
    measures, 279–282
    therapist adherence to model, 276–278
    therapists, 275
Miller, W. R., 150
Minnett, A. M., 135
MIS. see Mastery–Insight Scale
Models
    of dream work, xiii–xiv
    Hill cognitive–experiential dream. See Hill cognitive–experiential dream model
Moving on with life (task 4), 180–183

Nakayama, E., 248
Narcotics, 204
Networks, support, 208
New areas of therapy, 102–105
Nightmare(s), xiv, 203–220
    action stage of working with, 215–216, 218–219
    benefits to exploring, 208
    changing the, 76–79, 236
    decreasing emotional temperature of, 29
    definition of, 206
    exploration stage of working with, 209–213, 217–218
    frequency/chronicity of, 203–204
    Hill cognitive–experiential approach to working with, 206–207
    impact of, 203–204
    insight stage of working with, 213–215, 218
    onset/frequency/intensity of, 208
    pace of work with, 39
    recurrent vs. nonrecurrent, 204–205
Non-REM sleep, 205
Nonverbal behaviors, 211
Normative male alexithymia, 194
Notepad, 101
Notetaking, 21

Oedipal conflict, 54–55, 232
Old Testament, 149
O'Neil, J. M., 194
Ongoing psychotherapy, 97–114
    adapting the model to, 101–102
    dreams that facilitate therapeutic process and behavior change in, 108–111
    dreams that open new areas of, 102–105
    dreams that summarize progress in, 111–113
    dream work contributions to, 97
    educating clients about dream work in, 100
    identifying clients for dream work in, 98–99
    introducing dream work to clients in, 99

teaching clients to increase dream recall in, 100–101
transference/countertransference issues in, 105–108
Onset (of nightmares), 208
Openness to experience, 204
Open questions, 19, 27

Pace (of exploration), 39, 209
Pain of the grief, working through the, 174–177
Paranoid schizophrenia, 43
Parents, 54, 55
Participants
  as term, 226
  in training, 227
Parts-of-self level of insight, 52–54, 58, 78, 232
Past dreams, 83
Past experience, 51
Patient (term), 10
Pennebaker, J. W., 137, 140
Perls, F., 232
Personal control, 133
Personal experience, 230
Personality dynamics, 52–59, 232–233
Personal meaning, 4
Peterson, A. B., 247
Peterson, D., 138
Pharmaceutical companies, x
Planning, 86
Positive imagery, 216
Posttraumatic stress disorder (PTSD), xiv, 204
Privacy, 134
Progress, markers of, 111–113
Projective identification, 52
Psychodynamic dream theory, 8
Psychological General Well-Being, 166
Psychologically minded clients, 260–261
Psychotherapy, ongoing. *See* Ongoing psychotherapy
Psychotic, 99
PTSD. *See* Posttraumatic stress disorder

Race, 263
Rapid eye movement (REM) sleep, ix, 204, 229
Reactance, 266
Readiness for change, 73

Reading materials, 227
Reality of the loss, accepting the, 171–174
Recall (of dreams), 219
Recency (of dreams), 22–23, 264
Recording dreams, 101
Recurrent nightmares, 204–205
Re-experiencing (of dream), 27–29
Reflections
  of feelings, 19, 27–28
  of waking life, 230, 233
Reik, T., 59
Relationships, 52
Relaxation exercises, 29
  and bereavement, 175, 176
  and nightmares, 76, 209, 212
Religiosity, 151
Religious tradition, 149–150
Relocating the deceased, emotionally, 180–183
REM sleep. *See* Rapid eye movement sleep
REM-suppressing drugs, 204
Repetition, 76
Reprocessing, 205
Research, 245–283
  on client suitability for dream work, 260–266
  on components of the model, 269–273
  on effectiveness of dream work, 251–259
  future, 282–283
  on involvement of clients, 267–268
  methodological issues in, 274–282
  on self-help methods, 141–143
  summaries of, 246–250
  summary of findings in, 273
  on Therapists vs. self-help, 266–267
  volunteers for, 259–260
Resistance, 191, 206, 215
Respect, 117
Restatements, 19
Restrictive affectionate behavior among men, 195
Restrictive emotionality, 195
Retelling the dream, 20–23
Richmond, C., 135
Rituals, 9, 83–84, 237
Rochlen, A. B., 142, 192, 247–249, 262
Rosen, G., 140

Safety, 207–209
Santrock, J. W., 135

Schizophrenia, 43
Scogin, F., 135
"Searching behavior," 171
Seeman, R., 246, 252
Self-care, 208
Self-efficacy, 180, 183
Self-healing, 7, 72
Self-help, 133–146
    benefits of, 134–135
    case study of, 143–145
    and dreaming, 135
    and ethical issues, 140–141
    future research on, 145–146
    and Hill model, 135–137
    manual for, 138
    methods for using Hill model in, 137–140
    research on methods of, 141–143
    and timing issues, 140
Self-help movement, 266–267
Self-understanding, 5
Seligman, M. E. P., 133
Senses, 25
Sensitivity, 204
SEQ. *See* Session Evaluation Questionnaire
Sequels (to dreams), 76
Sequential exploration, 25
Session Evaluation Questionnaire (SEQ), 251, 253
Session Impacts Scale—Understanding subscale (SIS–U), 252, 253
Sex offenders, 43
Sexual abuse, 104
Sifneos, P. E., 194
SIS–U. *See* Session Impacts Scale—Understanding subscale
Skills
    action stage, 72
    for behavioral changes, 81
    insight stage, 42
    of therapist, 5–6, 19, 230
Sleep, REM. *See* Rapid eye movement sleep
Sleep disorders, 208
Sleep research, ix–x
Smyth, J. M., 137
Snow, J. S., 251
Social influence theory, 242
Software. *See* Computer software
Somnia a Deo Missa (dreams sent by God), 151

Speisman, J. C., 60
Spiritual adjustment, 180
Spiritual–existential concerns, 56–58, 234
Spirituality in dream work, 149–167
    action stage of, 164–165
    and associations, 162
    case study of, 152–165
    and client summarization of action stage, 165
    and client summarization of insight stage, 163–164
    defining, 150–151
    and dreams, 151–152
    exploration stage of, 152–158
    future research on, 166–167
    and grief work, 173
    insight stage of, 158–164
    questions for exploring, 159
Spiritual Well-Being Scale, 166
Stephens, G., 135
Stiles, W. B., 142, 251, 257
Storytelling, 100
Stress, 204
Structure, 117
Subjective Units of Discomfort Scale (SUD), 212, 216
Success, 194
SUD. *See* Subjective Units of Discomfort Scale
Support networks, 208
Surrealists, ix
Survey, 293–296
Symbolism, 99
Symbols, 100

Tallman, K., 268
Talmud, 8
"Tasks of mourning," 170–183
Taylor, J., 116
Temporal lobe epilepsy, 204
Therapeutic techniques, 5–6
Therapist-Rated Adherence Measure, 295–296
Therapists, research on value of, 266–267
Therapy, ongoing. *See* Ongoing psychotherapy
"Thin" mental boundaries, 204
Time allowance (for training), 226
Timing
    of dreams, 24

and ongoing psychotherapy, 102
and self-help, 140
of stages, 38
Title (of dream), 237
Trainer
qualifications of, 228
as term, 226
Training clients, 262
Training therapists, 225–242
about action stage, 235–238
about exploration stage, 230–232
about insight stage, 232–235
agenda for, 241
didactic portion of, 228
dyad training, 240, 241
experiential portion of, 238–240
goals for, 230
introduction stage of, 229–230
participants in, 227
participants' reactions to experiential portion of, 240–241
preparation for, 226–228
and qualifications of trainer, 228
reading materials for, 227
research on, 241–242
sample presentation of, 228–241
and stages of model, 230–238
thoughts about, 234–235, 237–238
time allowed for, 226
Transference reactions, 105, 108
Traumatic life events, 205, 229
Trust, 207–208, 264
Two-chair exercise, 53–54, 173

Ullman, M., 60, 116
Umemoto, D., 263
Unconscious, 100, 152
Understanding of the dream
choosing among insight levels in, 57–59, 234
client's level of, 43–45
conflicts originating in childhood as reflections in, 54–56
expanding on client's initial, 48–59
as the experience itself, 49–50, 232
inner personality dynamics as reflections in, 52–59, 232–233
spiritual–existential concerns in, 56–58, 234
waking life triggers for, 50–52, 233

Valence (of dreams), 264
Value of the interpretation, accuracy vs., 61
Valuing (of client's perspective), 42
Van de Castle, R., x
Vividness (of dreams), 264
Vivino, B., 246, 254

WAI-S. *see* Working Alliance Inventory
Waking life changes, 79–85
and continued dream work, 84–85
and rituals to honor dream, 83–84
specific behavioral, 80–83
training therapists about, 236
Waking life interpretations, 57, 58
Waking life triggers, 23, 34–35, 50–52
Waking thinking, continuation of, 4
White-Lewis, J., 265
Wonnell, T., 248, 250, 259, 264, 268
Worden, J. W., 170, 171, 173, 177, 180
Working Alliance Inventory (WAI-S), 254, 255
Working through the pain of the grief (task 2), 174–177
Working With Dreams in Psychotherapy (C. E. Hill), 135
Writing methods, 137–138

Yalom, I. D., 56

Zack, J. S., 84, 140, 142, 247, 249, 264

ABOUT THE EDITOR

Clara E. Hill earned her PhD at Southern Illinois University in 1974. She started her career as assistant professor in and is currently professor and co-director of the Counseling Psychology Program at the Department of Psychology, University of Maryland. She has been the president of the Society for Psychotherapy Research, the editor of the *Journal of Counseling Psychology*, and the winner of the Leona Tyler Award from Division 17 (Society of Counseling Psychology) of the American Psychological Association. She is North American editor-elect of *Psychotherapy Research*, the journal of the Society for Psychotherapy Research. Her major research interests are dream work, the psychotherapy process, and training therapists in helping skills. She has published more than 120 journal articles; 20 chapters in books; and 5 books, including *Therapist Techniques and Client Outcomes: Eight Cases of Brief Psychotherapy, Working With Dreams in Psychotherapy, Helping Skills: Facilitating Exploration, Insight, and Action* (American Psychological Association, 1999), and *Helping Skills: The Empirical Foundation* (American Psychological Association, 2001).